MONKS AND MAGIC

NIAS – Nordic Institute of Asian Studies
NIAS Classics Series

Scholarly works on Asia have been published via the Nordic Institute of Asian Studies for more than 40 years, the number of titles published exceeding 300 in total. Since 2002, this work has been continued by NIAS Press. All of those NIAS books published in the earlier decades have been long out of print. However, the Press has begun work to digitize all of our titles so that these will again be available (and this time to a global readership).

As part of this process, NIAS Press has launched a new NIAS Classics book series, comprising selected titles from the NIAS backlist that have been judged to be of enduring value. In each instance, not only will the original book be reproduced (sometimes unchanged) but also supplementary material will be added that locates the work in its contemporary scholarly discourse.

All titles appearing in the series will be published both in printed and digital format.

First titles in the series

1. *Hunting and Fishing: Revisiting a Classic Study in Southeast Asian Ethnography* by Damrong Tayanin & Kristina Lindell
2. *Monks and Magic: Revisiting a Classic Study of Religious Ceremonies in Thailand* by Barend Jan Terwiel
3. *Going Indochinese: Contesting Concepts of Space and Place in French Indochina* by Christopher E. Goscha

NIAS Press is the autonomous publishing arm of NIAS – Nordic Institute of Asian Studies, a research institute located at the University of Copenhagen. NIAS is partially funded by the governments of Denmark, Finland, Iceland, Norway and Sweden via the Nordic Council of Ministers, and works to encourage and support Asian studies in the Nordic countries. In so doing, NIAS has been publishing books since 1969, with more than two hundred titles produced in the past few years.

UNIVERSITY OF COPENHAGEN

norden
Nordic Council of Ministers

MONKS AND MAGIC

Revisiting a Classic Study of Religious Ceremonies in Thailand

BAREND JAN TERWIEL

nias PRESS

Nordic Institute of Asian Studies
NIAS Classics series, no. 2

First published in 1975 by Curzon Press Ltd
Second and third editions published in 1979 and 1994
This fourth revised edition published in 2012
by NIAS Press
NIAS – Nordic Institute of Asian Studies
Leifsgade 33, 2300 Copenhagen S, Denmark
Tel: +45 3532 9501 • Fax: +45 3532 9549
E-mail: books@nias.ku.dk • Online: www.niaspress.dk

British Library Cataloguing in Publication Data

Terwiel, B. J.
Monks and magic : revisiting a classic study of
religious ceremonies in Thailand. -- New ed.
-- (NIAS classics ; 2)
1. Buddhism and culture--Thailand. 2.
Buddhism--Thailand--Customs and practices.
I. Title II. Series
294.3'48'09593-dc23

ISBN: 978-87-7694-065-2 (hbk)
ISBN: 978-87-7694-101-7 (pbk)
ISBN: 978-87-7694-066-9 (e-book)

Typesetting: Donald B. Wagner

Printed in the United Kingdom by Marston Digital

CONTENTS

ILLUSTRATIONS

Figures

Maps

Tables

PREFACE TO THE FIRST EDITION

The preparation for the research of which this book is a result began in 1964, when Dr Robert van Gulik lent a textbook and gramophone records for the study of the Thai language[1] to a group of undergraduate students at the University of Utrecht. For more than two years these students held regular meetings during which they covered the greater part of the course. Most of them persevered with the study of this language because a plan had been developed to form an anthropological 'expedition' to a small community in Thailand. It was intended to set forth in 1967 and, once in the field, each member would gather data almost independently from other members of the group. In order to prevent duplication of work, and to spread the scope of the research as wide as possible, each member had to choose a certain topic within the anthropological discipline upon which to base fieldwork. One decided to concentrate upon decision-making and authority (the 'power structure' as it was then called), one would look closely at land tenure, another would deal specifically with problems related to kinship and genealogy, whilst the author of this study would focus his attention upon the religious aspects of social life. Since these plans were conceived while the students involved had only recently commenced their academic studies, it was possible for some of them to map out several courses which would prepare them for the planned fieldwork. The author was thus able to incorporate the reading of Sanskrit and Pali texts and the history of Buddhism in the programme of the *doctoraal* examination in cultural anthropology.

The conditions attached to the allotment of funds for this joint fieldwork proved too demanding, and the plan for the 'expedition' was abandoned in 1966. However, the preparatory work of several years proved fruitful in at least one instance when, in December 1967, the Australian National University admitted the author as a research scholar.

Before taking up the scholarship, it was possible to travel extensively in central and northern Thailand. The main object of this journey was to select a community where the circumstances seemed favourable for anthropological

1 Mary R. Haas and Heng R. Subhanka, *Spoken Thai*, Holt Spoken Language Series, 1945.

fieldwork, where the inhabitants would not be opposed to prolonged intensive research which would centre upon their religious observances.

No effort was made to ensure that the community to be selected would be 'typical' or 'average', since it was virtually impossible to form a firm opinion on such matters at that stage of the research. It was argued that, if the selected community should prove markedly different in its religious practices and beliefs from those of other communities, this would by no means invalidate the research. In such an event, analysis of the differences between the religion studied in detail and the religion of other communities would elucidate the topic of research and so would analysis of the situation where no marked variation could be traced. In retrospect it can be said that the religious observances of the community in question did not differ in any major aspect from those of other communities visited in central rice-growing areas of Thailand.

PREFACE TO THE SECOND, REVISED EDITION

Within two years the first edition of *Monks and Magic* was sold out and the Scandinavian Institute of Asian Studies began considering a second edition. I used this opportunity to rewrite certain sections, to bring the text up to date and to make the text more accessible by providing an index.

PREFACE TO THE THIRD, REVISED EDITION

Twenty-five years have passed since the fieldwork upon which *Monks and Magic* was based took place. During this quarter century central Thailand has been transformed and I studied and experienced many of the multifarious changes. Probably the scope and pace of change was greater in Wat Sanchao (the community where fieldwork was conducted) than in surrounding areas, for in 1967 the people of Wat Sanchao, through a series of circumstances beyond their control, were isolated from the nearby provincial capital. Since then, the area has become almost like an outer suburb of the town of Ratchaburi.

The decision to reprint this book is, however, not because my notes and photographs have acquired antiquarian value. There has been a steady demand for this work. In 1986 a third edition, updated and newly illustrated had been prepared when unfortunately the business handling the version went bankrupt and I was unable to trace the whereabouts of the new map, the photos and the relevant computer tapes. The motivation to start the work of revision once more stems from the fact that in 1991 and 1992 I taught anthropology, with special relevance to mainland Southeast Asia at the Ludwig-Maximilians University of Munich. During lecture preparation and seminar discussions I had to consult *Monks and Magic* and found to my surprise that this work is still relevant, particularly when updated.

PREFACE TO THE FOURTH, REVISED EDITION

When I was asked by Gerald Jackson, the editor in chief of NIAS Press, whether I would be willing to cooperate with a new edition of *Monks and Magic*, at first I was somewhat sceptical. After all (as mentioned in the preface to the third edition) once before I had helped prepare a reissue, a work that never came to fruition. Moreover, twice I had given permission to have the work translated, once in the French language and once in Thai, and these translations had also not eventuated. However, while discussing the matter in more detail with Gerald during the recent EUROSEAS conference in Göteborg, the plan seemed realistic and I agreed to assist with the rebirth of the book that now has been out of print for many years. I had already had the impression that this work, begun more than forty years ago, still retains relevance, for it has been extensively cited and occasionally large segments were reproduced.[2] My main motivation, however, for agreeing to once more spend much time and energy on the book is that it provides me with a chance to improve the book.

In the first place, *Monks and Magic*, being the first book I wrote in English, showed clearly that at that time I had an even more limited experience of writing in that language than at present. Over the years, as I gradually acquired a feeling for expressing my thoughts on paper, I noted that the wording of many sec-

2 Three times substantial parts were reprinted namely in John S. Strong, *The Experience of Buddhism, Sources and Interpretations*, (the most recent edition Belmont: Thomson Higher Education, 2008, pp. 249–53); a shortened version of the book appeared in the Dutch language as *Boeddhisme in de Praktijk*, Terreinverkenningen in de Culturele Antropologie, Assen: Van Gorcum, 1977, and finally a selection out of *Monks and Magic* was reprinted under the title: *Boeddhisme*, in the series *Religieuze Levensbeschouwingen*, Part 1C [Tilburg: Vereniging Ons Middelbaar Onderwijs 1989]) Smaller parts were placed in the Internet, notably paragraphs dealing with tattooing and amulets.

tions did not exactly match that which I had intended to write. Going through the whole text with a critical eye provided me with a chance to eliminate grammatical mistakes, to be more precise and to add a few comments. In the second place, when the first version of this work was written, it was a cut-and-paste effort with the help of a common typewriter (an instrument now almost obsolete). At that time it was virtually impossible to combine Latin and Thai script in the text. It is therefore a pleasure to be able to introduce Thai concepts and book titles, not only in transcription, but also in Thai script. Thirdly, the inclusion of illustrations has become so easy with modern computer technology that also in that respect the new edition could be enriched.

The preparation of the new edition motivated me also, in November 2010, to pay another visit to Wat Sanchao, where I met once more with members of 'my' family (about whom more below) and it was a joy to find my former research assistant still in good health, now the patriarch in his compound. More than forty years earlier, during the time that I was a Buddhist monk, the rules of the Sangha made it difficult for me to take photographs. I therefore selected a young man, Somkhuan Suthichai by name, who was willing to learn to make photos, not limiting himself to the customary formal posed group pictures, but concentrating on sequences of ritual acts. At the end of first fieldwork period I presented him with a camera. Somkhuan then went of his own accord to major events, first in his own province and later further about, where he took pictures. The best of them he sold on a free-lance basis to the print media. In 2010 he could look back on a successful career, now attached to two national newspapers, in the possession of impressive professional equipment.

Returning to my study I compared my most recent set of photographs of the monastery with those I took in the 1960s, and this inspired me to write the mini-essay that appears in the epilogue.

ACKNOWLEDGEMENTS

A first version of this work appeared as a dissertation, submitted in 1971 for the degree of Doctor of Philosophy in the Australian National University. For four years the Australian National University granted me a scholarship and fully financed the last two periods of fieldwork. For initial assistance, encouragement and supervision I am indebted to Professor J. A. Barnes, now of the University of Cambridge, England, to Professor A. L. Basham and to Dr H. H. E. Loofs of the Australian National University. Whilst rewriting I received stimulating critical comments from my colleagues Miss Wipudh Sobhavong and Dr R. B. Davis.

I am most grateful to the people in and around Wat Sanchao, who put up with my inquisitive presence. I hope that I managed to represent and interpret their views realistically. Amongst these informants I would especially like to mention the late Yom Sangiam Charoenchan, the Venerable Phlìk who has recently become the abbot of Wat Sanchao, the Venerable Bunrot of Wat Sanchao, the late Phrakhru Methithammanuyot of Wat Latmethang, Phrakhru Wimonthitì of Wat Phanoenphlu and Somkhuan Suthichai, who became my trusted assistant and friend.

A NOTE ON TRANSLITERATION

In the first two editions Thai words were generally transliterated into romanized spelling with the use of the phonetic system devised by Mary R. Haas, and which is used in her *Thai–English Student's Dictionary*. Only when words are widely known in a different orthography did I deviate from her phonetic system. In the following two editions I have used a system that may be described as a simplified Library of Congress transcription. In the fourth edition, all Thai words, when first introduced, are also given in Thai script. Also, in the glossary, Thai words are first given in transcription and then in Thai. With references to Thai books and articles, only the title of the work is given in Thai (followed by an English translation of the title); Thai names are only presented in transcription.

When Thai words have been derived from Pali or Sanskrit, this is indicated in the glossary. Whenever Pali formulae are cited, the common Pali spelling is maintained, although it ought to be kept in mind that this does not correspond fully with Thai oral usage.

CHAPTER I

TWO ORIENTATIONS IN THE PRACTICE OF BUDDHISM

The research on the practice of religion in rural Thailand, of which this study is a result, was partly inspired by the observation of discrepancies and opposing views in the literature on the subject. On the one hand there are those whom I would like to call syncretists who maintain that the religion in Theravada Buddhist countries is a harmonious blend of Buddhism and local creeds. Other scholars, however, distinguish clearly between two or more distinct strata in the religion.

During the fieldwork[1] it was possible to solve at least part of this controversy. A factor that is neglected by many authors is that the whole Buddhist population cannot be described under a single rubric. There appear to exist at least two fundamentally different approaches towards religion in Thailand, and, by inference, in other Theravada Buddhist countries as well. The basic principles underlying rural, unsophisticated Buddhism appear to be fundamentally different from the Buddhist religion of the highly educated classes.

In my view, some syncretists draw their conclusions from the observation of the untutored population, and some authors who compartmentalize the religion base their views upon statements of members of the educated classes. The two groups of authors would have avoided apparent controversies had they made clear that their description of Buddhism does not encompass the whole Buddhist population, but refers only to certain sections of it.

Amongst the authors who mention the fact that Buddhism and non-Buddhist beliefs and practices have, in the course of the centuries, become

1 The three periods of fieldwork in Thailand upon which this study is based were a preliminary survey from October 1967 to November 1967, the main period which lasted from April 1968 to March 1969 and a period from October 1969 to January 1970. Since then I have revisited the community on numerous occasions, but never for a prolonged time.

so intermingled that it is at present impossible to draw a distinction between them[2] is Anuman Rajadhon. In his essay on the traditional culture of Thailand he describes two strata of belief: animism and Buddhism (the latter with elements of Brahmanism and Hinduism). In his view their interrelation may be described as follows:

> In Thai popular Buddhism, these two layers of beliefs and conceptions among the mass of the Thai people have become intermingled in an inextricable degree.[3]

The use of words such as 'popular Buddhism' and 'the mass of the people' indicates that Anuman Rajadhon is of the opinion that the syncretism between Buddhism and animism is particularly true for the religion of the unsophisticated people.

Some researchers who obtain their data on religion from the highly educated sections of the population tend to stress the discrepancy between 'pure Buddhism' and 'accretions'.[4] They are continually aware of the philosophical content of the teachings of the Buddha, and when observing religion they can always tell whether a ritual, or an aspect of a ritual conforms to the Buddhist stratum in religion or must be placed among the magico-animist stratum. An example of this compartmentalized approach is given by Wales:

> The lower one goes in the social scale in Siam, as perhaps in every other country, the more one finds that superstitions and the belief in the existence

2 Such views are expressed, for example, by John E. de Young, *Village Life in Modern Thailand*, 1955, p. 110; Frank N. Trager, 'Reflections on Buddhism and the Social Order in Southern Asia', *Burma Research Society Fiftieth Anniversary Publications*, Vol. I, 1960, pp. 533–4; E. Michael Mendelson, 'The Uses of Religious Scepticism in Modern Burma', *Diogenes*, Vol. 41, 1963, pp. 94–116; Gananath Obeyesekere, 'The Great Tradition and the Little in the Perspective of Sinhalese Buddhism', *Journal of Asian Studies*, Vol. 22, 1963, p. 140; William J. Klausner, 'Popular Buddhism in Northeast Thailand' in *Cross Cultural Understanding*, edited by Filmer S. C. Northrop and Helen H. Livingston, 1964, pp. 89–90; June C. Nash, 'Living with Nats: An Analysis of Animism in Burman Village Social Relations', *Anthropological Studies in Theravada Buddhism*, 1966, pp. 117–35; Jasper Ingersoll, 'The Priest Role in Central Village Thailand', *Anthropological Studies in Theravada Buddhism*, 1966, p. 51; and Michael A. Wright, 'some Observations on Thai Animism', *Practical Anthropology*, Vol. 15, 1968, p. 1.

3 'The Cultures of Thailand', *Journal of the Siam Society*, Vol. 38, 1951, reprinted in Phya Anuman Rajadhon, *Essays on Thai Folklore*, 1968, p. 33.

4 These views appear to underlie statements in works of Sukumar Dutt, *Buddhism in East Asia*, 1966, p. 78; Melford E. Spiro, 'Religion: Problems of Definition and Explanation', *Anthropological Approaches to the Study of Religion*, edited by Michael Banton, 1966, pp. 93–4 and in his *Burmese Supernaturalism*, 1967; Akin Rabibhadana, *The Organization of Thai Society in the Early Bangkok Period, 1782–1873*, 1969, p. 11 and recently also by Jane Bunnag, *Buddhist Monk, Buddhist Layman*, 1973, pp. 18–23 and Robert L. Mole, *Thai Values and Behavior Patterns*, 1973, Chapter II.

> of spirits who require propitiation come to the fore at the expense of the established religion. So it is that in Siam, despite the teachings of Buddhism, which especially denounce such beliefs, the spirits of the dead and other innumerable varieties of *phī*, all more or less objectionable, make considerable demands on the time of the Siamese, at least of the uneducated classes, in order to keep them at bay.[5]

When I interviewed villagers in central Thailand on the relationship between Buddhist and non-Buddhist aspects of their religion, a variety of reactions were observed. The more sophisticated informants generally stated that the Lord Buddha had never forbidden rituals of ancient origin. Other persons hesitatingly made up their minds with regard to the orthodoxy of a ritual, but on subsequent occasions contradicted their previous judgement. Many were at a loss to classify rituals or beliefs under rubrics such as 'Buddhist' and 'non-Buddhist'.

It soon appeared that the categories under discussion had little relevance in their minds. Therefore it was decided to follow the syncretist model during the analysis of rituals and beliefs of the farmers. This proved a much more fruitful approach[6] and throughout the fieldwork the questions of orthodoxy and the relationship to textual Buddhism were seldom raised.

The farmers, as well as the educated classes, call themselves Buddhists. It should be recognized, however, that the two types of Buddhism can be quite distinct. Some studious people appear to be aware of the philosophical message of the teachings of Siddhartha Gautama and its implications for those who wish to follow his path to salvation. Most others who call themselves Buddhist, on the other hand, have little or no idea of the philosophy of Buddhism. Instead, the practices and beliefs that are derived from Buddhism appear to have been reinterpreted in a local religious framework that fits the local worldview.

A distinction between the Buddhism of the highly educated and that of the relatively untutored has been remarked on by many scholars.[7] Usually, however, this difference is considered to be gradational. Thus, the highly educated

5 Horace G. Quaritch Wales, *Siamese State Ceremonies*, 1931, p. 300.

6 See Barend Jan Terwiel, 'A Model for the Study of Thai Buddhism', *Journal of Asian Studies*, Vol. 35, 1976, pp. 391–403.

7 For example in Phra Sarasas, *My Country Thailand*, 1942, pp. 248–9; Mendelson, *op. cit.*, pp. 106–7; Michael M. Ames, 'Magical-Animism and Buddhism: Structural Analysis of the Sinhalese Religious System', *Journal of Asian Studies*, Vol. 23, 1964, pp. 40–1; Chandra Jayawardena, 'The Psychology of Burmese Supernaturalism: A Review Article', *Oceania*, Vol. 41, 1970, p. 18, and Edmund R. Leach, 'The Politics of Karma', *The New York Review*, November 1971, p. 44.

Buddhist is often depicted as placing a strong emphasis upon the doctrinal and philosophical aspects of religion, whilst in the view of these scholars, the farmer appears to be more preoccupied with the ceremonial side of Buddhism.

The model of Theravada Buddhism adopted in this study differs from that proposed by most scholars in that it shows a fundamental discrepancy between the principles underlying the religion of the farmers and the axioms of that of the highly educated classes. The religion of the farmer is basically magico-animistic, whilst those among the elite who adhere to religion may be regarded as having organized an intellectual appreciation of Buddhism. It is because of the incorporation of Buddhism in the magico-animistic worldview that the villagers 'do not feel that they are members of several different religious systems at the same time'.[8] On the other hand, the sophisticated Buddhist may well consider that there exists a discrepancy between the Great Tradition and what they feel to be manifold accretions.

Though the farmer uses the same Buddhist institutions, concepts and ideas with which the elite are familiar, he gives them a different meaning. In the course of this book it will be seen that in rural areas the role of the monk is intimately connected with the idea of creating a certain type of magical power. Similarly, whilst the educated Buddhist may accept the five precepts as an ethical guide, in the countryside the recitation of these precepts is more a cleansing ritual. While the acquisition of merit is important for both types of Buddhists, in the eyes of the farmer the concept of merit is closely connected with beneficial magical power and good luck.

Table 1 gives the framework of the distinction between the two types of Buddhism. It must be considered an overall approach, a broad generalization, and it is probably too rough a model to describe all Buddhists of Theravada countries. There will be a number of semi-educated persons who fall between one type and the other. Moreover, both these ideal-types are likely to cover a range of religious approaches, from the sceptical to the deeply involved, and can probably be further subdivided. For the purpose of this study, however, where most attention is given to syncretist Buddhism, the model is useful.

Recognition of the fundamentally different approaches to religion within the population can provide a researcher with concepts with which the dynamics of Buddhism can be studied. The interaction between the two categories of Buddhists may well be one of the major factors in the process of religious change in Southeast Asia.

8 Edmund R. Leach, 'Pulleyar and the Lord Buddha: An Aspect of Religious Syncretism in Ceylon', *Psychoanalysis and the Psychoanalytical Review*, Vol. 49, 1962, p. 84.

Table 1: Two fundamentally different religious approaches within the Buddhist population

	Syncretist Buddhism	*Compartmentalized Buddhism*
Basic approach towards religion	The animistic worldview prevails and Buddhist concepts and beliefs are incorporated in magico-animism.	Buddha's teachings are considered superior to beliefs and practices that are obviously animistic.
Typically found among	Lower income earners such as farmers, fishermen, servants.	Upper ranks of the government officials, church dignitaries, nobility and the wealthy leisure class.
Usual residence	Rural areas, poor quarters in towns and cities.	Towns and cities.
Formal education	None beyond a few years of elementary schooling.	Secondary education or higher.

This book, however, is limited to an analysis of syncretist Buddhism. The religion of a group of farmers in central Thailand is shown to be primarily based upon magico-animistic principles, in which Buddhism has been transformed to suit the animistic worldview.

The Diachronic Perspective

Most references to the history of Buddhism in Thailand favour what I have called the compartmentalized approach, that is, they maintain a distinction between Buddhism and non-Buddhist religious practices. Usually this view is strengthened by the notion that non-Buddhist practices represent a deeper historical layer. For the animist aspect of popular Buddhism, Klausner has to 'reach further back',[9] deYoung refers to 'earlier animism',[10] and Akin, speaking about the first records of the Thais, surmises that the indigenous beliefs of the Thai must have been animist, and that these continued to be practised side by side with the imported Buddhism.[11] It seems to be accepted by most scholars that in Thailand originally an animistic religion prevailed until the moment that Buddhism and Brahmanism were introduced.

9 William J. Klausner, *op. cit.*, p. 89.

10 John E. de Young, *op. cit.*, p. 110.

11 Akin Rabibhadana, *op. cit.*, p. 11. In common with Thai usage, Thais are indicated by their first name.

A careful examination of historical sources shows, however, that the evolution of Thai Buddhism did not occur in such a simple manner.

From approximately the second half of the sixth until the eleventh century A.D. the region that is now called central Thailand is historically known as Dvāravatī There are indications that even before the Dvāravatī period the religion had been influenced by the Indianized Funan region. The population was basically of Mon stock.[12]

Archaeological remains of Dvāravatī provide a picture of the religion of the ruling class. Cult buildings and religious objects can easily be recognised as of Indian derivation.[13] The most prevalent religious image is that of the Buddha, but portrayals of Brahma, Indra, Gaṇeśa, Tāra, and especially Viṣṇu are also found. The presence of some images of various Hindu gods does not necessarily mean that in Dvāravatī rivalry existed between Buddhism and forms of Hinduism. Sculptures in which the Buddha appears flanked by Brahma and Indra indicate a blending of various Indian traditions and have been interpreted as showing at least a preponderance of Buddhism.

There has been a tendency, however, to characterize the religion of Dvāravatī simply as orthodox Theravada Buddhism. Such a view is found throughout Wales' monograph on the region.[14] Evidence suggests, however, that the reality was rather more complicated. In the first place many religious objects have been found there that do not fit in with the orthodox Buddhism propounded by Wales. Secondly, in line with the model proposed above, it can be argued that the religion of the region may not have been adequately covered when it is specified under a single rubric. The evidence that has survived mainly seems to favour the religion of the Dvāravatī elite.

With regard to the first objection it should be noted that in the Dvāravatī period a great number of Viṣṇu images, lingas and Mahayanist bodhisattvas have been found. This suggests that aspects of Vaiṣṇavism and Śaivism were incorporated in the Dvāravatī type of Buddhism. When confronted with Mahayana objects Wales finds them problematic and tries to explain them with a suggestion that a small party of Mahayanist monks from Western India may have wandered into Dvāravatī.[15] To me they may rather be indications that the region was on a major long-distance trade route and that its inhabitants came

12 Georges Coedès, 'A propos de deux fragments d'inscription récemment découverts à P'ra Pathom', *Comptes-Rendus de L'Académie des Inscriptions et Belles-Lettres*, 1952, p. 146

13 Pierre Dupont, *L'Archéologie Mône de Dvāravatī*, 1959.

14 Horace G. Quaritch Wales, *Dvāravatī, The Earliest Kingdom of Siam*, 1969.

15 *Ibid.* pp. 62–3.

into contact with various types of Indian people from which they adopted certain symbols. It would be wrong, however, to assume that these symbols always retained the same meaning that they originally had on the Indian subcontinent.

The second objection to the view that the Mons of Dvāravatī can be adequately described as Theravada Buddhists is that there is insufficient evidence to warrant a discussion of the religion of the people as a whole. The archaeological and historical evidence with regard to Buddhism comes from the political centres, where cult buildings and images may have been closely linked with state ceremonies and the rulers' religion.

A variation in the type of stone images, such as the Mahayanist ones mentioned above, need not therefore be related to a group of proselytizing monks but could, for example, be interpreted as a sign of political upheaval. In Wales' opinion the Mon population 'remained devoted Hīnayānists', who 'were probably never even tempted by the Mahayanism and Hinduism'.[16] I doubt whether the general population of that time was ever motivated by the sectarian feelings that Wales ascribes to it. Rulers and elite may have weighed religious objects on a scale of relative orthodoxy or according to a written norm, but the average subject most likely did not possess the type of information necessary for such weighting. Whatever the images the rulers decided to present as articles of worship, they automatically would become symbols of power to the ordinary man. There is simply no hard evidence to construct a picture of the religion of the farming community, but this gap in our knowledge should not cause us to leave that part of the population out of the imagined past.

From the eleventh until the thirteenth century the Khmers dominated the political scene in most of the region now known as Thailand. Vassalage to Angkor had a profound influence upon the religious art and architecture. Many statues that date from this period can be related to Mahayana and Hindu mythology.[17] It is generally accepted that Buddhism remained the predominant religion. Coedès words it as follows:

> Although it is clear from the Khmer inscriptions of Lop Buri that, during the eleventh century at least, Hinduism was practised there as well as Buddhism, the predominance of Buddhist temples and statues both at Lop Buri and in other western provinces of ancient Cambodia shows that, even

16 *Ibid.* p. 80.

17 See for example Silpa Bhirasri, *Thai Buddhist Art, Thai Culture,* N.S. 1970, pp. 3–5, Guide to the National Museum, Bangkok, 1970 and M. C. Subhadradis Diskul, *Art in Thailand, A Brief History,* 1972, pp. 9–10 and 38–42.

under Khmer rule, Buddhism retained the pre-eminence it had enjoyed in this region during the time of the kingdom of Dvaravati.[18]

During the twelfth and thirteenth centuries, and possibly even a little earlier, Tai[19] speaking tribes had been settling in the valleys of what is now northern Thailand. This was part of a series of Tai conquests involving also parts of the regions now known as northern Laos, northern Burma and eastern Assam. The Tai invasions seem to have been triggered by a large-scale armed conflict between the Tais and the imperial Chinese armies during the middle of the eleventh century, which ended in a devastating Tai defeat.[20]

Many scholars have tried to trace the Tai-speaking tribes back much further, usually by equating Tais with one or more of the southern tribes in the Chinese annals.[21] Much of this research remains speculative and the question of the origin of the Tai speakers has not yet been resolved in a satisfactory manner.[22]

One of the persistent myths regarding the early history of the Tais is their involvement with the kingdom of Nanchao, which had its centre around Lake Tali in Yunnan. Probably it was Terrien de Lacouperie who originally proposed this when he remarked that the Shans formed the leading family in the Nanchao agglomeration.[23] Early in the twentieth century this idea found its way into virtually all history books and it has been presented as proven fact. At

18 Georges Coedès, *The Making of South East Asia*, 1966, p. 122.

19 Tai refers to the wider language family, whilst the term Thai has been reserved for matters relating to Thailand.

20 J. G. Barlow, 'The Zhuang Minority Peoples of the Sino-Vietnamese Frontier in the Song Period', *Journal of Southeast Asian Studies*, Vol. 18, No. 2, Sept 1987, pp. 250–69; see also James R. Chamberlain, 'A New Look at the History and Classification of the Tai Languages', in *Studies in Thai Linguistics in Honor of William J. Gedney*, Jimmy G. Harris and James R. Chamberlain (eds.), 1975, pp. 49–66.

21 Some Thai views on the origin of the Tais can be found in Prince Damrong Rājānubhāb, 'History of Siam in the Period Antecedent to the Founding of Ayudhya by King Phra Chao U Thong', *Selected Articles from the Siam Society Journal*, Vol. III, 1959, p. 37; Likhid Hoontrakul, *The Historical Records of the Siamese-Chinese Relations*, 1953; and Kachorn Sukhabanij, 'ถิ่นกำเนิดและแนวอพยพของเผ่าไทย' [The Origin and Migration of the Thai], *In Memoriam Phya Anuman Rajadhon*, Tej Bunnag and Michael Smithies (eds.), 1970, pp. 111–28.

22 For an overview of many opinions, see B. J. Terwiel, 'The Origin of the T'ai Peoples reconsidered', *Oriens Extremus*, Vol. 25, Pt. 2, 1978, pp. 239–58: an elaborate update of this article appeared in Thai, 'การค้นหาแหล่งกำเนิดของชาติไทย' [Reconsidering the Origin of the Thais], in B. J. Terwiel, Anthony Diller and Chonthira Sattayawathana, คนไท(เดิม)ไม่ได้อยู่ที่นี่, [The original Thais did not live here] Bangkok: Muang Boran, B.E. 2533 (1990), pp. 8–78.

23 A. E. J. B. Terrien de Lacouperie, 'The Cradle of the Shan Race', in A. R. Colquhoun, *Amongst The Shans*, 1885, p. xxix.

present, however, most historians agree that Nanchao had little to do with Tai tribes.[24]

The spread of the Tai over a vast area of mainland Southeast Asia has often been described as a gradual merging with local cultures. Coedès describes the process as an infiltration of immigrants. Supposedly over a period of time they took positions of command, settled amongst the sedentary agriculturalists already present and assimilated their culture.[25] It may well be argued, however, that the Tai expansion represents a journey of conquest. From local histories such as the *Ahom Buranji*,[26] it may be inferred that the Tais established with overwhelming might. Especially during the troubled times of the twelfth and thirteenth centuries, when the older mainland Southeast Asian kingdoms were unable to protect their outer regions, the Tai expansion went unchecked.

In what is now called northern Thailand, not far from the present town of Chiang Mai, the capital of a Mon territory could be found from the eighth century until the late thirteenth century, when Tai speakers took over. This territory, which was known as Haripuñjaya and whose capital was Lamphun, is best known to us from local chronicles[27] and a series of stone inscriptions[28] The languages in these inscriptions are Pali and Mon. The use of Pali, the fact that all these inscriptions refer to religious donations and also the context show a clear predominance of Theravada Buddhism, at least amongst the ruling elite.

From the end of the thirteenth century onwards, inscriptions appear in Pali and Thai. A powerful Thai dynasty was set up in Sukhothai from approximately 1250 onwards. The pre-eminence of Theravada Buddhism in

24 Wilhelm Credner, *Cultural and Geographical Observations Made in the Tali (Yunnan) Region with special Regard to the Nan-chao Problem*, translated from the German by E. Seidenfaden, 1935, as quoted by F. M. Lebar (*et al.*), *Ethnic Groups of Mainland Southeast Asia*, 1964, p. 187; G. Luce, 'The Early Siam in Burma's History, *Journal of the Siam Society*, Vol. 46, 1958, p. 141; M. Blackmore, 'The Ethnological Problems Connected with Nanchao', *Symposium on Historical, Archaeological and Linguistic Studies*, 1967, pp. 59–69; Li Fang-kuei's remarks, as reported in Barry M. Broman, *Early Political Institutions of the Thai: Synthesis and Symbiosis*, 1968, p. 23; and F. W. Mote, 'Problems of Thai Prehistory', *Social Science Review*, Vol. II, 1964.

25 Coedès, *The Making of South East Asia*, p. 102.

26 Golap Chandra Barua (transl. and ed.), *Ahom Buranji (with parallel English translation) from the Earliest Time to the End of Ahom Rule*, 1930.

27 Translated in Georges Coedès, 'Documents sur l'histoire politique et religieuse du Laos Occidental', *Bulletin de l'École Française d'Extrême-Orient*, Vol. 25, 1925, pp. 1–202 and Camille Notton, *Annales du Siam*, Vol. II, pp. 1–68.

28 R. Halliday, 'Les inscriptions môn du Siam', *Bulletin de L'École Française d'Extrême-Orient*, Vol. 30, 1930, pp. 86–105, and A.B. Griswold and Prasert ṇa Nagara, 'An Inscription in Old Mon from Wieng Manó in Chieng Mai Province', Epigraphic and Historical Studies, No. 6, *Journal of the Siam Society*, Vol. 59 (1), 1971, pp. 153–6.

Sukhothai is a well-documented fact. Thus, king Ram Khamhaeng has many passages in his inscription of 1292 A.D. that prove this.[29] The first reference to Buddhism on Ram Khamhaeng's stone pillar may have some bearing on the distinction between the religion of the elite and that of the farmer, referred to in the beginning of this chapter. Griswold and Prasert ṇa Nagara in their article on the text of the pillar[30] translate:

> The people of this city of Sukhodai like to observe the precepts and bestow alms. King Rāma Gaṃhèṅ, the ruler of this city of Sukhodai, as well as the princes and princesses, the young men and women of rank, and all the noblefolk without exception, both male and female, all have faith in the religion of the Buddha, and all observe the precepts during the rainy season.[31]

Though common farmers are mentioned in other places of the inscription, they are not included in the enumeration of people adhering to the faith. This omission cannot be regarded as proof of different orientations toward religion within the population, but it certainly indicates that Buddhism occupied the role of court religion.

Further references in Ram Khamhaeng's inscription show not only that Buddhism was not merely a theory or a philosophy, but that ceremonies were held every year to mark the end of the annual retreat, much in the manner that can be witnessed in present-day Thailand:

> At the close of the rainy season they celebrate the Kaṭhina ceremonies, which last a month, with heaps of cowries, with heaps of areca nuts, with heaps of flowers, with cushions and pillows: the gifts they present [to the monks] as accessories to the Kaṭhina [amount to] two million each year. Everyone goes to the Araññika over there for the recitation of the Kaṭhina. When they are ready to return to the city they walk together, forming a line all the way from the Araññika to the parade-ground.[32]

How well established Buddhism was can be deduced from other references in the text that mention different types of monasteries, three classes of monks and many statues of the Buddha.

29 Since writing this there has been a debate on the authenticity of this inscription. For those who are in doubt whether the inscription is genuine, see Barend Jan Terwiel, *The Ram Khamhaeng Inscription: The Fake that did not Come True*, 2010.

30 A. B. Griswold and Prasert ṇa Nagara, 'The Inscription of King Rāma Gaṃhèṅ of Sukhodaya', Epigraphic and Historical Studies, No. 9, *Journal of the Siam Society*, Vol. 59 (2), 1971, pp. 179–228.

31 *Ibid.* p. 209.

32 *Ibid.* pp. 209–10.

The last mention of a religious nature on this pillar refers to a sacred mountain:

> The divine sprite of that mountain is more powerful than any other sprite of this kingdom. Whatever lord may rule this kingdom of Sukhodai, if he makes obeisance to him properly, with the right offerings, this kingdom will endure, this kingdom will thrive; but if obeisance is not made properly or the offerings are not right, the sprite of the hill will no longer protect it and the kingdom will be lost.[33]

With the intellectual appreciation of Buddhism that characterizes the writings of many scholars, Dutt evaluates the reverence for a mountain as a kind of superstition, a form of 'demon-worship' which the populace of this region retained in spite of the teachings of the Buddha.[34] I would prefer to consider this from a different perspective.

While, as pointed out above, in present-day Thailand members of the intellectual elite may recognize and keep separate in their minds two or more strands of religious practices, whereby they value Buddhism as the superior strand, such a model need not necessarily apply to the region seven hundred years ago. During the late thirteenth century Theravada Buddhism no doubt played an important role, but that does not necessarily mean that this new religion stood in rivalry to other long-established indigenous beliefs. It is quite possible that Buddhism was widely accepted for reasons embedded in local religion and that it would be wrong to presuppose a scene of conflicting ideologies. Participation in placatory rites for the god of the mountain may not have been seen as a reason for religious qualms; it is more likely that it was part of the universally accepted system of beliefs. We may also speculate as to the nature of these 'proper' offerings twice mentioned in the inscription. If the descriptions of placatory rituals for local spirits for northern Thailand and Laos may be taken as a guide, it is likely that this involved a buffalo sacrifice.

The next major event in the religious history of the Thais falls in the first half of the fourteenth century. It is known that king Lö Thai of Sukhothai, who succeeded Ram Khamhaeng, sent a message to the abbot of the Sīhalabhikkhus in the Mon region of Martaban, requesting monks qualified to perform the acts

33 *Ibid.* p. 214.

34 Dutt, *Buddhism in East Asia*, 1966, p. 78. Wales also interprets this as a sign that animism vied for first place with Buddhism (H. G. Quaritch Wales, *Early Burma – Old Siam*, 1973, p. 110).

of the Sangha.[35] This should not be interpreted as a petition for missionaries to convert the court, for we know from the preceding passages that Theravada Buddhism was well established in Sukhothai.

Instead, it can be considered from the angle of diplomatic contacts between Martaban and Sukhothai. The Sīhalabhikkhus had only recently founded a monastery not far from Martaban. These Araññavāsī, or forest-dwelling monks, were famous for their learning and austerity. Some of their repute was derived from the fact that they could claim to belong to a Ceylonese sect of great fame. They could boast of one of the purest lines of succession in Theravada Buddhism.

At various stages of the history of the Sangha there had been a preoccupation with the validity of ordinations. If, in the course of the centuries, a mistake had crept into the text of the ritual the whole monastic succession was in doubt. Sects could accuse each other of not truly representing the Sangha because the ordination ritual was not, or had not been, performed according to the ancient tradition. A group of monks who feared that their ordination was invalid could be re-ordained in the most orthodox fashion. The Sīhalabhikkhus were considered to be monks whose ordination was of unassailable validity, and therefore it was considered an asset to have a branch resident in one's country.

King Lö Thai's request was granted and representatives of this extremely orthodox sect settled in Sukhothai. If Lö Thai had made his request in a bid to bolster his status vis-à-vis other Tai principalities, his attempt remained unsuccessful, for during his reign Sukhothai lost its hold over many of its former vassals.

Another religious matter that appears prominent in the inscriptions and architecture of this time is the cult of relics. In Wat Mahathat (Monastery of the Great Relic) at Sukhothai it was proudly believed that there were held remains of the Buddha himself, and that these remains performed a number of miracles.[36] Sukhothai may have boasted possession of a relic of the Buddha himself, but it is interesting to note that other towns also vied to possess mighty relics and that virtually every important town housed a Mahathat monastery within its walls.

These towns must have occupied a prominent position in the worldview of both their inhabitants and that of the surrounding population. They were the

35 For the information on this episode I am mainly relying on the recent study by A. B. Griswold and Prasert ṇa Nagara, 'King Lödaiya of Sukhodaya and his Contemporaries', Epigraphic and Historical Studies, No. 10, *Journal of the Siam Society*, Vol. 60 (1), 1972, pp. 21–152.

36 *Ibid.* pp. 80–134.

habitat of the wealthy, they constituted places of refuge in times of uncertainty and upheaval. The town stood for written knowledge, authority and the force of law; it was the place where, ideally, redress could be obtained if an injustice had taken place. The town was in many respects the centre of the world and the ruler, as guardian of the realm, therefore fulfilled an important ceremonial role.

It is unlikely that Theravada Buddhism gained acceptance as a focus in the ceremonial life of the court merely by virtue of its philosophical doctrine, its persuasive message, or the impressive quality of its advocates. It is more likely that Buddhism proved efficacious in providing ceremonies intending to ensure the town's wealth and prosperity. In addition Theravada Buddhism played a political role in that it allowed a rationale for accepting the ruler's right to authority and at the same time prescribed a number of guidelines that safeguarded, at least in theory, against excesses of the crown and propagated values directed towards a harmonious social life. The role of Buddhism ought not to be overstated, however, in terms of conflict with indigenous beliefs and practices. As mentioned above, questions of orthodoxy may have been irrelevant when the king had to perform the annual rites to propitiate the spirit of the mountain.

During the time of king Lö Thai in the fourteenth century, it was not possible for a town to exist in isolation: political life appears to have been dominated by the formation of alliances and attempts to acquire vassals through diplomacy, strategic marriages, intrigue, intimidation and warfare. Centres of alliances, usually towns of strategic importance, celebrated their enhanced importance with monumental buildings and greater pomp and ceremony, and it is in this atmosphere that we may see the cult of relics.

The Mūlasāsanā (most of it written a century after Lö Thai's reign) tells how the venerable Sumana found an important relic. This Sumana was one of the Sīhalabhikkhus sent from Martaban. His relic was brought in procession to the nearest town, Sisachanạlai, north of Sukhothai, where Lö Thai's son ruled. Astonishing miracles occurred when the relic was lustrated by the viceroy of Sisachanalai. The fame of the relic spread to Sukhothai and Lö Thai sent officers of the Crown with a message to the Mahāthera Sumana requesting him to bring it to the capital city.[37]

The Mūlasāsanā reports that the relic failed to perform a miracle for Lö Thai. Whilst there is some doubt about the accuracy of this statement, Griswold and

37 A. B. Griswold and Prasert ṇa Nagara, 'King Lödaiya of Sukhodaya and His Contemporaries', p. 64.

Prasert ṇa Nagara believe that this failure did happen.[38] It would have been an excruciatingly awkward moment for the king, for the failure would throw doubt on his suitability as guardian of the realm. If true, the episode could help explain the ineffectiveness of his reign. The detailed account of wondrous events surrounding the installation of other relics in Sukhothai later in his reign may have been inspired to counteract the negative impact of the relic's failure to perform. If this account was not based on a disappointing lack of a miracle, it could be an indirect judgement on Lö Thai's ineffectiveness.

An interesting document that may be seen as a measure of the independent development of Thai Buddhism is the *Traiphūmikhāthā* (Sermon on the Three Worlds), first written in the middle of the fourteenth century by Phaya Lü Thai, heir-apparent to the throne of Sukhothai.[39] Using more than thirty sources of the classical Buddhist literature, Lü Thai boldly created a new local cosmology. Upon ascending the throne Lü Thai took the title of Great Dhamma King (Mahādhammarāja) and, in a vow reminiscent of Mahayana Buddhism, promised to work for the salvation of all beings.[40]

An intimate relationship between statecraft and religion is also apparent in the history of Ayutthaya. This city was a rival of Sukhothai probably already before the middle of the fourteenth century.[41] Because of its strategic position Ayutthaya gradually grew to be one of the most important cities in Southeast Asia. Because of its proximity to Angkor, Khmer influences were strong in Ayuttaya. After the Thais of Ayutthaya captured and looted Angkor in 1431–2 the Khmer influence must have increased, because when King Trailok (whose long reign fell in the second half of the fifteenth century) reorganized the administration of his realm he used an Angkorian model. Khmer inspiration can be found in the art and architecture and language development, and also in the court religion. Much of the customs and rituals that later came to be called court Brahmanism probably date back to Trailok's time.[42]

38 *Ibid.*, p. 69.

39 There are good translations of this text in European languages: in French by Georges Coedès and Charles Archaimbault, *Les trois mondes (Traibhūmi Brah Ruaṅ)*, 1973, and in English by Frank E. Reynolds and Mani B. Reynolds, Three Worlds according to King Ruang, 1982.

40 See Barbara Watson Andaya, 'Statecraft in the Reign of Lü Thai of Sukhodaya (ca. 1347–1374)', in Bardwell L. Smith ed., *Religion and Legitimation of Power in Thailand, Laos and Burma*, 1978, pp. 2–19.

41 For arguments that Ayutthaya was founded prior to 1351, see B. J. Terwiel, *Thailand's Political History: From the 13th Century to Recent Times*, 2011, pp. 13–4.

42 See for example, H. G. Quaritch Wales, *Siamese State Ceremonies*, 1931, and his *Ancient Siamese Government and Administration*, 1934.

This court Brahmanism should not be regarded as a rival religion, threatening to supplant Theravada Buddhism. Instead it was a corrolary of the general trend of Khmerization that can already be noted in Sukhothai during the reign of Lü Thai. Court Brahmans were needed to assist the government with their specialist knowledge. Royal life-cycle rituals were their domain and they felt responsible for the well-being of the king and his family. Their greatest asset was probably their inherited astronomical and astrological knowledge. The court Brahmins calculated the most favourable moments when the king ought to implement his decisions, such as declaring war and setting out to subdue a rebellious vassal state.

Theravada Buddhism had been firmly established for centuries and flourished in countless monasteries. Brahmanism, with its limited and distinctly administrative role, offered no alternative for the monastic organization of the Sangha. Buddhism and court Brahmanism shared religious concepts and their respective pantheons overlapped, so as to facilitate a degree of mutual penetration.

Throughout the Ayutthaya period Theravada Buddhism enjoyed the status of being the realm's chief religious orientation and it did not have to compete with alternative creeds, which prescribed different paths to salvation. While in the region now called Thailand Buddhism formed the only soteriology, without serious competition from other systems of thought, it would be rash to think of this form of Buddhism as being 'pure' or 'doctrinal' according to the Theravada school as this has been described in the general literature on Buddhism.

It is plausible that the great majority of those who considered themselves Buddhists adhered to a form of religion in which local magico-animist principles were dominant. While Buddhism undoubtedly had a monopoly in the region, it must not be forgotten that it was allowed to develop its own interpretation of the scriptures. Khmer-inspired Brahmanic ritual in the capital city may be seen as an enrichment and diversification of the established system of beliefs. The court Brahmins were seen to manipulate powers that had already largely been accepted in the Buddhist context.

How strong the magico-animist orientation of Thai Buddhism may have been is indicated by an episode in the history of the northern Thai kingdom of Lanna, where in the first half of the fifteenth century the king, Sam Fang Kaen (r. 1401–41), repudiated Buddhism in favour of a local 'animistic' cult.[43] The episode remains an exception, however, the general trend in Thai Buddhism being one of tolerance of and accommodation to local creeds.

43 Coedès, *The Making of South East Asia*, p. 150.

In general, archaeological and historical data on the development of Thai religion is heavily biased towards the ruling classes and the urban environment. Scholars have noted this phenomenon and interpreted it in various ways. Thus, writing about Cambodia during the thirteenth and fourteenth centuries, Bechert assumed the existence of an urban–rural dichotomy. He assumes that Theravada Buddhism generally spread in the villages of the Khmer empire before the court adopted it in favour of the Hindu–Mahayana syncretism it had adhered to up to then.[44] While his hypothesis may need to be strengthened by taking the continuing role of Buddhism in the Khmer urban setting into account, as well as the effects of the local power shifts in favour of the Thais, his view that the Indian culture of Southeast Asia in the Khmer period was mainly an urban phenomenon, and that there was a marked difference between towns and villages agrees with the model of Thai Buddhism selected for this study.

Another scholar who assumes a fundamental dichotomy between village and town is Reginald Le May who described the religion of the Tai-speakers at the time of their invasion of Mon territories in what is now northern Thailand. He thinks that the villager did not fundamentally change his religious beliefs when he came in contact with Buddhism:

> It must not be forgotten that to the vast majority of Siamese (and Burmese) peasants Buddhism is, and always has been, what I call 'The Decoration of Life', and the people themselves have remained at heart animists.[45]

At first sight, this view fits in with the model proposed in this book. However, developing this theme further Le May pictures a fully compartmentalized rural religion. According to le May Buddhism is used by the villager for purely other-worldly reasons, whilst animism is needed to cope with everyday life:

> Their lives fall into two parts. They pay their devotion and give their offerings to the Lord Buddha, so that their merit may increase and their Karma may enrich them in future lives, but in the present life there are a host of '*p'i*', or spirits, to be propitiated if evil is not to befall them, and the latter are, therefore, continually courted and feasted to this end.[46]

In my opinion Le May has not fully appreciated the role of Buddhism in the village setting by describing it merely as a veneer and as a tool to be used

44 H. Bechert, 'Living Buddhism in East Bengal: A Comparative View', mimeographed, p. 22.

45 Reginald Le May, *The Culture of South-East Asia*, 1964, p. 163.

46 *Ibid.*, p. 163.

solely for other-worldly ends. Instead, I have come to believe that the peasants gradually adopted Buddhism as part of their religious system, but in a manner quite distinct from that of the urban elite. The peasant accepted Buddhism not primarily because he became convinced of the truth of the Pali canon, but rather because it could be grafted upon ideas he held previously.

In the urban centres the preponderant themes of the leading monasteries may well have been directed to stimulate a devout acceptance of the Buddhist moral code. Salvation from the eternal cycle of lives by a strict following of the path outlined by Siddhartha Gautama could have motivated the sophisticated city monks. In the countryside, however, Buddhism appears to have been incorporated in the pre- existing animistic, manipulative, magic-oriented religion. When Buddhism spread to the Thai farmers in the first centuries of the second millennium they fed, housed, sponsored and themselves became Buddhist monks, not because they wished to escape rebirth, but primarily to acquire magical power. The ritual code of behaviour of the Sangha was considered efficacious in bringing about increased chances of prosperity and Pali texts were used as spells to ward off danger and illness.

This hypothesis on the introduction of Buddhism in the rural areas can be neither substantiated nor contradicted by historical evidence. Rural culture leaves very few traces, especially in a tropical climate where religious buildings, images and books are made from plant material. Nevertheless the hypothesis of a rural restructuring of Buddhism whereby it can justifiably be called animistic Buddhism is made plausible by reference to the rapid spread of Buddhism, and to parallels with Tai-speaking tribes outside Thailand, and also by a consideration of the evidence of present-day rural religion.

Firstly, with respect to the spread of Buddhism it can be pointed out that there are few or no indications of active proselytism. Even when local religious practices flagrantly contravened basic Buddhist tenets this was not met in a confrontational manner. The best example of this lies in the gradual suppression of animal sacrifices. Even after many centuries of Buddhist influence the buffalo sacrifice was still not fully eradicated.[47]

Another aspect of the spread of Buddhism lies in the fact that no formal legalistic threshold has to be crossed before an outsider is allowed to attend most Buddhist ceremonies, a few rituals reserved for members of Sangha being

47 Note that animal sacrifices were not completely eradicated. The buffalo sacrifice is reported for Laos and Northern Thailand. See Paul Lévi in *Kingdom of Laos* (ed. René de Berval), 1959, p. 162 ff. In central Thailand villagers may buy a pig's head and trotters and display them on an altar to propitiate certain spirits.

the exception. Any layman can take part without having to repudiate other beliefs. There is no examination of intentions, no formal conversion ritual, no initiation ceremony. Instruction in the Buddhist doctrine is not a specific requirement for the lay devotee who wishes to sponsor the Buddhist monks and partake in their ceremonies.

Furthermore, in order to understand the spread of Buddhism to the countryside, it is necessary to notice the method of recruitment of Buddhist monks. Any villager who fulfilled the traditional stipulated conditions of age, health and good name belonged to the field from which the Sangha drew its numbers. On village level, while elaborate preparation may have been common to help propel a man into his new exalted status, these preparations involved little or no doctrinal knowledge. From the perspective of the Sangha, as long as a man had found a proper preceptor, and as long as he actively and accurately participated in uttering the whole ordination text using the Pali language, there was no cause to bar him from joining the order as a fully-fledged member. Such village monks were enfolded in the rules of the Sangha, they learned to chant sacred texts and thereby became esteemed monks. Whether or not they acquired knowledge of the Buddhist teaching was a matter of personal choice.

The religious beliefs of the aspirant monk are not brought into question during the ordination procedure. In rural areas, up to the present day, it is quite common and widely accepted that a man joins the Sangha for reasons that appear to be primarily magico-animistic. When a villager finds himself in mortal danger he can resort to a prayer to the invisible powers in which he promises to become a monk for a specified number of days, months or even years, if only he is rescued. If he escapes unscathed, he must fulfil his promise and find a preceptor. This practice, apparently not in line with the principles guiding the brotherhood of monks in the written code, has been widely accepted in the Thai countryside. It is quite likely that the motivation of many farmers to join the Sangha during the past centuries may have been equally far removed from orthodox Buddhism. Hence, the representatives of Buddhism par excellence, the monks, can on the village level adhere to beliefs that need not conform with orthodox Buddhism.

References to the religions of Tai-speaking tribes of the twentieth century cannot simply be used as evidence to determine the religion of Tai-speaking farmers living in the Chao Phraya valley at the time of early Sukhothai and Ayutthaya. Instead they can provide us with knowledge about the variations that have developed in the course of time and aid us in placing the Thai farmers in a broader perspective.

At present, Tai-speakers can be found in southern China (notably in Yunnan, Kweichow and Kwangsi provinces), northern Vietnam, Laos, Thailand, northern Burma and northeastern India (Assam). Summary descriptions of the religions of the most important Tai groups[48] mention a mixture of magico-animism with one or more dominant, widespread religion. Thus Tai tribes in Kweichow follow many Taoist practices, there are groups in rural north Vietnam that practice Mahayana Buddhism and some communities make use of a mixture of Buddhist, Taoist and Confucian rituals. In Laos, Thailand, Burma and south Yunnan, most Tais are called Theravada Buddhists.

All reports of the religions of Tai speakers mention a strong magico-animism. The adherence to Taoism, Confucianism and Buddhism appears to be derived from an eclectic approach to religion. Writing about the tribal Tai as a whole, the compilers of a gazetteer on the region[49] notice that the fundamental religion is centred upon propitiation of ancestors and of a multitude of spirits.

> There are phi of all kinds: guardians of the earth and village, the evil spirits of those who suffered a violent death, bearers of disease, tormentors, who watch over the crops etc. Outside each village is a small pagoda for the guardian of the village, and inside each house are one or more altars for the ancestors and the guardian of the hearth. The religious practitioners are the heads of the families, who are responsible for the ancestors, and the various classes of shamans, generally hereditary, who know how to find lost objects, commune with the spirits, cure the sick, interpret dreams, etc. A few local festivals are held, for the New Year, for the dead, and the harvest . . . .[50]

This basic magico-animism that characterizes tribal Tai also underlies the religion of the farmers in lowland Thailand. The Thai farmers use the same concepts, practise similar ceremonies and use identical paraphernalia during many rituals. It cannot be accidental that the white Tai in north Vietnam and the Thais in central Thailand recognize the symbol of a central pole or pillar as the symbol for a central authority and that both call it by the same name: *lak mueang*, a more formal term of the Thais is *chaopho lak mueang* (เจ้าพ่อหลักเมือง)[51] Other such striking similarities will be noted in the course of this study.

48 Frank M. Lebar, Gerald C. Hickey and John K. Musgrave (eds.), *Ethnic Groups of Mainland Southeast Asia*, 1964, pp. 187–244.

49 *Ethnic Groups of Northern Southeast Asia*, Cultural Report Series No. 2, Yale University Southeast Asia Studies, 1950.

50 *Ibid.*, p. 123.

51 G. Maspero, *Un empire colonial français: L'Indochine*, Vol. I, 1929, p. 239 and F. M. Lebar *et al.*, *Ethnic Groups of Mainland Southeast Asia*, 1964, p. 225.

As far as the history of rural Thai religion is concerned, it can be inferred that the farmers adopted the same eclectic approach that their distant relatives in the valleys of other parts of mainland Southeast Asia have taken. When their hereditary leaders accepted Buddhism, these farmers did not fundamentally change their religious outlook. They remained 'animists', and continued to propitiate their ancestors and the different kinds of spirits remained in the foreground.

When Buddhism was introduced, it became subservient to magico-animism. Buddhist monks were revered because their Pali chants proved effective as spells to ward off evil. The image of the Buddha joined the ancestor shrine in the houses and the Buddhist monastery occupied a place just outside the community where among non-Buddhist Tais the shrine for the guardian of the village stood. In the course of the centuries the role of Buddhism gradually became more prominent in village religion. Rural magico-animism slowly became magico-animistic Buddhism. Under the influence of Buddhist principles the animal sacrifice was replaced by different kind of offerings. But even this ancient sacrifice has not totally been supplanted. In central Thai villages there are occasions when a pig's head and trotters – bought for the occasion – form the central gift in a ceremony to propitiate the gods.

During the nineteenth and twentieth centuries, when the central government established effective control over much of its rural areas, the role of Buddhism expanded markedly. The central administration directed its efforts towards standardizing the Pali texts used by the monks, distributing textbooks for newly ordained members of the Sangha, and sponsoring an elaborate examination system for the Buddhist church. We may surmise that the prestige of the monks has risen in accordance with their increase in knowledge. No rural community is now complete without a monastery from which at all times it can recruit a chapter of monks to chant blessings over a newly married couple, to inaugurate a new house, to ward off illness, to perpetuate a spell of prosperity and to bring solace to the dead. But while the Sangha and Buddhism therefore pervade religious life in the villages, this does not necessarily mean that the villager accepts the philosophical tenets of Buddhism or adheres to its soteriology. The Buddhist concepts can be interpreted in such a way that they fit in with magico-animistic presuppositions. In the following chapters it is demonstrated how Buddhism has been cast in such a magico-animistic mould.

CHAPTER II

THE SETTING AND THE FIELDWORK

The central rice-growing area of Thailand is depicted in Map I. In the southwest corner of this region lies the provincial capital Ratburi on the river Maeklong. The town is an important traffic centre, not only because a large river flows through it, but also because a major highway and a railway cross the river at this point. Its strategic position is emphasized by a large garrison.

Like all Thai provincial capitals, Ratburi (or in the official spelling Ratchaburi) provides a centre of trade and commerce, and is frequented by people from the surrounding rural regions. Apart from a huge market place, there are work yards, specialist shops and branch establishments of banks. The town is famous for its manufacture of huge earthenware water pots which are distributed by truck throughout the country. The government administration is represented by a post office, a police station, a court of justice, a cadastral office, a hospital and various institutions providing education up to tertiary level.

The monastery that was selected for the main period of fieldwork is situated only about five kilometres from the market of Ratburi.[1] Notwithstanding its proximity to town it could be called a rural monastery because it lay relatively isolated from urban influence. In 1967 it was connected with the network of bitumen roads only by a rough path and a rickety footbridge. The most convenient method of reaching the monastery was by boat.

Since the period of fieldwork the situation has changed drastically. In February 1974 I noticed that a bridge had been built which made it possible that motorized traffic reached the monastery. Consequently the influence of urban life was visible everywhere. New houses were built, the monastery

1 In the mini-essay 'Wat Sanchao revisited', written as an epilogue to this latest edition, I have described how I found 'my' village in 1967 through a chance encounter five years earlier.

and many houses had been connected with electricity. In a recently erected roadside cafe I noticed the first television set. By 1977, motorized traffic went directly past the monastery and the community began to look more and more under the influence of Ratburi town. In the early 1990s one could safely say that the monastery lay on the outskirts of the town and the region developed suburban characteristics. In 2010 the region had almost completely lost all features that characterized it in the 1960s. The footpaths now were roads, the monastery was now surrounded with a solid wall, most of its buildings were now of concrete, and in its direct vicinity some two-story buildings lined the street. Most rice fields had given way to fruit and vegetable gardens.

The origin of this monastery cannot be determined with certainty. One of the resident monks, the Venerable Phlik, told that even his grandfather had not been able to recall the time of its founding. From an analysis of genealogical charts that were made with the help of some older inhabitants, it appears that the ancestors of the present population arrived around 1850 to settle on the riverfront and to open up rice fields, but it is not clear whether they built the monastery themselves or settled at a site where a monastery had already been established. According to oral tradition, the original name of the monastery was Wat Kaewfa, 'Monastery of the Blue Crystal', and it was founded by a monk who had been born in northeast Thailand. Approximately one century ago the name appears to have been Wat Paknam, 'Monastery at the River Mouth'. There are older people who can trace the names and origin of the last nine abbots.

Early in the twentieth century the name of the monastery changed again, this time to Wat Sanchao, 'Monastery of the Guardian's Shrine'. The latest name was derived from the fact that a shrine was built for a Chinese god on some land adjacent to the monastery. A Chinese person constructed it after he had won a big prize in the Huai Kokho lottery. This was a very popular lottery in Thailand from 1835 until 1916, and the shrine must therefore date from this period.[2] The shrine's upkeep is in the hands of a Chinese caretaker and its worshippers come from the Chinese population of Ratburi. The shrine and the monastery represent different cultures and there is virtually no communication between the two.

Wat Sanchao is situated on a rectangular piece of land of eight *rai* (ไร่)[3] or 1.28 hectares on the south bank of the river Maeklong. Like most Thai rural monasteries, Wat Sanchao can be considered the community centre of the

2 For further details on this lottery see B. O. Cartwright, 'The Huey Lottery', *Journal of the Siam Society*, Vol. 18, pp. 221–39.

3 The *rai* is a Thai square surface measure, equal to 1,600 square metres. Eight *rai* corresponds thus with 1.28 hectares.

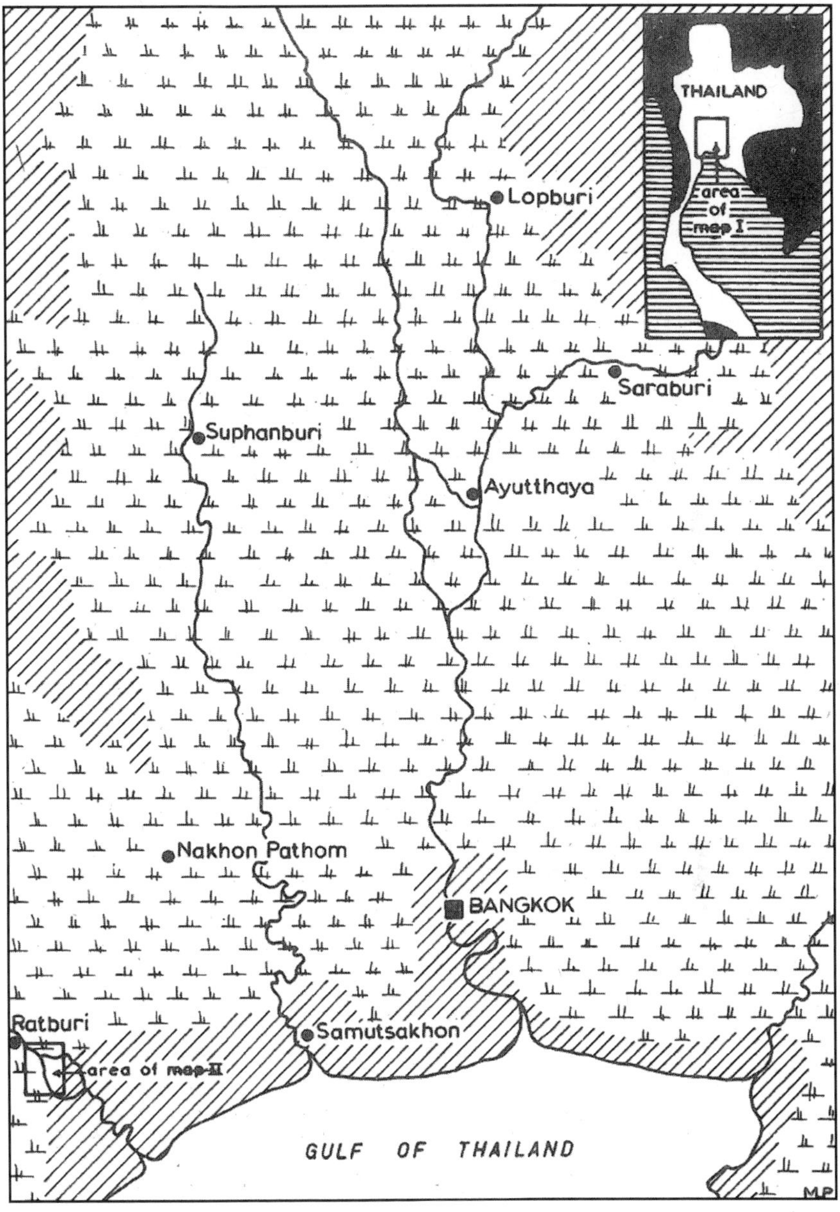

Map I: The main rice-growing areas of Central Thailand

population that sustains it. A visitor can easily see that great care has been taken to make a good impression. A row of ornamental trees near the riverbank is pruned in the shape of candles. Three jetties provide access from the river and each of them is provided with a small shelter. It is a cool place from where to watch the vessels on the Maeklong, and at lunchtime the schoolchildren can often find a woman selling fruit or sweets here.

All footpaths are somewhat elevated so that the buildings can easily be reached on foot even when most of the area is flooded in an exceptionally wet rainy season. The high footpaths are used during the dry periods of the year also, because, in accordance to their discipline, monks and novices should avoid walking on grass lest they inadvertently tread on insects.

The buildings are kept in reasonable repair and are often richly adorned. The most important structure is the *bot* (โบสถ์),[4] or temple. In olden days, the rural temple was invariably a wooden building, usually erected on a brick platform. At the beginning of the previous century the old *bot* of Wat Sanchao was derelict and the villagers constructed the present temple in 1932 and 1933. They made it according to the latest fashion, with thick brick walls plastered white and a roof covered with glazed tiles. When the present structure has to be replaced again, probably a more ornate building will be decided upon, with a concrete base and a multi-tiered roof.[5]

Among the most essential buildings are two parallel rows of *kutì* (กุฏิ),[6] or monks' cells. In Wat Sanchao they are joined by a central meeting hall where many of the ceremonies involving laymen take place. A second meeting hall is less often in use. Other structures on the monastery grounds in 1967 were the bell tower, a pyramidical building called *cedi* (เจดีย์),[7] a cremation platform and the primary school. Since 1967 much has changed. The *bot* has a new roof, two meeting halls have been replaced with a modern building and the open cremation platform has been supplanted by a crematorium. Along the river frontage a concrete retaining wall has been built, new *kutis* have been erected, and a new school complex completes the virtually total renovation during the last forty years.

To the east, south and west lie the households of the farmers who regularly support the monastery with food, services and money. From the monastery, most houses can be reached on foot as well as via one of the waterways. In 1967 the total number of households called upon by the monks of Wat Sanchao when they collected food early in the morning was 116. The farmers' houses

4 From the Pali word *posatha,* or Sanskrit *poṣadha,* meaning a Buddhist fasting day.

5 Contrary to my expectations, in 2010 the old *bot* was still standing, only its roof had been renewed.

6 From the Pali or Sanskrit word *kuṭi,* meaning a shelter.

7 Pali *cetiya,* Sanskrit *caitya.*

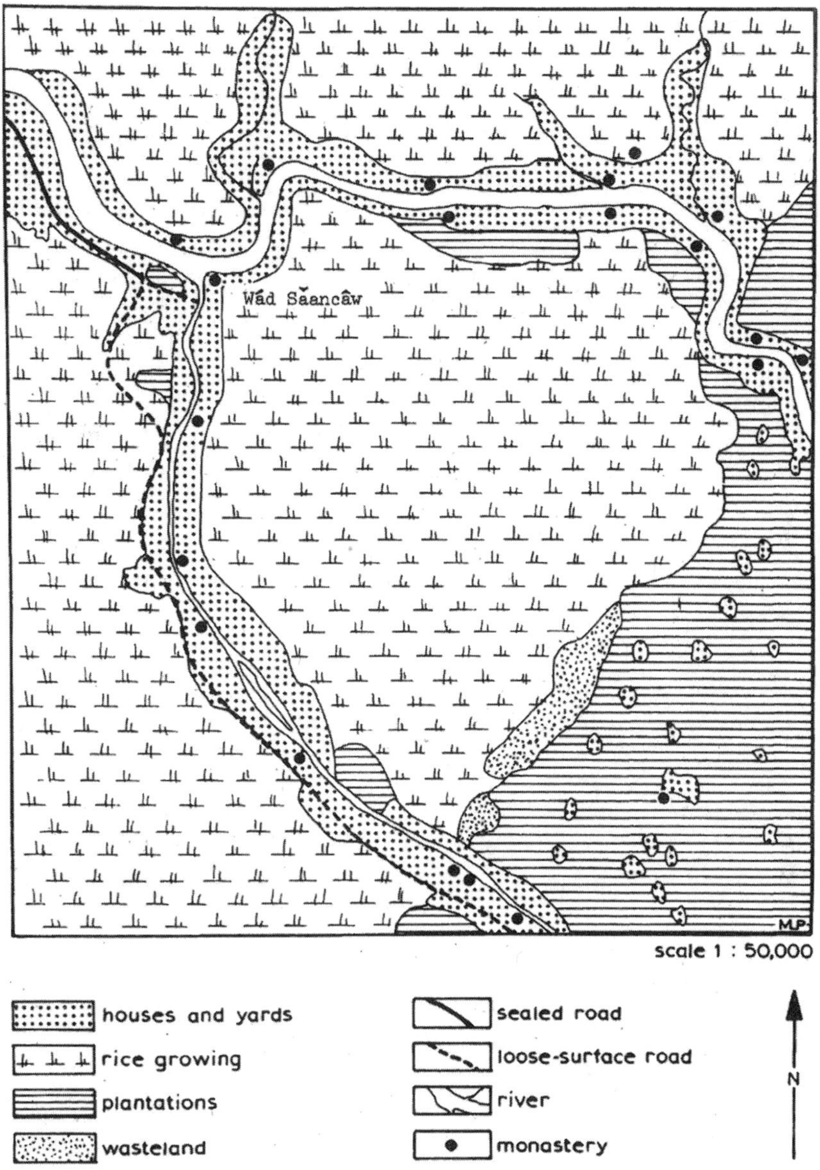

Map II: Habitation, vegetation and rivers around Wat Sanchao

lie scattered about on the south bank of the river Maeklong and on both sides of the river Om, which branches off from the Maeklong at Wat Sanchao.

Map II, which shows the surroundings of Wat Sanchao in the year 1967, depicts two distinct ecological systems. On the one hand there is the region in which Wat Sanchao itself is situated, characterized by the cultivation of rice; on the other there is an area that suddenly begins a few kilometres to the southeast of the monastery where no rice is grown, but where people draw their livelihood mainly from coconut plantations. The latter type of environment is part of a wider area covering much of the delta of the river Maeklong. In this estuary the salinity of the soil prevents the growing of rice. Scattered throughout these plantations single homesteads can be found. Recently many plantation owners have put their incomes on a somewhat broader basis by combining their plantations with poultry farming.

The habitat around Wat Sanchao differs greatly from the plantation area; it conforms to the rice-growing regions in the rest of the central alluvial basin of Thailand. After 1967, however, some enterprising farmers began converting parts of their rice fields into orchards, no doubt a result of the introduction of controlled irrigation.[8] In contrast to the people living in the coconut plantation area, the people connected to Wat Sanchao live on the borders of the main waterways. The growth of the population has caused virtually all riverbanks to be divided up in homesteads, so that on either side of a river an almost continuous stretch of gardens can be found, here and there interspersed with the expanse of a monastery. Thick vegetation hides most houses from view. The plants growing in a compound usually comprise a few clusters of bamboo, many trees of which the fruits or leaves are edible, an areca palm,[9] a betel plant and sometimes a kapok tree, and if there is a small relatively open space left this is likely to be covered with a variety of vegetables.

The stretches of inhabited land are divided into small administrative units, the *muban* (หมู่บ้าน). In many areas of Thailand a *muban* forms a distinct hamlet or a small village, but around Wat Sanchao, as in much of the central plain, there is no visible boundary between different *muban*. The farmers in these populated riverbanks are aware of the fact that they live in a certain *muban* through their dealing with officials from the post office, from the provincial cadastral office and from the Department of Irrigation. Several *muban* are combined administratively into a precinct, a *tambon* (ตำบล). A number of *tambons* form an *amphoe* (อำเภอ), and several *amphoes* constitute a *changwat* (จังหวัด), or province. The farmers do not readily identify themselves with these larger administrative units. Apart from their families, the main unit with

8 This trend continued, so that in 2010 such plantations and various vegetable crops dominated the landscape.

9 *Areca catechu*. The seeds of the Areca plant are often referred to as betel nut, an unfortunate name since it is not a *betel* nor, botanically speaking, a nut.

which many farmers are firmly linked in thought and deed is usually the nearest monastery.

Enclosed by the main waterways and their fringes of gardens and houses are the regions used for agriculture. Generations of farmers have cleared the soil of almost all flora and have constructed rectangular fields, which are separated from each other by small dykes that also serve as a footpath and along which at irregular intervals a few sugar palms can be found. Each year at the beginning of the rainy season, during the months of May, June and July young rice-plants are transplanted in the best fields and rice seed is distributed over the less favourable plots, and in November, December and January, during the cool season, the crop is harvested.

The extent of land-holding varies considerably from farmer to farmer. In the region surrounding Wat Sanchao, a man possessing a hundred *rai* is considered a big landowner, while a farmer with five *rai* to his name is regarded as very poor. Many farmers possess between 30 and 40 *rai*. A field is not necessarily cultivated by its owner; big landowners and old people without children often rent their land to farmers with small holdings. In 1968 a *rai* of fields could be rented under the condition that the owner received a certain part of the yield of those fields. The customary fee was 10 *thang* (ถัง),[10] or 200 litres of rice per *rai*, regardless of the total yield, but in special circumstances a different price could be agreed upon. Since the harvest of one *rai* usually yields between 25 and 50 *thang* of rice, the customary rent amounted to a share of the produce ranging from 20 to 40 per cent of the total. Another common practice was to draw up a tenancy agreement according to the *baeng ha* system, in which the tenant was allowed to keep three-fifths of the produce of the rented field on condition he surrendered two-fifths to the owner. By 1978, probably as a long-term result of irrigation, a new system was in operation, named *chao mao*, or *chao khat tua*, in which a farmer agreed to pay a fixed amount of money to the lessor.

After harvesting and threshing, part of the rice must be reserved for private consumption and another portion for planting during the subsequent year; sometimes a certain amount must be used to pay for rent of land or draught animals,[11] but the remainder can be sold to a dealer. The money received for his surplus of rice usually represents the greatest part of the yearly cash income of the farmer. Other sources of income during the year come from the sale of surplus vegetables, fruit and fish in the provincial market and sometimes from

10 One *thang*, or 'bucket', is a unit of capacity equal to 20 litres.

11 During 1968, the rent of an ox was estimated to be 30 *thang* of rice per year.

selling sweetmeats or products of handicraft. The poorer farmers can derive additional income from working as unskilled labourers during the slack periods of the year, for example in the time between the harvest and the planting of the new crop. Some farmers may derive an extra income from breeding draught-oxen, whilst others who can be assured of irrigation water may grow a second crop on a few of their fields. In the region around Wat Sanchao the second crop usually consists of small green peas.[12]

While the great majority of people in the region of Wat Sanchao derive their income from agriculture, some also derive part of their income from other sources. In the first place there are some local industries. A few families have dug large clay pits in their compounds and bake bricks. Some of these clay pits are larger than the houses so that it can be deduced that this home industry has been established for a long time. This brick-making is confined to a small region east of Wat Sanchao on the south bank of the river Maeklong, where the deposits of alluvial clay are suitable. Another family derives most of its income from the manufacture of bronze images of the Buddha with a few Indras as a sideline.[13]

Secondly, there are farmers who spend a great deal of their time trading goods. Some go from house to house in a small boat, slowly paddling along a waterway, announcing their wares. Others, whose houses are situated favourably at a crossroad or next to a monastery, convert part of their homes into a shop. They sell household goods such as soap powder, matches and cigarettes. These shops often serve as coffee-houses, where one can obtain soft drinks as well as alcoholic beverages.

A third group of people who derive an income from sources other than agriculture consists of those who receive remuneration from the government. Under this heading fall the headman of the *tambon*, the schoolteachers, men in military service and those who draw a state pension.

Up to the time of the Second World War, the flow of goods from the provincial capital to the region of Wat Sanchao was very small. The farmers built their own houses and their monastery from local materials. In many households a loom was in constant use for the production of cloth. During the Japanese invasion which lasted from early 1942 till mid-1945, Wat Sanchao found itself

12 *Phaseolus mungo*.

13 This reflects the economic situation of the 1960s and is no longer true. Investment in the infrastructure (notably road- and bridge-building and electrification) soon resulted in the establishment of a large clothing manufacturing factory, as well as the development of market gardens and orchards.

involved in war-time activities, because the provincial gold reserves were buried there, a fact that was successfully kept from the Japanese. During the war the flow of goods from the central market in Ratburi dried up almost completely. The older inhabitants of the region recalled that in the last year of the war they had to press their own oil in order to light lamps, and the scarcity of matches made it necessary to rely on flint-stones in order to make fire. Since the war, however, many new goods and ideas have been introduced in the region. In 1968 the farmers had become actively involved in the economy of the provincial capital, and ten years later the community had been fully drawn out of its erstwhile isolation.

Many of the recent innovations have proven beneficial; access to modern medical equipment and new pharmaceutical products in the state hospital has relieved some of the harsh sides of the life of the farmer. Mechanization of transport and irrigation systems opened the way for new initiatives and the accumulation of a measure of wealth.

Most recent innovations, however, have side-effects that have only gradually come to be realized. Transistor radios, for example, link many households with the national broadcasting system and much valuable information may be disseminated through this medium. In actuality, however, when a radio is switched on for hours on end in order to provide background noise, this prevents the type of relaxed conversation of pre-radio times. The art of storytelling, once a favourite evening pastime, is incompatible with the transistor radio. Motorcycles provide splendid opportunity to travel rapidly along the footpaths. The effect of speeding bikes on pedestrian traffic can be quite dramatic. The young adults on their bikes cause many breaches of traditional etiquette by forcing their elders to jump for safety.

Similarly, the outboard motor has greatly increased the efficiency of the transport system on all waterways, but nobody has assessed the damage of the increased waves, or measured the accompanying noise in decibels.[14] Mechanical pumps do relieve the anxieties of waiting for rain, but at the same time it makes the farmer dependent upon expensive fuel.

The monastery has played an important role in the modernization process. It is the place where in the days before the community was connected to the provincial electricity network the combined effort of the farmers made it

14 The problems connected with speedboats of the late 1960s rapidly disappeared when an efficient road network was established. The bitumen road network has proven more economical. Passengers and goods have moved to buses and trucks and consequently peace has once more descended upon the waterways.

possible to rent a generator, install electrical wiring, and enjoy modern goods, such as brilliant lights, record players, amplifiers and loudspeaker boxes. On festive occasions there was no longer the need to hire a band of musicians, as the record player can produce more sound and for a longer period. The monastery, built and maintained by the whole community, reflects the modernizing aspirations of the surrounding farmers.

The Fieldwork Situation

When an anthropologist remains for a prolonged period among a relatively small group of people, often he cannot avoid becoming a disturbing influence in the community under study. Upon his first introduction into the group selected this may already become apparent. When he is not able to explain his presence in a manner that is acceptable to his future informants he may jeopardize the whole project.

Usually the researcher comes as a stranger to the community. The argument that he has come to do research to foster the development of a discipline in a scientific manner will not be easy to transmit and, if understood, it may be met with utter disbelief. Understandably the people may suspect that the researcher has arrived for a special reason that he can not or will not divulge in public. Especially in relatively isolated rural communities where some activities would be regarded as illegal by a central government, the members of the small community may suspect him of having come in order to spy.

Such a situation hampers ethnological research, because information gained from people who are suspicious of the researcher's motivation tends to be of limited value. All answers to the anthropologist's questions may be given with caution, his informants, being constantly on guard may tell deliberate untruths. For these reasons it is advisable, especially during the early stages of fieldwork, for the anthropologist to try and find a role which helps explain his presence in the eyes of his informants. Depending on the situation he can, for example, assume the role of schoolteacher, shopkeeper, tractor-repairer or irrigation expert. If a role can be found that is intimately linked with the aspect of culture under study, the practical advantages of assuming such a role may be great.

Since the research in question centred upon the practice of religion in a Thai rural setting, the role that immediately presented itself was that of a Buddhist monk. In central rural Thailand almost every adult man will become a member of the Sangha for some period of his life. In the rural areas a young man's taking of the vows of the order for at least one Lenten season is regarded as an essential preparation for adult life. It is a fortunate circumstance that, under certain conditions, the Thais do not take exception to a foreigner who wishes to become a monk. As long as the aspirant-monk is prepared to behave in a manner befitting a full member of the order, to learn a certain number of Pali sentences by heart, and to demonstrate to all that he is restful, happy and content in the role of a Buddhist monk, they will be inclined to help and encourage this man. In a rural monastery he will be admitted only if the local abbot is convinced that laymen are willing to guarantee the continuous supply of additional food which will be needed for the extra member of the order.

The author had the privilege to be a member of the Sangha in Wat Sanchao from 20 April 1968 until 3 November of that year. This role proved to be advantageous to the researcher in many respects. In the first place, the anthropologist had little difficulty in explaining his presence, for, in the eyes of the members of the community, he had come to lead a very useful life. Secondly, the role of Buddhist monk is in principle open to all males: it is not necessarily reserved for men born in the community that sustains the monastery. Therefore the adoption of this role by a foreigner does not necessarily upset the total situation. In the third place, as a newly ordained monk, the anthropologist was required to learn a set of skills that are of prime importance for an understanding of the practice of Thai religion. Learning to chant Pali texts, to preach from palm-leaf manuscripts, and to meditate and study with fellow monks was of aid in the understanding of many formal aspects of the religion.

In addition, participation in a great variety of ceremonies, from services for the laity such as the first haircutting of a child, blessing a marriage, praying for rain and assisting with cremations, to ceremonies reserved for members of the Sangha, provided a stimulating introduction to the kaleidoscopic experiences a newly ordained monk can undergo. Moreover, many of these ceremonies were attended repeatedly, and this gave rise to a realization that rituals of the same name may not always take exactly the same form.

As a monk in Wat Sanchao, the researcher was drawn into participating in many different activities. Ultimately this proved very useful in reaching an understanding of many aspects of rural life. He became linked in a network of obligations towards his benefactors, pupil of some senior monks, classmate to other recently ordained members of the Sangha, comrade of some monks and laymen and occasionally instructor to some children who were assigned to the monastery. It is the author's hope that the fact that this foreign researcher was so obviously involved with the religion of the community assisted in making much of his tedious repeated questioning about details of religious ceremonies excusable to his informants. When such questioning took place, the answers were often given as a matter of course, in a spontaneous manner.

Finally, the ritual superiority of a full member of the Sangha over all laymen facilitated the questioning of people who were much older than the researcher himself. If the researcher had been a layman, the difference in age would have placed him in a subservient position to some of the most knowledgeable members of the community.

The role of a Buddhist monk also brought some disadvantages from the anthropologist's point of view. A monk cannot move freely, during the Lenten season he should obtain permission from his abbot before leaving the precincts of the monastery, he should avoid mingling with crowds, and he should keep at a distance from sporting events and military parades. At all times he ought to be aware of his thoughts and movements and remain aloof from women. His rules forbid him to participate in gambling, to drink alcoholic beverages, to fish or to work in the fields. In addition his superior ritual position prevents him from participating in those kinds of religious activities which involve paying homage to those non-human powers that are ritually inferior to monks. In order to overcome the limitations imposed by the monk's role, the first year of fieldwork was divided into two parts; the first portion of just over six months consisted of the time as a member of the Sangha, the second part was a period of five months during which the researcher remained in the vicinity of Wat Sanchao as a layman.

During the second part of the main fieldwork period, the participant-observer technique remained in the foreground. Every occasion to participate actively in the religious life of the farmers was grasped. Therefore it was decided not to live in isolation, but to accept an invitation to take up residence with a farmer's family,[15] whose house was situated about one kilometre distance from Wat Sanchao. From here it was possible to go out and attend further rituals, whether a fund-raising ceremony at a neighbouring monastery, the building of a new house, the celebrating of a marriage, or listening to a famous preacher. In addition I was allowed to take part in the work on the farm. Especially during the period of harvesting and threshing rice many days of hard physical work were spent in the fields.

Much of the information upon which this study is based has thus been obtained with the help of the participant-observer technique. This technique

15 I am greatly indebted to the family of the late Sangiam Charoenchan. They allowed me to take part in their private lives and gave real friendship, thus making this period of research not only immensely interesting but emotionally rewarding as well.

has its difficulties and shortcomings. While the researcher is physically actively engaged in some aspect of social life, for example, while he is helping to pound rice kernels into a paste, or learning how to weave a basket, and meanwhile asking questions about some related beliefs and values, it is difficult to record the information received.

A tape-recorder could only be used in extremely formal circumstances, such as during a preaching or whilst the monks were chanting sacred texts. It was virtually impossible to record casual conversation because invariably the conversation was diverted towards the recorder itself[16] and most people showed marked inhibition to having their ordinary daily language recorded. Moreover, the researcher felt that continual use of the tape-recorder did not agree with the role adopted for the duration of the fieldwork. It became therefore necessary to type or write notes in an abbreviated form at free moments. Sometimes it was many hours before these notes could be worked out in detail and be incorporated in the rest of the data. It is apparent that under these circumstances no word-for-word record could be made. Relying on his memory, guided by a few key words jotted down, the researcher could only reconstruct the gist of the various interesting conversations. Accuracy was sacrificed to a certain extent in order to obtain volunteered, spontaneous information.

For this reason, a check on accuracy seemed necessary. Near the end of the main fieldwork period it was therefore decided to employ one member of the community living around Wat Sanchao, and to read aloud in the Thai language to this informant all accumulated data. The informant was encouraged to make critical comments. This check eliminated certain inaccuracies and rectified some misunderstandings on the part of the author; in addition the notes themselves proved a most fruitful store of topics of conversation, and some new data were unearthed. These sessions lasted for one month and this period represents the only time that a paid informant was used.

The Framework of Definitions

Unlike many other sciences, anthropology does not appear to possess a set of axioms that are generally accepted. There is no unanimity of opinion on what should be the definition of culture, religion or ritual; the definition of anthropology itself is not beyond discussion. For this reason it is relevant to set out in a concise manner what meaning is given to some of the concepts that are crucial to this study of religion and how these concepts are interrelated.

16 The tape recorder was at that time a bulky machine and the turning of the large spools had a very distracting effect.

The theoretical framework drawn up in this section rests upon a system that is by no means original; a similar model has been devised, for example, by Homans.[17]

The basic assumption in this theoretical framework is that the aspect of culture that social scientists primarily wish to elucidate is social activity. By the social activity of a person is meant that type of activity that is directed towards, or implies the existence of, other actors. The word 'actor' should be used in a broad sense indeed: it is not solely reserved for human actors; it can include all kinds of non-human or imagined agents. This ensures that the theoretical model encompasses religious activities among the social activity studied.

The social activities observed by the researcher invariably take place in an environment that contains other actors and agents who recognize, or are believed to recognize, most of each other's activities; in other words, who partake in the same culture. Different sub-disciplines of social science study different aspects of social activity. Most anthropologists are often intent on investigating the norms that exist in a certain community.

By the concept 'norm' is understood the opinion of a certain number of actors that under certain circumstances certain activities should be engaged upon or avoided.[18] Since non-human agents can be regarded as a type of actor in social activity, it is apparent that ethics and morals can be seen as specific types of norms.

Each norm is the product of a historical chain of events: there must have been a set of precedents in the past which have resulted in its being generally known that in certain circumstances one ought to behave in a prescribed manner. The constant influx of new circumstances, which brings about new precedents, combined with the fact that in the course of time the members of a culture do not remain the same individuals, makes it understandable that norms change continually in all societies.

There are norms, however, which, with the help of historical records, can be traced over a long period of time. Even if such a norm does not appear to have changed during many centuries, this does not warrant the conclusion that the norm can be evaluated in a similar manner over that whole period of time. Since all cultures are in constant flux, a norm should be interpreted in its contemporary context: in relation to the whole cultural situation of a particular time.

17 George C. Homans, *The Human Group*, 1951, and *Social Behavior, Its Elementary Forms*, 1961.

18 Homans, *Social Behavior, Its Elementary Forms*, p. 46.

Thus it was noted that the people of Sukhothai in the fourteenth century worshipped sacred relics. Similar beliefs can probably be established in the same region six centuries later. However, for a proper understanding of the importance of relics in Sukhothai times it is necessary to attempt to put together as much information about fourteenth-century Sukhothai as possible. Factors such as the size of the population, methods of communication, the system of slavery, the means of production, religious concepts, the position of the ruler as guardian of the realm, and the likely political impact of a religious validation of the ruler through the intervention of miraculously found relics must all be taken into account.

Consistent with the framework of concepts drawn up so far, the definition of religion is based upon the concept of religious activity. Religious activities are hereby defined as those social activities or aspects of social activities that involve human actors in relation to culturally postulated immaterial non-human agents.[19]

The words 'immaterial non-human agents' are used in preference to the more generally accepted 'supernatural beings', since the word 'supernatural' has connotations such as 'more than natural', 'beyond nature'. While activities showing the aspect of 'more than natural' can sometimes be regarded as religious, the exclusive use of the term 'supernatural' limits religious phenomena too much. After all, it is likely that there are cultures in which at least some invisible religious agents are seen as an intrinsic part of nature. Such seems to be the case in rural Thailand.

For a similar reason the term 'superhuman' was avoided in the definition of religion, since 'superhuman' has connotations of 'more than human', 'above human', and while much of the religious activities can be caught under a definition that uses this term, it is not necessarily a classification that comprises all religious action. It is quite possible to envisage religious agents that are 'other than human', or even 'below human'. Some of the spirits of Thai religion may well fall under the latter heading. Since the morphological classification of religious agents will differ from religion to religion, it was therefore decided to make the wording as wide as possible and use the terms 'immaterial non-human agents'.

In contrast with the approach of some anthropologists of the functionalist school, religion is here not thought of as a social system, as a sub-system, or as

19 I arrived at this definition partly by critically appraising Melford E. Spiro's definition of religion from 1964: 'a cultural system consisting of culturally patterned interaction with culturally postulated superhuman beings' in: 'Religion and the Irrational', *Proceedings of the 1964 Annual Spring Meeting of the American Ethnological Society*, p. 103.

an institution in its own right.[20] Instead, religion is considered an aspect of social behaviour; it is usually found in combination with non-religious activities. Many anthropologists who have learned to compartmentalize human behaviour fail to realize how rare 'purely' religious behaviour is. Even in the institutionalized areas of religion, for example during certain ceremonies with a stated religious aim, it is always possible to discern aspects which have direct bearing on quite different areas of the culture. For example, when a group of villagers gather in Wat Sanchao on a Buddhist holy day in order to offer food to the monks and listen to the recital of sacred texts, non-religious aspects can be crucial for a full understanding of the ritual. Some laymen may take part to gain merit, but others attend because staying home would give rise to gossip, or because they wish to meet certain other villagers. The positioning of the laymen in respect to each other, who sits next to whom during such a gathering, is of anthropological interest, but may have little to do with religion. The amount of food donated may be seen from an economic angle and the verbal exchanges between laymen may be of great scholarly interest for a variety of reasons that, again, do not necessarily relate to religion.

While the activities in the Buddhist monastery can be interpreted from non-religious perspectives, the reverse is also true. Many activities in the houses and in the fields, when carefully analysed, reveal a religious aspect. Before cutting a large tree, a farmer may address the spirit he believes to inhabit that tree. When he is setting out on a hazardous journey, precautions may be taken that are of religious significance. Religion thus pervades all aspects of life and it can be studied in virtually all social situations in rural Thailand.

In line with a general trend among anthropologists, in this study no distinction is made between religion and magic; the latter is seen as part of the rich field of religion as a whole. Magical activities are those religious activities whereby the human actors manipulate the non-human agents for a practical purpose of their own.

Social activity, culture, norm, religion, and magic having been defined, there remains a concept crucial to the study of Thai religion: the ceremony or ritual. A ceremony is hereby defined as the performance of a number of related social activities in a prescribed manner. They provide a researcher with a formal demonstration of a set of interrelated norms. In many societies the enactment of a ritual is considered important, and care is taken to adhere to the manner traditionally observed. In Thailand, where some traditional lore is

20 Notably Melford Spiro, *loc. cit.*, and his 'Religion: Problems of Definition and Explanation', in *Anthropological Approaches to the Study of Religion*, ed. by Michael Banton, pp. 96–7

preserved in handbooks and reinforced by formal teaching, ceremonies tend to preserve an interrelated network of norms of a period prior to the time of enactment. The study of ceremonial can thus be an aid to historical insight while, on the other hand, historical data may be helpful to an understanding of the inclusion of certain elements in the analysis of contemporary ceremonies.

Ceremonies, having been defined in relation to social activities in general, are therefore not necessarily part of religion. There are many ceremonies that are centred around a religious theme, but much religious information is embedded in rituals which are primarily concerned with other aspects of social activities.

Much of the evidence brought forward in this study of Thai rural religion is based upon the analysis of a multitude of ceremonies. Although the analytical statements can ultimately be traced back to data obtained from the observation of specific rituals, usually the details of actual ceremonies have been left out so as to keep this study concise as well as comprehensive. The presentation of rituals in this book is often one level removed from direct observation. For the benefit of the reader, rituals are presented in their basic normative form. A ritual is often first described in its essential core: the minimal activity without which the ceremony has no validity in the eyes of the performers.

This essential ceremony gives clues about the nomothetical structure behind the activities. However, the wealth of ideographical detail has its own analytical value. Therefore after the elementary core is described, usually a description of common elaborations follows, in which is shown what aspects of the core ceremony are generally embellished by those who have the means and the inclination to do so.

While the analysis of many ceremonies has been chosen as the major key towards understanding certain fundamental principles underlying rural Thai religion, the order of presentation is derived from a general awareness of a simple sociological truth: the individuals who make up a society are of great diversity, each possessing a unique genetic code. All persons differ in their appreciation of their own culture.

In the first place there is a great difference in the grasp and complexity of religious beliefs between persons of different ages. The religious knowledge of a person during the first formative years of his life is essentially different from the understanding an adult may have acquired. The religion of a man who has been a Buddhist monk may well be at variance with that of a person who has not had that privilege. A man setting up a family may be supposed to have a different outlook from a person in his old age. Secondly, within each age group, women may differ from men in religious experiences and access to religious knowledge,

In order to impart these principal notions, the ceremonies that are discussed in this book are ordered along a developmental scale, and from time to time a distinction between the sexes is mentioned. Thus a picture of religion is developed in a manner somewhat like that in which religion unfolds itself to the Thais.

In order to impart an idea of the techniques used during the different stages of the fieldwork, some additional methods and technical devices have to be mentioned.

(a) A picture of the historical background was obtained mainly through discussions with the older members. All available documentary records of the monastery were checked. Altogether this comprised 346 books and pamphlets in Thai and Pali, as well as several handwritten sources. Most of the books, however, were old copies of texts used by monks to prepare themselves for state examinations. The handwritten sources were exercise books in which was recorded all individuals who had contributed to religious ceremonies held in the monastery. Altogether the printed and written documents were interesting, but of very limited historical value.
(b) In line with the participant-observer technique, information was obtained from in-depth interviews rather than from questionnaires. In general it can be stated that when a certain point remained unanswered, or when the researcher failed to understand a particular remark or statement, this was noted in a booklet especially reserved for this purpose and followed up in subsequent questioning.
(c) Genealogical charts were constructed, comprising all households that regularly supported the monastery. These charts included all people already deceased who could be remembered. It was recorded of all males in the charts whether or not they had ever been a monk, and if this question was answered in the affirmative, how many times they had been ordained, in which monastery and for how many years.
(d) On some occasions when the researcher was prevented from attending an important ceremony through overlap with other engagements, a photographic record was obtained. For this purpose, an informant was instructed in the use of photographic equipment. The resulting photographs were often instruments in further conversations and interviews.[21]

21 How an anthropologist unwittingly can precipitate change in the community under research is demonstrated by the fact that this informant gained employment at first as a freelance photographer, and later was employed by several newspapers to supply relevant photographs.

(e) While the use of the tape-recorder was restricted for reasons mentioned earlier in this chapter, it was possible to make recordings of much of the chanting of the monks. These recordings were later used to compare the chanting of the Wat Sanchao monks with the texts issued by the Department of Religious Affairs and by the Mahāmakuta Educational Council of the Buddhist University in Bangkok.

(f) Furthermore, it should be mentioned that attempts were made to evaluate the instrument upon which the whole project depended in the first place: the anthropologist himself. Nobody who for a prolonged time immerses himself in an alien culture can remain objective. The personality of the researcher is involved, not only when he chooses his path through the multitude of information which unfolds itself daily around him, but also when he selects contacts with members of the community. The values and attitudes of a person influence his manner of observation, his basic classification, his line of analysis.

When a psychologist at the Australian National University[22] was approached before setting out for the main period of fieldwork, it was with two aims in mind. In the first place, realizing how subjective human perception is, the researcher felt necessary to obtain some sort of assessment of his values and attitudes. Secondly, it was considered that it would be interesting to discover whether any marked change in his personality would occur as a result of the new experiences during the fieldwork.

It was decided to try and obtain a picture of the attitudes and values of the researcher by administering at two distinct moments of time a certain number of tests, as set out in Table 2. The first set of tests was given in March 1968, just before the researcher set out for Thailand, and the second series took place in April 1969, immediately upon his return from the main period of fieldwork. In addition, extensive interviews were recorded.

The major findings resulting from the analysis of the tests and interviews can be summarized as follows:

(1) The topic of the thesis and the role of a monk were chosen, not only for the purpose of intellectual enquiry, but also because the researcher hoped and expected that it would enlarge and enrich his personal experiences.

(2) After the research he was disappointed in some measure to realize how ordinary and understandable the experiences were.

22 Mrs Margaret Evans of the Australian National University spent many hours of her time in order to prepare answers to my questions.

Table 2: Tests administered to the researcher before and after the main period of fieldwork

	March 1968		April 1969
1	Eysenck Personality Inventory Form A	1	Eysenck Personality Inventory Form B
2	Thematic Apperception Test	2	Thematic Apperception Test
3	Rorschach	3	Rorschach
4	Cattell's 16 P.F. Form A	4	Cattell's 16 P.F. Form B
5	Minnesota Multiphasic Personality Inventory	5	Minnesota Multiphasic Personality Inventory
6	Allport-Vernon-Lindzey's Study of Values	6	Allport-Vernon-Lindzey's Study of Values
7	Leary Interpersonal Check List	7	Leary Interpersonal Check List
8	Willoughby Personality Schedule	8	Willoughby Personality Schedule

(3) Although he participated in many ceremonies and rites, he never possessed faith.

(4) He himself felt that he did not personally change greatly from these experiences.

(5) The tests revealed no significant changes in his personality as a result of these experiences.

CHAPTER III

CHILDREN AND RELIGION

In many traditional societies ideas concerning the principles governing the conception of a child are strongly influenced by religious beliefs. In Thailand, as can be expected from a Buddhist country, adults see the conception of a child as related to the principles governing rebirth and karma.[1] In rural areas it is believed that a woman who regularly has sexual intercourse with a man becomes pregnant when a *winyan* (วิญญาณ), a soul or spirit,[2] settles in her womb. Coitus provides the circumstances wherein the *winyan* can grow and eventually be reborn. It has been reported that a woman can obtain knowledge of the character of the child through a dream soon after she has conceived,[3] but no such instances can be reported from the region around Wat Sanchao.

If a child is stillborn or if it dies soon after birth, the *winyan* of the infant is considered to have possessed bad karma. The fact that such an unhappy event occurs to a certain family is also seen related to the bad karma of the parents involved.

The woman who finds herself pregnant usually takes great care to protect herself and the foetus from harm. In light of the attitudes towards unhappy events described above it may be asked why the Thais should take elaborate precautions against a mishap, since the doctrine of karma appears to indicate a world view based on a theory of predestination. It could thus be reasoned that an individual with good karma will be free from mishap, whatever actions he or

1 Literally: 'doing', 'action'. The Thai spelling indicates that the Thai word *kam* (กรรม) is derived from the Sanskrit *karma,* rather than the Pali *kamma.*

2 Pali *viññāṇa,* life force, also extending over rebirths.

3 H. G. Quaritch Wales, 'Siamese Theory and Ritual Connected with Pregnancy, Birth and Infancy', *Journal of the Royal Anthropological Institute of Great Britain and Ireland.* Vol. LXIII, 1933, pp. 442–3. Phya Anuman Rajadhon, *Life and Ritual in Old Siam,* 1961, pp. 109–10. It is related to the belief that all dreams can be interpreted. Whenever a person has a vivid dream or a nightmare he or she may try to find out its meaning by consulting textbooks or knowledgeable persons.

she takes and that a person who possesses bad karma will not be able to avoid a horrible fate. However, the place of the karma doctrine in the Thai world-view is quite different; in no way can the religion of the Thais be called fatalistic or deterministic.

As an illustration the agricultural pursuits of a farmer can be taken. The man who plants a crop and tends his fields has a chance of reaping a harvest, whilst the man who decides not to plant will surely run out of food. The methods of dealing with the environment in order to maximize the chances of obtaining profitable results have been handed down through the generations. Magical manipulations form part of the traditional knowledge, and it is generally accepted in Wat Sanchao that these have proven successful in many instances. Sometimes, however, a person does not obtain the desired result notwithstanding the fact that he took proper precautions. Small misfortunes can be explained in several ways: the techniques may have been applied in the wrong manner or at the wrong time, the persons involved may have been inexperienced, or the propitiation of outside powers may have been insufficient. It is only when a man has continuously used the proper methods and still receives setback after setback that he has to acknowledge that his bad karma must be the overriding factor.

The store of karma from past lives is for most people a mixed bag, some positive but also a certain amount negative. In ordinary daily life references to this ultimate decisive factor of a person's circumstances are seldom made. Only in special circumstances during a run of exceptionally bad fortune, but also when there is an otherwise inexplicable amount of good luck, will reference be made to a person's karma. In general, the karma doctrine is therefore used *ad hoc*, as an ultimate explanation for the occurrence of events.

The karma doctrine and magical manipulations are therefore not fundamentally opposed in the eyes of Thai farmers. Placing a karmic system in opposition to a magical system, as Robert Textor does for a village in central Thailand, seems to be based on the apperceptions of that researcher rather than those of the farmers themselves. This becomes even more evident when he gives the karmic system the epithet 'moral', and calls the magical system 'amoral'.[4] The karma doctrine does not exclude the principles underlying the application of magical power. On the contrary, the two systems are complementary. Someone who neglects magical protection, relying solely on his good karma, is like a gambler trusting his luck. A man who takes the appropriate

4 R. B. Textor, *An Inventory of Non-Buddhist Supernatural Objects in a Central Thai Village.* 1960, pp. 8–11 *et passim.*

magical precautions before engaging upon important activities is more secure. If things turn out badly for the latter, at least it is not due to his neglect of the non-human agents around him.

Therefore a pregnant woman will do all she can to protect herself and her child. Even if she personally is not inclined to do so, her relatives may ensure that she takes magical precautions, because if she fails to do so she is a potential danger to her immediate surroundings. If she were to die with her as yet unborn child, she becomes a very dangerous spirit, likely to blindly revenge her sorrows on innocent members of the community. The common precautions taken include a special diet, the wearing of certain talismans and special rules of behaviour during bathing. Many of the traditional prescriptions for pregnant women have been described in detail by Phya Anuman Rajadhon under his pen-name of Sathian Koset and they need not be repeated here.[5]

Usually a child is born at home. Even the farmers who live within easy reach of a hospital ask for medical help only in exceptional cases. This reluctance to use modern medical facilities is partly due to the expense involved. Additionally, many women prefer to give birth in the ancestral home because there they can freely surround themselves with magical precautions which have no place in hospitals. Moreover, many women fear that the obstetrician may be a male and do not wish to expose their bodies to the cold, clinical eyes of medical personnel. When the child is born in the village, an older female assists and a loose cloth over the lower parts of the body gives privacy.

Ceremonies surrounding the birth of a child vary according to the wealth of the family into which it is born and the number of children that have already been born to the couple in question. When the family is poor or when the child has already many brothers and sisters, often only the essential ceremonies are observed.

As soon as the labour pains begin, the midwife is called. When the midwife enters the house she must be presented with a ceremonial gift: a tray with a quantity of unhusked rice, a coconut, some bananas, areca fruit, candles, incense and a sum of money. Wat Sanchao farmers can recollect the time when the amount of money was four or six *baht*,[6] but in 1968 the midwife could expect to receive twenty *baht* if she worked for friends, and as much as

5 Sathian Koset, ประเพณีเก่าของไทย, 1957, pp. 10–35. An English translation can be found in *Life and Ritual in Old Siam*, pp. 110–120.

6 The *baht* is the monetary unit of Thailand. In 1968, the pound sterling equalled approximately forty-nine *baht*, or one US dollar equalled twenty *baht*. More relevant for the rural setting: a labourer's wages were approximately twenty-five *baht* per day.

forty *baht* when she worked for a family with whom she was not particularly intimate.

The midwife formally accepts the tray, but it is immediately taken away and set in an honourable place of the house. She does not take possession of it until three days after the delivery. The midwife assists the pregnant woman with her skills, which usually include the application of ointments, the use of medicine, the uttering of spells and manipulation. As soon as the child has been born, mucus is removed from the mouth and the nose of the baby by sucking. The umbilical cord is cut with a knife made from *mai ruak*, a type of bamboo.[7] The placenta is collected, salted and placed in a jar that is kept in the room for three days. The day of the week and the lunar month are noted, so that the child may use this knowledge later when making decisions for which astrological calculations are necessary.

Under the house, directly beneath the place of confinement, a heap of thorny branches has been laid. This acts as a cover for the body liquids and excreta that may fall during and after the confinement. The thorns prevent not only animals, but also malevolent spirits from feeding on the offal.

On the third day after birth, the child is ceremoniously accepted into the world of his relatives. The infant is laid on a *kradong* (กระด้ง), a large round winnowing tray. The midwife moves the tray three times in a clockwise direction, while chanting slowly: 'Three days, child of the spirits; four days, human child – who will receive this child?'[8] An older relative, who has a good standing in the community and who has the reputation of being able to raise children successfully, accepts the small infant from the hands of the midwife and has to pay a ceremonial sum for this honour. On this occasion the child receives a string of cotton thread bound around his right wrist,[9] a ritual intended to reassure the soul of the infant.[10] After this precaution, the baby is bumped softly on the floor in order to acquaint it with the fact that harsh and startling events may occur in the world of the humans where it has now been received. After the infant has thus been introduced to its relatives, the midwife receives her payment. The jar containing the afterbirth can be buried under a tree somewhere near the house. This establishes a link between the tree and the infant: if the tree thrives, the

7 Thai: ไม้รวก, *Thrysostachys siamensis* (G. B. McFarland, *Thai-English Dictionary*, p. 689).

8 For a similar rhyme amongst the Tais near the Laotian-Vietnamese border see A. Bourlet, 'Les Thay', *Anthropos*, Vol. 2, 1907, p. 361.

9 This ritual is mentioned for ancient India in the *Sāṅkhāyana Gṛhya Sūtra*, I, 25, 12 (*Sacred Books of the East*, Vol. XXIX, p. 51).

10 The ceremonies of reassuring the soul are mentioned in more detail later in this chapter.

child should be healthy and happy; if the tree droops or dies, it bodes ill for the infant and he or she should be guarded carefully.

The elementary ceremonies surrounding birth close with the tonsure of the child. On an auspicious day, some time after mother and child have left the place of confinement, a member of the family who is skilful with a big razor shaves the head of the infant.[11] If the child seems ailing and the family fears that it may not be sufficiently strong enough to face life, it may be decided to leave one or more tufts of hair growing. In that case, during the following years, the rest of the head should be shorn regularly, leaving the tufts to grow. When the child is ten or more years old, this hair, which may have been plaited or knotted, will be shaved off at an auspicious moment. Many children who soon after birth appear perfectly healthy may never have such a topknot. The tonsure not long after birth can be regarded as a purification rite; it serves to cleanse the baby's head, which has been treated disrespectfully and which has come into contact with unclean matter.

Farmers who can afford to pay for elaborate ceremonies may decide, before a child is born, to have the place of confinement purified and protected. They invite a ritual specialist, who can be a Buddhist monk or an older layman, to do this. The specialist strings a white cotton thread, known as *sai sin* (สายสิญจน์),[12] around the place of confinement in the form of a square, several feet above floor level. Whenever such a cord is placed around an area or an object it sets the enclosed area apart as a sacred space. The ritual specialist then sacralizes a bowl of water, by reciting from memory a number of auspicious verses in the Pali language whilst holding a lighted candle above the surface of the water in the bowl. During this recitation, the specialist holds the candle at such an angle that it drips wax onto the surface of the water. After sacralization, the water is known as 'mantra-water', or *nam mon* (น้ำมนตร์). Immediately after the *nam mon* has been prepared, it can be sprinkled in and around the area of confinement. The householder may keep some of the *nam mon* in order at a future date to extinguish the fire that traditionally formed an essential part of the post-natal treatment.

11 The tonsure ceremony was commonly used in ancient India. It is described in detail in the *Gṛhya Sūtras,* in the *Manu-smṛti* and dealt with in Kane's *History of Dharmaśāstra,* Vol. II, p. 260 ff. It is by no means certain, however, that the leaving of a topknot is derived from India. See G. E. Gerini, *Chūlākantamaṅgala, the Tonsure Ceremony as Performed in Siam,* 1976.

12 This word means literally 'sprinkling cord'. It is related to the Sanskrit word *siñcana,* or the Pali *siñcanaka.* The connection with water lies probably in the ritual of sacralization of this water.

So as to ward off evil influences the ritual specialist may have prepared and brought along various kinds of sacred objects: small banners and magical drawings. The banners are usually made of gaily coloured pieces of paper cut in the shape of a triangle and fastened by one side to a small stick. The magical drawings, known as *yan* (ยันต์),[13] are usually made on paper or on cloth. Often they consist of intricate geometrical designs in which small characters in the sacred Mūl script are inserted. Both the banners and the *yan* are placed above and around the place of confinement.

Many older women around Wat Sanchao have been through a period of *yu fai* (อยู่ไฟ), or 'staying at the fire' after giving birth to a child. Nowadays it is considered old-fashioned and not worth the trouble. Only a single case was reported recently.[14] For this reason *yu fai* was not included in the description of the elementary birth ceremonies to which it formally belonged. Nowadays it may be regarded as a kind of elaboration and thus is mentioned here.

Before the child is due to be born, an oven is prepared from a layer of banana leaves covered with a generous amount of sand. The farmer collects an ample supply of firewood, which he heaps up neatly, and covers with a thorny branch to keep evil spirits away. The wood ought to be of good quality, so it will burn steadily for a long time. He should not, for example, collect bamboo for that burns unevenly. Moreover, bamboo was traditionally used to cover corpses and to cremate bodies. Its association with death is the reason why young persons should not even plant bamboo.

As soon as the child is born, a big fire is lit in the earth oven, and the mother's bed is placed as close to it as she can endure. The fire is kept burning for days and the mother and child should not leave the place of the confinement until it has been ritually extinguished. Usually *yu fai* lasts an uneven number of days, and a woman may remain as long as fifteen days on the confinement bed.

The older women relish their periods of *yu fai* in their memory. During this time they are the centre of attention in the household. The men are employed to keep the fire burning, and female relatives are in constant attendance. Many friends come to visit the lying-in woman and cheer her up with interesting stories. Visitors avoid mentioning the heat of the fire, because it is believed that if such a topic were broached the lying-in would become unbearable. The

13 A word derived from the Pali *yanta* or the Sanskrit *yantra*. Originally the word meant 'aid' or 'tool', to be used in meditation. The Thais often use it in a restricted sense, namely as 'mystical diagram'. The original meaning can be found in the Thai language in the word for mechanical engineering: '*wichayantakam*' (วิชายันตรกรรม).

14 Personal communication, Sangiam Charoenchan, 14 November 1969.

period of lying by the fire is considered to have a very positive medicinal effect. The fire warms the belly, dries up the liquids, cleanses and heals. It is believed that a woman who has had a period of *yu fai* will live to a ripe age without suffering from pains in the back or in the belly.[15]

An elaboration of the ceremony of the winnowing basket, three days after birth, consists of a ceremony known as *tham khwan* (ทำขวัญ). A ritual specialist invokes non-human powers to come and assist in the ritual. In order to cause these non-human agents to assist he folds some *bai si* (ใบศรี), conical structures folded from banana leaves, and places an egg atop of each of these. Around the *bai si*, other foods that the powers like, such as bananas and sweetmeats, are placed. The ceremony is intended to strengthen the *khwan* (ขวัญ) of the child. *Khwan* is a word that does not translate easily into English; it may mean 'ego', 'soul', 'morale', 'grace', or 'prosperity'. In order to increase the courage and reassure the soul of the infant, it is dressed with glittering ornaments and the whole family, sitting around the child in a circle, passes around three lit candles, from which each member wafts the smoke towards the centre. During the ritual, the specialist binds a piece of cotton string around the baby's wrist, anoints the child's forehead and implores the child's soul to be unwavering, to stay firm and to enjoy its pleasant surroundings.

The *tham khwan* ceremony may be repeated at various periods of a person's life. For example, it may be undergone when a person has had a severe shock as a result of which it is feared that he is losing his zest for life. It is also customary to hold a *tham khwan* ritual during the elaborate preparations for ordination as a Buddhist monk. *Tham khwan* is a feature of the house building ritual and it may be performed over the rice harvest, immediately before threshing.[16]

Finally, the tonsure of an infant may be subject to elaborations. Well-to-do farmers may use the occasion of the first shaving of their child to invite a chapter of monks who will perform a ceremony at home. These monks sacralize a bowl of water and, while they chant a final blessing, the head of the child is shaved. If the infant is a boy, the leader of the chapter of monks, usually the abbot, may remove the first lock of hair. A small girl has to be handled by laymen only since the rules of the Sangha, at least in their Thai interpretation, forbid a monk to touch females.

15 For an overview of the spread and meaning of the custom of lying by the fire, see Lenore Manderson, 'Roasting, Smoking and Dieting in Response to Birth: Malay Confinement in Cross-Cultural Perspective', *Social Science and Medicine*, Vol. 15 B, 1981, pp. 509–20.

16 More details can be found in Phya Anuman Rajadhon's 'The Khwan and its Ceremonies', *Journal of the Siam Society*, Vol. 50, 1962, pp.119–64 and in Ruth-Inge Heinze, *Tham Khwan: How to Contain the Essence of Life*, 1982.

Not long after birth, when it appears likely that the child will live, its name is chosen. There are two types of children's names, which I shall call the private name and the nickname. The private name must be selected with care, for an unsuitable appellation may cause its bearer to become sickly and listless. Before deciding upon a name many parents will consult friends who have access to a booklet with choices, or they will ask suggestions from a monk whom they trust in these matters. The person who advises will be mainly guided by the time and day of the week when the child was born. A person born on a Monday, for example, should avoid vowels in the written form of the name, whilst the Sunday child can make use of all vowels.

Often the private name will have an auspicious, pleasant or highly valued connotation. Thus a person may be called with the word for a respected trait in people, such as 'Polite, Clean, Beautiful, Happy, or Gentle'. Others may carry the name of precious or semi-precious metals: 'Gold, Silver or Copper'. There are names which are especially suited for boys, such as: 'Firm, Extreme, Brave, Battle, Grasp, Impressive', whilst girls may be referred to by names like: 'Fascinating, Full of Auspiciousness, or Attractive'.[17]

There are people who believe that a small child should not be called by its private name for it reflects characteristics that the infant still does not possess. It will be only after the years of childhood are over that a person can make full use of the name that has so carefully been chosen for him. Therefore, a nickname is used during the child's tender years, and in the choice of this nickname the parents carefully avoid reference to beautiful or auspicious objects or concepts. They select 'neutral' words instead, which are neither auspicious nor inauspicious. They may choose the generic name of a domestic animal: 'Pig, Chicken, Dog, or Cat', or a common adjective: 'Little, Fat, Red, or Plenty'.

A special characteristic of the child may prompt the nickname and this leaves room for choosing a rather humorous name such as: 'Beaming, Big Vessel, Tiny, Squeal, Turtle, or Frog'. Sometimes the nickname is formed from an abbreviation of the real personal name, choosing one of the syllables of the latter. There are families in which the nicknames of all children begin with the same consonant.

It has been repeatedly mentioned in the literature that the use of nicknames in Thailand is derived from a custom to deceive evil spirits into thinking that there was no child in the house, that, when parents call out to their child, it is

17 The many rules of name giving are extensively dealt with in Wiriyaburana, ประเพณีไทย [Customs of the Thais], 1967, pp. 78–117.

only the cat, the dog, or an innocent, harmless word being called.[18] Informants who live around Wat Sanchao, however, when confronted with such statements, did not wholly agree. In general, they considered the idea that people gave ugly nicknames in order to deceive spirits ingenious, and it could be true for other regions or may have been so a long time ago. It was not the reason why the farmers of Wat Sanchao give nicknames. Some nicknames are neutral, simply because it is too soon to use the real name, but names such as 'Pig' and 'Dog' are chosen in the hope that the baby will need as little attention and care as a dog or a pig. In this respect it is relevant to notice that the nicknames given to children never refer to inauspicious objects or to objects which are considered magically powerful. Names that cannot be used are those connected with footwear, pain, death, poverty, ignorance, heat, fire, tools, and rice.

Generally, the Thai child spends its first two years on earth in a relaxed environment. Children are taught to walk, to speak and to control the body excretory functions without any form of punishment. They meet with practically no restrictions: they eat when they are hungry and sleep when they feel tired. Instead of receiving censure for a clumsy movement or a wrongly pronounced word, they are praised for each successful step and every attempt to utter a word is met with encouragement.

Before a child is one year old it should be able to make several polite gestures. Every time a child wishes to receive something, and immediately after obtaining something from an older person, be it milk from the breast of the mother, or a toy from an the hands of a grandparent, he has to raise his hands, palm to palm. During the first six months the relatives have to guide the arms of the baby to help him perform the gesture, but by the time the child is one year this gesture has become a conditioned reflex.

Another gesture that infants learn often before they are able to speak is the prostration: placing the hands palms down on the floor and lowering the head until it rests between the hands. Both gestures are extremely important in Thai culture; they are part of almost every religious ceremony, and the order in which these gestures are made and the exact manner of execution reveal the hierarchical positions of the participants in a ritual.[19]

18 Kenneth P. Landon, *Siam in Transition,* 1968, p. 169; K. Chandruang, *My Boyhood in Siam,* 1969, p. 37; Howard K. Kaufman, *Bangkhuad, A Community Study in Thailand,* 1960, p. 145. The same belief is reported for China in J. A. Meijers and J.C. Luitingh, *Onze Voornamen, Traditie, Betekenis, Vorm, Herkomst,* 1963, p. 19.

19 For further details about the execution of both gestures, see Phya Anuman Rajadhon, 'Thai Traditional Salutation', *Thai Culture,* New Series, No. 14, 1963, reprinted in *Essays on Thai Folklore,* 1968, pp. 178–89.

The infant can freely observe how the household's ritual leader, usually its eldest member, pays obeisance to the ancestors. Little children are usually greatly attracted by the lighting of candles and incense and are encouraged to imitate the elder's prostrations. Gradually, as the child grows older and begins to understand language in its finer nuances, the training in proper behaviour becomes more serious. At this time, round about the age of two, the infant is slowly weaned from the breast of its mother and encouraged to eat without the supplementary mother's milk. Now, if the child acts naughtily with the apparent knowledge that he breaks a rule of behaviour, he is punished by verbal reproach or, if deemed necessary, by a mild slap.

From about the age of two, the education of boys begins to differ in character from that of girls. Small girls are taught to do errands for their mother, to help watch over a younger relative and to make themselves useful in the household. The boys on the other hand are allowed to wander about and explore their surroundings. The only chore that automatically falls to a male child is to keep an eye on the buffaloes or oxen when they are allowed to graze, or to pluck grass for these domestic animals. The difference in treatment between the sexes is stressed from a very early age in the different ways of clothing. When they can afford it, parents will dress a baby girl with a string around the waist from which a small metal shield, called *chaping* (จะปิ้ง),[20] hangs over the lower abdomen as *cache-sexe*, whilst small boys may walk about naked. A girl is made to wear short pants at least from about the age of four and from about nine they must cover all the lower part of the body. Boys may wear short trousers from about the age of six.

One of the strictest rules impressed upon girls is that they should never come close to a Buddhist monk. All women, regardless of age, must keep their distance from members of the Sangha, so that the monks can conform to the rules in the strict manner that these are interpreted in Thailand. A small boy is not kept away from monks. On the contrary, parents often like to present their small sons to a monk when they meet, and note with approval how their child is touched and blessed.

A young girl ought to be near the house. She should help in the kitchen, assist in cleaning the house, and sweep the compound. She is given charge over a younger child, thus learning to handle infants skilfully at a very early age. In her autobiography Prajaub recollects her experiences:

20 The small leaf-shaped shield is made of gold, silver, or base metal, depending on the wealth of the family. It is intended to hide the genital area.

> Sometimes, while Mother was away on her short errands, I had to look after my little brother who could crawl very well now. My goodness! To keep him from falling off the verandah was the same as trying to keep a living crab to stay on a tray.[21]

Part of the household duties of a girl may consist of the offering of food to the monks every morning at dawn. Tambiah puts forward the suggestion that young men avoid feeding the monks because they 'find it uncongenial to approach their peers who have temporarily renounced the world . . .' .[22] Such a motivation cannot be ascribed to the men of Wat Sanchao. It is true that few men give food to the monks in the early morning, but their absence can be readily accounted for. Early in the day, when the sun is low, most able men will be in the fields. When men happen to be available they perform this ceremony willingly. Another reason why this task falls almost automatically to the women lies in the fact that women prepare the rice and curries. Therefore they are often better judges of the amount that can be distributed to others without depriving the household.

A child's first acquaintance with the monastery usually dates from a very early age. On the Buddhist special day of worship, *wan phra* (วันพระ), which is held four times each lunar month,[23] children are often brought along whilst their parents attend the ceremonies. During the periods of the service when the monks chant sacred texts, most laymen sit in a polite posture, with the hands raised palm to palm in front of the chin or chest. Some children readily follow the example of their parents, but if the chanting persists for too long young people usually relax from their polite position. No child will be reproached for not keeping his hands up. Only when a youngster threatens to interrupt the ceremony will he be mildly restrained or carried outside.

Some ceremonies in the monastery can be accompanied by festive elaborations. In order to attract a great number of people who will donate money, the organizers of some major ceremonies provide a selection from a variety of attractions, music, classical theatre, popular drama, shadow theatre, films, or acrobatics. On such occasions great crowds of children flock to a monastery

21 Prajaub Thirabutana, *Little Things,* 1971, p. 18.

22 S. J. Tambiah, 'The Ideology of Merit and the Social Correlates of Buddhism in a Thai Village', in *Dialectic in Practical Religion,* ed. by E. R. Leach, 1968, p. 66.

23 *Wan phra* is held on the day of full moon, the eighth day of waning moon, new moon and the eighth day of waxing moon. These are exactly the days reserved by the Buddhist monks for recitation of the teachings in the early days of Buddhism. See *Mahāvagga* II, 1, 1–11, 2,1; *Sacred Books of the East,* Vol. XIII, pp. 239–41.

and they enjoy watching the entertainers free of cost. Through the theatre performances especially they become acquainted with the splendour and pomp of royalty, the might and beauty of gods, the fearful looks and bad behaviour of demons, the antics and power of the semi-divine monkey Hanuman, and the nobility and heroism of Rāma, one of the *avatāras* of Viṣṇu.

The attitudes of many children towards the monastery may well be ambiguous. The splendour of the gods is counteracted by the fearful impressions left by the demons. The normally so friendly and pleasantly spoken monks suddenly appear inaccessible during the impressive sonorous chanting of sacred texts. The lofty buildings are reported to be the habitat of dangerous spirits. In part of the beautiful monastery grounds corpses are stored, awaiting the annihilation of the body on the funeral pyre. Children may watch older people handle the decaying bodies immediately before cremation. It is common knowledge that, at night, spirits roam around in the monastery grounds and beyond. When the dogs of the monastery start to howl it is reputedly because they can see these spirits even if men sometimes cannot. Children are told about these monastery spirits; beings, often dressed in a white shroud, sometimes deceptively looking like ordinary humans, but capable of suddenly changing into skeletons trying to grab people.

Much of the lore surrounding evil spirits has been laid down in the form of a film entitled *Mae Nak Khanong Rak*.[24] This film is full of examples of the powers of different kinds of spirits. Various versions of this film have been circulating in rural central Thailand for many decades and it is probably Thailand's most popular horror film. Many Wat Sanchao people have seen the film on more than one occasion.

At night, a multitude of strange beings threaten the humans. These spirits often lurk in patches of dark vegetation and stories about their characteristics vary, depending on the accounts of eyewitnesses. Sometimes the only indication was a sudden rustling noise, a peculiar sound, or the appearance of a pair of luminous eyes. The wise person does not stay to investigate: he hurries home to tell of a narrow escape from the terrible shock of an encounter with an unknown evil power.

Some of the spirits that a person may encounter are well known from lore If a man meets one of them he would certainly recognize the spirit for what it is. A great looming shape with a small head that makes a piercing noise must

24 Produced in the beginning of this century by M. L. Anusak.

be a *pret* (เปรต),[25] a being suffering for the heavy sins of a past life. The *pret* is considered not very dangerous; if one encounters it, one should have pity on them and offer some merit with an appropriate sentence.

Much more dangerous are the *phi krasue* (ผีกระสือ), ghosts that feed on excrement. A *phi krasue* is shaped like a human head with entrails hanging underneath.[26] They reveal their position during the night by intermittently sending out a small red light. During the daytime these ghosts live in the body of an ordinary-looking person. As soon as the person in whom a *phi krasue* lives falls asleep, the ghost can roam about and search for food. If someone succeeds in capturing a *phi krasue* outside the body of its host, the ghost will plead to be released and reputedly will offer great amounts of money in return for its freedom. The person in whom the *phi krasue* lives during the daytime may not be aware of the fact that such a ghost lives as a parasite in his body. Being possessed by *phi krasue* is regarded as hereditary and, if it becomes known that a certain family is prone to carry these ghosts, pressure may be exerted to have them removed from the district.[27]

Extremely malicious is the class of spirits called the *phi taihong* (ผีตายโหง), literally: 'spirits who died wrongly'. In this category fall all those who died in an inauspicious manner: from cholera, poisoning, a snakebite, or from a bullet- or knife wound inflicted in anger. Each time a person dies unprepared and very much against his own will he may become a *phi taihong*. The most dangerous of this type comes into being when a woman dies when pregnant or during childbirth.

Much less dangerous are the *phi ban* (ผีบ้าน), also known as *phi ruean* (ผีเรือน), the ghosts of the ancestors who hover around the house that once was their own property. These house-spirits jealously watch what their descendants do with the property. If the *phi ban* become offended by an activity of one or more occupants of the house, they may express their discontent by causing nightmares or illnesses. During the daytime their spirit is believed to reside near a shelf in a high place in the house where some of their ashes and sometimes a picture are the material witnesses of their former residence as humans in the home. At night they may roam around the house and the compound.

25 Related to the Sanskrit *preta*.

26 The same type of spirit is described for Malaya under the name *penanggalan* by K. M. Endicott in *An Analysis of Malay Magic*, 1970, p. 61.

27 C. Hardouin, in 'Traditions et superstitions siamoises', *Revue Indo-Chinoise*, April 1904, pp. 415–8, describes in detail how the *phi krasue* are transferred when a possessed person dies. See also Phya Anuman Rajadhon, *Life and Ritual in Old Siam*, pp.118–20.

The present householder usually lights some incense and a candle on the shelf every evening and reports to the *phi ban* that everything is well. Unpleasant news is usually carefully omitted in the daily account, lest the *phi ban* become upset and irritated.

A different category of powers is the *chaophi* (เจ้าผี), tutelary spirits living outside the homes of people. These powers may reside in the forest, in a mountain cave or in a tall tree, but sometimes people have been able to entice one to come and live in a shrine. These powers are usually addressed by the title 'Lord father' or 'Lady mother', depending on which sex they are believed to be. From time to time they should be presented with an offering. Some pleasant aroma from a bundle of incense or from some flowers, a candle alight, or the essence of some food or liquor are reputed to attract such powers. In return for these gifts, the persons who offer them may ask that these powers provide assistance in difficult ventures. When it is an important matter, the aid of a 'Lord father or 'Lady mother' may be obtained by promising an even greater gift if the venture comes off.

Children are well aware of the existence of these different, potentially dangerous powers. They hear stories of terrifying encounters and of people who suddenly became violently ill as a result of offending such a spirit. A child will be taught to behave politely, and to make appropriate, polite gestures to the different spirits. In addition, a simple spell can be taught which will be protective in all circumstances. Thus Kumut Chandruang learned to say 'Namo',[28] probably derived from 'Namo Buddhāya' (In Name of the Buddha). Other protective measures taken are in the form of small Buddha images and amulets. Most protective objects tend to be reserved for boys. Girls are rarely seen with objects that have the power to protect; on the few occasions that a girl carried a Buddha image on a string around the neck, it was reputedly a 'small one', 'not a powerful one', or 'more for decoration than for protection'.[29]

Around their necks, many boys wear a cord from which one or more objects dangle that have the power to protect. Often it is an image of the Buddha or a medal, cast in honour of a famous monk. Sometimes there also hangs a small container containing a tiny scroll. These scrolls, *takrut* (ตะกรุด), may be of paper, cloth, or metal and usually are tightly rolled up inside the container, but sometimes are rolled directly around the cord itself. Their protective value is derived mainly from the fact that *yan*, magical drawings, have been made on

28 Kumut Chandruang, *My Boyhood in Siam*, p. 68.

29 Since the time of fieldwork in the 1960s, this has changed. It is no longer unusual to see a woman wearing the same size images of famous monks and of the Buddha as men do.

the material by a person skilled in magical lore. Some boys wear beads, made from the seeds of the tamarind. Some may have a cord around the waist with a talisman attached, but when it is worn so low on the body, the protective object cannot depict the Buddha or a monk. Instead it usually is a small wooden or metal phallus reputedly powerful enough to make evil spirits recoil.

The boy who wears protective objects is instructed to handle them with care. The cord around his neck is so long that it can be taken off, for example, when the boy lies down to sleep. Under no circumstance should an amulet be placed on the floor or in any other low position where someone may inadvertently step on it. When washing or relieving himself, the boy may put the amulet into the mouth, or temporarily hang it at the back so that it cannot be insulted.[30] The object on the cord around the waist cannot be taken off so easily and at inauspicious moments when the wearer does not wish to insult the amulet, it can be shifted to the back, out of sight.

Formal Education

Especially since the abolition of the absolute monarchy in 1932, the Thai government has accelerated the programme to bring primary education within the reach of the whole rural population.[31] The introduction of government schools has resulted in some far-reaching changes in the social life of the farmers.

Before the time of government schools, formal education was in the hands of the monks. The skills of reading and writing were taught to a select group of small boys, the *dek wat* (เด็กวัด), literally: 'monastery children', who lived in the monastery as servants to the monks. Lessons were given every afternoon, five days per week, by a monk who could read and write with ease. No formal instruction was given on *wan phra* or on the day preceding *wan phra*. Apart from the intricacies of the Thai alphabet, instruction often included the learning of some Pali formulae and the mastering of a sacred script; in central Thailand this is called *Khom* (ขอม) writing. The *Khom* alphabet, also known as Mūl writing, is a form of Cambodian writing (Khom being one of the words for 'Cambodian'). Kaufman was probably misinformed about the position of this script in the whole of central Thailand when he reported that for his community most of

30 These rules of behaviour resemble the Hindu practices regarding the *yajñopavīta*, or sacred cord.

31 B. J. Terwiel, 'The Development of a Centrally Organized Education System in Thailand' in K. Orr (ed.) *Appetite for Education in Contemporary Asia*, 1977, p. 47.

the monks were Cambodian and used their own books.[32] In most monasteries of central Thailand books in *Khom* script can be found and this is no indication that those who read these books are of Khmer descent. It is only since World War II that the Thai government has stopped printing Pali in *Khom* characters. The script is still widely used in the more esoteric skills of tattooing and in the drawing of *yan*.

The road to learning was therefore reserved for the boys in the monastery. Girls were automatically excluded from monastery schools, at least until the beginning of the twentieth century. Young women were traditionally kept under the supervision of elder relatives at home until they married. Nowadays, however, most rural monasteries have reserved part of their grounds for a co-educational government school. Usually the monks do not possess a teaching certificate and are therefore not allowed to teach in these schools.

When children are about six or seven, both boys and girls have to attend school. The first time a child attends lessons, parents usually accompany him in order to present the new pupil to the guardian spirit of the monastery in the grounds of which the school is situated. The tutelary spirit of the Wat Sanchao compound is called the Venerable Father Cha. He lives close by the temple and the place where he usually resides used to be marked with a stone monument, a miniature temple on a pedestal, and a table for placing gifts. During the 1980s the residence of the spirit has been totally refurbished in the form of a special shrine and a life-size image of Father Cha himself. When a new child is introduced, the parents light a candle and some incense, offer some flowers, usually in the form of a garland, and speak to him in the local vernacular. Father Cha is politely informed of the fact that henceforth this child will come regularly to the monastery for the purpose of being educated. The parents then ask the spirit to take notice of the fact that this child will be in and around the school buildings and from time to time will be playing in the monastery compound. They ask Father Cha to cause the child to be happy and successful. After this prayer to the spirit the child can proceed towards the school.

All children are instructed to be always polite near Father Cha's shrine and to lower the head respectfully when passing close by. It would be unwise to forget to inform this tutelary spirit of events of importance in the monastery, because if the spirit becomes annoyed he may retaliate.

> Some years ago, there was a *dek wat* who suddenly fell ill. He had contracted a high fever, and the abbot was called to examine him. Another *dek wat* told

32 H. K. Kaufman, *Bangkhuad*, p. 84.

Figure 3.1: The Venerable Father Cha is also told when a young man is preparing to be ordained in the monastery.

> the abbot that he had seen the sick boy earlier that day playing near the shrine of the Venerable Father Cha and that some incense sticks had been taken away from the shrine. The abbot immediately understood the cause of the fever and hurriedly sent someone over to light new incense sticks near the shrine. Half an hour later the sick boy had recovered, his fever had almost completely gone.[33]

The school curriculum is determined by the Department of Education in the national capital, but in practice many details of what is actually taught are left to the discretion of the teachers. Most of the time in school is devoted to learning to read and write the Thai language with ease. Some teachers use about one hour per week for religious or moral instruction. A variety of subjects can

33 Translated from a personal communication with *Phra* Phlik, on 5 November 1969. Later *Phra* Phlik added: 'Each monastery has its own spirit, and its characteristics vary. Our Venerable Cha happens to be easily offended.'

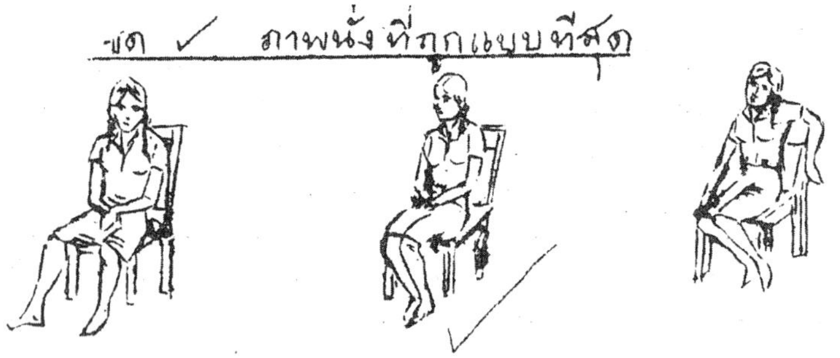

From an exercise book. The Thai text says: 'Indicate with √ which is the most polite way of sitting'.

Figure 3.2: The respectful sitting posture.

be caught under this heading. Apart from the story of the life of the Buddha and some essential ideas from some famous Buddhist texts, religious teaching can include lessons about ethics, morality, and proper physical behaviour, including etiquette. Each child should respect four classes of superiors: his parents, his teachers, the king and the Buddha.

Towards his superiors every child should behave in a proper manner, with the use of polite speech and respectful gestures. The body should be in a proper position when in the presence of one's elders: never on a superior horizontal plane, always avoiding pointing the feet in their direction. Figure 3.2 indicates how this is carried over in a classroom situation. Children are often reminded of the fact that they are deeply in debt to their parents and teachers who have provided them with life, with the essential provisions, with loving and anxious supervision and with knowledge.

The king and the Thai government, it is taught, should be respected as institutions that uphold and propagate morality and the Buddhist faith. In teaching, nationalism and Buddhism appear to be closely interlinked. Such a connection between the two is clear, for example, during the flag-raising ceremony that marks the opening of each school day. All children have to stand neatly dressed in their uniform in orderly lines in front of the school buildings while the flag is raised, and they sing a few bars of the national anthem. A schoolteacher will then lead the children in a communal recitation of some well-known Pali words:

Teacher:	'Arahaṃ sammāsambuddho bhagavā . . .
All:	Buddhaṃ bhagavantam abhivādemi'.

Teacher:	'Svākkhāto bhagavatā dhammo . . .
All:	Dhammaṃ namassāmi'.
Teacher:	'Supaṭipanno bhagavato sāvakasaṃgho . . .
All:	Sanghaṃ namāmi'.

Translated:

Teacher:	'He is the Holy one, completely aware, the Lord . . .
All:	I honour the Lord Buddha'.
Teacher:	'The moral instruction is well preached by the Lord . . .
All:	I will pay homage to the moral instruction'.
Teacher:	'The community of the disciples of the Lord is of good conduct . . .
All:	I pay homage to the community of the disciples'.

Most children do not know the exact translation of these words, but virtually all are aware that they refer to the Triple Gem: The Buddha, the Dhamma and the Sangha. Also they may recognize that the monks often use these sentences in their official chanting: they are the opening clauses of three paragraphs.

During term the children flock to the monastery grounds five days a week. Those rural schools that still adhere to the monastery calendar close their doors on *wan phra* and the day preceding *wan phra*. However, all but the most isolated schools now conform to the practice in the provincial capitals and follow the government policy by closing on Saturday and Sunday instead.

Before school and during lunchtime the children can play in the monastery grounds, and thus they have ample opportunity to become acquainted with the daily affairs of the monastery. Children can see the monks eat during the morning, they can look into the cells when the doors are left open. They are able to witness the monks when they read, talk or rest. Monks can stroll to groups of playing children and stop to chat with children they know particularly well. Girls will be reminded of the fact that they will have to keep physical distance from monks at all times. The members of the Sangha can be freely observed when they perform public ceremonies, repair a building, or walk to the river clad only in their yellow bathing cloth in order to wash themselves. Even during classes, children are often aware of the daily routine in the monastery, for they can hear the big monastery drum beaten around eleven o'clock in the morning which warns the monks that in an hour's time they have to start their daily fast. Moreover, at regular times the schoolchildren will be able to discern the sound of the monks' chanting sessions.

The Dek wat

Although the monks' monopoly of primary education has been broken by the general introduction of the government schools, the institution of the young male servants of the monks, the *dek wat,* is still important. For 1967, for example, the Department of Religious Affairs reported for the whole of Thailand just over 108,000 *dek wat.* By 1975 this had risen to more than 118,000.[34] The number of *dek wat* per monastery in municipal areas is probably lower than the average number of *dek wat* per monastery in rural areas. In the region around Wat Sanchao there are usually as many *dek wat* as there are monks.

With the loss of the educational privileges that in the past were bestowed solely upon the *dek wat,* the recruiting pattern has changed. While previously parents sent their young boys to serve in the monastery so that they would learn to read and write, nowadays other reasons prevail. A small boy can be assigned to a monastery where an older relative has become a member of the Sangha, and this boy may have to serve that particular relative as a family obligation. Sometimes a small boy is encouraged to serve in the monastery because there he will be able to eat free meals. Parents who can ill afford the expense of feeding their children may well decide to send one or more sons into the service of the monks.[35]

The age of the *dek wat* usually varies between seven and fourteen, and therefore their tasks in the monastery are interrupted by the school curriculum. Their duties are not very heavy. At night they sleep on the floor of a monastery building, huddled together, using some discarded cloth to keep warm. Monks' robes that are beyond repair are often reserved for this purpose. The monks' robes are considered to be of special value as long as they serve to cover the body of a member of the Sangha. When they are finally discarded they can be used for any purpose, even for wiping floors.

Just before six o'clock in the morning they are awakened by the monks, so that they have time to wash their faces before joining the monks for the customary tour around the houses of the laymen to collect food for the day. Only the monks who go begging individually, while paddling a small boat, do not need the services of *dek wat.* Similarly, in urban areas monks often collect food without lay helpers. It is especially in rural regions like Wat Sanchao that small boys accompany the monks. The *dek wat* always must walk behind the

34 Kromkansasana, รายงานการศาสนาประจำปี ๒๕๑๐ [Annual Report on Religious Affairs, B.E. 2510], p. 97 and รายงานการศาสนาประจำปี ๒๕๑๘ [Annual Report on Religious Affairs, B.E. 2518], p. 159.

35 See also Tsuneo Ayabe, '*Dek Wat* and Thai Education; the Case of Tambon Ban Khan', *Journal of the Siam Society*, Vol. 61 (2), 1973, pp. 39–52.

monks. Whilst the monks carry their big metal begging bowls, the boys carry multi-compartmental layered food containers, called *pinto* (ปิ่นโต). Monks receive rice and occasionally some fruit or packed sweetmeats in their begging bowls, but most other kinds of food, such as curries, soups, fish or meat, are collected by the boys. The *dek wat* must store different foods in separate compartments of the *pinto* and this requires some manual skills on their part.

Around seven o'clock in the morning they return heavily laden to the monastery and help arrange the foods in the place where the monks usually partake of their communal meal. If there are members of the Sangha who prefer to eat alone, these have their portion placed in the privacy of their own cells. It is common practice that all foods are shared, so that those who cannot beg because of physical infirmities will not be disadvantaged.

When the monks gather to eat their joint meal, each platter of food and each bowl of rice has to be ceremoniously offered to them. This is the result of a strict interpretation of the rule that food may not be taken unless it has

Figure 3.3: The *dek wat* are well-fed in rural monasteries.

been presented. During the transfer of the food from the households to the monastery the *dek wat* have touched various items and to make certain that no rules are broken, all is formally given again. Even if, during a monk's meal, a lay person were accidentally to touch some item of food that had already been transferred to the Sangha for consumption, that layman should immediately renew the presentation. This ceremonial offering of goods to the monks, known by the verb *prakhen* (ประเคน), is one of the most important tasks of the *dek wat*. Throughout the day, for example when a monk prepares some food for his own consumption before the fasting period of the day begins, or when a monk wishes to drink some liquid other than water, he can call upon any *dek wat* to come to present the plate or the vessel in the proper manner.

After waiting on the monks during their morning meal, it is the turn of a *dek wat* to eat. After a hurried meal they have to help wash the empty food containers and sweep the floor of the building. Then all boys don their school uniform and are inspected by some monks for any sign of dirt before they are allowed to join the flag-raising ceremony in front of the school building.

During the time that a small boy is assigned to serve a certain monk, this member of the Sangha should act as father and mother to the child. A monk can punish a *dek wat* when he does not perform his tasks well. These punishments vary from a verbal reprimand to a thrashing, depending on the gravity of the offence.

Outside school time, a *dek wat* can be called to perform small services for the monks, such as carrying messages, hauling water, buying refreshments, or *prakhen*-ing an item of food. When a monk is invited to perform a ceremony somewhere outside his monastery, he may decide to take his *dek wat* along. However, if travel would interfere with school tasks, permission to accompany a monk should be obtained from the head of the school. This can create an awkward situation: a monk is ritually superior to a layman such as a schoolmaster and should not ask favours from inferiors. Moreover, in this situation, the head teacher will find it very difficult to refuse. Most monks therefore avoid this embarrassing situation and, if the time clashes with the school curriculum they prefer to go without a small servant.

Unlike the days before the arrival of the government primary schools, there is no formal instruction of the *dek wat* in many monasteries. In Wat Sanchao, the abbot may at times call the *dek wat* together and impress upon them that they should behave in a proper and dignified manner, that they are not like ordinary boys who do not have the advantage of living in a monastery, and that they should try to observe the Five Precepts as conscientiously as they can.

The intelligent boy can obtain an extensive knowledge about the life of the monks during the period that he is a *dek wat.* Daily he hears their chanting, and the Pali texts that are most frequently repeated may soon be etched upon his mind. He has a chance to witnesses many ceremonies and will soon understand the difference between various types of ordination. He never misses a theatre performance in his monastery grounds and is in the front of the crowd during cremations.

A *dek wat* is not confined to the monastery; he can observe religious events beyond its boundaries. During fund-raising ceremonies in neighbouring monasteries he may accompany the monks who are invited to attend. If a monk has to travel for business to the provincial capital or beyond, he may take the cleverest boy along in order to let him handle money (a commodity that, ideally speaking, a monk should not touch). *Dek wat* can be taken to private ceremonies in the houses of laymen where they observe how water is sacralized. If a boy is a servant of the monks for a long time, he will witness the chanting for rain in the fields, the blessing of a new house, and the chants to ensure longevity in a sick person.

The Novices

While in 1975 the Department of Religious Affairs reported more than 118,000 *dek wat* for the whole of Thailand, the number of novices reached almost 122,000.[36] This represents an average of four novices per monastery. A breakdown of the figure shows, however, that the distribution of novices is uneven. In the north and northeast of Thailand and in the country's capital, the average is as high as seven novices per monastery, but in rural central Thailand the average is only two novices per monastery. The great number of novices in the north and north-east correlates with a relatively small number of monks, and it seems that in these areas the novitiate has taken on some of the functions of the order of monks in other regions. In the north and northeast many a man is considered adult after having been a novice, while in rural central Thailand having been a novice does not entitle a man to be called fully adult: he should have been fully ordained before he can claim that status. With regard to the high incidence of persons in novitiate in the capital, this is probably related to the excellent schooling facilities in some monasteries in Bangkok.

Before the introduction of state schools in rural areas, if a young boy who had not yet reached the age of twenty (the age when he could become a monk)

36 Kromkansasana, รายงานการศาสนาประจำปี ๒๕๑๘ [Annual Report on Religious Affairs, B.E. 2518], p. 159.

wished to obtain formal education at an advanced level, he could only do so by becoming a novice. At present, a boy looking for secondary education will find that the state schools offer a programme suited to the demands of modern society, while becoming a novice no longer prepares a young man for secular life. Only a shimmer of the aura of the elite surrounds the institution of novitiate in central Thailand. Often it is the parents who can ill afford the expense of sending a son to secondary school who may encourage their child to become a novice.

Monks as well as novices are expected to prepare for the yearly religious examinations that are sponsored by the government and administered by the Department of Religious Affairs. A bright novice can pass several degrees of ecclesiastical learning. If he successfully sits for his examinations he may well decide to embark upon a career in the order. Especially in recent times, many offices in the Buddhist church have been allotted to young monks who have attained a superior degree of religious education. No position of authority is given to a novice in central Thailand and the brilliant novice will have to wait until he is twenty before he can begin to acquire seniority. He usually must have been a monk at least five years before he can become abbot.

A novice is ritually inferior to a monk. Novices follow only ten precepts while the monks are obliged to regulate their lives to the 227 precepts that have been handed down in the Pali *Pāṭimokkha*. Novices are excluded from the decision-making meetings of the Sangha, and therefore they are not allowed to attend the final part of the ceremony of the ordination of a monk. They are also not allowed to join the monks during the times that the *Pāṭimokkha* is recited, and they do not change their names when they become members of the order. At present, the novitiate does not carry great prestige in central Thailand. If a novice fails his yearly examination, his parents may well ask him to give up his yellow robes and to return to the household in order to work on the land.

At the beginning of this chapter the magical protection of pregnant women and of small children was mentioned. Much of these customs and related beliefs may well reflect the insecure circumstances of the past. A few generations ago, the risk of giving birth to a child was much greater than it is now, and the incidence of small children suddenly succumbing to illness was much higher than at present. But still there is a risk involved in delivering a child, and nowadays children may also unexpectedly contract diseases. The continuing anxiety of the parents will ensure that some sort of magical means will be employed in the future.

When children are still very young they learn proper polite behaviour, and this extends not only to the great number of elder relatives, teachers and monks, but also to the potentially dangerous powers in the house, the compound, at certain places along the roadside and in the monastery.

An important theme related to the understanding of the religion is the diverging religious experiences of boys and girls. This is apparent in the variance in behaviour with regard to members of the Sangha and the types of magical protection which are given, but it is even more obvious in the fields of religious education. Traditionally boys were the only members of the community who had a chance to learn to read and write. Whilst the girls are now equally admitted to the state schools, small boys retain most of the monopoly on religious knowledge through the institutions of *dek wat* and the novitiate. The difference in access to religious knowledge between boys and girls becomes even more pronounced in the period of adolescence, discussed in the following chapter, and during the period when many young men become monks, in early adulthood, which is the subject of Chapter V.

CHAPTER IV

ADOLESCENTS, AMULETS AND TATTOOING

Adolescents and Religion

After successful completion of their primary education, children can, in theory, continue their formal education in a school that prepares them for matriculation into a secondary school. As mentioned in the previous chapter, the boys among the pupils have an additional chance of obtaining a schooling by becoming novices. However, in the region around Wat Sanchao, the incidence of children opting for further education is rare.

In the genealogies of people sustaining the monastery, 790 males of more than 14 years appeared. Of all these men it was ascertained whether or not they had been novices. Only eleven affirmative answers were obtained, which corresponds with 1.4 per cent of the eligible men. Of all adults who had been brought up in the Wat Sanchao community, people could recall only three persons who had completed secondary education in a state school. It was remarkable that these three were siblings; probably the successful schooling of the eldest boy influenced his younger brothers in choosing to attend secondary school as well. However, the number of persons who obtain secondary education in the state school may rise sharply in the future, because in 1969 there were eight children attending preparatory school and one boy enrolled in a secondary school.[1]

Many parents seem reluctant to allow their children to study after completing primary education. To these parents, the advantages of further schooling may seem purely hypothetical and at best many years ahead. Sending a child to school when

1 In 1975, the first stage of a new school was opened and the curriculum was expanded from 4 to 7 years, in line with government policy. In 1978 the second stage was under construction and a year later festively opened.

he is more than twelve years old deprives the household of valuable manpower. Moreover, since the cash income of the farmer depends largely on the size of the rice crop and since that can fluctuate greatly from year to year, the steady financial burden of a school-going child is something not lightly undertaken.

Therefore, after formal primary education, the great majority of children in the Wat Sanchao community do not continue their formal schooling. Instead, they are employed on their parents' farms. Boys learn to plough and to harrow the fields, to transplant young rice shoots, and to maintain the irrigation channels. They obtain knowledge about the many different varieties of rice plants and the ways to improve the soil. As their skill and physical strength increase they become indispensable in the household. Often a hardworking son is rewarded by his parents with the ownership of a plot of land. Girls gradually take over many of their mother's tasks. They learn to cook, tend fruit and vegetable plants in the garden, and look after the younger children in the household. In addition they must help with the lighter duties in the fields.

Work on the fields is intensive during several months of the year, but there are periods when there is little labour on the land. During the slack periods traditionally the boys were allowed to wander around with friends of their own age. They went fishing, playing, or visiting the provincial capital in small groups. This was the milieu in which they learned to smoke and obtained a first taste of alcoholic beverages. Some of them might have fought among themselves, others got involved in gambling, visited a brothel, or tried the effect of opium. Girls were not allowed to roam about; they were carefully kept under the supervision of elder members of the family. In the house there was always something to mend and in a spare hour the young women could make themselves useful by weaving cloth or making bamboo baskets. Nowadays, however, especially since a sealed road has been constructed between Wat Sanchao and the provincial capital many teenagers seek work in town during the periods of agricultural 'holidays'. Both young men and women commute between the farm and the town where they are often engaged as unskilled workers on construction sites.

After they leave school, teenagers usually have little contact with the monastery. Many young people generally find it tedious to sit attentively while the monks chant the sacred stanzas and they are rarely interested in the topics of sermons. Thus there are very few teenagers who attend the regular services of *wan phra*. Moerman reports the same for a community in northern Thailand.[2]

2 Michael Moerman, 'Ban Ping's Temple: The Center of a "Loosely Structured" Society', in M. Nash (ed.) *Anthropological Studies in Theravada Buddhism*, 1966, pp. 143–4.

This lack of interest is regarded by older people as something quite natural and parents do not try to coerce their children to attend sessions in the monastery. In these matters each child is considered fully responsible for himself. It is recognized that young people do not worry about the form of their future rebirths, because death still seems far away to them. Unlike older people they do not grasp every opportunity to increase their store of good *karma*.

However, on special occasions young people do come to the monastery in great numbers. During the annual major ceremonies in the monastery they will readily join the rest of the community in the traditional joint food offering early in the morning. The New Year festival in mid-April gives youngsters an occasion for some mildly licentious behaviour. Also during the night before an ordination takes place, there may be music and dancing, which is followed the next morning by a procession where some strong drink circulates and, encouraged by the stirring music, many join in a spontaneous dance. A group of young women play a different role during such processions: young unmarried women are needed to carry the ornate gifts used during the ordination ceremony. It is a chance to display their most beautiful clothes and to appear at their best, walking gracefully under the admiring glances of relatives and others who have come along.

Since the maintenance of the monastery is a costly matter, every year the lay leaders, in consultation with the monks, organize a fund-raising ceremony. They may choose one of the annually recurring major ceremonies for this purpose, but sometimes a special ritual can be organized solely for the purpose of raising cash. Great crowds are expected to come to the monastery on such days, and young people are expected to play their part during the preparations. The grounds must be clean and orderly, the grass has to be cut, footpaths have to be weeded, and some of the buildings have to be decorated before the day when thousands of persons will flock to the monastery. Women occupy the monastery kitchen to prepare food for all who help embellish the monastery. If a chief financial sponsor is expected to come from afar, meals for him and his party also need to be cooked. An older, quick-witted woman takes charge of the kitchen. She, the *mae khrua* (แม่ครัว) or 'mother of the kitchen' has bought the provisions and divided the work; she makes sure that nobody is idle and that flirtations between men who have finished their tasks and the younger women under her charge remain within bounds.

The fund-raising ceremony itself is attractive to young people, not so much for religious reasons, but mainly because there is usually much entertainment in the form of theatre, music, or films. For those of courting age it is an excellent opportunity to see members of the opposite sex, not only from their own community but from the whole surrounding area. In former days this was one of the few occasions when a young man might have a good look at marriageable girls from outside his own community. Nowadays, communication with the provincial capital and new economic factors have altered the picture. There is now ample opportunity to meet girls on the way to town and while working part-time during the slack seasons, and the attraction of the monastery fund-raising ceremonies must have waned accordingly.

The relations between adolescents and the monastery seem therefore to have little to do with religious matters. The adolescents are absent during most of the religious services; they are drawn to the monastery only when there is attractive entertainment.

Amulets

From a very early age onward, boys wear objects that reputedly protect them against diseases, witchcraft and accidents. When a boy becomes adolescent these objects with protective power become increasingly important in his life. There is a great variety of objects which can serve as amulets, as Wood noted:

> It would be possible to write a biggish book about charms to ward off sword or bullet wounds. There are dozens of different kinds – tattoo marks, written formulas, knotted strings, tiny images of Buddha, precious stones, dried seeds, needles in the body, and others too numerous to mention.[3]

Undoubtedly the most popular object that is worn on a cord or chain around a man's neck is the image of the Buddha. These images can be cast from metal, carved out of a piece of wood, ivory or resin, but the most common traditional ones are manufactured from a mixture of many different ingredients, pressed in a mould and baked. In modern times coloured plastic ones have become quite popular. The Buddha images vary in size; their height may be as small as two centimetres but can extend to seven or eight, their width varies from about one to five centimetres.

Although laymen are not excluded from making these small protective Buddha images, their manufacture is largely in the hands of older monks. In order to make a pressed or printed image, commonly known as *phra phim* (พระพิมพ์), a monk needs, apart from the mould, a recipe, the proper ingredients, and considerable knowledge of spells, the sacred script and magical drawings.

3 W. A. R. Wood, *Consul in Paradise,* 1965, p. 88.

Figure 4.1: Buddha images and medallions. 1–4 Various Buddha images. Number 4 is made out of a bullet. Numbers 5, 6 and 7 are medallions of various monks. Number 8 depicts King Chulalongkorn.

Historians will be sad to hear that one of the common ingredients of *phra phim* is the ash obtained from burning the oldest handwritten sacred books of the monastery.

Almost as popular as Buddha images are the metal protective medallions, which depict the head of a sacred person and often some *Khom* writing and a simple *yan* on the other. Very popular are medallions with the face of King Chulalongkorn, but even more popular are those depicting the face of a Buddhist monk, one who is famous for his magical power. These medallions are made by commercial firms, usually on order by the organizing committee of a fund-raising ceremony (see Fig. 4.1, second row).

On the chain or cord from which a Buddha image or a medallion dangles, other amulets can be hung. In Chapter III the *takrut* (paper, cloth or metal scrolls, inscribed with mystical diagrams) have already been mentioned. A small container on this cord may hold an amount of sacred cotton thread or some twine used during the dedication ceremony of a temple. A splinter of wood taken from the most important supporting pole of the ancestral home has protective value to a man, and so has a small piece of cloth given to him for this purpose by his mother. Around his waist a man can carry a cord with a small wooden or stone phallus or a tiger's tooth.

It is quite easy to obtain protecting objects. They are readily for sale in the market of the provincial capital, they are hawked by travelling salesmen and many monks distribute them freely among other members of the Sangha and laymen. Amulets are sometimes distributed as a memento of a particular ceremony and friends may exchange amulets as a gesture of their friendship or appreciation of each other.

The amulets derive their protective power partly from the association with powerful things. The *phra phim* are made from sacred ingredients. It may occur that a piece of wood or resin has naturally the shape of a Buddha figure, and such an object is highly valued for its miraculously taking this shape: it is sacralised by nature itself. A Buddha image made from a bullet (Fig. 4.1, no. 4) is in this context not such a strange combination: the transformation of the shape will surely protect its wearer from bullet wounds. The use of the image of the Buddha, of a highly revered king, or of a famous monk is in itself understandable from this point of view: the innate sacredness of the subjects is a guarantee of beneficial power. Similarly, a phallus or a tiger's tooth is obviously connected with force and the use of these objects illustrates the principle that a wide range of things that are associated with power can be used in order to protect humans magically.

In some instances it is not immediately clear to an outsider why certain objects are chosen as amulets. It is not until the ceremonies connected with building a house are taken into account that it can be appreciated why a splinter of wood taken from the main supporting pole of a house is chosen as an object with protective power.[4] The use of a piece of cloth given to a man by his mother is also difficult to grasp at once. A woman's *phanung* (ผ้านุ่ง), the lower garment, a piece of which a mother may give to her son for magical protection, is considered antithetic to protective powers of the amulets when the cloth has been worn by a woman who is not one's mother. The reversal of the rule can be seen as symbolic of the exceptional relationship between mother and child.

4 See Chapter VII.

The child is a product of his mother's reproductive organs and therefore her bodily secretions are not harmful to his magical power.

In general, the inherent quality of the amulets is considered insufficient to ensure protection to the person who wears them. Apart from being made from auspicious material and depicting powerful symbols, the amulets usually ought to be sacralized. This sacralization can take many forms. The most elementary sacralization ritual, called *pluksek* (ปลุกเสก), can be observed, for example, when a monk gives a small Buddha image to a layman. Taking the image in both hands, the monk brings it close to his mouth and murmurs a short Pali formula. While uttering the final syllable of the spell, the monk may blow sharply upon this Buddha image. Some monks prefer to draw a simple *yan* over the amulet with the index finger of the right hand or with a pencil while saying the Pali words. The layman who receives the small image should press it against his forehead for a short period in a gesture of the highest appreciation.

The elaborate ceremony primarily designed to sacralize amulets is called *phuthaphisek*.[5] The concentrated effort of monks that has been described in the elementary ceremony above is also the core of the *phuthaphisek* ritual. It is one of the rarer fund-raising ceremonies that a committee of laymen, in consultation with the monks, can organize. This ceremony should be held on a day when the 'spirits are strong': an ominous, portentous day on which it is inadvisable to cremate corpses, such as a Saturday or a Tuesday. The fifth day of the fifth lunar month is especially suitable for sacralization. That is also why there is a great demand for tattoos on this day. This has also been reported for Bang Chan in central Thailand by Robert Textor.[6]

As soon as the date for the *phuthaphisek* ceremony has been determined, a chapter of renowned monks is invited and the event is widely announced. Any man who wishes his collection of amulets to be sacralized wraps the objects in a bundle and hands them to the organizing committee. The objects are counted, the exact number is written down in a book, and a label is attached to each bundle. No mistakes should be made in the registration of the objects, because these amulets are highly valued by their owners, and a major argument would erupt if, at the close of the ceremony, some objects were found to be missing. The committee receives a fee for including an amulet in the sacralization ceremony, and the more people who come to 'charge' or 'recharge' their charms, the greater will be the total sum of money that is raised for the monastery. In

5 Thai: พุทธาภิเษก. From the words Buddha and *abhiṣeka* (Sanskrit: anointing, consecrating).

6 R. B. Textor, *An Inventory of Non-Buddhist Supernatural Objects in a Central Thai Village*, 1960, p. 104.

addition, the organizers may order a special medallion cast for the occasion, or a special type of Buddha image made. These can be included in the sacralization ceremony, and sold afterwards in order to boost the finances of the monastery.

The ritual can take place in the temple, the most sacred place in the monastery. For the *phuthaphisek* ritual, four tall, many-tiered umbrellas are erected at the corners of the elevated platform on which the monks usually chant. There is always an uneven number of tiers, sometimes five, or seven, but usually nine of them. At a height of about 1½ metres above the floor the sacred white cotton thread, *sai sin,* is strung so that it encloses the rectangular area of the elevated platform. The thread is taken around the back of the main Buddha image, so that this huge object is within the delineated sacred precinct. All the objects that have to be sacralized are placed in the middle of the marked-off area.

The monks who have been invited to perform the ritual take their places around the three free sides of the platform, in such a manner that they, together with the huge Buddha image, enclose all amulets. Each monk places a begging bowl partly filled with water on a metal ring directly in front of him. (The begging bowls are rounded at the bottom so that they cannot be stood on a flat surface without rolling over. Among the monk's standard equipment is therefore the metal begging bowl's resting ring.) More strings of cotton thread

Figure 4.2: Beneficial power flows through the *sai sin*.

are unrolled from a central ball resting among the amulets towards each of the monks.

At the outset, all monks prostrate themselves before the Buddha image, and each monk lights a candle. Often the candle is affixed to the rim of the begging bowl so that it will drip wax on to the surface of the water without intervention on the part of the monk. Some monks prefer to fasten a coin to the bottom end of the candle and gently lower it into the vessel until it rests upright on the bottom of the begging bowl, the top of the candle protruding above the water surface. The chapter of monks remains for a long period within the temple, usually four or five hours, during which time they chant Pali texts in unison and meditate. Thus they jointly emit so much beneficial power that the objects in the centre become charged with it. During the whole time the monks are thus engaged, all the doors and windows of the *bot* should remain closed to prevent secular influences interfering. The amount of power thus generated is so great that it is believed that the cotton thread which has been used during the ritual becomes permanently charged. The organizing committee can sell short pieces of this *sai sin* as amulets in their own right.

Thus, sacralization of auspicious objects takes place when monks say Pali formulae over them, draw *yan* on them, blow upon them or meditate in their proximity. In the examples given, the consecration is intentional and goal-directed. Sometimes, however, amulets can be charged without the knowledge of the monks who bring this about. A small bundle of amulets can be placed under the edge of the cushion on which a monk sits chanting, preaching or reciting the *Pāṭimokkha,* the rules of the discipline. The monk in question may be totally unaware of the fact that, while performing his monastic task, he adds to the power of some amulets. The custom of placing amulets in the begging bowl that is used during the ordination ceremony can be seen in the same light. This custom, as well as being often seen in central Thailand, has also been reported for the northeast of the country by Francis Cripps.[7] The ordinand may know that friends have placed amulets in his begging bowl, but the chapter of monks that accepts him as a member of the Sangha may not be aware of this. At some point of the ordination ceremony, when the ordinand must prostrate himself while the metal bowl remains strapped to his back, the amulets may get displaced and suddenly rattle loudly. When the amulets thus reveal their presence, everybody, the ordainer included, may smile amusedly,

7 F. Cripps, *The Far Province,* 1965. p. 84.

well aware of what caused this noise. Sacralization can therefore take place unintentionally; proximity to a major ritual is considered sufficient.

Not all objects need the intervention of monks to become charged with power. A lay person who knows the proper actions and spells can charge objects with power. In general it can be said that the intervention of a monk is needed only for protective and beneficial power. Lay specialists often manipulate the more aggressive and dangerous types of magic.

Sometimes no human intervention is needed to sacralize objects. It is believed, for example, that during the *Loi krathong* (ลอยกระทง) festival, which is held in November on the night of full moon of the twelfth lunar month, the water in all rivers is charged with beneficial power. During this *Loi krathong* night it is wholesome to bathe in the river and to fill the big earthenware water vessels that every farmhouse possesses. A spectacular sacralization took place on 25 September 1968, when lightning struck the *bot* of Wat Sanchao. Scorched pieces of plaster were immediately collected by some of the monks, later to be ground up as an ingredient for the manufacture of *phra phim*.

When donning a string of amulets, a man should raise the objects to his forehead and say some auspicious words over them. Some men have learnt a proper spell, *khatha* (คาถา),[8] suitable for this particular action, often consisting of a mixture of Pali, Sanskrit and Thai words. One such *khatha* begins as follows:

> Buddhakāmo rathedhammamạ dhammakāmo rathebuddhaṃ aṭṭhikāyo kāyādevānaṃ oṃ srī oṃ srī brahma raṃ srī māmate.[9]

These opening words are obviously a mixture of Pali and Sanskrit. It seems that some words have been changed during the process of oral transmission, or that they are part of an esoteric body of knowledge. Therefore it is better to refrain from a conjectural translation. The sentence which concludes the *khatha* is in Thai and can be translated as: 'I ask from the *ṛṣis*[10] and also from these amulets that they give me worthiness.'

If a man does not know any spells that are specifically designed for the moment of donning a string of amulets, he may use some general auspicious Pali words like: 'Buddha ārakkhaṇaṃ, dhamma ārakkhaṇaṃ, Sangha ārakkhaṇaṃ,' which may be translated as: 'Buddha protection, Dharma protection, Sangha protection.' Or he can repeat three times the famous sentence: 'Namo tassa

8 Sanskrit or Pali: gāthā.

9 Recorded from the Venerable Phlik, 7 July 1968.

10 The Thais use the Sanskrit word *ṛṣi* to indicate the legendary mystical wizards who were the original possessors of knowledge.

Bhagavato arahato sammā sambuddhasa,' which means: 'Reverence to the Lord who is worthy and completely awakened.'

The amulets are not worn continually, but are reserved for special occasions. Men wear their string of protective charms when they go out and can expect to meet many people; they will take care not to forget them when they expect or fear a potentially dangerous situation to arise. The fear of dangerous spirits, the *phi,* acquired during early childhood often does not disappear when a person grows up. Somebody who has to walk home in the middle of the night without company may well become extremely apprehensive, and a sudden noise or a moving shadow may suffice to convince him that something dangerous lurks in the dark. It is not considered unmanly to be afraid in the dark.

The *phi* are not the only dangerous element in the surroundings of a young man. When travelling in buses or cars he faces the danger of becoming involved in a traffic accident; when going out with friends he may drink too much alcohol and become embroiled in a fight; when gambling takes place, tempers may rise and the losers may become violent; when engaged in unlicensed betting all participants run the risk of being arrested by the police. A man's amulets can be of assistance in all such circumstances. The amulets may cause him survive a traffic accident unscathed, or, if injured, at least escape death. Wearing a powerful string of protective objects may cause his body to become invulnerable so that, if a gun is fired at him or a knife is thrust, his skin will not be pierced. Amulets may also cause the wearer to be pleasant and inoffensive in the eyes of other persons so that nobody will feel the urge to vent his rage upon him.

Apart from their protective value, the amulets are often *objets d'art.* A man will wear his string of amulets when a display of neat clothes is required: during important ceremonies or secular meetings. The charms may reflect a person's wealth, because he who can afford it will buy a gold necklace, and encase his best amulets in gold. The choicest objects will be hung in the middle. During the course of the years each person is likely to acquire many more protective objects than he can hang around his neck. He will keep them in a box and store them in a high place at home. There are special albums for sale in the provincial capital in which small Buddha images or medallions can be stored. There are avid collectors who display hundreds of these small sacred objects in a glass case on the wall of their house.[11] Whenever a group of men are together and there is a lull in the conversation, one of the group only has to ask someone

11 There are collectors' journals such as *Lanpho, Suea lae Phrakhrueang, Tamnaan Phrakhrueang, Phuthandon Traiwet* and *Nitayasan Amata Phrakhrueang.*

to show his amulets, and the conversation is likely to centre upon these for a long period. Everyone is willing to explain in detail from where a prize amulets hails, how rare it is, and what powers it possesses.

Tattooing

During the period that boys serve as *dek wat* in the monastery, they may often have the opportunity to witness a tattooist, the *khru sak* (ครูสัก) or *achan sak* (อาจารย์สัก),[12] performing his skills upon young adult men. If the *dek wat,* impressed by the ritual, ask the *acan sak* to tattoo them as well, the tattooing specialist may be persuaded. He may place a small geometrical design, the picture of a butterfly, or the shape of a little fish on the lower arm of the *dek wat.* For a while the young boys will be very proud of their decorations. They feel that they have shown themselves to be quite adult and brave in willingly having undergone this painful ordeal. They feel a bond with the older men who are ostentatiously tattooed. However, it will not be long before somebody explains to them that the marks they received cannot be compared with the tattooing of older people, and that their designs are simple decorations lacking all the power ascribed to the more intricate patterns that their seniors received. What appeared to them to be a mark of adulthood is soon felt to be a sign of childishness that cannot be erased. 'Proper' tattooing is not given to men until they are adult: when they have reached the age of about seventeen. Traditionally, nearly every man in rural areas of Thailand used to be subjected to tattooing of one kind or another. Monks as well as laymen can be *achan sak,* but there is a difference in the scope of their work.

Monks as well as laymen can be *achan sak,* but there is a difference in the scope of their work. When a member of the Sangha exercises magical skills by tattooing young men he is limited in the application of this skill by the fact that he is a monk. As a member of the Sangha his essential role should be earning good *karma,* thereby generating beneficial power, for himself, for the persons who sponsor him, and for his ancestors. When tattooing, he is therefore customarily limited to the bestowal of beneficial, protective power upon the man who receives his indelible marks. As a result of his monastic role he can therefore tattoo only on the higher, most respected parts of the body: the chest and the upper arms, but particularly the man's head. The marks he bestows are often directly related to his monastic occupation and consist of mystical

12 The word *khru,* as well as the word *achan,* means teacher. They are related respectively to the Sanskrit words *guru* and *ācārya. Sak* is possibly derived from the word *śalākā;* see Monier-Williams, *A Sanskrit-English Dictionary,* 1964, p. 1059.

diagrams and rows of syllables in the sacred *Khom* alphabet. They are applied by the monk whilst he murmurs a few sacralizing formulae. Another tattooing sometimes performed by a monk is the marking of the tongue, whereby he does not really pierce the tongue's skin: a perfunctory touch with the tattooing needle suffices. It is believed that the beneficial power from a tongue-tattoo pervades the whole body via the saliva. The tattoos made upon the body by a monk protect a man from mishap and often are believed to have the power to make a man popular and favoured with his fellow human beings.

A lay ritual specialist, not limited by his role to pure, protective, beneficial powers, can offer his clients a much wider choice of body decorations. Not only can he execute the designs that monks use and thus usually has in his repertoire a variety of *yan* and many groups of syllables in the sacred alphabet, but in addition he can apply many theriomorphic and anthropomorphic designs.

A young man can be motivated to receive a tattoo for a variety of reasons. To many it is a sign that they are grown up and proof that they have bravely faced the painful process. The designs themselves are often aesthetically pleasing and therefore some men may be prompted by vanity. Others may be especially attracted by the thought that the tattoos will increase their power and charm. Many boys receive an extra incentive when they discuss tattoos with their comrades; they do not wish to be outdone in courage by their age-mates.

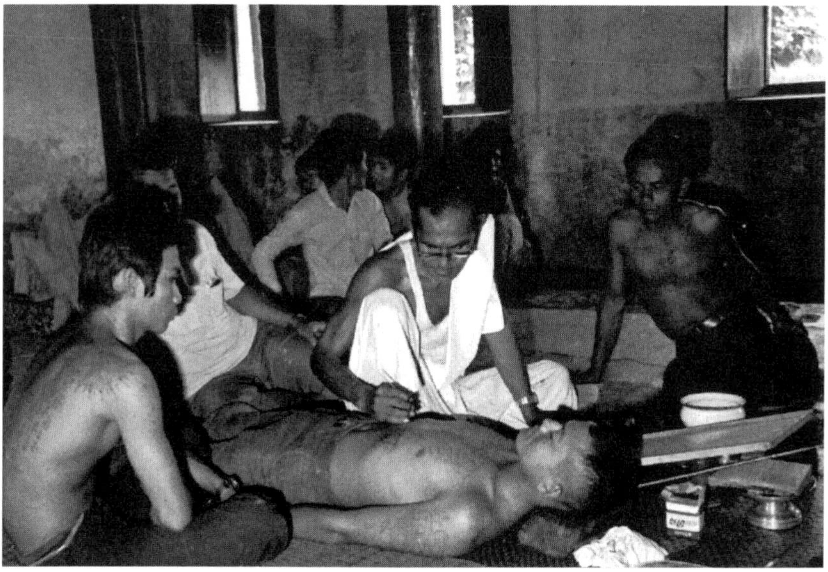

Figure 4.3: The painful process is witnessed by age-mates.

When a young man has decided upon a certain *achan sak,* he must approach this ritual specialist with proper deference in order to make an appointment for the first session of tattooing. Often the *achan sak* will decide that a Tuesday or a Saturday is the most appropriate because, as mentioned before, reputedly on such days of the week the 'spirits are strong'. On the appointed day, the young man must come to the house of the tattooist, carrying a candle, some flowers and the fee. Payment for these types of magical services should traditionally be connected with the number six. Older people remember the days when they used to pay six *salueng,* which is equivalent to 1½ *baht,* but nowadays the fee is often six *baht* or a multiple of that amount. The young boy should kneel down with his face towards the east, light the candle and incense and offer them together with the flowers to the 'teachers', to those who in the dim past handed down the knowledge of tattooing. This ceremony is called *wai khru* (ไหว้ครู), and is presided by the *acan sak.* It is a common ritual also among Thai actors, dancers, musicians and boxers.[13]

After the *wai khru,* when respect has been paid to the original possessors of the knowledge used, the *achan sak* begins to make the tattoo. He employs a wooden shaft with a sharp metal tip that can contain a small quantity of ink. The tattooist guides the instrument over thumb and index finger of the left hand on to the skin of the young man, making rhythmical, powerful strokes in order to pierce the skin, pausing often to refill with ink. The person who undergoes this treatment should not cry out in pain, lest he be the laughing-stock of all who have suffered stoically. One design, covering maybe twelve square inches of skin, is usually sufficient for the first session; if the man still wishes to receive other designs he should wait a few days until the swelling of the recently tattooed skin subsides a little.

While he is being tattooed, a man is sometimes advised to repeat a short Pali spell such as: 'ehi ehi sammā', which can be translated as: 'O come, come properly'. It is likely that such formulae are meant to make the recipient open to receive magical qualities which go together with the designs. The *achan sak* himself continuously murmurs formulae. After finishing a design, the tattooist says a final spell while rubbing his fingers in the mixture of blood and ink that wells up from the recently tattooed skin and terminates the session by blowing with all his might upon the design.

13 For details of elaborate *wai khru* rituals, see Dhanit Yupho: 'The Custom and Rite of Paying Homage to Teachers of Khon, Lakhon and Piphat', *Thai Culture, New Series,* No. 11, 1970. For Thai boxing *wai khru,* see C. Yanawimut, หลักวิชามวยไทย [The theory of Thai Boxing] 1966, pp. 19–23.

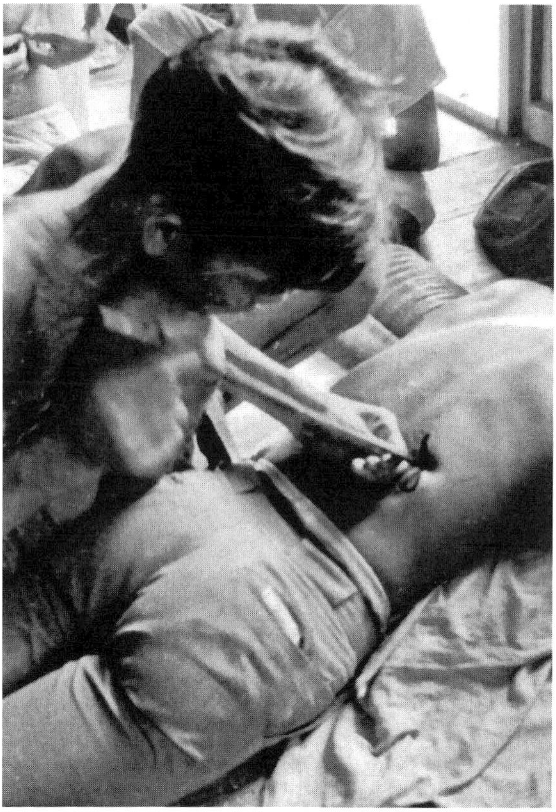

Figure 4.4: The tattooist makes powerful strokes to pierce the skin.

After a man has received as many tattoos as he wishes, a process that may last several weeks (because of the intermittent periods without tattooing), he still must undergo an effecting or charging-up ritual. This ceremony is generally known as *yok khru* (ยกครู), literally: 'to raise the teacher'. Not only newly tattooed men, but all those who feel in need to boost the powers that they believe to be inherent in their tattoos may join in. This ritual may take place in a monastery, near a Buddha image; it may even be staged in its most sacred place: on the monks' raised dais in the *bot*. During one such ceremony the platform was made attractive to the non-human powers by the offering of appropriate foods: a pig's head, eggs, sweetmeats, candles, incense and flowers. First the powers have been invoked and then the *achan sak* will perfunctorily pierce the skin on top of the skull of each of his clients several times with his tattooing needle, thus effectuating all his clients' tattoos.

From this moment onwards, the tattoos are empowered: their strength resides in the body. The tattooed person should observe some taboos to preserve these powers intact. In no circumstances should a man who has been tattooed be in an inferior position to a woman during copulation lest he lose all the magical qualities of his tattoos. Another prescription often given to a recently tattooed man is that he should be aware and attentive when relieving the body so as not to let any of his magical power escape. In both these rules of behaviour a common theme can be discerned: a man is considered vulnerable during the moments that material, be it semen, faeces or urine, leaves the body.

In addition, many tattooists will prescribe that a man refrain from eating certain food. In the region around Wat Sanchao, the tattooed men were usually advised to keep away from the *mafueang* fruit. This is the fruit of the *Averrhoa aarambola,* also known as cucumber tree (มะเฟือง).[14] Informants were unclear as to why this particular fruit is forbidden to tattooed men. A possible explanation could be that the fruit is also known as *sida,* the name of the heroine of the Ramayana. This association with so feminine a name may be a reason for prescribing to men who are filled with sacred power that they should refrain from eating this fruit.

Apart from advising his clients to refrain from acts which will cause the recently acquired powers to dwindle, the *achan sak* reveals to the men how they can induce the latent powers to rise. The recently tattooed men receive spells, *khatha,* to arouse the dormant forces.

In order to show that the body has now been properly tattooed, the *achan sak* may, after the *yok khru* ceremony, test the men's invulnerability. He will order one or more of the recently tattooed men to lie down, facing the floor. The *achan sak* will brandish a bamboo knife and show the bystanders how sharp the point is. After saying a formula over a tattooed area of skin on the back of the person lying on the floor, he will suddenly forcefully stab the knife into that area. Afterwards, invariably the point of the knife can be shown to have broken off and, when examined, the skin proves to have remained intact. It is difficult to say for certain how the tattooist ascertains that he does not accidentally pierce the skin; it is quite possible that he himself breaks the point of the knife immediately before thrusting it upon the back of his client.[15] After having thus proved that the powers work, the tattooist urges his clients to use their powers only when in dire need. The forces are not to be abused.

14 G. B. McFarland, *Thai-English Dictionary,* 1954, p. 637.

15 When the author was subjected to this treatment he could hardly feel the impact of the knife.

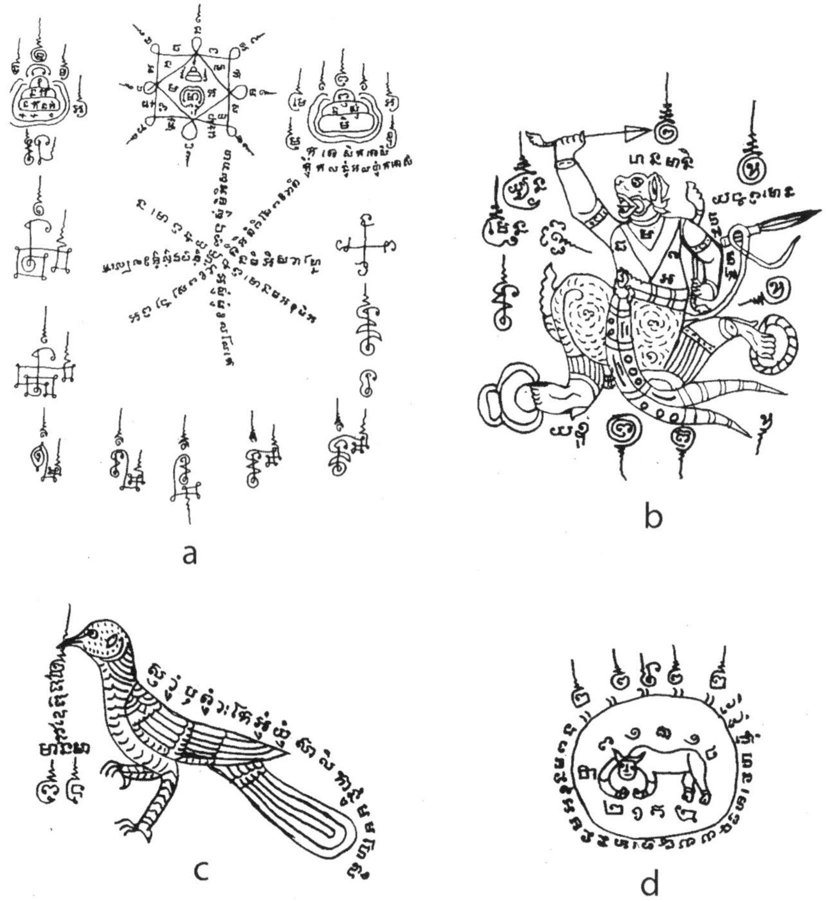

Figure 4.5: Some tattooing designs.

An examination of the distribution of various designs over the body reveals certain norms. Thus the designs show a decreasing eminence when the eye traverses over the body downwards. On top of the skull purely geometric designs (such as in Fig. 4.5, a) or the outline of the Buddha image surrounded by mystical diagrams are likely to be encountered. These are believed to protect the head in case of an attack, but above all they serve to make the wearer popular and favoured. The face is usually kept clear of elaborate tattoos, it being felt that tattoos would interfere with the features and facial expressions. A single dot can be tattooed on the cheek by way of protection for the whole face. In this context it is relevant that in Thailand a mole on the face may be considered a sign of beauty.

The chest and upper arms can be used for strings of sacred syllables, sometimes decorated with *unalom* (อุณาโลม). The *unalom* is a conically shaped figure often placed above or around a design in order to draw attention to its importance. In Buddhist texts the *uṇṇā* is one of the 32 signs of a great man that were also present on the Buddha: it is a small tuft of hair between the eyebrows.[16] This conical symbol has been traced by Jan Boeles to a representation of the Vedic magic syllable *Oṃ*.[17] The chest and upper arms can also be decorated with some esteemed anthropomorphic or theriomorphic designs. This is the region of the body where the heroes of the Ramayana are depicted: Rama, his twin sons Kuśa and Lava (known to the Thais as But and Lop), Aṅgada and especially Hanuman (Fig. 4.5, b), each holding one or more appropriate weapons. On these areas of the body an *achan sak* may tattoo a strong and valiant animal: the *garuḍa* (ครุฑ), the *haṃsa,* the lion, the tiger, or the panther. When a human or animal motif is tattooed on the body, the *achan sak* usually surrounds the picture by secondary motifs, small mystical diagrams, and single *Khom* letters, often crowned with *unalom.*

The lower part of the arms, from elbow to wrist, can be used for miscellaneous designs. Some men carry there the marks they received when they were *dek wat,* others have placed just above the wrist the number of the regiment they served when conscripted into the army. A design once found on the lower arm is the picture of the *garuḍa* fighting a snake. This latter theme is well known in ancient India; it probably arrived in Thailand with the Ramayana in which the battle between birds and serpents also features. Other designs that are suited for the lower arm are a lizard with two tails, or a dove holding the top of an *unalom* in its beak (Fig. 4.5, c). The knuckles of the hands may each receive a single syllable.

High on the thigh near the hip joint a man may receive a picture of the *ling lom* (ลิงลม), the slow loris, also known as the wind monkey (Fig. 4.5, d). It is a small, tailless nocturnal animal which, according to a popular belief, exercises some influence over the wind.[18] On the right thigh the monkey is depicted within a circle, on all fours. This is the usual shape of this design. In the more rare case that somebody obtains a decoration on the left thigh as well, the *ling lom* stands free, on its hind legs, not surrounded by a circular border. When Textor described the more common form of this tattoo he tried to explain the circle around the monkey as follows:

16 See *The Pali Text Society's Pali-English Dictionary,* 1966, p. 130.

17 J. J. Boeles, 'The Migration of the Magic Syllable *Oṃ*', *India Antiqua,* 1947, pp. 40–56.

18 G. B. McFarland, *Thai-English Dictionary,* p. 745.

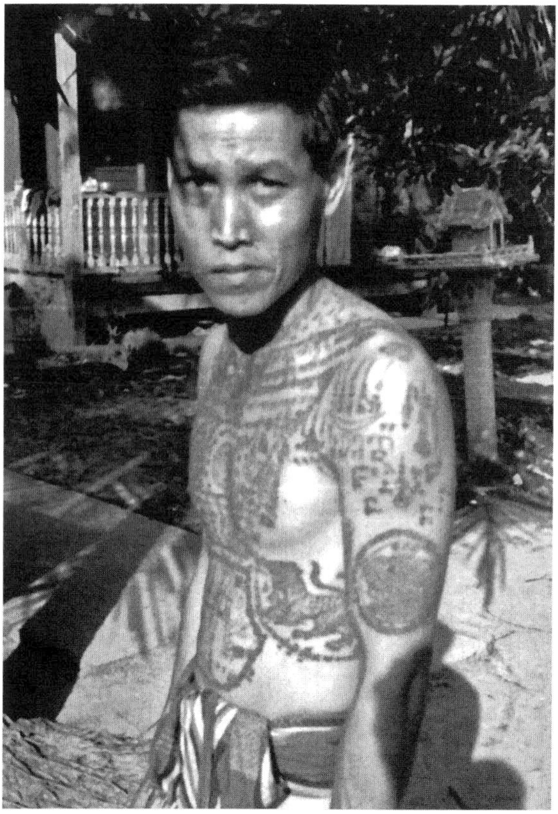

Figure 4.6: The proud result of many tattooing sessions.

> The reason for the circular border, which is otherwise not common, is conceivably that *ling lom* in fast speech sounds somewhat like *ling klom,* that is, 'round monkey' or, by extension, 'monkey in a circle'. My guess is that tattooing artists found it difficult to represent wind, and so settled on the circle instead.[19]

This is an ingenious train of thought, but it does not do full justice to the complexity of the system of symbolic representations used by the tattooist. We should note that usually a line of letters is tattooed above the back of the monkey as well as below the feet of the animal, usually a series of letters is tattooed. One professional tattooist explained that one of the lines represents water and the other line of symbols stands for fire.[20] If it is realized that the word

19 Textor, *An Inventory,* p. 102.

20 *Achan* Nuan, 6 October 1968.

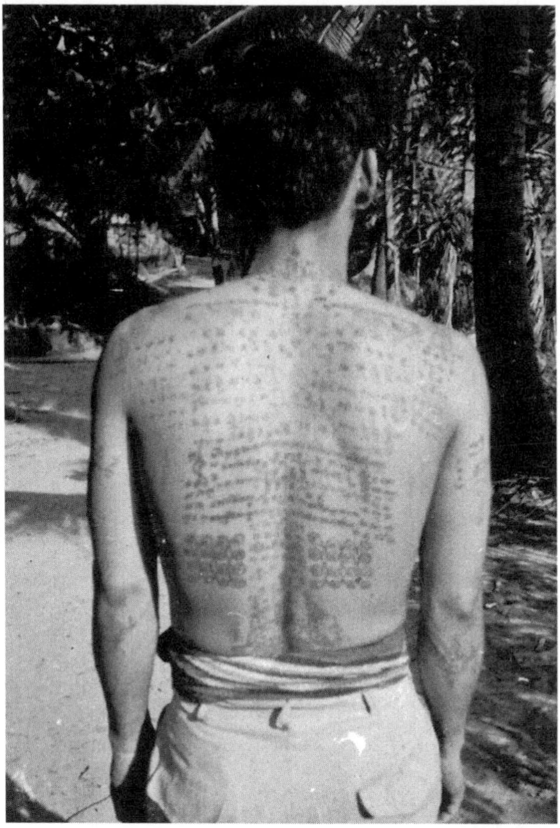

Figure 4.7: The back offers space for spells in the Khom script . . .

ling lom means literally 'wind-monkey', it is apparent that the circle around the monkey, the water and the fire, represents the fourth element of the universe: earth.

Lower still on the body, between the hips and the knees, miscellaneous tattooing of a less esteemed, sometimes outright dangerous kind can be made. This is the region of the body where a picture of a naked woman with an exaggerated vulva can be worn. This type of tattooing is considered very powerful and dangerous. It is usually reserved for those who have strong reason to wish to wield aggressive magical power. A professional tattooist can receive such a tattoo from his own teacher, or he may tattoo it on his own thigh. Another aggressive type of tattooing sometimes found on the upper leg is the phallus, depicted with an *unalom* as if it were emitting semen. On the lower part of the legs, very little tattooing is found. A single dot or a few unadorned syllables on

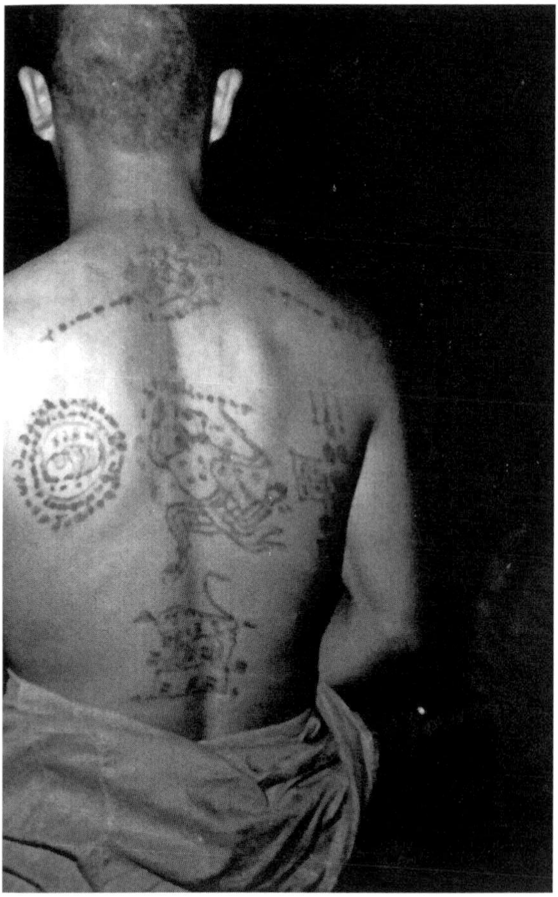

Figure 4.8: . . . or a combination of spells and theriomorphic icons.

the ankles sometimes suffice to protect a man against snake bites, but usually the tattooing needle does not come so low on the body.

The distribution of tattoos on a man's body reveals some aspects of the magical evaluation of the different parts of the human body. From the waist upwards, the more important parts of the body are crowned by the head. Lower down, where the excretory body apertures are situated, is a magically dangerous area. Further down, man's lesser parts begin, ending in the least respected and magically almost ignored members: the feet. The lower arms and hands constitute a rather ambiguous area of the body: farmers' hands are active in many respects and are engaged in activities that range from direct contact with dirt to handling sacred books.

This magical perspective of the body underlies some of the behaviour in respect to amulets. A small Buddha image or medallion should not be worn in a trouser pocket, or even worse, be placed in such a position that someone could step on or over it. Contravening such rules would not only greatly offend onlookers; it would destroy or at least diminish the sacred power that has been invested in the amulet.

It has also become clear that not all tattoos and amulets are equivalent in their magical charge: some are purely positive, some are believed to be replete with aggressive power, and others are downright dangerous. The positively charged objects and tattoos are closely connected with the monastic discipline, with Pali texts, and with the power of meditation. The aggressive tattoo designs begin on the chest, with pictures of tigers and leopards. Lower on the body we find the wooden phallus and dangerous, negative, even anti-social decorations.

It is generally believed that dangerous tattoos influence the behaviour of a man and that a heavily tattooed person will, as a result of his decorations, have acquired an aggressive and restless character. The *achan sak* is well aware of the possible danger of the powers he bestows and he takes care that he does not give designs that are too strong in their effects. A picture of an ancient sage or that of a devil would surely cause the receiver to go berserk. For this reason the tattooist can deliberately omit a detail of a design, in order to weaken its effect. Thus he may leave out the last syllable of a spell or, when tattooing a tiger, depict the animal without its tail.

Because of the fact that many aspects of magical tattooing are connected with equipping a man for an aggressive role and with anti-social behaviour, violence and roguishness, the Thai government discourages the practice. The government may well have been stimulated in this policy by the relatively recent European influence in the capital. To many foreigners who were brought up around the Second World War, who were unaware of the religious background of many tattoos, the body decorations appeared objectionable. In the 1970s, when a man would seek a position as a junior government official, he might have been asked during the interview to take off his shirt and show that he is not heavily tattooed. Nobody could foresee that from the 1990s onward, a veritable tattooing hype would conquer the international world. While the art of tattooing in the 1960s seemed to be clearly on the wane, especially in municipal areas, some men did find a compromise in being tattooed with *namman nga* (น้ำมันงา), the oil from sesame seed, which leaves no visible trace.

In the remote rural regions many men still consider it a privilege to be able to obtain magical powers from an *achan sak.* A major factor that sustains belief in the tattoos is the occasional occurrence of a case that 'proves' their powers. If a man is savagely attacked and escapes unscathed, or if he is involved in a major traffic accident and receives little or no injury, his good fortune is often ascribed to magical power. If he was wearing a strong amulet, he may well believe that this protected him; if he is of the opinion that his tattoos have saved him, he will be happy to proclaim their proven value. Events that do not corroborate the current beliefs in the protective quality of the magical designs and amulets may be explained by surmising that there was some overruling factor: a man may have lost the protective powers by not behaving in the manner his *achan sak* prescribed, he may not have 'awakened' the dormant forces with the proper *khatha,* or, if no direct explanation comes forth, the man may have possessed an extraordinarily great amount of bad *karma.*

In the late 1960s it was is common for a Thai woman to wear a small ornament on a necklace and sometimes these ornaments may appear very similar to the amulets worn by men. Among these objects are Buddha images of miniature size, sometimes as small as one centimetre in height. Another ornament often worn is the image of *Nang Kwak* (นางกวัก), the depiction of a woman who beckons with her hand. The miniature Buddha images and *Nang Kwak* are believed to bring luck, the latter especially during financial transactions. These objects worn by women are regarded by many men as second-rate in comparison with 'proper' amulets. Although they may be luck-bringing, they are not filled with magical power bestowed by an official sacralization process.

Women are excluded from wearing 'proper' amulets and it will be hard for a woman to find a tattooist who would be willing to invests her with magical tattoos. The most obvious reason for this almost total exclusion from this aspect of religious life lies in the fact that women are considered antithetic to many kinds of magical power from time to time because they exude dangerous power every month during menstruation. Menstrual blood is seen as polluting and diametrically opposed to beneficial power. All substances that may come into contact with menstrual blood are thus suspect and therefore a man should take care to keep the tattoos of the upper part of his body and his amulets that are charged with beneficial power away from the lower part of a woman's body and her lower garments.

In this light the newspaper report about a non-Thai woman who '... caused a major furore by hanging her underwear on the rails in the bathroom above

Table 3: The range of magical powers

	Dangerous	*Ambiguous*	*Beneficial*
Primary sources	Polluted substances, excreta, *namman phrai*	Esoteric spells uttered by a layman with sacred knowledge.	Meditation; uttering of Pali texts, especially when performed by monks.
Amulets	Objects used in aggressive love magic.*	Those worn on a cord around the waist: a tiger's tooth, a phallus.	Small Buddha images, *takrut,* medallions, objects which come from a strong ritual.
Tattoos	Naked woman tattoo, always placed on the thigh.	Anthropomorphic and theriomorphic designs, often on the chest.	Sacred syllables, *yan,* Buddha image, on the shoulders and on top of the head.

*__Note__: Such objects will be discussed in Chapter VI.

the heads of any men who might enter the room'[21] should be now be clear. This also explains why a woman should not possess an object charged with protective power; inadvertently she is likely to spoil its magical value.

There are other dangerously powerful, often polluting substances in the environment. Excreta from humans and from animals are polluted *per se,* and by extension the soil around a house and those creatures that devour excrement are to be avoided. The feet, which at least in traditional farmers' lives frequently come into contact with dirt, are therefore often associated with contamination. Outside every house, at the foot of the ladder leading up to the living area, a big water vessel filled with river water provides the means with which people who arrive barefoot can rinse their feet. In this context it is relevant to note also that before entering the Thais do not rub their feet clean with the hands. The usual method of cleansing consists of pouring some water on the feet from a ladle, while skilfully rubbing one foot with the other.

Another major source of pollution and dangerous magical substances is derived from corpses, especially from the bodies of people who have died violently and whose spirits may be expected to be enraged. A ritual specialist may use a corpse of a human who has died inauspiciously to extract some fluid, called *namman phrai* (น้ำมันพราย) with which very aggressive magical practices can be undertaken.[22] Some tattooists who specialize in powerful, aggressive designs re-

21 *The Bangkok Post,* 13 November 1969.

22 See Chapter VI.

putedly mix a small quantity of *namman phrai* with their ink in order to increase the dangerous power of their tattoos.

Sources of magical power

Nature can provide the farmers with unexpected seats of power. A termite hill not far from Wat Sanchao has a considerable reputation. Its power, when properly invoked, is often used to increase luck in business. A smooth round stone of fist size or even bigger that is dragged up from the bottom of the river should be kept in the rice storage hut, for it possesses the power to make the rice goddess happy. Another example of a magical object provided by nature (already mentioned above) is a lump of resin in which the shape of a Buddha image can be recognized.

Among the human activities that are reputed to generate magical power, two are conspicuous: the uttering of sacred words and meditation. In this respect both monks and laymen can be a source of power. In practice there is a division of labour between them. The monks, who professionally spend a great deal of their time in reciting Pali texts and controlling mind and body in meditation, are often the appropriate persons to make objects sacred. Only when their exalted position prevents them from doing so, namely when a ritual is directed primarily towards politely requesting spirits to assist human endeavours, are monks excluded from the actual supplication. A monk is considered to be higher on a hierarchical scale than a spirit.

It has been noticed in this chapter that some material is considered to be invested with dangerous magical power because it is polluted and offensive. Examples of this type of powerful substance are excrement, menstrual blood and a liquid extracted from certain corpses.

Amulets can in many instances be regarded as secondary seats of magical power: they derive much of their protective value from having been exposed to the blessing of a monk or some more elaborate empowering ritual. Similarly, the magical tattooing is characterized by the saying of sacred words and esoteric spells.

In the course of this chapter different types of power have been recognized. Some forces are considered beneficial, others are dangerous, and between these extremes there is an ambiguous region. In Table 3 the range of powers is set out and some examples are given to illustrate this ordering. On the dangerous end of the scale are sources that represent moments of great uncertainty, when people are likely to be thrown out of balance. The ambiguous section can be related to moments of importance and magnitude in the life of a person of which the outcome can be good, but which also may turn out unfavourably. On the beneficial end of the range the forces are solely connected with positive actions.

CHAPTER V

THE FIRST PERIOD IN THE SANGHA

As soon as a man reaches the age of twenty he is eligible to become a fully ordained member of the Sangha, in Thailand usually called *phiksu* (ภิกษุ).[1] Although many people around Wat Sanchao cannot state with precision exactly on which calendar day they were born, they are aware of the year in which their birth took place and can easily calculate when a person is eligible to become a monk.

In Thai Buddhism, ordination as a Buddhism monk is regarded as a kind of *rite de passage*, a circumstance that may well be typical of mainland Southeast Asia.[2] While, in theory, every man in Thailand is supposed to become a *phiksu* for at least one period of his life, in reality not all men are willing to take this step. Information on the number of monks, monasteries, and size of the eligible population is set out in Table 4. It can be seen at a glance that the number of monks is, in relative terms, decreasing. From 1927 to 1970 the estimated number of eligible men increased more than threefold, but the number of monks increased only by 50 per cent. Or, as Mulder has calculated, in 1927 one out of every 16.5 eligible was a monk and in 1970 the figure had become one out of every 34.7 adult Buddhist males.[3]

A closer examination of the figures shows that the number of monasteries gradually increased, but the column 'number of monks' presents quite a different picture. In 1948, 1949 and 1950 the number of monks gradually increased and rose to over 175,000. From 1951 onwards the number drops markedly and it was not until 1966 that the figure for 1949 was matched. The increase dated

1 From the Sanskrit *bhikṣu*. The spelling *phikkhu* derived from the Pali word *bhikkhu* is also known in Thailand.

2 In the Pali ordination text the aspirant monk solemnly promises to follow the monastic rules 'tante yāvajīvaṃ' or 'for the duration of his life', but Thais are usually not aware of this, and if so, do not feel that they are bound to such a promise.

3 J. A. N. Mulder, *Monks, Merit, and Motivation: Buddhism and National Development in Thailand*, 1973, p. 10.

Table 4: Thai monks, monasteries and population (rounded to thousands)

Year	*Number of monks*	*Number of monasteries*	*Population*	*Adult Buddhist males*
1901			7,491,000	
1909			8,087,000	
1919			9,966,000	
1927	130,000	17,000	11,600,000	2,150,000
1929	125,000 *	16,000	12,433,000	
1937	150,000	17,000	14,549,000	2,750,000
1947			17,657,000	
1948	162,000	19,000		
1949	175,000	20,000		
1950	176,000	20,000	20,000,000	3,740,000
1951	166,000	20,000		
1952	160,000	21,000		
1953	155,000	21,000		
1954	157,000	21,000		
1955	155,000	21,000		
1956	150,000	21,000		
1957	155,000	21,000		
1958	156,000	21,000	24,800,000	4,640,000
1959	150,000	22,000		
1960	159,000	23,000	26,990,000	
1961	153,000	23,000	27,210,000	5,050,000
1962	152,000	23,000	28,054,000	
1963	152,000	23,000	28,923,000	5,330,000
1964	167,000	23,000	29,820,000	5,500,000
1965	173,000	24,000	30,744,000	
1966	175,000	24,000	31,691,000	5,964,000
1967	186,000	25,000	32,680,000	
1968	185,000	25,000	34,000,000	6,358,000
1970	195,000	26,000	36,100,000	6,750,000
1975	213,000	26,000	42,000,000	
1986	285,000	33,000	53,000,000	

Sources: W. Trittel, *Thailand,* 1943, p. 34 and p. 45 (figures for 1901, 1909 and monks and monasteries in 1937); J. Bourgeois-Pichat, 'An Attempt to Appraise the Accuracy of Demographic Statistics for an Underdeveloped Country: Thailand', as quoted in J. C. Caldwell, 'The Demographic Structure', in *Thailand, Social and Economic Studies in Development,* ed. by T. H. Silcock, 1967, p. 35 (population figures for 1919, 1929, 1937 and 1947); Credner, *Siam, das Land* der *Tai,* p. 199 and p. 341 (monks, monasteries 1929); *Thailand Statistical Yearbook,* Number 27, 1966, p. 438 (monks, monasteries 1948–1957 and population estimates 1961–1967); รายงานการศาสนาประจำปี [Annual Report on Religious Affairs] *2508, 2509,* 2510, 2513, 2518 (monks, monasteries 1958 onward); Caldwell, *op. cit.* p. 35 (population 1960) and J. A. N. Mulder, *Monks, Merit and Motivation,* 1973, p. 10 (figures for 1927, population for 1950, 1958, 1959 and 1970; figures for adult Buddhist males).

***Note**: Credner's statements are not linked to a specific date; it is deduced from the context that the figure given is for 1929 (Credner, *op. cit.,* p. 199 and p. 341).

Table 5: Men of Wat Sanchao and their ordination up to 1968

Category	*Living*	*Deceased*
Ordained in Wat Sanchao	164	101
Ordained in other monasteries	85	21
Not ordained	36	13
Planning to be ordained, just over 20 years of age	21	–
Chinese religion	3	18
No information given	18	15
Eligible male population	327	168

from 1964 and continued to 1975. It is likely that the sudden increase in the number of monks is related to the post-war population 'explosion' nineteen years earlier.

However, it may be noted, with the figures of Table 4 in mind, that the relative number of monks is decreasing for the whole of Thailand, the information is not as straightforward as it may seem. In the first place it must be borne in mind that the figures are taken in the middle of the rainy season, the months of religious intensity. Outside this period of the year the number of monks in Thailand is much smaller. Secondly, the figures on the number of monks give no information on the turnover that takes place every year. Before these statistics can tell anything about the degree and type of decrease of the monastic institution it is necessary to assess the average length of time that a monk remains in the order. Unfortunately, only for 1970 is such information available.[4] In that year approximately 24 per cent of all monks in Thailand had been ordained recently. Without similar information over a large number of years it is impossible to determine the character of the apparent relative decrease.

When the genealogies of the people who live near Wat Sanchao were being collected, among the questions asked of males were: 'has this man once been a monk?' 'in what monastery (or monasteries)?', and 'for how long?' This information was obtained for 495 males; it included men born in communities other than Wat Sanchao but related to Wat Sanchao people through marriage. It went back several generations, as far back in history as people could recollect with certainty. Table 5 shows the results of these enquiries.

Under the category 'Ordained in other monasteries' two different types of persons can be distinguished. On the one hand there are households that, although situated near Wat Sanchao, send a young man elsewhere to be a

4 รายงานการศาสนาประจำปี ๒๕๑๓ [Annual Report on Religious Affairs, 2513], p. 166.

monk. There is no firm obligation to send a boy to the nearest monastery; other considerations occasionally have priority. Often a reason given is that the monastic education is believed to be better in the other place of residence. On the other hand, into this category fall some men who, having been monks in another community, have married local girls and settled near Wat Sanchao. A further complicating factor not shown in Table 5 is that a man can be ordained in one place and may choose to live in another one immediately afterwards. Moreover, the number of 'Not ordained' in the column 'Living' is not necessarily a final figure. Many of these are men who married before they were twenty years old and whose responsibilities for the upkeep of their family make it difficult for them to become monks. Some have other reasons for never having been ordained. They may not be eligible for the Sangha because of physical or mental disabilities, they might have disqualified themselves by getting into debt, or they may have been overawed by the strict rules of behaviour or the heavy burden of learning.

Under the heading 'Chinese religion' fall those who are of Chinese descent and who do not wish to adhere to the Theravada form of Thai Buddhism. Just over a hundred years ago several Chinese settled in Wat Sanchao, married locally, and became rice growers. Their children usually felt themselves to be Thai, rather than Chinese. They often changed their Chinese name into a Thai one and followed the Thai religion. Usually they did not seek contact with the Chinese who entered Thailand in more recent times and who tended to bring their own Chinese wives. These relative newcomers did not become farmers but on the whole they settled in the towns. The assimilation of the older Wat Sanchao Chinese is clearly reflected in the marked difference in numbers between 'living' and 'deceased' in this category.

Excluding the members of the Chinese religion, disregarding the category of those 'planning to be ordained', and taking the 'No information given' category as 'Not ordained', it appears that of the already deceased men 81 per cent did become monks during their lifetime. Of the living it seems that as much as 82 per cent have been or are at present monks. It may thus be concluded that at least for the region around Wat Sanchao a very high percentage of Buddhist men become a member of the Sangha. The information given in Table 4 suggests that a similar picture may not be expected in many other regions. It is quite possible that the high percentage for Wat Sanchao is related to its essentially rural and conservative character and that the increasing influence of the nearby provincial capital will soon be reflected in a much smaller number of men becoming monks.

The question of why so many rural men go through an expensive ritual of ordination and subject themselves to a set of rigorous rules can be approached from various directions. From the point of view of the individual Thai farmer it should be understood that a person who is to be ordained for the first time in his life may have a rather distorted picture of what being a member of the Sangha entails. If he has been a *dek wat* he will probably remember the power and authority of the monks whom he served. Also he can be aware of the life of a monk from his contacts with members of the Sangha when they come to collect food early each morning, from witnessing ceremonies in the monastery as well as in private houses when monks sit in rows, chanting sacred texts. Every man knows the superior ritual position of the monk, a position enhanced by the many rules of behaviour.

This incomplete knowledge of the monastic life may present a rather attractive picture; from the moment of ordination onward all laymen will be ritually inferior, and there will be no exhausting labour in the rice-fields. Moreover, if the rules prove too hard to follow, it is common knowledge that each monk can leave the order with impunity. If he manages successfully to complete one rainy season he can withdraw honourably, without any loss of face.

Although the overall picture these young men have of the life of a *phiksu* may not be completely negative, this alone seems an insufficient reason for deciding to become a monk. Kaufman indicates that young men may do so against their will when he reports that the older monks regard newly-ordained members of the Sangha as: '... serving their time more as a result of outside pressure than from their own volition'.[5] Pressure from other people certainly can be a major factor in a young man's decision to become a *phiksu.* The persons who sponsor his ordination gain prestige and earn a great amount of good *karma* by helping a man join the Sangha, and they would be upset if the candidate decided to remain a layman.

A candidate is often encouraged most strongly by his mother. The woman who guides and helps a son to attain the status of monk, and who takes the responsibility to provide the monastery with the food necessary to feed the extra inhabitant, will earn an immense amount of merit. In Thailand, where a woman is excluded from entering the Sangha, the closest she can come to that exalted position is to sponsor a son in the order.

In addition, a candidate will be influenced by the fact that other men of his age will be monks. Not only will he feel more secure in the monastery when he

5 H. K. Kaufman, *Bangkhuad*, p. 120

shares his experiences with some of his comrades, but also he would risk – if he were to refuse to become a *phiksu* – becoming an outsider in his age-group. Within the community, a person who has never been a monk is regarded as a non-adult. He is a *khon dip* (คนดิบ), an unripe person. Such a man can more easily be called by his nickname without much consideration of his age.

During ceremonies where monks and laymen come together there is usually a moment in which one of the laymen will have to ask in the Pali language for the Five Precepts.[6] Every man should be able to lead the lay community during this part of the ceremony. Those who have not been monks, and consequently cannot lead the lay community in chanting in Pali, may be teased about their lack of knowledge. Outside pressure is therefore certainly a factor to be considered when answering the question of why a young man decides to become a monk. However, it is a mild pressure, and there is no constant harassing, no barring from communal pleasures. Those who are well over 30 years of age and still have not been monks will, when asked, readily admit that they have thus far missed the opportunity, but they do not walk about dejectedly as if ashamed of themselves.

While the fact that becoming a monk is an accepted social custom may assist some men in deciding to join the Sangha, considerations of a more private nature may be relevant as well. Credner, observing the Thais in the 1920s, wrote about the personal motivation of those who become monks in words that can be translated as follows:

> Behind the monastic institution of Buddhism hides certainly much laziness and a pleasure in having an idle life, but also can one find much serious piety and a striving for spiritual completeness.[7]

However, these extremes have little or no relevance for the rural scene. The man who wishes to be idle and enjoy an existence without work should not, like most candidates, join the Sangha just before the beginning of Buddhist Lent; he would be bitterly disappointed by the regime of chanting, studying, and meditating many hours per day. On the other hand, piety and a striving for spiritual completeness are very rarely thought about by young aspirant monks. Such thoughts may be relevant for some of the older men who join the Sangha at the stage when their lives are coming to a close.

A young man may be personally motivated in a variety of ways that often having little religious significance. He may, for example, wish to avoid being

6 See Chapter VIII.

7 W. Credner, *Siam, das Land der Tai*, p. 341.

conscripted into military service, and if he studies hard and passes his religious state examinations, he may succeed in doing so. Other reasons, so well known that the Thais sometimes enumerate them in a little rhyme, are:

buat kae bon (บวชแก่บน)	(ordination to fulfil a promise)
buat kae chon (บวชแก่จน)	(ordination to escape poverty)
buat ni mia (บวชหนีเมีย)	(ordination to flee from a wife)
buat ni thuk (บวชหนีทุกข์)	(ordination flee from sorrow)
buat ha khong kin (บวชหาของกิน)	(ordination to eat [good] food)
buat ha phuean (บวชหาเพื่อน)	(ordination to join one's friends)
buat duai sathan (บวชด้วยสถาน)	(ordination out of respect)

The seventh reason, 'out of respect' is the most proper one. Another acclaimed reason a young man can give for deciding to join the Sangha is that he wants to learn. For this reason the first ordination of a man can be called *buat rian* (บวชเรียน) as Sitsayamkan pointed out, 'ordination in order to gain knowledge'.[8]

In order to distinguish between young men who join the Sangha at the age of twenty usually for a period of just over three months, and monks who remain *phiksu* for many years, several authors classify the monks under the headings 'temporary monks' and 'permanent' or 'career' monks.[9] There are some drawbacks to this categorization. In the first place, the temporary nature of a young monk's residence can only be judged in retrospect. There are ordained persons who originally planned to leave the order at the end of Lent but who decided to remain *phiksu*. Every year there are young monks who appear to be suited to their role and who are urged to stay on for at least another year. In the second place, the permanence of the monks who remain members of the Sangha for a period longer than one Lenten period is no matter of certainty either. Every monk in the country can decide to return to the status of layman; no stigma attaches to him who acts thus and no monk or layman should reproach him for doing so. Once, during World War II and just months before the Lenten period, the abbot of Wat Sanchao himself decided to leave the order. Notwithstanding the fact that this decision severely upset the organization of the monastery, it was never publicly criticized.

Moreover, the Thais themselves do not divide their monks into groups that can be recognized as 'temporary' and 'permanent'. The distinctions between

8 Luang Sitsayamkan, *Some Useful Information on the Buddhist Religion as it is Taught and Practised in Thailand*, 1963, p. 6.

9 Kaufman, *Bangkhuad*, p. 107 ff; J. A. N. Mulder, *Monks, Merit, and Motivation*, 1973, pp. 9–11; J. Bunnag, *Buddhist Monk, Buddhist Layman*, 1973, pp. 36–7.

Figure 5.1: The night before ordination an elaborate *tham khwan* is held.

monks who probably will serve for one Lenten season and those who have been in the order for years may be subsumed in a hierarchical scheme. Two principles can be distinguished in this hierarchy: seniority and rank. According to the rule of seniority, a monk who has joined the Sangha at an earlier date than another monk is the senior of the two. An interruption is considered to erase the status: when a man joins the order for a second time he again begins at the lowest level. The ranking principle often overrules seniority: an abbot takes precedence over a monk who has spent a greater number of seasons in the order.

The difference between monks joining the order probably for one Lenten season and those who remain for longer periods is therefore not adequately described under rubrics such as 'temporary' and 'permanent', but it is designated better by the terms 'inexperienced' and 'experienced'. When the inexperienced monk lives one *phansa* (พรรษา),[10] one Lenten season, in a monastery he is

10 Like many Thai religious words, *phansa* is probably derived from the Sanskrit *varṣa*, rather than the Pali word *vassa*. The Lenten period lasts from mid-July until mid-October.

Figure 5.2: The ordination procession to the *bot* is led by music and dance.

usually obliged to partake in an intensive learning process, while the experienced monk, even when he joins the order anew and begins again at the bottom of the hierarchy, does not need to attend classes. The inexperienced monk is often preparing for life and looks ahead to raising a family and living in his own home as soon as he has left the order. The experienced monk, however, often looks ahead to a career in the Sangha and if he is an older man his period in the order may be seen as a preparation for death and rebirth.

The knowledge an inexperienced monk has to acquire can be subsumed under two headings. Firstly there is traditional learning, which comprises the skills a monk ought to acquire according to the ancient rules that probably date from long before the time the state examinations became important in the rural scene. Secondly a monk often has to take part in the preparation for the nationwide religious examinations. In the remainder of this chapter these two rubrics will be elucidated.

Figure 5.3: Young women carry the gifts for the new monk and the Sangha.

Traditional Learning of the Inexperienced Monk

Ordination

It has been customary that before ordination the aspirant monk lives for a while in the monastery where he will be ordained. Once this preparatory time may have been as long as several weeks;[11] in Wat Sanchao people believed that one week was customary. In actual practice two or three days are often considered sufficient. During this period of preparation the young man must perform some menial tasks; he helps with the mopping of floors and fills the water containers that are for general use. In return for these tasks he will be instructed in aspects of his future life as a monk.

In this period he is taught how to don and wear robes, leaving one shoulder bare within the monastery boundaries but covering both shoulders outside the

11 J. Bunnag, *Buddhist Monk, Buddhist Layman*, p. 40.

Figure 5.4: Sometimes the candidate rides a horse, reminding us of the way that Siddhartha Gautama left his palace.

sacred precinct. He is also instructed in the daily routine of the monks, and thus it is expected of him that he joins the morning round collecting food as a servant to the *phiksu*. Doing this not only serves to familiarize him with the etiquette surrounding the ritual reception of food items but also introduces him to a large number of households as a person who is preparing for ordination. The most important task of the aspirant monk consists of the preparation for the ordination ceremony. The text of the ordination is found in the booklet *Suatmon Chet Tamnan*,[12] the standard handbook for all inexperienced monks. The whole ordination text is learned by rote: each sentence is repeated aloud in some quiet corner by the aspirant monk until he can recite it without looking at the pages. The whole text is in the Pali language, so that most words are

12 สวดมนต์เจ็ดตำนาน [Chanting the Series of Seven], B.E. 2510 (1967).

Figure 5.5: The guardian spirit of the monastery must be informed.

unintelligible to the average candidate. Near the end of his preparation time an experienced monk will go through the whole ordination text with him and elaborate instructions are given regarding the sequence of actions that take place during ordination.

When the time of the ordination arrives, the aspirant monk is usually very nervous and is likely to make mistakes in the recitation or to forget the text altogether. If this occurs, the ordainer will prompt him with the appropriate key word until the text comes back to mind. If he still cannot recollect the right words he will be guided all the way, word for word. This prompting does not invalidate the ceremony; the important aspect of the ritual is that the words have to be said by the aspirant monk. The prompting, if it occurs, may give rise to a little ridicule from the spectators: superior smiles from those men who performed better at the time when they were ordained, compassion from those

Figure 5.6: The aspirant-monk presents himself to his preceptor.

who met with the same difficulties. As soon as the ceremony is over, the text for the ordination can be forgotten.[13]

Immediately after the ordination, the new monk is made aware of his exalted ritual position by the use of special words that are reserved for activities of monks. While laymen can speak of themselves eating, drinking, sleeping and relieving themselves, a member of the Sangha must use special sacerdotal language to designate these activities when they are related to himself or another member of the Sangha.

13 The best sources in the English language for the procedure of the Thai ordination are still K. E. Wells, *Thai Buddhism, Its Rites and Activities*, 1960, Chapter V, and H.R.H. Prince Vajirañāṇavarorasa, *Ordination Procedure*, 1966, pp. 20–45. The rural ordination is best appreciated in Worakawintho's poem, translated into English by T. H. Silcock, published as *A Village Ordination*, 1976.

The inexperienced monk also has to become used to a new terminology for addressing many members of the community, and at the same time he will have to become accustomed to the fact that all laymen address him with great respect. The recently ordained monk does not have to change the terms of address for older monks; as a layman he could have addressed the abbot and other older monks as *luang pho* (หลวงพ่อ) 'reverend father' or *luang ta* (หลวงตา) 'reverend uncle' and may continue to do so. However, he used to refer to many inexperienced monks by the term *luang phi* (หลวงพี่) 'reverend older brother'; from now on they are his colleagues and can be called by their names or nicknames.

Within the Sangha, the recently ordained member has thus to adjust his mode of address in the lower echelons. The reverse is true for his terminology with regard to laymen; here the older and most respected persons must suddenly be addressed differently. From the moment of ordination a monk avoids in his speech all polite prefixes that he formerly had to use for older relatives. Honoured laymen can be addressed by a monk with the special sacerdotal pronoun for parents: *yom* (โยม). All laymen will refer to the newly ordained monk by his name, preceded with the prefix *phra* (พระ), by using the new monastic name that was conferred upon him at ordination, also with the prefix *phra*, or by adressing him as *luang phi* (reverend older brother).

From the moment of his ordination a monk has to become accustomed to his ritual superiority towards all laymen. When a passer-by raises his hands palm to palm in the customary polite form of greeting, a monk should not answer by returning the gesture. He can only acknowledge the greeting verbally. When walking, a layman will walk a step behind him, when sitting, a layman will choose a lower level to sit. Many inexperienced monks are acutely aware of the fact that this deference on the part of the laymen is not the result of their personal accomplishments, but is the automatic result of their belonging to the exalted order. It may stimulate most newly ordained members to observe the strict discipline and try to become worthy of the great respect shown everywhere.

Chanting

The *Suatmon Chet Tamnan*, the regular handbook for inexperienced monks, contains many of the Pali texts that are often chanted by the monks. They are a mixture of passages from the canon and short verses composed in later times by famous monks. There are chants for early in the morning and for late in the afternoon, chants for auspicious occasions, hymns with deep philosophical meaning, reflections on food and clothing, and texts to be recited at funerals. Most of these texts have been adequately translated into English.[14]

During the Lenten season the monks chant Pali texts in unison many times a day, sometimes for prolonged periods, but on other occasions the recitation may last only a few minutes. In most monasteries there are four major chanting sessions: before sunrise at four o'clock, at nine, early in the afternoon and just before sunset. During these longer chanting periods the monks sit in orderly rows facing a Buddha image, the hands raised palm to palm in front of the chest. The abbot sits in front, the most recent additions to his chapter sit at the back. The abbot indicates which text will be used by chanting the first word of that text. All the monks join in, with loud voices at the same pitch. An inexperienced monk usually does not know these Pali texts by heart. During the communal chanting sessions in the monastery when no laymen are present he is allowed to take his copy of the *Suatmon Chet Tamnan* with him. Therefore he is able to chant in unison with the experienced monks as soon as he has found the printed text in his handbook.

Since the monk can use a book during these communal chanting sessions, there would seem to be no need for him to memorize the passages. However, during spare moments many industrious recently ordained monks can be seen reading these Pali texts in a loud voice while committing them to memory. One of the main incentives for learning the texts by heart is the consideration that during ceremonies when laymen are involved no textbooks may be used. On each *wan phra* during *phansa,* four times a month, a numerous lay congregation gathers in the monastery and observes the monks perform certain ceremonial acts that include chanting auspicious stanzas.

In addition there are often ceremonies outside the monastery at which a chapter of monks is invited to chant for a group of laymen. These ceremonies can be connected with the stages of the life cycle such as birth, first haircutting, marriage, and death, or with the fertility of the fields, rainmaking, entering a new house and the increase of the prosperity of a certain family. During all these ceremonies when the members of the Sangha perform a ritual for laymen, the monks sit on a dais facing the laymen. The monks recite Pali texts for a considerable period; sometimes it is as short as a quarter of an hour, but often it is much longer, thus causing a bowl of water to be charged with beneficial power.[15] Usually all the texts that are recited can be found in the *Suatmon Chet*

14 K. E. Wells, *Thai Buddhism, Its Rites and Activities,* and H.R.H. Prince Vajirañāṇavarorasa, *Ordination Procedure,* pp. 72–111.

15 See Chapter IX.

Tamnan. A detailed description of the texts chanted in the presence of laymen in northeast Thailand shows great similarity with central Thai practices.[16]

On *wanphra* all inexperienced monks participate in the ritual, but especially in rural areas newly ordained monks may also be invited to chant at private homes, notably when the ritual takes place in the house of close relatives. At such occasions the laymen can observe whether a newly ordained man can already join in the chanting of texts or whether he has to sit silently while his fellow monks recite. After a man has been a *phiksu* for several months, it is expected of him that he take part in most chants. Inexperienced monks may feel quite embarrassed when the leader of a chapter of monks chooses a text that they have not yet mastered. Some monks may try to hide their lack of knowledge by extending a breathing pause, or by simulating a cough during difficult parts of the text, and then resume the recitation during the easy, repetitive parts. However, they have little chance to mislead the audience with such simulated knowledge of Pali texts, because most of the adult men in the audience have been monks themselves and are quite capable of detecting the inexperienced monks' degree of ignorance.

One of the incentives for learning the texts by heart is therefore the wish to avoid embarrassment during ceremonies involving laymen. In addition, a monk who is known as someone who chants well may be invited more often to perform ceremonies for laymen than the monk who cannot recite with ease. As it is the custom to reward all monks who perform ceremonies outside the monastery grounds with money as well as with other gifts, there is also a financial incentive for learning to chant expertly.

The money presentation is always kept apart from the presentation of additional gifts, because the rules of the order forbid monks to handle money. Rural people interpret these regulations concerning monks and money rather loosely and in many instances these rules are broken openly. This is discussed later in this chapter; for the purpose of this description it suffices to note that the written rules have at least an influence upon the moment and manner of ritual presentation.

The traditional gifts to the members of a chapter of monks always include incense, a candle, and a flower. In addition there is often a presentation of some useful practical objects such as a plate, a toothbrush, soap powder, toilet paper and matches. It is customary to donate identical gifts to all monks who participate. The decisions regarding donations rest, however, with the lay

16 S. J. Tambiah, *Buddhism and the Spirit Cults in North-East Thailand*, 1970, pp. 201–6.

organizers, and variations occur sometimes in the amounts of money distributed to the individual monks. For example, if one of the monks outranks the other members of the Sangha by far, the lay organizers may donate a greater amount to this monk than to the remaining *phiksu*.

In a rather unusual decision, the laymen of Wat Sanchao decided to remunerate the experienced monks with a greater amount than the inexperienced ones:

> 1 June 1968:
> . . . a well-to-do layman invited thirteen monks from three different monasteries to chant in his house. Many of the monks happened to be inexperienced, recently ordained monks, and the oldest, highest ranking monk present was more than 80 years old. This venerable *phiksu* chose to chant texts which almost none of the other members of the chapter knew, and the sound of the recitation became very meagre indeed.
>
> The house-owner conferred softly with several other laymen present, and after the ceremony, when publicly announcing the amount of the donation, he stressed: 'In this case we donate fifty baht to each of the four members of the Sangha who used their voices, and only half that amount to the remaining monks'.

On any ordinary day during the Lenten period, the total time spent by the monks in communal chanting without a lay audience varies possibly from two to four hours. During the chanting sessions of a rural monastery, the abbot seldom varies the first and last text. In addition, during the periods of communal recitation the abbot gradually works through the various texts that can be used on special occasions, such as funerals or housewarmings. Both types of texts occur in the *Suatmon Chet Tamnan*.[17] Usually the abbot chooses from the texts those which the monks have not chanted recently and each section of common chanting will be recited in unison at least once a week. Often it will take a monk two Lenten seasons before he masters all major texts; it is only the exceptional individual who commits them all to memory during his first year in the Sangha. Most monks end their first Lenten period being capable of reciting only the texts that are used every day.

Even the most experienced monks find it difficult to chant individually. During the recitations in unison with others each individual can rely on the

17 In this respect, Tambiah appears to have been misinformed when he writes: 'The *tham watr* are not memorized from printed texts' (*Buddhism and the Spirit Cults in North-East Thailand*, p. 123). These collections of chants appear in *Suatmon Chet Tamnan*, pp. 63–73.

memory of those around him. The drone of many voices is slightly soporific and the experienced monk often chants in a completely relaxed manner. If, however, asked to chant alone, a monk may find that even an 'easy text' suddenly becomes difficult. When chanting alone a monk is suddenly forced to remember sequences of words that he normally produces automatically in unison with others.

Monastic Behaviour

In theory, every monk should follow the rules of behaviour as they are laid down in the *Vinaya Piṭaka*. These rules consist of the 227 that can be found in the famous formulary *Pāṭimokkha*, as well as the many additional guidelines which are known as *thūlaccaya* (serious transgressions) and the *dukkhaṭā* (ill deeds). These additional guidelines consist of many rules that came into existence after the final redaction of the *Pāṭimokkha* had been accepted.[18]

When a young man is accepted in the order he cannot be expected to appreciate the intricacies of all these different rules. Some of the older experienced monks who have never had the opportunity to study for the religious state examinations have only a vague idea of the wording of most rules. Still, they can behave in an exemplary manner, and function as experienced monks in the community, regardless of the fact that they cannot recite the *Pāṭimokkha*, or quote any other text on behaviour.

If such a venerable experienced monk, who is not schooled according to the new curriculum, instructs a recently ordained inexperienced monk on the rules of behaviour he will undoubtedly begin by stating that the most important rules are the four *pārājikā* precepts. These are cardinal rules that a monk cannot break without automatically losing membership in the order. There are other classes of rules, but for the exact number and wording he might have to look up in an appropriate manual. The four *pārājikā* rules of the *Pāṭimokkha* are the only rules on which even the oldest monks can discourse at length.

When these four rules are mentioned in the literature on Thai Buddhism, they have sometimes been paraphrased rather carelessly. Kaufman, for example, translates them as follows: '1) Do not kill any human creature; 2) Do not steal; 3) Refrain from all sexual activities; 4) Do not tell lies'.[19] The Thai monks word these four rules in a much more specific manner, thereby closely guided by the Pali text. Their version usually corresponds with something like:

18 T. W. Rhys Davids and H. Oldenberg, *Vinaya Texts*, Part I, pp. xxv–xxvi.

19 H. K. Kaufman, *Bangkhuad*, p. 135.

1. A monk completing sexual intercourse with a living being is no longer a member of the order.
2. A monk stealing an object worth more than five *māsaka*[20] is no longer a member of the order.
3. A monk who intentionally kills a human being thereby expels himself from the order.
4. A monk who lies about his magical powers is no longer a member of the order.

The inexperienced monk is told in words that cannot be misunderstood that breaking one of these *pārājikā* rules would result in a disastrous situation. Not only would immediate expulsion result, but the person who becomes a layman in such an ignominious manner would be a social outcast. He would be talked about throughout the province. No one would want to be seen with such a man, no woman would marry him.

In these circumstances it is most unlikely that a man who broke such a precept would talk about it. It is not a subject on which frankness can be expected. It is therefore quite amazing to read in Kaufman's book the following statement:

> No doubt there is some homosexual activity, at least during the Lenten period, when so many young men are suddenly thrown into celibacy. Two men in the village informed me of such occurrences during their stay in the *wat*.[21]

All Thai informants to whom I translated this passage were convinced of the fact that this cannot represent the truth. It is possible that Kaufman meant something much more specific when he broached the subject of homosexuality that his informants when they answered his queries. It is not unknown, and indeed a subject that can be openly discussed, that young monks develop strong attachments among each other. However, it remains most doubtful that the two informants of Bangkhuad referred to activities that would automatically result in expulsion from the Sangha. In the region of Wat Sanchao all monks were aware of the fact that ejection of semen with assistance of a living being, be it female, male, or animal, would mean that a *pārājikā* rule had been broken.

20 The *māsaka* is a small coin of very low value of ancient times. It is not known in Thailand. Modern Thai exegesis takes five *māsaka* to be approximately equivalent to one *baht*.

21 Kaufman, *Bangkhuad*, p. 136.

All other types of sexual contact, not resulting in emission of semen, fall under less important categories.

A parallel case may possibly be the one reported by Welch for Chinese Buddhist monasteries. One of Welch's informants stated that a great deal of homosexual practices went on in monasteries. When pressed for details it became clear that there was no evidence of physical consummation.[22] It seems likely that Kaufman's informants referred to similar emotional attachments. In this context it is relevant that two monks walking while holding hands, or with their arms around one another's shoulders, may not be regarded as evidence for homosexual behaviour. In Thailand these are regarded as a normal friendly gestures that do not necessarily have connotations of aberrant sexual inclinations.

Most of the older monks who never followed official religious instruction cannot give the wording of any rules other than the *pārājikā* section of the *Pāṭimokkha*. However, if they are not aware of the letter of the remaining precepts, the meaning of proper monastic behaviour is clear to all. A monk should be aware of his thoughts and actions at all times. He should behave in a subdued, friendly, and calm manner. He should never allow himself to become excited, argumentative, angry, or rude, and therefore he should avoid running, jumping, or dancing. A monk should not gamble or drink alcoholic beverages. Instead he should always be polite, sober, clean, and unselfish.

When a monk sits, his limbs should be arranged in a proper manner; when he walks his arms should not swing about: a *phiksu* should continuously be aware of the proper position of his robes. It follows that a monk can laugh, but not unrestrainedly, can join in conversation with laymen, but does not gossip. A monk may look at a football game, but does not cheer, let alone take part; he may bathe in the river, but is not allowed to swim for pleasure or splash with water. When a monk eats he should show no greed, he ought not to even indicate that he is hungry. Instead he should eat slowly and casually as if unaware of the quality of the food.

Some of the restrictions regarding the consumption of food will be known to the newly ordained monk who once served as *dek wat*. Thus he is aware of the fact that he may only consume food that has been ceremoniously presented by a lay person (*prakhen*, described in Chapter III). After midday no solid food may be taken unless a monk is ill and the return of his health depends on breaking the daily fast. A *phiksu* may eat only in the time between

22 H. Welch, *The Practice of Chinese Buddhism, 1900–1950*, 1967, p. 118.

sunrise and noon. This fasting does not appear injurious; many of the monks appear well-fed; there are even some quite obese members of the Sangha. While laymen generally appreciate the thought of an ascetic monk, at the same time they do not object to corpulent monks, probably because the latter are the living proof of the generosity of the sustaining population. Usually the monks eat communally, and table manners are strict. However, the amount of food is ample and the abbot grants his monks sufficient time to satisfy the appetite. During the afternoon and evening the monks may drink tea, coffee, or lemonade, chew betel leaf with areca fruit and lime, and smoke tobacco. Some monks may drink coffee mixed with condensed milk, or take a glass of Ovomaltine, but others will refrain from using milk products during the periods of fast (some avoid milk products altogether).

One of the most important areas of controlled behaviour centres around the avoidance of contact with females. No monk should touch a woman, a female animal or even an object that is being held by a woman. Even if the mother or the grandmother of a monk wishes to present him with some medicine or some food, the object cannot be transferred directly from her hand to his. The monk in question will have to produce a piece of cloth, which he rolls or spreads on a surface before him. The woman can place the gift on this cloth while the monk holds on to an edge of the material. A woman is not allowed to speak with a monk in private: all verbal contact should take place within earshot of at least a third person. The recently ordained monk has to be instructed to be alert in public places lest he inadvertently bumps into a woman. At the same time, if a woman notices a *phiksu* in his yellow robes, she should move out of his path. In public transport, monks are given seats where they cannot accidentally come into physical contact with women. Before stroking a dog or cat the monk should ascertain that the animal is male.

Many of these rules of behaviour are closely related to the ideas on the monks' sanctity current among the rural population. The traditional knowledge of the rules can in general be described under two rubrics: activities that are prescribed and those that are forbidden. In the view of the Wat Sanchao people the monks' prescriptions are intended to increase their beneficial power, while the prohibitions are there to prevent the loss of this sacred protective force.

The principles of this magico-animism can be illustrated by analysing the ritual act that takes place when a woman presents a gift to a monk, described immediately above. In the first place, it can be seen that some type of contact, even if it be indirect, is deemed necessary during the ritual presentation. This continuity is needed to make it possible that some reward reaches the donor at the moment of giving. Her gain in the transaction is some luck-bringing force, a bit of beneficial power that flows from the fingers of the monk, via the cloth, through the object to her fingers. The second aspect of the monk's ritual receiving of a woman's present, which reveals a principle underlying religious behaviour, is the public demonstration of the physical distance between monk and woman. It could be argued that the monk keeps himself aloof in order to demonstrate publicly his abstinence. After all, in the eyes of the farmers, monks derive some of their magical power from abstention in sexual conduct. Whilst this is true to a certain extent, there is another factor involved in the maintenance of distance from females. Women are associated with a type of magical power that is believed to be diametrically opposed to that of the monks because of the feminine capacity to menstruate. Menstrual blood is considered highly charged with dangerous magical power and even a casual contact may destroy some of the beneficial force of the members of the Sangha.[23]

Formulae

Twice a month, on the last day of the waxing moon and the waning moon respectively, one of the experienced monks, usually the abbot, has to recite the whole text of the *Pāṭimokkha* for the congregation of monks. This recitation is in the Pali language, and may last for as long as three quarters of an hour. In rural areas, where outside the Lenten season an abbot may not be assured of a quorum of four monks, this solemn recitation takes place only during *phansa*.

While Tambiah was probably mistaken when he wrote that newly ordained monks have to learn the *Pāṭimokkha* by heart,[24] for this would be an immense burden needlessly imposed, the inexperienced monks have to say a short formula as part of the preparation for the recitation. This formula is known as the *sadaeng abat* (แสดงอาบัตติ), 'exposing the ecclesiastical offences', sometimes known in the literature as the monks' confession. The confessing *phiksu* approaches a monk of his own choice, squats and raises his hands palm to palm. The confessor acknowledges the situation by taking a similar position close by the confessing monk and by returning the hand gesture.

In theory, the Pali formula for confession should be repeated for each category of mistakes which the monk wishes to expose. Moreover, the exact

23 The same seems to be the case for northern Thailand. See Shigeharu Tanabe, 'Spirits, Power and the Discourse of Female Gender: The *Phi Meng* Cult of Northern Thailand' in Manas Chitikasem and A. Turton (eds.), *Thai Constructions of Knowledge*, 1991, pp. 188–9.

24 Tambiah, *Buddhism and the Spirit Cults*, p. 122.

wording should vary according to whether the monk has transgressed only once, twice or more often in the category of mistakes.[25] The confession per category of offences requires a thorough knowledge of the different categories of ecclesiastical rules as well as a working knowledge of Pali and it is therefore seldom used in rural areas. Instead, a single formula that covers most transgressions is used. Accordingly Wat Sanchao it consists merely of a short barrage of questions and answers in the Pali language.

Sadaeng abat is compulsory immediately before the recitation of the *Pāṭimokkha*, but a monk may approach a fellow *phiksu* for confession any other time he wishes. Especially after the main meal, many monks may take advantage of the proximity of a friendly fellow monk to recite the formula. In some cases the preference for this time of the day may also be related to a wish to avoid part of the communal task of cleaning the eating-place. The formula is easy to remember, and one month after ordination most monks will be able to recite it without hesitation.

In Wat Sanchao the confession is not an asking for forgiveness for specific misdemeanours, nor is it a relieving of a mind burdened by guilt feelings; and it may also not be regarded as a private discussion of specific breaches of precepts, as was the case in early Buddhism.[26] In rural Thailand the formula is said in a language many monks do not understand, it is often recited within earshot of other members of the Sangha without the slightest embarrassment, and the ritual is regularly performed without a sign of reluctance. For these monks the meaning of the confession is a renewal of the 227 precepts of the *phiksu*; it is a ritual cleansing that has nothing to do with feelings of shame or guilt.

Although some monks feel that the confession literally 'washes away the mistakes', thus taking the idea of cleansing in its direct meaning, others are aware of the fact that such cannot be the case. In the Theravada Buddhist doctrine there is not such an easy way for undoing sins. The monk who has received a certain amount of religious education should know that once a mistake has been made it automatically produces an amount of harmful *karma* and that a subsequent token of remorse will not undo the effect of an evil deed. A future incident of bad luck is the equaliser. That is why the Thai Buddhist 'is not weighed down by a great burden of guilt, the latter being thought of as a very unskilful mental attitude productive of future sufferings'.[27]

25 The details can be found in Vajirañāṇavarorasa, *Ordination Procedure*, pp. 54–62.

26 See *Mahāvagga*, II, 27, 1; and *Cullavagga*, V, 20, 5; VII, 3, 7.

27 Khantipālo Bhikkhu, *Buddhism Explained*, 1968, p. 33.

Figure 5.7: *Kruat nam* is a solemn moment.

Another type of formula that a monk regularly uses falls under the category of *kruat nam* (กรวดน้ำ), literally 'sprinkling of water'. This expression is used both literally and metaphorically; in the latter case it refers to the generous dispersal of good *karma* to beings other than oneself. It is possible that it derives from the ancient Indian custom of satiating gods and deceased persons by presenting libations of water: the *tarpaṇa* ritual.[28] In early Buddhism this developed into a dedication by pouring water, and it is mentioned as such in the *Tipitaka*.[29]

In Thailand, the *kruat nam* ritual may be performed by laymen as well as by monks, but there is a difference in the methods used. A layman who has performed an act that carries a good deal of good *karma* uses a vessel that contains some clean water. He or she pours the water over the index finger of the right or the left hand, whilst dedicating a share of the good karma to individuals of his or her choice. This dedication can take place in silence, by thinking intensively of those to whom the merit is offered, but there are some who use words in Thai or in Pali. The individuals to whom the merit is offered may be living persons, but usually the ancestors are the recipients. This ritual

28 *The Laws of Manu, Sacred Books of the East*, Vol. XXV, II, 176; III, 70, 74, 81–82, 283; V, 69–70, 88–90; VI, 24.

29 *Mahāvagga*, I, 22, 18 and VIII, 30, 4.

may occur privately, for example immediately after a layman has placed food in a monk's begging bowl, or it may occur publicly, for example after performing a ceremony in the *bot*. When monks are presiding at a public ceremony, the *kruat nam* of the laymen takes place whilst the monks chant their concluding blessing.

Members of the Sangha are continually performing deeds that carry good *karma* and it is considered proper that they transfer a share to the secular world. However, the monks do not *kruat nam* in public, and when they transfer merit they do not pour water. Their *kruat nam* is communal and is accompanied by words. Every day, after the late afternoon chanting and meditation session, the abbot guides his monks into the recitation of one of the texts for transferring merit. The most common Pali chants for *kruat nam* are given on pages 74 and 75 of the *Suatmon Chet Tamnan*. After the joint recitation of such a text, a short period of silence is observed, during which the monks think of those on whom they wish merit bestowed. It is interesting to note that the official Pali words indicate that they give merit to all beings, to the world in general. During their moment of silence, however, most think intensely of their benefactors, their parents, the people who sustain them, and their ancestors.

Many formulae of the monks are not found in textbooks. They are passed on in an oral tradition. Most inexperienced monks of Wat Sanchao keep a notebook in which they write down useful formulae. Experienced monks may instruct them to say certain auspicious syllables when cleaning and rubbing the begging bowl – this will have the effect of inducing laymen to be generous when ladling out food. Another spell is used by a monk when pinning an amulet to his robes, so that he will be protected from accidents whilst travelling. The rules forbid a monk to adorn himself and therefore he cannot wear a string of amulets as laymen can. Many monks pin their favourite amulet on the inside of their robes, out of sight.

A widely used formula consists of a few syllables muttered over the first spoonful of rice in the morning. It reputedly ensures that the food will strengthen and embellish the consumer. The private notebooks of the recently ordained monks also contain various formulae that they may need later after leaving the order. There are spells that reputedly will stop a bullet from injuring, others will make a knife miss, and some cause a person to be invulnerable to clubs and sticks. Each formula is commonly accompanied by instructions for its use, for example, whilst uttering a certain spell a particular *yan* ought to be drawn.

Some of the most common spells consist of syllables, arranged in a seemingly haphazard manner:

'i ka vi ti'
'i svā su'
'pā su u jā'
'ka ra ma tha'
'thī ma saṃ aṃ khu ā pā ma u pa saṃ i dhā pu ka ya pa'

These collections of syllables are often transmitted from one monk to another without mention of the meaning or origin of the particular spell. The only information needed is its reputed effect. Such spells are thus clearly part of an esoteric tradition. There are cases where the syllables can be traced to a Pali text. For example, the syllables 'i svā su' can be traced to the words *itipiso, svākkhāto* and *supattipanno* that are prominent words in one of the best-known Pali texts.[30] In a similar manner, 'bā mā nā u ka sa na du' is related to another famous chant which can be found in the booklet *Suatmon Chet Tamnan.* The four syllables 'na ma ba da' reputedly epitomize the four elements: earth, water, fire and wind, but the reason for this particular choice of syllables is not clear. It therefore appears that the seemingly unrelated syllables often represent abbreviations of more complex words and ideas. They can be seen as an extreme example of abbreviation of canonical passages common in some Indian schools of thought. Thus many of these spells may be related to the Indian *mantra,* the *paritta,* the *dhāraṇī,* the *yamala* and the *kavaca.*[31]

Preaching

On every *wan phra* during the Lenten season it is customary to hold two preaching sessions. Traditionally, the abbot gave the sermons himself, or he appointed an experienced monk to preach. The monk who gave the sermon had time to select a text inscribed on palm leaf from the ornamental bookcase in the *bot,* and to familiarize himself with the inscriptions. The texts on palm leaf were written or sometimes printed in the *Khom* alphabet and it required much preparation before the text could be read with ease. Moreover, the monk was expected to chant the sermon, something that required extra practice.

Thus it was only a very experienced monk who traditionally preached for his fellow-monksand the lay congregation. The lay supporters and the monks were fully aware of the difficulties involved in the reading from palm leaves,

30 *Suatmon Chet Tamnan,* p. 15.

31 For the background to this tradition in mainland Southeast Asia, see F. Bizot, 'Notes sur les yantra bouddhiques d'Indochine, in M. Strickmann (ed.), *Tantric and Taoist Studies in Honour of R. A. Stein,* 1981, pp. 155–91.

and realized the exalted nature of the texts, which often consisted solely of Pali sentences. It is only since the 1850's that Thai words have been introduced in sermons. The lay people attending a sermon would each light a candle and some incense, so that the monk would be provided with sufficient light and be enveloped in a pleasant fragrance. All monks and laymen present lifted their hands palm to palm for as long as the preaching lasted. The meaning of the text read was often beyond the understanding of most of the audience, and could even be unintelligible to the preacher himself. The main task of the monk in the preaching chair was to transform the sacred words on the palm leaves into sound. The best preachers chanted the words in an even pitch, varying the tone only in the last syllables of a stanza.

Nowadays the sermon is a slightly different affair. Since 1940 the government has stopped printing and distributing sermons in *Khom* script, and instead uses palm leaf texts in Thai writing.[32] The Pali content has been greatly reduced. Even the sermons that deal with philosophical concepts consist usually of a single Pali sentence that in the remainder of the text is explained and elaborated upon in the Thai language. Many sermons contain subjects of general interest, dealing with mythological stories or episodes from the *Jātakas*. At present, most inexperienced monks have little difficulty in reading these palm leaves fluently, and with the proper intonation. Experienced monks have thus lost their former advantage, when they were the sole persons able to decipher the sermons.

While the first sermon of *wan phra,* which is held during the morning, is still reserved for the experienced monks of the monastery, the abbot may ask one of the recently ordained monks to preach the second one, at night. The relatives of the inexperienced monk who preaches will not fail to attend, and will proudly witness how the sacred message is read by the young man who only a short while ago was a common layman. The parents of the newly ordained monk may even invite their son to preach in his ancestral home, so that they will be able to show relatives and neighbours, as well as the ancestors, to what height of scholarship their son has risen.

Meditation

One of the skills, intimately linked with beneficial magical power, which greatly increases the store of merit and which carries great prestige is the concentration

32 Further details about Thai palm leaf manuscripts can be found in C. Velder, 'Die Palmblatt-Manuscriptkultur Thailands', *Nachrichten der Gesellschaft für Natur- und Völkerkunde Ostasiens,* Vol. 89/90, pp. 110–4.

in a proper manner: the practice of meditation. All inexperienced monks in rural monasteries have to take part in communal sessions and are expected to practise the skill in private. There are indications that meditation is less important in the urban setting where traditional skills have sometimes been supplanted by the study for certificates.[33]

During the Lenten season, the abbot of Wat Sanchao leads the monks when they chant *tham wat yen* (ทำวัตร์เย็น), the late-afternoon chanting. After the recitation of general texts that can be found in the *Suatmon Chet Tamnan* and before the *kruat nam* ritual he usually inserts a period of communal meditation. At a sign from the abbot all monks depart from their 'polite' chanting position and seat themselves comfortably with the legs folded in front of the body and the hands placed palm upwards, the right hand on top of the left one, in the lap. The abbot then instructs the inexperienced monks in various techniques of meditation. They should close their eyes and breathe slowly but deeply. As an aid to breathing properly, he advises them to think of an auspicious word whilst they breathe. For example, with the auspicious name *Phuttho* (from the Pali *Buddho*), the meditating monks should think of the syllable *Phut-* while breathing in and of *–tho* during the exhalation. If the word *arahan* (from the Pali *arahant*) is used, *ara-* is reserved for inhalation, *-han* to breathe out.

Apart from the instruction on purely technical matters, the abbot may introduce a theme upon which to concentrate. Usually he holds a short monologue during which he introduces a subject that will help a monk to obtain the proper attitude towards his environment. A common theme is the inevitable decay of all that surrounds us, people grow older and die but so do plants and even the buildings of the monastery will last only a while before falling to ruin. Or he speaks of the futility of the hankering after pleasures, notably those that cause a person to accumulate harmful *karma*. The abbot may recite the *pañcakakammaṭṭh*āna, a formula that mentions the five elements that can be found in all men and the larger animals: hair on the head, hair on the body, nails, teeth, and skin. These formulae serves to put the monks in the right frame of mind.

During the abbot's monologue, all monks sit with their eyes closed, and practise the breathing technique whilst concentrating on the topic the abbot has chosen. When the abbot has finished speaking it becomes very quiet in the *bot*; only the sounds from the world outside still penetrate the building. In this atmosphere each monk should try to lower his consciousness while

33 Bunnag, *Buddhist Monk, Buddhist Layman*, pp. 53–4. See also S. J. Tambiah, *World Conqueror and World Renouncer*, 1976, pp. 417–23.

remaining fully alert. The inexperienced monks may find it difficult to relax and at the same time remain concentrated. After a few minutes some usually cannot remain quiet; they begin to fidget, look around, or feel that they should clear the throat. These interruptions are usually soon followed by the abbot's announcement that the meditation is finished for the day and that the monks may take up their praying position again for the *kruat nam* recitation. However, near the end of the Lenten season, when all monks have been members of the Sangha for at least several months, the communal meditation sessions can be prolonged without any disturbance from the recently ordained monks.

The precepts of the monks as laid down in the *Pāṭimokkha* forbid any monk to talk about extraordinary experiences during meditation. The most severe category of rules, the *pārājikā* section discussed earlier in this chapter, contains a clause that forbids a monk to lie about his magical powers. In Thailand this rule is understood to include lies about strange experiences while meditating. It is less generally known that a rule from the fifth category of prescriptions, the *pācittiyā*, forbids monks even to tell the truth about their magical experiences.[34]

Although many monks will therefore not speak about their feelings when practising meditation, these restrictions do not apply once the monk has become a layman again. It is commonly known, particularly among men, that there are some people who are rewarded for their efforts by visions of colours and unidentifiable shapes. Some report hearing extraordinary sounds. It may safely be assumed, however, that the communal sessions are of too short a duration to bring about such experiences, and many a monk will try to induce them in the privacy of his cell. Times that are especially recommended for private meditation are early in the morning, before the food collecting takes place, and late at night, just before lying down to sleep.

More Recently Introduced Learning Tasks of the Inexperienced Monks

State Examinations

The Thai state has apparently always had a stake in the organization and management of the Sangha. When, during the second half of the nineteenth century, largely as a result of the direct and indirect challenges posed by contact with representatives of the colonial powers, the Thai government reorganized

34 Ñāṇamoli Thera, *The Pāṭimokkha, 227 Fundamental Rules of a Bhikkhu*, 1966, pp. 48–9. This may well have been the reason for the Ayutthaya monks to reply only in very vague terms when questioned as to the techniques used during meditation as reported by Bunnag, *op. cit.*, p. 54.

itself, it also increased its involvement in Sangha affairs. One of the areas where state involvement is most apparent is that of the nation-wide ecclesiastical education courses.[35] The government has supervised the advanced courses since 1893, and from 1910 onward it has taken responsibility for a primary course as well.[36] At present, there are ten different levels of ecclesiastical scholarship recognized in Thailand. In order of increasing difficulty these levels are: *Nak tham* III, II and I, followed by *Parien* III to *Parien* IX. *Nak tham* (นักธรรม) means 'Skilled in the Buddhist teachings' whilst *Parien* (เปรียญ) is probably derived from the Pali *pariñña*, 'knowing, recognizing, understanding'.

The *Parien* religious education is confined to municipal regions, but the preparation for the *Nak tham* examinations lies within the scope of most rural members of the Sangha. In most monasteries the recently ordained monks are prepared for the *Nak tham* III examination by an experienced fellow monk, but even if no classes are held in a monastery a person who wishes to qualify can study privately from textbooks. As an illustration of how widely the *Nak tham* examination is known, the figures for 1970 can be given. Of a total number of 311,000 monks and novices who constituted the Thai Sangha in that year, almost 123,000 sat for the easiest examination, 35,000 tried to pass *Nak tham* II, and 16,000 enrolled for the examination for the highest *Nak tham* I degree.[37] For 1975 there were 335,000 monks and novices of whom 111,000 sat for *Nak tham* III, 30,000 for II and 26,000 for the highest of these three levels.[38]

There are several textbooks written especially for *Nak tham* III students, and of these the three most important ones are:

1. The *Nawakowat* (นวโกวาท). The title is derived from the Pali *navakovāda*, or 'Advice to the Newly Ordained Monk'. It contains a commentary on selected parts of the *Vinaya Piṭaka*, with special reference to the *Pāṭimokkha*. The second half of this book is devoted to Buddhist ethics. It was written by the late Supreme Patriarch Prince Vajirañāṇavarorasa. In 1966 it was printed for the sixty-fourth time, an issue of 100,000 copies.
2. The *Phutthasasanasuphasit* (พุทธศาสนสุภาษิต), by the same author. It is a book of 500 Buddhist proverbs in Pali and Thai, topically arranged. The year 1968 saw its 24th printing, with 50,000 copies.

35 R-I. Heinze, *The Role of the Sangha in Modern Thailand*, 1977, pp. 26–35.

36 K. E. Wells, *Thai Buddhism, Its Rites and Activities*, 1960, pp. 14–5.

37 รายงานการศาสนาประจำปี ๒๕๑๓ [Annual Report on Religious Affairs, 2513], p. 221.

38 รายงานการศาสนาประจำปี ๒๕๑๘ [Annual Report on Religious Affairs, 2518], p. 32.

3. The *Phutthaprawat* (พุทธประวัติ), the biography of the Buddha in three parts. The first two booklets are written by Prince Vajirañāṇavarorasa, but volume 3 is from the hand of another late Supreme Patriarch named Sa.
4. The *Pathomsomphot* (ปฐมสมโพธิ), or 'First Step to Enlightenment', edited by Supreme Patriarch Pussathewa. This is a commentary on various important Buddhist sutras. In 1967 it was printed for the fifteenth time, an issue of 15,000 copies.

In the monasteries where the inexperienced monks are prepared for the *Nak tham* III examination, lessons are held five days a week. On *wan phra* and on the day before *wan phra,* called *wan kon* (วันก่อน), 'the day before', no lessons are given. Most of the teaching time is devoted to the first part of the *Nawakowat,* the part in which many rules of behaviour are discussed and in which a Thai translation of most of the *Pāṭimokkha* is given.

By way of preparation for the lessons, the students are told to learn a certain number of passages of the *Nawakowat* by heart. The teacher will explain the exact meaning of these passages during the following lesson, and he will instruct his pupils to memorize a few subsequent paragraphs. In this manner the pupils work through most of the *Nawakowat.*

In order to depict the teaching methods of a good teacher a fictitious example of instruction has been set up. It is based on actual experience, not from Wat Sanchao, because no school for inexperienced monks was held there, but from a monastery on the north bank of the river Maeklong.[39]

> It is a day in the beginning of August, 1.30 p.m. The room commonly used to teach *Nak tham* III students is occupied. The teacher sits in front of the class at a desk, well elevated above the level of the desks of his pupils. (See Fig. 5.8).
>
> The teacher has just reached the fifth category of precepts in the *Pāṭimokkha,* the *pācittiyā.* He asks one of his students to stand up and recite the first of the 92 *pācittiyā* rules. The student indicated immediately stands up and in a glib and rapid manner recites the rule in question. For good measure he will add several more of the rules before the teacher can stop him. After acknowledging the student's skill in memorizing, the teacher repeats the first rule of the *pācittiyā* category, but this time slowly and deliberately: 'An intentional lie is a *pācittiyā*'.

39 I am indebted to the abbot of Wat Phanoenplu for his patient instruction in the subjects necessary to sit for the *Nak tham* III examination. This fictitious example is also intended to express some of the skill and humour with which he gave his lessons.

Figure 5.8: Preparing for the *Nak tham* III examination.

He continues with a detailed explanation of this rule:

'A monk who is aware of the fact that he makes a false statement, and who is not deterred by that awareness, commits this offence, which falls under the category of faults which are expiable. If a lie is uttered, and nobody heard the statement, the monk can consider himself lucky, for he will then not have broken a precept of this category. However, the monk in question is still at fault, but his mistake will fall into a less important category, one that need not be expiated.

'Under the first of the *pācittiyā* rules must be included false statements made in writing, and even a lie by a gesture. If, for example, a member of the Sangha answers a question by nodding affirmatively, while knowing that the reply should have been negative, he commits a *pācittiyā* offense. Whether the person who is the recipient of the false statement believes the lie, or does not believe it does not make any difference; in both cases the precept in question has been broken.'

After this careful explanation of the first rule of the *pācittiyā* category the teacher may ask:

> 'If a monk went around saying that during meditation he saw the god Indra and if this statement were not true, what type of precept did the monk break?' The teacher chooses a rather dull student to answer him, and in the context of the lesson the answer is likely to be:
> 'Pācittiyā, sir!'
> The teacher now asks the students one by one until he obtains the right answer:
> 'Lying about one's magical accomplishments falls in a special category, the most severe one, *pārājikā*, which causes expulsion from the order.'

Almost all lessons dealing with the *Nawakowat* proceed in the manner indicated by this example. The lesson lasts about two hours, and at the end of the instruction period the teacher selects a few questions from a book that contains a great number of questions asked in previous years in the official *Nak tham* III examination. He takes care to select questions that have direct relevance to the subjects discussed during the lesson. To continue the fictitious example, the teacher might write on the blackboard:

> 1. A monk writes a letter to a friend in which he tells a deliberate lie. The letter gets lost in the mail and never reaches its destination. What precept has the monk broken?
> 2. A monk is asked: 'What time is it?' and answers: 'Two o'clock' (after having consulted the monastery clock). Later he finds out that the clock indicated wrongly. Has this monk broken a precept, and if so, what category of precepts?
> 3. The teacher of a monks' school asks a pupil whether he has studied the previous night. The student has not even opened his books during that night, but nods his head affirmatively. Has this student broken a precept, and if so, what precept?

The teacher then instructs the class to write their answers in the notebooks. He may tell the class to place the notebooks with the answers neatly written down on his desk as soon as they are ready, and he then leaves the room. Most students will look in their own copy of the *Nawakowat* to see if they can find the answers to the questions. They may discuss in a soft voice the possible answers with one another and many students may copy the answers that the brightest among them has written down. By 5.00 p.m. all notebooks must be placed on the desk of the teacher, because at that time the students should be on their way to the *bot* for the late afternoon chanting and meditation session.

Most of the teaching hours are thus devoted to exegetical exercises with regard to the rules of the *Pāṭimokkha*. In addition the students must be taught to write a page-long treatise on the meaning of a religious concept. The curriculum of the monk's school also encompasses the reading of the *Phutthaprawat*, the elaborate biography of the Buddha, and the pupils must take note as well of the ethical aspects of the teachings of the Buddha as they are discussed in the latter half of the *Nawakowat*. The teacher will usually ask the students to write a page of prose on a certain religious concept during the day before *wan phra* and during *wan phra* itself when no classes are held. One of the teaching days of the week may be devoted to ethics and the communal reading of the story of the life of the Buddha, so that four days per week remain for the discussion of the rules of behaviour and the precepts of the monks.

Shortly after the Lenten season the yearly state examinations for the ecclesiastical degrees are held simultaneously in hundreds of the more important monasteries throughout the country. During the examination there is strict supervision, the students are not allowed to consult their notes. In 1975, approximately 70 per cent of the candidates for *Nak tham* III failed to pass.[40]

Behaviour

In the section on the traditional learning of the inexperienced monk, the subject of monastic behaviour was already broached. It was shown that traditionally, the behaviour of the monk should be oriented towards calmness, tranquillity, peacefulness, awareness at all times and the public display of contentedness, and that very few precepts were traditionally memorized.

In contrast, a thorough knowledge of the exact wording and interpretation of most of the rules is a prerequisite for the more recently introduced *Nak tham* III examination. During the formal training in the jurisprudence of the precepts many newly ordained monks notice that the general intention of many rules is identical with what the older monks may have told them. Also they will come across many precepts that are archaic, which refer to circumstances that have disappeared in the more than two millennia since the *Pāṭimokkha* was composed, and which simply cannot be applied to monks in present-day Thailand. Under these rules fall especially the many that deal with behaviour towards the *bhikkhunī*, a class of female members of the Sangha rarely found in Thailand.

It is interesting to note that the thorough schooling in the rules of behaviour may also bring about awareness that there are certain precepts that are regularly

40 รายงานการศาสนาประจำปี ๒๕๑๘ [Annual Report on Religious Affairs, 2518], p. 32.

broken. In rural areas there is a discrepancy between the accepted manner of behaviour and the official precepts, for example with regard to the handling of money. The eighteenth rule in the category *nissaggiyā-pācittiyā* states clearly:

> Whatsoever Bhikkhu shall receive gold or silver, or get someone to receive it for him, or allow it to be kept in deposit for him – that is a Pākittiya offence involving forfeiture.[41]

According to this precept, which is endorsed in the *Nawakowat*, monks may not possess or handle money, and after having confessed a breach of this rule they must forfeit the money handled. In principle, it would be possible for the Thai monks to live without possessing or handling money. After all, individual monks are provided with all basic material goods. The monk receives free clothing and food, free medicine in state hospitals and is assured of a roof above his head. When he performs a ceremony for lay people he often receives presents that include common household goods, such as toothpaste and soap, so that he need not depend on buying them.

In practice, however, there are few rural monks who do not regularly break the rule. A monk handling money is a common sight; he may be seen paying for transport, for only the municipal bus services of Bangkok provide free travel for members of the Sangha; on long-distance buses monks pay half price. The fare in taxis and boats is usually full price. A travelling monk may be seen paying for his morning meal in a restaurant. In rural monasteries, many monks buy tobacco, tea and Ovomaltine.

It is not only the fact that many monks are used to spending money which makes it difficult to change the monastic behaviour more towards the letter of the rule; the laymen themselves often insist on giving money to individual members of the Sangha. It is a generally accepted custom that all monks who assist a ceremony in the house of a layman are remunerated for this service. All the invited monks come to the layman's house expecting to be rewarded financially, and their expectations are never in vain. Poor people will give less than rich ones, and it is not by accident that a chapter of monks often chants considerably longer in the house of a rich farmer than in the house of one who cannot afford to donate a great amount.

The people insist on making cash donations because they believe that there is a clear connection between the amount of money offered to the monks and the amount of beneficial *karma* received in return. As Hanks pointed out:

41 T. W. Rhys Davids and Hermann Oldenberg (translators), *Vinaya Texts,* Part I, *Sacred Books of the East,* Vol. XIII, p. 26.

> Contrary to the Christian gospel, a poor widow, giving her all to the priest, remains less blessed than the rich man; both have performed meritorious acts, but the Thai observe that the effectiveness of ten thousand baht far outweighs the widow's battered coin.[42]

The giving of money to monks, though it contravenes an official rule, remains important to the people because they believe firmly in the possibility of an instantaneous effect of the beneficial *karma* that they gain through their donation. This immediate effect of merit is protective power, the keeping away of accidents, and good luck.

Accepted practice and the letter of the rule are thus in open conflict, and the widespread schooling in the skills needed to sit for the *Nak tham* III examination has caused the inconsistencies to become more widely known than before in rural areas. This awareness has probably given rise to some new patterns of behaviour. When presenting money to a monk, a layman may use a Thai formula, stating that the money involved has been collected so that the monk can buy a new begging bowl or new robes. This manner of presenting does not mean that the monk will be restricted in the methods in which he can spend the money; he spends it as he wishes and all laymen are aware of this. The formula possibly stems from a rather vague knowledge of the eighth, ninth and tenth rules of the *nissaggiyā-pācittiyā* category of the *Pāṭimokkha*, in which mention is made of householders who have collected money to purchase a robe for a monk. Although these rules are not intended to encourage laymen to present money to individual monks, it is possible that they have been interpreted to mean that under these circumstances, when money is presented for a good cause, it is not in disaccord with the *Vinaya*.

A common method used to avoid the actual moment of giving cash to monks in public is the presentation of a document known as a declaration of intention. These declarations can be obtained from shops in the provincial capital, and are usually printed leaving open the name of the donor and the amount donated. At the end of a ceremony in a private house, the householder may present each monk with an envelope containing such a declaration of intention. Later, in the privacy of their cells, the monks will receive the equivalent in banknotes.

Another method often used to avoid embarrassment is to wrap money in paper so that a monk does not actually physically handle the currency. Many

42 Lucien M. Hanks, 'Merit and Power in the Thai Social Order', *American Anthropologist*, Vol. 64, 1962, p. 1248.

people realize that wrapping money in paper does not really solve the problem of the monks acting against a precept, but at least it is not so bad as openly handling that commodity. Many a monk will avoid handling cash in public, knowing that his public image suffers by his touching banknotes and coins. When in a shop, monks are often allowed to perform money transactions in the private atmosphere at the back, out of the public gaze. Others try to take along a *dek wat* who should handle all cash.

The dealings with money represent an instance where the religion of the villagers conflicts with the written tradition, where the two orientations in the practice of Buddhism, outlined in Chapter I, are in disagreement. In order to demonstrate how far removed the villager's ideas about monks and money are from what can be expected from a perusal of the *Pāṭimokkha,* the gist of a conversation at Wat Sanchao regarding the-monks and the state lottery is presented. It must be kept in mind, however, that this is not a translation from a verbatim report; the fieldwork situation forbade direct recording. The conversations were noted down whenever the researcher had a moment of privacy, often late at night.

July 31, 1968
During a friendly talk, a monk complained that he had hoped to pay off his debts, but he had not won in the lottery this week. He had not spent any money on the lottery for some weeks now, but had the feeling that this time he might be lucky. Unfortunately it did not come true.
Question: Did you ever win a prize?
Answer: Yes, last year I got 200 *baht* for my 10 *baht* ticket.
Question: What would you do if you won a million *baht*?
Answer: I would give a generous sum to the monastery to build something, did you know that that is how the big *cedi* had come to be built, as well as the school on the monastery grounds? Of course I would keep a good amount to set up a pleasant life.
Question: Do all monks buy in the lottery?
Answer: No, only a few can afford it. The Venerable [name suppressed] buys every week because he has a small pension from the government because his son was killed in the war.
Question: Does a monk have the same chance to win a prize as a layman?
Answer: Probably a monk has a better chance, after all he is apart by virtue of his discipline. But you cannot count on good luck, you never can reckon on the fact that merit will work instantaneously.

All the monks realize that gambling is officially frowned upon. Still, because it does not interfere with their private religious beliefs, they readily engage in such matters. The only concession to the written rules is that they usually engage a lay friend to purchase the lottery tickets.

With regard to the conflict between official rules and the accepted behaviour of village monks it can be noted that the strict interpretation of the *Pāṭimokkha* as given in the *Nawakowat* is gaining more and more acceptance. The trend towards monastic behaviour according to the letter of the rules is enhanced by the existence of a sect within the Thai Sangha that prides itself on a close adherence to the Teachings. This sect, the *Thammayuthika nikai* (ธรรมยุทธิกานิกาย) 'The Assembly of the Dharma Laws', formally established in 1894, now comprises less than five per cent of the order; the rest of the Sangha is known as *Maha nikai* (มหานิกาย), 'the Great Assembly'. The monks who belong to the *Thammayuthika nikai* set themselves high standards indeed with regards to public behaviour. They take care to dress in a simple uniform manner, they do not walk out of step when begging for food. They are cautious not to be seen handling money and will refrain from the use of sandals. Their lunar calendar has been calculated with greater precision than that of the rest of the country, and their chanting methods are slightly at variance with those used in other monasteries.

Whilst it can be said that the *Thammayuthika nikai* monks behave in an exemplary manner, the opposite cannot be said of the *Maha nikai*. Among the latter many interpretations of the ecclesiastical laws can be found, from the extremely rigid to the very lax. But as communication with the centrally organized Sangha now reaches even the remote rural monasteries, a stricter adherence becomes generally adopted. Laymen in general favour the very proper behaviour. The farmers of Wat Sanchao think that the monks who act fully according to the precepts generate more and stronger beneficial power than those who are less strict, and the former ought to be supported in preference to those who do not make such efforts. When asked, they often think, however, that the *Thammayuthika nikai* exaggerate in some respects, and they do not ask from their own monks, for example, that they should walk barefoot in the heat of the day.

In this chapter, the role of the Buddhist monk has been described in the complex setting of a rural tradition that is increasingly linked to the nation-wide organization of the Sangha. In order to understand fully the exalted position of the Wat Sanchao monk, it is not sufficient to refer to the principle of merit, as is often the case in the literature on rural Thailand.[43] It is true that the monk

43 For example in Kaufman's *Bangkhuad*, p. 183, DeYoung's *Village Life in Modern Thailand*, p. 130, and in Kingshill's *Ku Daeng*, p. 8 *et passim*.

increases his own store of merit, as well as the good *karma* of his benefactors and ancestors, and that a monk offers a continual opportunity for laymen to perform meritorious deeds. The ritual of *kruat nam* points to the importance of the aspect of merit. While the idea of the acquisition of beneficial karma is of assistance in explaining the religious behaviour of the monks, in rural areas the role of the Buddhist monks can be further interpreted by taking the magico-animistic worldview into account. The fundamental ideas surrounding the origin and the value of beneficial power have bearing upon the behaviour of the monks and the attitudes of the laymen towards the Sangha. It has been established that monks who chant Pali texts, who meditate or who preach are believed to emanate a protective power, and that objects and persons in their proximity can become charged with this beneficial power.

This magical aspect of the activities of the monks is by no means incompatible with the belief that the monk's activities increase their merit. On the contrary, it reinforces that idea; the greater the store of beneficial *karma* a monk possesses, the stronger the power he generates. In the magico-animistic interpretation of Buddhism, protective magical power can be seen as the immediate aspect of merit. This immediate magical aspect is needed to understand the role of rural monks. It is because of the protective power that emanates from a monk that a father presents his son to such a 'charged' man, and is pleased to see the child 'bask' in the luck-bringing force. It is a factor underlying the tradition of inviting monks to chant sacred texts in the private homes. It is also an aspect to be considered in answering the question of why laymen listen for hours to sermons they may barely comprehend. The principle of emanating power is needed to explain the ceremonial manner in which a woman presents a gift to a monk, and it also helps to understand why certain behaviour of the monks, though in conflict with the official rules, persists.

In the last part of this chapter the recent encroachments of intellectual, compartmentalized Buddhism, resulting in some changes in the behaviour of the monks, were demonstrated. However, the two interpretations of Buddhism appear to be able to live side by side; the officially sponsored orientation does not prevent rural people believing in the efficacy of magical power. In the eyes of the farmers, monks and magic belong to the same religious norm complex.

CHAPTER VI

LEAVING THE ORDER, COURTSHIP AND MARRIAGE

Leaving the Sangha

Unless a monk commits one of the *pārājikā* offences, he cannot be disrobed against his will; every monk should decide for himself if and when he will become a layman again. However, extraneous circumstances or outside pressure usually influence his decision. If a monk passes his *Nak tham* III examination and shows that he has an aptitude for a monastic career by generally behaving in a manner considered befitting the Sangha, elder monks as well as the more influential laymen may urge him to remain a monk. The longer such a man stays in the order the better, for not only will his skill in chanting Pali texts increase but in time he may be willing to relieve the abbot of some of his tasks, such as teaching the newly ordained monks or even chanting the complete *Pāṭimokkha* for the whole group of monks.

If such a promising monk succeeds in passing the remaining two *Nak tham* examinations, he arrives at the crossroads in his career. Either he remains in his rural monastery, makes himself many friends among monks as well as laymen and waits until he is asked to become an abbot in one of the monasteries in the neighbourhood, or he takes up residence in one of the municipal monasteries in order to be trained for the *Parien* degrees, thus opting for the higher ecclesiastical offices. At this point in his career a monk seldom considers leaving the Sangha; it would mean leaving a position that carries great prestige, that entails the supply of free food and lodging as well as free medical service in all state hospitals for the rest of his life.

Moreover, at this stage a monk may receive a reasonable income. Much of the remuneration comes from Sangha payment for religious services in the houses of laymen. In addition, after some years in the order, a monk can be elected to be preceptor during ordinations, which occur in great numbers just before the Lenten season. If he becomes religious head of a *tambon* and passes an examination that empowers him to ordain, his yearly income from that source alone may be as much as several thousand *baht*. Additionally, the government pays a small monthly stipend to monks above the rank of abbot.[1]

Those who do leave the order after several years of service are often men who have failed to pass the highest of the *Nak tham* examinations, or who have been frustrated in their wish to be chosen as abbot. An abbot is almost always chosen in close consultation with the lay supporters of the monastery. When the post of abbot has to be filled the chief supporters of the monastery may have to meet several times and discuss the various candidates. When they have found a suitable *phiksu* who is willing to serve, they petition the *chaokhana changwat* (เจ้าคณะจังหวัด), the monk in charge of the administration of religious affairs of a whole province, to make the official appointment. Ideally an abbot should possess leadership qualities, be of pleasing manners so that he will be able to receive guests in a proper manner, take the initiative in ventures to enrich the monastery, give guidance to monks and laymen alike, and be respected and liked by all.

Those monks who become laymen after many years of service carry over to their lay life only a little of their previous aura. Their profound knowledge of chanting and rituals will bring them some standing in lay life. The lay community depends on these men to be their spokesman and lead them during the major religious ceremonies.

Most newly ordained monks decide to leave the order after completion of their first Lenten season, after the *kathin* (กฐิน) ceremony has marked the end of the period of the year when religious life is most intensive.[2] The man who decides to leave the order must ask advice about an auspicious moment for doing so. A person with astrological knowledge tells him the most propitious day and usually insists that the ceremony should take place at the time of sunrise of that day. The insistence upon the moment of sunrise, the 'birth' of a new day, could be an indication that leaving the Sangha can be seen as a ritual rebirth; a man who 'died' to the world when ordained is 'born anew' when he leaves the order. Consistent with this view is the fact that ordination can take place on any day of the year. People do not try to select an auspicious day for becoming a monk; similarly, no special day can be set for death.

1 More information on the government stipend to high ranking monks can be found in Bunnag, *Buddhist Monk, Buddhist Layman*, p. 61 *et passim*.

2 See also Chapter VIII.

In the same vein Rabibhadana writes:

> A man who was born at an unfortunate time, i.e. when the stars are not favorable, could select a propitious time for leaving the monkhood. He might then have his horoscope made, taking the time of his leaving the monkhood as the time of his birth. It is believed that by this means, the man would be able to escape the bad influence of the stars . . .[3]

In present-day Thailand all men, regardless of the date of their original birth, seek the most auspicious time for leaving the Sangha. Choosing a wrong time is reputed to cause unhappiness, restless feelings, sickness, or even to invite major accidents. Although it is recognized that the man who leaves the order breaks with what is noblest in a man's life, the ceremony is not a sad event and no stigma is attached to such a man. Every man who has passed at least one Lenten season in the order has the right to claim a position in adult lay society. It is advisable that a person who is going to leave the order should be happy and content about his decision; a man who is dejected and unsure should remain in the security of the Sangha until he feels more certain.

The day before leaving the order, a man must take leave of his fellow monks by prostrating himself in front of each of them and by asking forgiveness for any offence that he may have caused through his negligence. On the morning of the ceremony, the monk should dress in clean robes and renew his vows with the *sadaeng abat* formula. He must take along some layman's clothes, candles, incense, flowers, his begging bowl in which he has poured some clean water, and a bundle of twigs that still possess their foliage. All the twigs are taken from plants which have auspicious names or fortunate associations, such as *bai ngoen bai thong* (ใบเงินใบทอง) literally 'silverleaf-goldleaf',[4] *ya phraek* (หญ้าแพรก), a hardy grass that is generally considered to epitomize sturdiness and health,[5] or leaves from the *mai mayom* (ไม้มะยม), a shrub with long graceful branches and feathery foliage that is often used in folk medicine.[6] With all these paraphernalia the monk must go towards the place where the ceremony will take place; usually this is the office of the abbot or the *bot*. He lights a candle and the incense and offers these together with the flowers while prostrating himself three times

3 Akin Rabibhadana, *The Organization of Thai Society in the Early Bangkok Period, 1782–1873*, p. 123.

4 *Graptophyllum hortense*, G. B. McFarland, *Thai-English Dictionary*, p. 491. It is a garden herb with leaves that are blotched with red, and it is often used medicinally.

5 *Cynodon dactylon*, McFarland, *ibid.*, p. 600.

6 *Phyllanthus distichus*, McFarland, *ibid.*, p. 638.

before the image of the Buddha. Meanwhile, the monk who is in charge of the ceremony has taken the begging bowl containing water and quickly murmurs some Pali formulae whilst holding a lighted candle above the surface of the water, thus consecrating the contents of the vessel. This leading monk is usually the abbot of the monastery where the monk has stayed for the Lenten season. It sometimes happens, however, that a man prefers to leave the order somewhere else. In that case he can travel to another monastery and agree with the abbot there to stay the night so that the following morning the ceremony can be performed.

The monk on whose instigation the ritual takes place is told that, if he wishes to change his mind about becoming a layman, he now has a last opportunity to do so. When he has indicated that he is certain, he is asked to repeat three times the prescribed formula: '*sikkhaṃ paccakkhāmi gihīti maṃ dhāretha*' which can be translated as: 'I leave the discipline, you should recognize me as householder'. From the moment that the word *dhāretha* has sounded for the third time, the man is a monk no more, and he must therefore change into lay clothing. Upon returning to the scene of the ritual, the man who has just left the Sangha must undergo several ritual acts that are intended to protect and guard him. The abbot sprinkles him with consecrated water, using the bunch of leaves as a brush, whilst the other monks who had to be invited as witnesses chant some auspicious stanzas. The ex-monk is then instructed to go and bathe himself thoroughly, to rub himself with soap, rinse well, and afterwards to return to the abbot. In the privacy of the abbot's room the layman is instructed to be a worthy member of the community, and is prompted to ask to receive the five precepts of the layman from the abbot.[7] He may also receive several protective objects. It is quite common for him to receive a cotton cord around his neck. This cord is made up of nine strands of loose cotton. The striking similarity between the use of this cord and that of the *yajñopavīta* of the *upayana* ceremony in ancient India[8] points to an Indian origin of this custom, Also, the abbot may draw a simple *yan* on the head of the layman, or press some gold leaf on his forehead whilst saying a blessing in Pali.[9]

Unless pressing reasons prevent him from doing so, the man who has just left the order is expected to still remain several days and nights in his monastery.

7 See Chapter VIII.

8 P. V. Kane, *History of Dharmaśāstra, Ancient and Medieval Religious and Civil Law*, Vol. II, Part 1, p. 287 ff.

9 For more details of the ritual of leaving the order of monks, see Phra Thammasenani, ระเบียบการลาสิกขาบท [The rules of Leaving the Discipline], B.E. 2496 (1953).

He should remove the traces he left whilst a monk; he ought to clean his former cell, the communal eating-place, and the toilets, and he should fill the communal vessels with fresh water.

When he arrives home for the first time since leaving the order he must prostrate himself before all his older relatives, especially those who supported him with gifts during his period in the order. When prostrated, the ex-monk politely lifts his hands palm to palm and in a soft voice offers a share in the merit that he has accumulated as a member of the Sangha. This act is called *baeng kuson* (แบ่งกุศล), or 'sharing good karma', and should not be omitted without offending the relatives. The custom of sharing merit is not only confined to this moment of leaving the order. It is common behaviour for anybody who has recently acquired a great deal of merit. After donating a great sum of money to a monastery, for example, a person can go to a good friend and share merit. It is believed that the sharing of beneficial karma causes people to be linked propitiously in future lives.

After a man has left the monastery, he may remain at home for a considerable time. It is expected from a young man who has just become a layman that for several months he behaves in a calm and subdued manner. Often he keeps away from public places until his hair has grown sufficiently to have his first haircut. After this moment, when there is no physical indication of his recent period as a monk, he is expected to take his position in society and as part of the taking of adult status he is expected to select a bride, marry, and raise a family.

Courting

Some men, especially those who are exceptionally attractive or relatively wealthy, have little difficulty in finding a suitable marriage partner, but most men in rural regions seem to feel rather insecure and anxious during the time of courtship. Traditionally, courting is an activity which should take place in the home of the young woman and the young man feels exposed to the scrutiny of the relatives of the woman he wishes to know better. She is continually chaperoned so that there is virtually no opportunity for a private *tête-à-tête*. Until her family has accepted a formal marriage offer, any suitor may come and try to impress the family with his prospects, good manners, and engaging personality. Rivalry between different suitors is not uncommon and the traditional place to outdo a rival is in the home of the girl, under the eyes of her relatives. This rivalry may express itself in a match of wits or a contest in politeness; aggressiveness, bragging, or brute force openly expressed do not win respect. Since many young people nowadays take temporary work in the provincial capital, courting has become less formal because members of both sexes can meet at work away from the supervision of elder relatives. This new situation does not prevent fierce competition.

In these circumstances, a man may avail himself of magical means in order to increase his chances of winning the bride of his choice. Thus, when courting, he will not forget to wear a chain of amulets that reputedly have the power to increase the popularity of the wearer. If he has been tattooed with designs that are alleged to possess the same power, he raises this energy by saying the appropriate *khatha* over them. Another method to ensure increased popularity is to say a *khatha* over the powder used to make up the face. In rural Thailand, people of both sexes and of all ages can use a form of make-up made with fragrant white powder paeng (แป้ง) mixed with water and applied to the face. The face can be completely blanched, a method called *tha paeng* (ทาแป้ง) 'smearing the powder', or white dots can be distributed over the face, using the fingertips, a method called *pa paeng* (ปะแป้ง).

Sometimes a man may have obtained from a ritual specialist a small glass bottle filled with some clear liquid that contains two small wooden images. One is made of black wood, and is about 1½ cm tall, the other is made of wood of a much lighter hue and reaches a height of approximately 1 cm. This bottle and its contents are called a *rakyom* (รักยม). It can be carried in the pocket of one's shirt. Reputedly it has a great amount of *mettā* (goodwill, compassion, sympathy or friendliness) and causes women to fall in love with the wearer.

In the context of analysing the rural interpretation of Buddhism it is relevant to note that the *rakyom* can be manufactured and blessed by highly respected monks. The members of the Sangha confer *mettā* through their meditation and sacred words, and this concept, derived from Pali, can in its Thai context, also be extended to include the more passionate form of friendship which we call love. It is therefore the ascetic monk who can invest the *rakyom* with so much *mettā* that a layman carrying the small bottle becomes irresistible to the opposite sex.

If these practices that are directed to boost a man's popularity in general do not have the desired results, he may resort to more goal-directed magical practices. One man reputedly won his wife by drawing a simple magical diagram, one of the category of the *yan napaṭhamaṃ* (see Figure 6.1 overleaf), while thinking intensively of the woman he wished to marry and saying the appropriate *khatha*. He waited seven days for the magic to take effect and, when approaching her, he noticed that she was more favourably inclined towards him.

Figure 6.1: A *yan napaṭhamaṃ*.

Yan napaṭhamaṃ means literally: 'The first, or foremost letter *N* diagram'. The letter *N* occurs frequently in Thai mystical drawings, probably because it may be regarded as an extreme abbreviation of the expression *namo buddhāya*, hail to the Buddha. In the literature on *yan* there are a variety of such diagrams, all called *napaṭhamaṃ*.[10]

10 Thus Thep Saríkabut, พุทธาภิเษกพิธี พิธีกรรมปลุกเสก พระเครื่องรางของขลัง [The Ceremony of Sacralization, Rituals of Blessing Objects that Cause Invulnerability], B.E. 2509 (1966), p. 127, Urakhin Wiriyaburana, คัมภีร์ยันต์ ๑๐๘, n.d. p. 122, and in his คัมภีร์คาถา ๑๐๘, B.E. 2509 (1966), p. 23.

Another method to ensure the love of a woman, also reported by Textor,[11] is to sit close by her while smoking a cigarette. The man should draw smoke deep into his lungs and, whilst softly saying the right spell, blow out the smoke so that it envelops her. A much stronger method consists of scooping up some earth with the big toe of the right foot, taking the earth in the right hand and rubbing it on the top of the head, whilst invoking the goddess of the earth, Mother Thorani (ธรณี), to assist in the acquisition of a bride.

The last two examples reveal that, as the magical practices become more strong and persuasive, less attractive material is used. It is not pleasant to be enveloped in smoke, and rubbing earth over one's head is an action no Thai will perform lightly. The earth is often associated with pollution because it can be the recipient of human waste and animal droppings. Moreover, scooping up a bit of earth with the foot must be regarded as an abnormal, 'inverted' activity. The feet are the parts of the body that are held in lowest regard, and reaching for something with the foot is regarded in Thailand as the epitome of bad manners. This is illustrated by the fact that the only instance of rural workers going on strike known to Wat Sanchao farmers occurred when a rich landowner pointed with his foot to some earth that still had to be removed. All his labourers walked off the job, deeply insulted.[12]

The use of dangerously polluted material in love magic occurs when a man resorts to the strongest magical means known to ensure the love of a woman. It entails putting a single drop of *namman phrai*, the fluid which magical practitioners extract from certain corpses,[13] in the food of the woman. Upon swallowing the food, she is expected to become totally enslaved to the man. Such love magic is rare indeed, because the real *namman phrai* is seldom obtained. Only a specialist with great magical powers will try to obtain that liquid from the corpse of a person who died inauspiciously, preferably from the most dangerous kind of corpse: that of a woman who died whilst pregnant or during childbirth. Reputedly, in the deep of the night the lay magical specialist approaches the place where such a corpse lies. He should grasp the dead body firmly in his arms and extract some liquid from the skull by holding a lighted candle under the chin of the cadaver. A terrible struggle may ensue before the corpse releases some of this *namman phrai*. The liquid is extremely dangerous and in present times there are only a few men who are reputed to possess it. Only a desperate man will try to use it as love magic, for while it is considered

11 R. B. Textor, *An Inventory of Non-Buddhist Supernatural Objects*, p.144.

12 Personal communication, Surija, 11 November 1969.

13 See Chapter IV.

certain that it causes a woman to be enslaved to a man, it is likely also to make her very ill. It is said that by consuming some of the liquid she may become mentally deranged for the rest of her life.

So far the magical means by which a man can win the attention of a woman have been discussed. Women can also resort to magic in order to attract a man, but they have recourse to different methods. Ideally they should be passive and demure. The magical practices of women are usually reported from older females, who often are already married but who feel that they are no longer the favourite of their husband. When a woman is convinced that her husband gives cause for jealousy she may make a potion or a powder that contains some of her vaginal excretion. If a man consumes some food that contains this potion or powder, he reputedly loses interest in all other women and devotes his complete attention to the woman from whose secretions the mixture was made. A woman who resorts to these means should take care to practise this kind of magic in secret; if the man finds out that his food has been treated in such a manner, he would be very angry indeed, for her vaginal excretion will surely have destroyed the power of many of his tattoos and amulets and rendered him vulnerable.

It is said among men that prostitutes use a similar magic. Reputedly a prostitute sprinkles some water that contains vaginal excretion at the door-posts and above the door of the house where she lives. A man walking near the door may suddenly be irresistibly drawn over the threshold. If he is wearing his string of amulets he should quickly take it off and give it to a friend in safe keeping before entering the house,

The principles involved in the magical practices of women are well illustrated by a passage in Textor's book where the ritual for undoing the effects of having come into contact with vaginal excretion is described. He reports that, if a woman fears that her husband has been treated with the vaginal excretion of another woman, she should obtain water from the bottom of three or seven taxi boats, and some moss from around the sanctuary of a monastery, or from the boundary stones of a *bot*. If her husband eats food containing a mixture of these materials, his previously alienated affection is restored.[14]

The substances chosen to counter the effects of aggressive love magic of another woman are obviously considered magically powerful in their own right. As such they can be placed somewhere in the range of magical powers drawn up in Table 3 (see Chapter IV). Water from the bottom of taxi boats

14 Textor, *An Inventory of Non-Buddhist Supernatural Objects*, p.152.

must be seen as polluted and aggressive: it is where the wood starts rotting, the stagnant water has often an unpleasant smell, and it may contain particles of dirt from the feet of countless passengers. Moss that grows on the sanctuary of a monastery appears more ambiguously charged. On the one hand, it can usually be found on ground level, and may have been dirtied by the many dogs that roam the premises. On the other hand, a small amount of the beneficial power that is continually generated in the building itself may have permeated as far as the mossy outside. It seems, however, that the aggressive aspects prevail for the moss is reported to be one of the ingredients of a magically highly potent substance used to kill enemies.[15]

It appears therefore that the magical practices to ensure the attention of a person of the opposite sex differ depending on whether the practitioner is a man or a woman. A man can resort to a much wider array of techniques. He can use sources of purely beneficial power, such as amulets worn on a string around the neck, obtain a proper *yan* or a *rakyom*, invoke gods, or resort to more aggressive, even harmful forces. A woman has virtually no access to the beneficial powers and if she wishes to influence other people by magical means she must use forces that can at best be seen as ambivalent, but usually fall in the aggressive category.

This difference in magical techniques can be seen as part of an overall ritual opposition of the sexes that becomes more and more pronounced as individuals grow from childhood to adulthood. It has been noted that boys can walk around naked for many years, whilst a small girl has her lower abdomen covered from a very young age. Boys can have contact with monks, whilst girls are instructed to keep away from the members of the Sangha. Boys acquire many objects that can protect them; hardly any are available for girls. Young men are likely to be tattooed and invested with the ancient powers of the *achan sak*, but women cannot partake in this aspect of life. At the age of twenty a man is expected to become a monk and spend several months in an intensive learning process; no such honourable positions are open to women. It is only at a much later stage of life that women obtain some access to sacred knowledge; while they are of childbearing age they remain ritually opposed to the men.

Marriage

The meeting *par excellence* of the ritually opposed sexes is sexual intercourse and in central Thailand such a meeting cannot be lightly engaged upon for

15 Phya Amman Rajadhon, 'Data on Conditioned Poison', *Journal of the Siam Society*, Vol. 53, Pt. 1, 1965, p. 80, reprinted in *Essays on Thai Folklore*, 1968, p. 149.

the first time. Unmarried girls are closely supervised and they may meet suitors only in the presence of witnesses. Fewer restraints are imposed upon unmarried couples as regards verbal advances; flirting with gestures of the eyes and hands is approved of and widely practised. A chaperone is only there to make sure that no physical contact such as touching or fondling takes place. Any sexual contact between courting couples usually has to take place secretly in the fields, away from the homes of people.

The reason for the general prohibition of physical contact between unmarried couples is usually given as: 'It insults the spirits of the ancestors'. Wood reports an anecdote concerning a cook who had committed a 'horrible outrage' by stroking the hand of the daughter of some Thai people, and writes amusedly of the reactions of the parents:

> ... not in our house. We have a spirit living in the roof which is extremely strict in morals, and which is rendered furious if it observes even the slightest familiarity between unmarried persons.[16]

This reaction of the parents of the girl indicates precisely the attitudes of rural people towards sexual intercourse of unmarried people. The ancestors are jealous and seem loath to leave their former property in the hands of their descendants. Before any stranger makes more than a short or casual visit to a house, the ancestors wish to hear about it and the newcomer must be properly introduced by the eldest of the house. This is done during the daily ritual of offering incense, a candle and flowers. If an unmarried couple stays overnight under the same roof and if they were to engage in sexual intercourse, the spirits of the ancestors who never sleep would be deeply mortified and insulted and they are likely to retaliate. Any misfortune that occurs in a community while an unmarried couple lives together will be seen as the likely result of the wrath of the spirits. The couple in question will be held responsible for the fact that a neighbour suffers from nightmares, that a child becomes ill, or a house burns down. Pressure will be brought upon them and their relatives to stop flouting the spirits.

This is the reason why the parents of a young woman will make sure that she does not find herself alone with a suitor; they guard her closely, especially when the time of marriage draws near. As mentioned earlier, in recent times the farmers find it increasingly difficult to guard their daughters because the young people travel often to the provincial capital to seek work during the slack

16 Wood, *Consul in Paradise*, pp. 94–5.

season and they may make arrangements to meet without knowledge of older relatives.

In line with the ideas concerning sexual intercourse and ancestors, the elementary, essential marriage ceremony consists of a ritual during which the spirits of the ancestors are informed of the fact that a certain couple will be husband and wife. The ancestors are made aware of the fact that a contract is made between the parties involved, and therefore these spirits should not be offended when sexual intercourse between the young people takes place. Similar beliefs are indicated for northern Thailand.[17]

Two meals for the ancestors are prepared on two trays, each containing, for example, a banana, a small ripe coconut, some boiled rice, some raw meat, an alcoholic beverage, and some sweets, the kinds of food which these spirits presumably like to receive. The even number of trays symbolizes that there are two parties involved; even numbers are a recurrent aspect of the marriage ceremony, especially in the elaborate rituals. Incense and candles are lighted and some fragrant flowers are donated to attract the attention of these invisible agents. The oldest members of the families involved will be spokesmen and -women for those who have gathered, and they will introduce the match in carefully chosen words. It is customary to indicate to the spirits that the contract is legally binding by showing the bride price to them. This need not necessarily be a very great amount of money; it depends upon the negotiations previous to the marriage. It must always be an even amount and can be offered in coins or bullion. Sometimes it represents years of savings of the bridegroom. If a woman deserts her husband for no reason considered valid, the bride price may be claimed back.

The bride and groom prostrate themselves before the place where the ancestors usually reside, usually near a shelf on the eastern, most honourable side of the house.' They also present themselves to their older relatives who bless them and wish them happiness. To ensure that no power will be offended, some food and liquor is also placed on the shrine of the spirit of the soil, not far from the house, and the couple should also inform this spirit of the marriage.

While the elementary marriage ceremony centres around propitiation, the elaborations cover a wealth of non-religious aspects as well as some details of interest to the student of Thai religion. Elaborate marriages usually unfold in three distinct parts, and the exact moment for the beginning of each part can be fixed at an auspicious moment by a ritual specialist.

17 Kraiśrī Nimmānahaeminda, 'Ham Yon, the Magic Testicles', 1966, p. 134.

An elaborate marriage ceremony begins with an official betrothal. From the family of the prospective bridegroom an emissary is sent to the family of the bride-to-be. This deputy can be male or female and to be chosen for this task is considered to be an honour, for usually only a person with an unblemished reputation, a thorough ritual knowledge, and a ripe age is asked to represent the bridegroom's family. The deputy takes two vessels, one containing some money or gold, unhusked rice, puffed rice, green peas, sesame seed and some leaves with auspicious names, such as silver-and-gold leaves; the other holds eight areca nuts and an even number of betel leaves. The contents of the vessels are determined by tradition. The different plants have to be included for symbolic purposes. In most cases the exact reason for the inclusion of a certain plant is not known by the actors of the ritual; they all know, however, that the total assortment must be seen as a polite request for a betrothal. There is only one vessel with areca and betel in contrast with the practice at a later stage, because at this moment it is only one party approaching another.

If the bride's family agrees in principle with the prospective match, they accept the gifts and discuss the details of the marriage with the deputy. It has to be decided whether the ceremony will take place in the house of the bride or that of the groom. Sometimes the couple will already possess a house of their own and prefer that the marriage will take place in that new residence. Other topics that have to be discussed during this meeting are the amount of the bride price and the date of the marriage. Auspicious times for marriages are usually days in the waxing phase of the moon of the second, fourth, sixth, eighth and twelfth lunar months. Obviously these months are chosen for their even numbers, symbolizing the fact that two families are involved in the ceremony. The tenth lunar month is excluded, possibly because around that time of the year most dogs in rural Thailand are in heat and make a public spectacle of copulation.

The second stage of the elaborate marriage ritual consists of a blessing by monks and relatives. Phya Anuman Rajadhon is of the opinion that the inclusion of the monks in the marriage ritual is a survival from the time that an elaborate marriage was always preceded by a blessing of a new house. The monks were invited to sprinkle some protective, sacralized water over the new building before the actual marriage could take place. This was accompanied by a ritual purification of the engaged couple. In present times, this act of purification has become an act of blessing.[18]

18 Phya Anuman Rajadhon, *Essays on Thai Folklore,* pp. 255–67.

On the day of the marriage the groom's family provides three ceremonial containers, one holding the bride price and plant material similar to that which accompanied the engagement money, the other to vessels holding areca nuts and betel leaves. At the betrothal, the single vessel with areca indicated the approach of one party, whereas the two containers stand for the coming together of two parties. The persons carrying the containers are received with proper hospitality.

At around ten o'clock in the morning the monks who have been invited for this occasion arrive, their *dek wat* carrying begging bowls. As in virtually all rituals where monks and laymen meet, the Five Precepts are recited, and as soon as the laymen have solemnly promised to adhere to these moral rules, the monks chant several texts which are known to be suited for auspicious occasions and which all can be found in the *Suatmon Chet Tamnan*. The begging bowls are placed immediately in front of the dais on which the monks recite, and during the chanting of Pali texts rice is offered into these bowls by all laymen present. The bride and bridegroom should be the first to place some rice in each begging bowl, using a single spoon that they should both hold at the moment of donating the rice. In this manner they perform a meritorious deed simultaneously, thus linking their individual stores of good karma. This ensures that they connect some of their future happy moments, not only in this life, but also in future existences.

Through their chanting the monks consecrate a bowl of water, and immediately afterwards the rice and all other dishes of food have to be ceremoniously presented to the monks. Again, the bride and groom should perform the ritual handing-over simultaneously. As always during auspicious ceremonies, the farmers make sure to include all powers, and a tray with a token of each kind of food is therefore placed in front of the Buddha image of the house, another tray with these foods is placed near the shelf with the remains of the ancestors, and a third food offering is brought to the shrine of the spirit of the soil just outside the house.

Wat Sanchao farmers can remember that a few decades ago the morning ceremony ended at this point. Just before noon the monks partook of the meal and the whole gathering had to wait until about four o'clock in the afternoon, which was considered the auspicious time for the lustration of the couple. It was customary to invite the same chapter of monks back so that they could initiate the afternoon ritual by sprinkling the couple with sacral water. This lapse of time between the morning meal of the monks and the sprinkling was inconvenient for the monks as well as for the laymen. The monks would have

Figure 6.2: Blessing the married couple by sprinkling them with *nam mon*.

to wait four hours before proceeding with the ritual, and if the house where the marriage took place were situated far away from a monastery it would not be worth while to walk to and fro. It was also inconvenient for the organizers of the marriage ceremony because, if the monks left the scene early in the afternoon and returned at four p.m., they would have to receive the members of the Sangha twice. If, on the other hand, the monks remained in the house, they would have to be constantly attended to in accordance with their exalted ritual position. Therefore it has now become customary to link the sprinkling ritual with the meal of the monks in the morning. It would, of course, not have been possible to shift the meal of the monks to the afternoon, since the rules of the Sangha forbid eating of solid food after midday.

Thus, immediately after the official meal has been concluded and the laymen have been able to offer a share of merit to relatives and ancestors in the *kruat nam* ritual, the bride and groom are sprinkled. They prostrate themselves before every individual monk in turn and as they go down the row the bowl of water is passed on. Each successive monk takes the bowl, dips into it a bundle of leaves that carry auspicious names and splashes some of the water over their heads while reciting an auspicious Pali phrase. For the marriage ceremony, a common plant from which to use twigs is the *Calotropis gigantea*.[19] Its inclusion is undoubtedly related to the fact that the leaves of this plant are called *rak*-leaves, and the word *rak* (รัก) means in Thai 'to love, to cherish'.

19 McFarland, *Thai-English Dictionary*, p. 515 and p. 700.

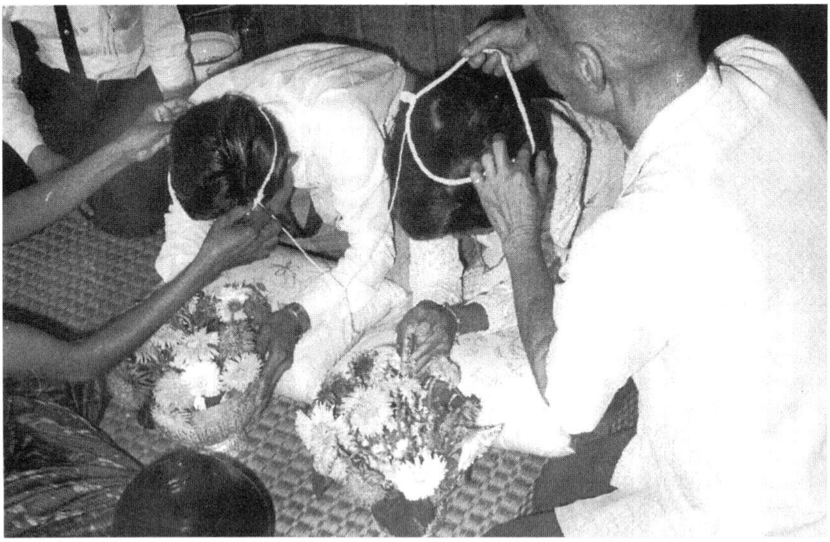

Figure 6.3: Putting on the twin crowns.

After the sprinkling, the monks return to their monasteries and the remainder of the marriage ritual is fully in the hands of the laymen. These continue the aspersion of the couple. The difference in rank between monk and layman is reflected in the fact that bride and groom do not have to fully prostrate when they are sprinkled by older relatives. The bride sits on the left hand of the groom. A person who knows an appropriate formula, usually a man from the community who is famous for his knowledge of ritual, approaches the couple and anoints their foreheads with a fragrant paste.

A spell for this occasion, recorded by Wirijá'buuraná', can be transcribed as follows:

> Sunakkhattaṃ sumangalaṃ supabhātaṃ suhiṭṭhitaṃ sukhaṇo sumuhutto ca suyiṭṭhaṃ brahmacārisu padakkhiṇaṃ kāyakammaṃ vācākammaṃ padakkhiṇaṃ padakkhiṇa manokammaṃ paṇidhi te padakkhiṇā padakkhiṇāni katvāna te labhantan te padakkhiṇe.[20]

This formula is made up of auspicious Pali words; the meaning seems obviously connected with a ritual circumambulation of the couple, which here be understood as a metaphor for a circular movement. The text seems slightly corrupt, however, but still may be translated as:

20 Urakhin, ประเพณีไทยฉบับพระราชครู [Thai Customs, the Rajaguru edition], B.E. 2510 (1967), p. 234.

Figure 6.4: An elderly relative pours scented water from a conch shell.

> A good constellation, a good blessing, a good dawning, a good rising, a good span and a good period. Perform a circumambulation, well offered among the brahmacārīs. Circumambulate with the action of the body, (circumambulate) with the action of the voice, circumambulate with the action of the mind. May they who are auspicious (circumambulate), having performed circumambulations, achieve (the fruit of) those circumambulations.

The 'going around' refers to the movement of a white cotton cord, which is three times wound around the head of the groom and a similar circular crown is placed on the bride's head. The 'twin crowns' as they are popularly called, are connected with a thin thread. Parents, relatives, and other guests now come forward one by one to sprinkle the hands of the couple with scented water from a conch shell whilst wishing them prosperity and happiness. After everyone has done this, the ritual specialist removes the 'twin crowns' simultaneously.

The third stage of the elaborate marriage ceremony is called *riang mon* (เรียงหมอน) or 'arranging the pillows'. It is usually held in the home of the bride, so that in some cases, notably where the chanting of the monks and the sprinkling ritual have taken place in the house of the parents of the groom, the whole party has to move to a different location. If the *riang mon* occurs on the same day that the sprinkling took place, the astrologer usually decides that the most auspicious time for the final stage of the ceremony is at seven or eight o'clock in the evening.

In the house of the bride a sleeping place has been arranged with great care. The bride price and some leaves with auspicious names, such as *rak*-leaves and silver-and-gold leaves, have been placed on this bed. Bride and groom must lie down on this bed, on either side of the bride price, the bride to the left, the groom to the right. While taking their position they should take care not to bump their heads together, since such a small mishap is interpreted as indicating that the marriage will be troubled by frequent vehement quarrelling.

A person who is reputed to have been happily married for many years has been invited to instruct the couple. This marriage instruction usually covers a wide range of subjects. Thus, the proper behaviour of the marriage partners towards each other is often broached. The husband is admonished to be just and considerate, whilst the wife ought to be gentle and understanding. Under no circumstances should they be forgetful with regard to the spirits of the ancestors.

Specific rules of behaviour that are auspicious in daily routine can be mentioned. For example, when getting up in the morning, a person should wash the face with clean water in a properly contemplative mood. The water can be blessed with a few Pali words before using it to rub the face. Some auspicious words such as *Namo Buddhāya*, or *Itipiso Bhagavā* may serve. Unless a person is sick he should not be found in bed at the moment of sunrise or sundown. Always, after a day's work, a person should bathe and perfume himself. The married couple should sleep with their heads towards the auspicious east. Husband and wife should not have sexual intercourse on *wan phra* or the day before *wan phra*. In addition there is a strong warning against sexual intercourse when a woman menstruates; such behaviour may result in the birth of unhealthy children. In accordance with the ideas of magical power, a woman should never be in a relatively higher position than her husband when they engage in sexual play lest the man lose some of his magical protection.

In former times, the couple was left alone after the marriage instruction until the next morning. At the present time, the moments of privacy often last only a few minutes; this is nothing more than a symbolization of the fact that from now on they are entitled to each other's company without a chaperone. Soon they join the guests for a final rejoicing in the occasion.

There are no fixed rules for the place of residence of a newly married couple. The decision to settle in a compound with the family of the groom, to reside with the family of the bride, or to live on their own depends largely on circumstances that differ from case to case.

The discussion of leaving the order, courting and marriage on the previous pages broached several aspects of rural religion that are of importance to young adults, but of which they were not aware of in their younger days. A short remark on symbolism and a more elaborate mention of auspicious moments are therefore warranted.

Symbolism

It is apparent to these young people that the paraphernalia used during ceremonies often serve a symbolic function. Some of these are almost self-explanatory. When betel leaves and areca nuts are used in a ritual they clearly indicate the concept of agreement, harmony, or understanding. Gold-and-silver leaves are present when it is appropriate to refer to the ideas of prosperity and wealth. *Rak*-leaves appear when it is necessary to stress the concept of love. It is more difficult in many cases to decipher the hidden messages of, for example, a tray with unhusked rice, puffed rice, green peas, and sesame seed. Such knowledge is reserved for the ritual specialist who prescribes and prepares the ingredients during elaborate ceremonies. The young people may regard it as esoteric lore.

Almost invariably a gift to an immaterial religious agent is accompanied by candles, flowers, and incense. The prime reason for the inclusion of these articles seems to lie in their pleasant scent. Spirits and divine beings are immaterial, and so is the fragrance of candles, flowers and incense. These articles may be seen as the paraphernalia that cause the spirits and gods to give their attention, and it is in line with this thought that they are always offered at the very beginning of a ritual.

Auspicious moments

It has been noted in both the ceremony for leaving the order and the elaborate marriage ceremony that advice may be sought with regard to the most auspicious moment on which the ceremony can take place. For major, elaborate rituals the farmer usually does not fix an auspicious time himself; he will have to consult a ritual specialist. This expert can be a monk or a layman who, when approached, usually has to consult some handbook before giving advice. Each type of ceremony has its own peculiar rules with regard to what is auspicious. In addition, the rules concern various units of time: the year, the lunar month, the day of the week and the divisions of the day itself. A further variant that

Daytime	06.01–08.24	08.25–10.48	10.49–13.12	13.13–15.36	15.37–18.00
Sunday	o o o o	X		o o	o
Monday	o	o o o o	X		o o
Tuesday	o o	o	o o o o	X	
Wednesday		o o	o	o o o o	X
Thursday	X		o o	o	o o o o
Friday	o o o o	X		o o	o
Saturday	o	o o o o	X		o o
Night-time	18.01–20.24	20.25–22.48	22.49–01.12	01.13–03.36	03.37–06.00

Figure 6.5: The *yan ubakong*.

needs to be taken into account is the moment of birth of the person or persons for whom the best moment is to be calculated.

Most farmers wish to choose auspicious moments for all decisive acts of their lives; they like to begin planting rice on the proper day, build a house in a favourable period, travel only when the signs are right, and discuss important matters only when the omens are good. For decisions of minor importance, most farmers will not take the trouble to visit an astrologer. Instead they may consult simple charts that give information about auspicious times in general. Such charts are widely distributed and in almost every household an astrological timetable of one sort or another can be found.

One of the most widespread timetables is the *yan ubakong* (ยันต์อุบากอง), of which an elaborate version is given in Figure 6.5. Each day and each night of the week is divided into five periods. The squares marked with four circles are the most auspicious times; the squares with a cross indicate the most inauspicious periods of the week. A blank square indicates an indifferent period that may bring luck but could bode disaster; the squares with two circles are mildly auspicious and those with a single one are slightly favourable. The *yan ubakong* can be seen chalked on a wall in a home; it may be printed on the back of leaflets which advertise a major fund-raising ceremony; sometimes a man can have it tattooed on the upper thigh. The *yan ubakong* shown in Figure 6.5 was found on the back of a propaganda leaflet for the general elections of 1969.

Other charts that are often found in the homes of farmers indicate which days of the lunar month are auspicious or inauspicious. Some tables can be used to find out to what degree people born on a certain day are compatible, others tell which type of rice will grow best during a certain year of the twelve-year cycle. This cycle, in which each year is known by the name of an animal, is used throughout mainland Southeast Asia but also in China and Tibet; probably the Thais adopted the system even before they migrated to the mainland. The Thai sequence of animals is: rat, ox, tiger, hare, big serpent, serpent, horse, goat, monkey, cock, dog, and pig.

A large number of charts are printed in relatively cheap handbooks that are widely distributed.[21] The different astrological handbooks may well contain contradictory information, and it is by trial and error that a farmer decides which charts seem to give best guidance. Ideally, a man should have a private handbook, one that has been drawn up by an astronomer using the personal moment of birth as base for all his calculations. The frequent use of astrology reflects the widespread feeling that the farmer's life is hazardous: sudden illness may strike, moneylenders may lose their patience, or crops may fail.

In this chapter, the range of magical powers has been further described, especially in the sections on love magic, where the whole gamut of forces can be used, A man can influence an unwilling woman by the use of beneficially charged objects, but sometimes the use of aggressive, even dangerous materials is not excluded. The use of polluted matter and body secretions is highly illuminative in the field of Thai magic.

The marriage ceremony has been approached only from a religious angle. The elementary ceremony was shown to be an occasion for informing the ancestors and asking for a blessing of the alliance from these spirits as well as from elder relatives, The elaborations involve a ritual meeting of the two families and propitiation of the ancestors, the Buddha image, and the spirit of the soil. The inclusion of a chapter of monks may not have been originally part of the ceremony, but at present Buddhist monks fulfil an important role. The beneficial power of the monks' chanting is used to bless the couple, to add to the auspiciousness of the occasion, and to increase the chances of a happy, long-lasting union.

21 For example: Urakhin, พรหมชาติ ฉบับหลวง ประจำบ้าน ดูด้วยตนเอง [The Brahman, Major Edition for the Household, for Self-use], Bangkok: Rongphim Luk S. Thammaphakdi, B.E. 2500 (1957). For an annotated translation of much of the information in such Thai astrological handbooks, see H. G. Quaritch Wales, *Divination in Thailand*, 1983.

Nhouy Abhay indicates that in Laos the monks can also be involved in the marriage ceremony.[22] When we take that information together with the evidence for central Thailand, it appears that Nash was not fully informed when he summed up the relation between monks and marriage in Southeast Asia, when he stated:

> . . . monks are present at marriage ceremonies in Cambodia, while in all other Theravada communities the Buddhist cleric is symbolically antithetical to marriage and procreation; . . .[23]

In rural Thai religion, there is an opposition between monks and women, as noted in Chapter V above, but the Sangha is not kept away from all matters concerning marriage and procreation. In this respect it can be recalled that it is the compassion of the monk that can fill a *rakyom* with *mettā* so that a layman can use it as an aid to win a bride. Possibly Nash is right only with regard to what has been described in this book as the other Buddhist orientation, the sophisticated compartmentalized religious orientation of the elite.

Other rules seem primarily related to a body of practical knowledge. When it is said that building a house is inauspicious from the sixth until the twelfth lunar month, this can be taken to mean that it is impractical, because the rainy season falls within this period and neighbouring farmers would be too busy to come to help with the construction. Removing mounds and tree trunks from the building site may displace jealous spirits, but at the same time it is technically sound to build on a smooth, level surface. Wood that is considered inauspicious for construction often proves to be just that which makes poor timber. Elements of practical wisdom, acquired in the past through trial and error, are thus handed down with religious validation.

The idea of a range of magical powers, from harmful and aggressive, through ambiguous to beneficial, has proven valuable at several instances in this chapter. It aided in explaining why during the elementary ritual for house-building there was a difference between the actions of a monk and those of a lay specialist. It also proved highly illuminative in the analysis of the *thorani san* ritual, where the positive power of the monks is needed to offset the effects of pollution.

22 Thao Nhouy Abhay, 'Marriage Rites', in *Kingdom of Laos* (ed. by R. de Berval), 1959, pp. 137–43.

23 M. Nash, in his Introduction to *Anthropological Studies in Theravada Buddhism*, p. viii.

CHAPTER VII

BUILDING A HOUSE[1]

In central rice-growing Thailand houses are usually rectangular and built on posts, so that temporary floods do not interrupt residence. A home on stilts has additional benefits: it gives protection against potential enemies, living in such a house gives a secure feeling, and it provides a place where someone can lie down to sleep without putting the head in an inferior position to that of a passer-by. The simplest houses are made mainly of bamboo, their roofs covered with *bai chak* (ใบจาก), the dried leaves of the Nipa palm tree. More expensive houses are at least partly made of hardwood. Recently other materials have become available to the well-to-do farmer: the posts upholding the house can now be manufactured from concrete, and roofs can be covered with tiles, sheets of fibre, or corrugated iron.

The floors of such houses are on different levels. The difference in height between adjacent levels usually varies between 20 and 40 cm. The simplest home has a floor plan with two levels, but more elaborate structures have a floor plan with three or more. The differences in height between different parts of the floor play an important role in the lives of farmers. They provide the means with which at any given instant objects, persons, and activities are ordered according to their relative importance: important ones should be on a higher level, the less important ones ought to be lower. For example, the objects used during the reception of an honoured guest, like the crusher of areca nuts and a mat of good quality, are kept on a high level, together with other prized possessions. A wiping cloth, pots and pans, mortar and pestle may all move around as circumstances require, but when put away, they belong to a lower level. When persons of markedly different status converse, those who are more important should sit on a higher level. If no raised areas of the floor are near, a simple mat or a piece of cloth can serve as an elevation.

1 A previous version of this chapter, illustrated with several photographs was published in *Anthropos*, Vol. 71, 1976, under the title 'Leasing from the Gods (Thailand)'.

During the hours of daylight, when farmers may be covered in perspiration, activities in the house, like eating and resting, tend to take place on low areas of the floor. In the evening, however, after all have bathed and changed into clean clothes, the whole floor space comes into play. At night-time the sleeping mats of the chief occupants are spread out on a high level, while servants sleep on a lower layer. Even in the relaxed atmosphere during an evening *en famille*, most people still adhere to certain rules of comportment that illustrate the importance of this vertical ordering:

> When somebody stretches out, his feet should not point directly in the direction of an honoured object, such as the head of another person who lies on the same floor.
> When moving about and passing close by a person who is older, the upper part of the body should not be in a higher position than the head of the older person.
> When moving around and passing close by a sitting person who is older. The upper part of the body should not be in a higher position than the head of that person.
> Even when an older person passes close by a sitting junior whose head happens to be markedly lower, the former should show a polite recognition by slightly bowing his head. This polite recognition may only be omitted altogether when the difference in age or status is too great to warrant a show of politeness, for example, when an old person passes close by a sitting child.
> Before engaging upon conversation with someone older, the junior should position himself on a relatively lower level.
> Servants must behave as if junior to all but very young children.
> When a monk is invited to enter a private home,[2] all laymen, irrespective of age, must arrange their sitting place so that they are lower than the monk.

The ordering of objects on different levels according to their relative status is not limited to different levels of the floor. The same principle is discernible in the distribution of the ornaments on the walls. The shelf for the ancestors will be placed high on one wall, about 1.60 m from the floor below. On this shelf rest the urns with some ashes of the ancestors and some portraits or photos of deceased relatives, but various objects that reputedly possess beneficial magical power can also be placed here. Thus, pieces of paper or cloth on which *yan*,

2 The Thais interpret the forty-third pācittiyā rule of the monks to mean that a monk cannot enter the house of a layman unless specifically invited to do so.

magical drawings and diagrams have been traced, can be found on or near the shelf. Sometimes an object that has the appearance of a banknote is fastened here. On close examination, however, it becomes apparent that, although it has many characteristics of Thai currency, the banknote depicts the image of a monk and some lines in the sacred *Khom* script. This 'sacred banknote' reputedly has the power of increasing the prosperity of a household. If a farmer possesses a horoscope, a book with spells, or a table showing the different auspicious and inauspicious times, these can also be kept on this shelf. Often it also contains the remains of daily offerings: remnants of candles, incense sticks and flowers.

More secular ornaments, like the picture of a living member of the family, or a calendar, tend to be placed at a marked distance from this shelf, preferably on another wall. If an ornament of secular nature is put near the shelf it has to be fastened in a lower position. A photograph of secular nature ought not to be placed above something ritually superior. Therefore a picture of the queen should not be hung directly above a photograph of a monk. Members of the royal family are god-like in status but ritually inferior to a Buddhist monk.

The arrangement on different levels is thus executed on the principle that a relatively more important object, person or activity should be placed higher.[3] Apart from this vertical collocation, principles governing on a horizontal plane can be added.

The east, where the sun rises, is associated with life and generally regarded as auspicious. The west, where the sun goes down, is associated with death and is inauspicious. A corpse is placed with the head in a westerly direction, but when a living person lies down to sleep, he should take care to position his body auspiciously. Nightmares would plague the person sleeping with his head in a westerly direction; the proper way to sleep is with the head towards the east.[4]

Taking the ideal auspicious position of the body of a sleeping person as point of departure, several architectural features of homes in rural central Thailand can be illustrated. The ancestor shelf has to be on the eastern half of the house; if it were on the western wall, the inhabitants of the house would insult their ancestors by stretching their feet in the direction of this shelf. Kraiśrī Nimmānahaeminda reports similar feelings among people of northern Thailand in respect of a shelf on which a Buddha image stands.[5] The entrance to the sleeping area, on the other

3 It is only during the course of the twentieth century that the Thais have come to terms with living in multi-storied buildings. Such a coming to terms means a shutting out of the thought that there may be people living directly above one's head.

4 Sathian Koset, ประเพณีเก่าของไทย [Old Customs of the Thais], p. 187.

5 'Ham Yon, the Magic Testicles', p. 133.

hand, cannot be on the eastern side, for thus people entering the area would be forced to walk close by the heads of those already resting.

Ideally, a house should therefore be built with the high levels of the floor on the east, and the lower portions on the western side. The stairway should lead to the low area but not directly towards the west. In practice most houses are not built strictly according to the east–west axis, and deviations of up to 45 degrees to either side are common. The exact position of the home often depends on the advice of a ritual specialist who, before deciding upon the direction of the house, will take the topographical circumstances into account. Building directly along a north–south axis is generally avoided in rural regions, as it would be *khwang tawan* (ขวางตะวัน), 'offensive to the sun'.

Not every man will come into such circumstances that he is obliged to build a house of his own. Those who inherit a dwelling and people who stay with relatives may never need to erect their own home. Those who feel obliged to build their own house usually observe certain rituals during the construction of the building. It depends mainly on the wealth of the builder whether only essential ceremonial must suffice, or whether more elaborate ritual is chosen.

The Elementary Ceremony

If a man who wishes to build a house can ill afford the services of an astrologer, he decides for himself the exact location of the new home. At the selected spot he traces out a rectangle of the size of the floor of the future house, taking care to avoid planning the main axis of the house in an inauspicious direction. The rectangle is cleared of all growth, and great care is taken to level out the building site and to remove all tree trunks, stones, pieces of glass, and other impurities. It is believed that any such impurity interferes with the happiness of the inhabitants of the future house. When the site has been well prepared, the owner often engages a ritual specialist, either layman or monk, to pacify the spirits who may be disturbed by the building process.

If the specialist is a monk, the ceremony consists simply of a profuse sprinkling of the site with sacral water whilst auspicious Pali words are uttered. However, if the specialist is a layman, a placatory gift is made. The lay ritual specialist can sprinkle the site with some sacral water and place incense, candles, flowers, and some foods on the earth, whilst invoking the different powers to allow the building of the home to take place.

It is interesting to note that a monk cannot offer an oblation to the spirits who may have a prior claim on the area of land. The fact that a monk should refrain from such behaviour can easily be interpreted as 'proof' of the fact that even in rural Buddhism the compartmentalization of pure religion and accretions has had its effects on ritual. People with the elitist type of Buddhism in mind may see it as an indication of a dichotomy between Buddhism and propitiation. However, seen from the perspective of the animistic type of Buddhism, the correct interpretation of the fact that a monk does not offer gifts to these powers is simply a matter of etiquette. A monk should never lower himself to ask favours from the spirits. The ritual position of a monk is more exalted than that of the spirits and godly powers around him.

When the site has thus been placated, when the spirits who may feel a claim to the land have been propitiated, holes for the poles of the house can be dug, and building can proceed without further ceremonial.

Common Elaborations

People who can afford to build a wooden home instead of constructing one of bamboo usually take more precautions to ensure the happiness of the future inhabitants. They engage a ritual specialist who will assist with the selection of the place on which to build, with the choice of wood and with the elaborate ceremonials.

In the time before the widespread devastation of Thailand's natural resources, the timber for building a house was not bought from another person, but had to be gathered in a forest by the man who built the home, accompanied and assisted by his intimate friends. They often took the ritual specialist along in order to decide which trees were auspicious. The specialist selected trees that grew in favourable positions, and made sure that the types of wood selected were considered suitable in ritual lore. Wood considered auspicious was, for example, *mai teng* (ไม้เต็ง) (*Shorea obtusa*) and *mai rang* (ไม้รัง) (*Pentacme siamensis*). A good timber tree, but dangerous because of its reputed attraction to certain spirits, was *mai takhian* (ไม้ตะเคียน) (*Serianthes grandiflora, Erythophloeun succirubrum*).

Most of the trees that were considered inauspicious were unsuitable for house building; they rotted quickly, were easily devoured by insects, were too wet or too heavy. One tree, although useful as timber, was avoided because its name *mai makha mong* (ไม้มะค่ามอง) (*Afzelia xylocarpe*), sounded inauspicious since the syllable *kha* was associated with the Thai word for 'to kill', 'to murder' (ฆ่า). In modern times, timber factories sell this wood under a new name, *mai charoensuk* (ไม้เจริญสุข), a name suggesting an increase in happiness. The woodcutters took great care to let the trees fall in an auspicious direction, and

Figure 7.1: The *san phiangta*.

the ritual specialist was at hand to interpret the creaking sounds in the wood just before it fell. These sounds were seen as a communication from the spirit of the wood, the *Nang Mai* (นางไม้).

Nowadays, the central area of Thailand has almost been wholly deforested, and timber merchants have to import wood from other regions. Therefore the customs regarding the selection and cutting of wood have virtually disappeared from this region. While selecting timber is now a purely commercial activity, the choice of the most auspicious building site is still decided by the ritual specialist. He examines in detail several situational and topographical characteristics of the plot of land. Before finally giving his advice, he takes into account which different plants grow there and in which direction these plants will stand in relation to the new house. In addition he looks at the slope of the land and the occurrence and exact position of anthills.

Usually, the elaborate ceremonies connected with the actual building of the house fall on two successive days. On the first day, offerings are made to placate the appropriate spirits and the holes for the supporting poles are dug. On the second day these poles are placed, the *sao aek* (เสาเอก), 'first pole' is raised, other posts put into position and the house is constructed. Traditionally, a house had to be built completely during that second day. Therefore the ceremony of raising the 'first pole' had to take place early in the morning, so that building could start just after sunrise. Many friends and relatives would turn up to assist in the construction. In order to ensure that enough manpower would be available, the house building had therefore to be planned during the periods of the year when work in the fields was slack. The owner of the new house had to note carefully who had come to help him, so that this service could be reciprocated at a future date.

All tasks of major proportion were shared in the traditional village economy. Voluntary, unpaid help was always reciprocal. If, for example, two members of a family helped during a whole day to build the home of a neighbour, the family of these two could be certain that it would receive a similar amount of man-hours in return whenever a comparable task arose. Nowadays, the big building tasks are often done by workers who are paid a daily wage and who receive free food. These paid workers toil shoulder to shoulder with the traditional-minded friends who help on a reciprocal basis. The same phenomenon can be observed during the harvesting period in the fields. If a family has accumulated many debt hours with another group of people and wishes to quickly rectify the balance, it is always possible to give appropriate financial assistance with one of the religious ceremonies of that group.

Although the custom of finishing the building on one day has largely disappeared, the raising of the 'first pole' still takes place at sunrise. Nowadays, a rich farmer feels obliged to build a home of such grandeur that it cannot be constructed in a single day. He now requires a well-laid hardwood floor, windproof walls, and a roof covered with prefabricated sheets of board or metal. His fellow villagers can be of only limited assistance to him; he needs to engage a professional carpenter. After the first day of building usually only the outer framework of the modern house has been assembled, and it may take many weeks before the home is habitable.

Prior to the first day of the elaborate ceremonies, the owner of the plot of land will have turned and levelled out the earth where the house will stand. Close by the building site he has to construct a *san phiangta* (ศาลเพียงตา), a 'shrine on eye level'. The ritual specialist has indicated to him exactly where this shrine should be erected, after having taken into account the astrological characteristics of the days of ceremony. This shrine rests on four, six or eight bamboo stakes. The front poles are about 1.60 m high, the back ones much taller. A horizontal framework connects all poles, giving the whole the appearance of a chair on tall props. A bar between the back poles provides the 'back rest'. Just before a ritual commences in which the *san phiangta* plays a role, a white cloth is draped over the top of the structure and a pillow in a white pillowcase is placed on the 'seat of the chair'. An umbrella fastened above the shrine completes the preparation of the *san phiangta*.

The specialist brings his ritual paraphernalia: white clothes which are regarded as the uniform of a 'Brahmin', a *phakhaoma* (ผ้าขาวม้า), which is a rectangular multi-coloured cotton cloth with a check pattern, worn only by men,[6] a number of rectangular pieces of plant material cut from an inner layer of the trunk of a banana tree, and two ritual food baskets. One of these food containers is triangular, the other is square with a circular inner vessel. Both ritual baskets are divided into a number of compartments, often nine, in which food for the powers to be placated is laid. He may also bring a vessel with sacral water, but if he has to travel far, he may prefer to sacralize some water at the place of the ceremony by muttering a series of sacred words and extinguishing a lighted candle in a bowl of water. The owner of the future house usually provides the other materials needed for the ritual, and will have bought an ample supply of candles, incense, flowers, food, and alcoholic beverages.

The specialist fills the compartments of the triangular and square baskets, each with food appropriate for the non-human powers: a bit of cooked rice, some puffed rice, green peas, sesame seed, a banana, a piece of sugarcane and different kinds of sweets. The full range depends often on what is available. If there is meat, a piece of chicken or duck is considered to be pleasing to the spirits involved. In the rural regions, the ordinary farmer could not explain the symbolic meaning of the different kinds of food. The general idea seems to be to offer a variety of foods that are of good quality and fragrant. The quantity appears to be immaterial, and therefore it can be presented in miniature containers.

The specialist places the triangle on the *san phiangta* and the square container on a mat, together with other ritual objects that he will need presently.

6 It can be used as loincloth, bathing trunks, towel, sash or as head-cover. For ritual purposes it is worn over the left shoulder, tucked under the right arm, like the *upavīta* in India.

On one occasion,[7] when asked for whom the gifts on the *san phiangta* were intended, the ritual specialist answered readily: 'For Phum (ภูมิ), the lord of the plot of land'. He then walks around the building site and, at every place where later a support of the house will stand, presses a twig into the earth to such a depth that, without falling over, it can support one of the rectangular pieces cut from the trunk of a banana tree. A twig upon which such a rectangular piece is fastened thus constitutes a receptacle, and every place where the earth will be deeply disturbed is indicated by such a small tray. On each of these little platforms an offering is placed, such as a small piece cut from a banana, or a minute piece of sugarcane, sometimes accompanied by incense. It is said that this gift is for *Phaya* Nak (พะยานาค), the king of serpents.

After these preparations he proceeds with an official invitation to the non-human powers. It may commence with words like:

> Oṃ Phra Phum, Phra Thorani, Krungphali, sahaparivarāya ehi sathaya āgacchantu paribhuñjantu svāhāya . . . .[8]

This formula appears to be made up mainly of Pali or Sanskrit words and may be paraphrased as follows:

> Oṃ[9] Venerable Phum, Venerable Thorani and Krungphali, come with your retinue; to the place let them come, let them enjoy the gift . . . .

After the invocation he sprinkles sacral water on the building site, and scatters some puffed rice, green peas and sesame seed. For a period of about a quarter of an hour all ceremonial action stops in order to give the invoked powers the opportunity to come and enjoy the different gifts. When the specialist is of the opinion that sufficient time has elapsed, he removes the receptacles with the gifts for *Phaya* Nak and indicates where the first hole should be dug, and in which direction the soil thus removed should be deposited. In order to decide where this first hole ought to be, he has to find out the exact position of the great serpent (*nak*, นาค). He may have to consult a handbook or private notes inherited from his teacher to determine the serpent's position.

Two books on Thai ceremonies[10] contained information from which Figure 7.2 could be distilled. The year is divided into four equal periods, of three lunar

7 Near Wat Sanchao, 14 December 1968.

8 Khim, 14 December 1968, recorded in field notes.

9 *Oṃ* cannot be translated, it is a sacred exclamation uttered at the beginning of a prayer.

10 Urakhin, ประเพณีไทยฉบับพระราชครู [Thai Customs, the Rajaguru edition], p. 258, and Sathian Koset, ประเพณีเก่าของไทย [Old Customs of the Thais], p. 265.

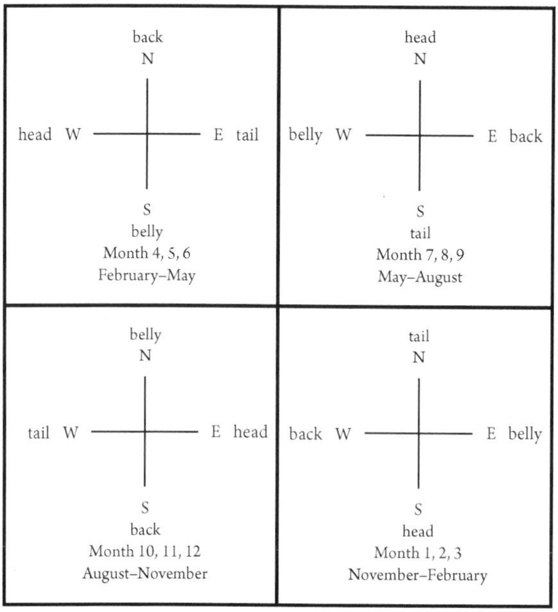

Figure 7.2: The positions of the *nak* during the year.

months each. In each of these quarters, the *nak* is in a different position. When the ritual specialist decides where to dig the first hole in the earth, he must imagine the *nak* on the building site. He should not dig where the head of the *nak* is; it is believed that such an act would cause the wife of the owner of the house to die soon. If the first penetration into the earth pierces the tail, it is almost equally inauspicious: the daughter of the house will kill another human being and have to flee the community. If the back of the *nak* is first dug into, the owner of the house himself will become very ill. It is only through the belly of the *nak* that there will be happiness and luck.[11] Following these instructions, it appears that during the months 4, 5 and 6, the first hole should be dug in the south, in the following quarter the first hole ought to be in the west, from the tenth till the twelfth month the north is appropriate, whilst during the months 1, 2 and 3 the first hole should be made in the east.

It can thus be noted that the seventh, eighth and ninth months, which are rather unsuitable for building a house because they form the rainy season, and work in the fields demands all attention, coincide with a *nak* in such a position that the first hole ought to be dug in the west, an inauspicious cardinal point.

11 Urakhin, *loc. cit.*

Similarly, the months during which it is most auspicious to build, namely the first, second and third lunar months, are those in which the *nak* is positioned in such a manner that the first hole has to be dug in the east, the most auspicious cardinal point.

Different rules govern the direction in which the earth coming from the holes ought to be deposited. For example, Phya Amman Rajadhon reports that, when the first hole has to be dug in the south, the spare earth has to be thrown in a south-easterly direction:

> During the three months number 4, 5 and 6, the *nak* has its head in the west, its tail in the east, its belly in the south, its back in the north. For the first digging, start in the, south first and place the loose earth to a southeasterly direction. Make the poles on which the house will stand lie with their ends in a southeastern direction.[12]

Customs with regard to house building collected from rural Cambodia by Mme Porée-Maspero show a striking resemblance between the practices in the two regions.[13] The Thai positioning of the *nak* and the prescribed direction to which spare earth has to be moved seems in this wider context to be yet another variant of several recorded. In her rendering of the position of the *nāki* from one of the manuscripts quoted it can be seen that the first hole ought to be dug between head and belly of the serpent, whilst the spare earth is thrown in the direction of the belly.[14] Without further information on the history of the Thai and the Cambodian sources it cannot be decided which variant represents a more authentic version. It is relevant to note, however, that in both regions a chthonic serpent is reckoned with, that this serpent is believed to have a head, tail, belly and back and that it rotates in accordance with the year.[15]

As soon as the first hole has been dug, all other holes that will later contain the base of the supports of the house can be made. All these holes will be about one metre deep. The ritual specialist then assists the owner of the future house to light incense, attach this to the square food container with nine compartments and deposit it in the hole first dug (see Figure 7.3). If this occurs while it is still daylight, the basket is placed upside down in the hole; at night an upright position

12 ประเพณีเก่าของไทย [Old Customs of the Thais], p. 265.

13 'Kròṅ Pāli et rites de la maison', *Anthropos*, Vol. 56, 1961, pp. 179–251, pp. 548–628 and pp. 883–929.

14 *Ibid.*, p. 552 and 563 ff.

15 Later I discovered that the rotating naga can be found throughout Southeast Asia and beyond. See 'The Rotating Naga: A Comparative Study of an Excerpt from the Oldest Tai Literature', *Asemi*, Vol 16, 1985, pp. 221–45.

is the proper one. A few drops of an alcoholic beverage and a coin can be added to this gift. On the bottom of each of the remaining excavations, an areca nut and some betel leaves suffice as an offering.[16] During the night all holes are covered, and the *san phiangta* is bared of its white cloth, pillow and umbrella,

The following morning, at sunrise, the holes for the foundation of the house are uncovered and it is ascertained that no insects or lumps of earth have fallen in. A new gift can be placed in all the holes, for example, a small coin or a few leaves of the silver-and-gold leaf plant. The *san phiangta* is provided again with its white cloth, pillow, and umbrella, and new food gifts are placed on it. When the participants in such a ceremony were asked for whom the gifts were intended, the answer was not unanimous:

> The ritual specialist Khim declared that they were for Krungphali (กรุงพาล) and Phra Phum. An older informant interrupted with the information that the Venerable In (Indra) was included among the recipients of the gifts. Further questioning made it clear that no informant was completely certain of the exact number and nature of the recipients of the gifts; in general they were those powers who could have a claim on the plot of land on which the house was built.[17]

While the gifts to powers like the Venerable Phum, Krungphali and Indra, that are placed on the *san phiangta,* can be accompanied by some meat such as chicken, a duck or a pig's head, a gift to Nang Mai should be free of meat. Nang Mai, the female spirit who lives in the wooden posts of which the basic structure of the home is made, should be placated with some fragrant gifts: candles, incense, flowers, some bananas and a small coconut.

The main ritual of the second day is the *tham khwan* or palliation of the *sao aek,* the 'first pole' of the house. The poles that will support the roof of the house vertically when the construction will be finished are placed in a row on the ground and the ritual specialist examines the general shape and the position of the knots in the wood of each of these pieces of timber. The pole that seems most attractive and auspicious is placed aside, aligned in the prescribed direction. A 'second best' pole is singled out and placed next to the *sao aek.* The remaining supports are ranged next to these two.

16 On reading this, a learned Thai informant remarked that she herself once had to represent her father in a house-building ceremony in Bangkok, and deposited nine kinds of semi-precious stones in the first hole (Achan Wipudh Sobhavong, personal communication, 21 May 1974).

17 Field notes, 15 December 1968.

Figure 7.3: The householder offers the gifts for the first hole.

Near the top of the *sao aek*, the ritual expert fastens a shoot from a banana plant and a young sugarcane. Later in the day, as soon as the first pole is raised in its final position, these plants will be set in the yard. If they thrive, it is interpreted as a good omen; if they die it bodes ill for the inhabitants of the new house.

Ornaments normally suitable for a woman (namely Nang Mai) are attached to this pole, for example, a golden belt, earrings, bracelets and a piece of hand-woven silken material. The 'second best' pole can also receive some ornaments, but these are of markedly less value than those of the *sao aek*. All the poles that will support the roof, including the first pole, are given a candle and incense, some gold leaf can be pressed near their top, and the ritual expert may perfume them. Finally he places a lotus leaf, a square of red cloth and a white piece of cloth on which he has drawn mystical diagrams on the top of each pole. If he wishes to simplify the ceremony, he may provide only the *sao aek* with these three layers. Diagrams often used for this purpose are the *yan trinisinghe* (ยันต์

Figure 7.4: The ritual specialist makes the offerings to the other holes.

Table 6: Names and domains of the nine different Phums.

Thai name	*Pali or Sanskrit Spelling*	*Realm*
Chayamongkhon ขัยมงคล	Jayamaṅgala	Houses, residences and different kinds of shops
Nakhonrat นครราช	Nagararāja	Camps, stockades, gates, doors, ladders, barracks
Thewathen or Thephen เทวเถร or เทเพน	Devathera or Devena	Stables, pens, barns, cowsheds
Chayasop ชัยสพ	Jayaśabaṇa	The rice storage hut and store-houses for other food supplies
Khonthap คนธรรพ์	Gandharva	Houses erected for festive ceremonies, bridal houses
Thammahora[a] ธรรมโหรา	Dharmahorā	Rice fields, open fields and mountain forests
Wayathat[b] วัยทัต	Vayadatta	Monasteries and other places of worship
Thammikarat ธรรมมิกราช	Dharmikarāja	Fruit gardens and vegetable plots
Thathara ทาษราชา	Dāṣadhārā	Brooks, lagoons, swamps, rivers and canals

a In Thongkham and Phit, ตำราพระภูมิ [The Manual for *Phra Phum*], p. 18, n. 4, it is said that some handbooks give the name Yawwaphaew (เยาวแผ้ว) for this Phuum.
b Urakhin, *op. cit.*, p. 288, gives Thewathen as an alternative for this Phum.

ตรีนิสิงเห),'three-in-lion diagram' (see Figure 7.5) and the *yan sipsong thit* (ยันต์ ๑๒ ทิศ) 'twelve-directions diagram', as drawn in Figure 7.6.

The builders can now put the supports in the foundation holes and fix the crossbeams on which later the floor will rest. As soon as the lower framework of the house stands firm, the *sao aek* is placed on its appropriate stilt, directly above where the first hole was dug. At the moment the *sao aek* is raised into the air, it is customary for one of the bystanders to raise his (or her) voice and chant the syllable '*Ho*', drawn out over a period of up to about five seconds, improvising on modulations and pitch. This is answered by all the other persons present with the shout: '*Hiw*'. This custom is also often observed during the *tham khwan* ceremonies of persons and at the beginning of a procession. Its entertaining character is an important aspect and different members of the audience try to elicit a great response by improving on the solo of a previous chanter. At the same time there seems to be a more serious undertone; it is

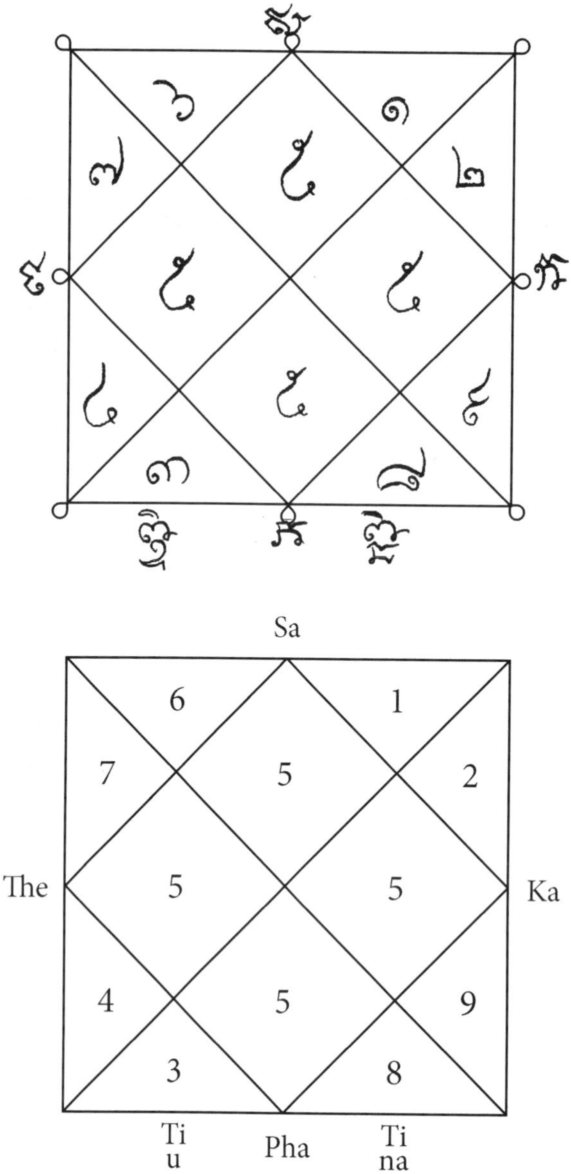

Figure 7.5. The *yan trinisinghe*, or 'three-in-lion' diagram.
Above, the Thai version as presented in Thawat, ตำราคัมภีเพชรัตนมหายันต์ [Manual of Gems of Yantras], B.E. 2509 (1966), p. 84. Beneath, a transliteration of the same yan is given.

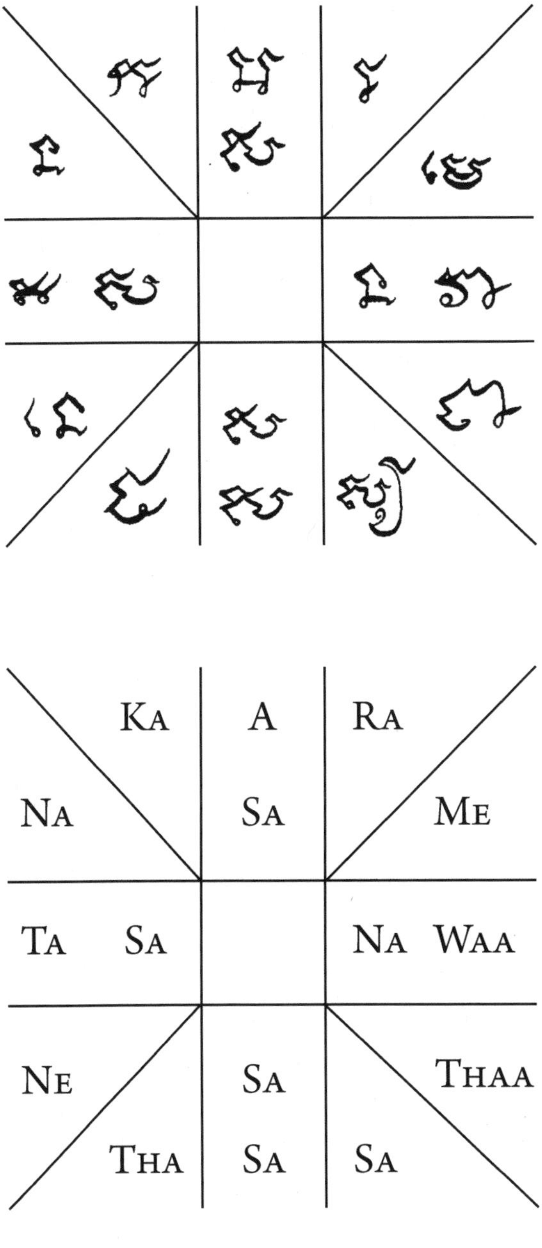

Figure 7.6. The *yan sipsongthit*, or 'twelve directions' diagram.
The top drawing in *Khom* letters, as in Thawat, *loc. cit*. In the lower version is the transcription.

a means by which the assembled community jointly focus their attention on the central person or object. It has possibly value as a means to scare away evil spirits. When this traditional chanting has been repeated several times, the construction of the building can proceed without further ceremonial.

A Closer Examination of the Different Powers Placated

During the ritual of building a new home, fragrant substances, food, liquor and valuables are offered to a multitude of different powers: Nang Mai, the Venerable Phum, Thorani, Krungphali, *Phaya* Nak and *Phra* In. Some of these powers need little explanation for the fact that they are included in the elaborate ritual, others require considerable research.

Nang Mai is the spirit of the wood; she can be heard crying and protesting during the time when a tree is felled. She can be expected to have become very unhappy during the cutting, transportation and fitting of the timber. The *tham khwan* ceremony of the *sao aek* and the other supporting poles is clearly intended to placate her.

The inclusion of Indra (Phra In) among the powers by a single informant seems to be incidental. Phra In is regarded as the most important king among the gods of the *Tāvatiṃsa* heaven. The fact that this god was mentioned can be seen as an indication that the elaborate ritual should not exclude any important power that may be involved in the breaking up of a plot of land.

The Venerable *Phum* derives his name from the word *bhūmi,* which stands in Sanskrit and Pali for earth, or soil. In Thailand he is often called *Phra Phum chaothi* (พระภูมเจ้าที); the epithet indicates that he is regarded as the owner of the land, the guardian spirit. The Venerable *Phum* is, however, not conceived of as a single personification of the earth: there are said to be several *Phra Phum,* each with his own realm. While the ordinary farmer usually knows only one of these *Phum* by name, to wit Chayamongkhon (ชัยมงคล), the guardian of houses, a ritual specialist should be able to recite several of them. Repeated questioning revealed that there are nine different Phum. This was confirmed in several Thai handbooks on customs.[18] The information is compiled in Table 6.

Chayamongkhon, who guards houses, is the best-known Phum in Thailand; he is the inhabitant of the *san Phra* Phum (ศาลพระภูมิ), the shrine in the grounds of nearly every home in central Thailand. The names of all nine appear to be of Indian origin. Only in some cases can a logical connection be shown between

18 Urakhin, ประเพณีไทย ฉบับพระราชครู [Thai Customs, the Rajaguru edition], pp. 287–8; Thongkham and Phit, ตำราพระภูมิ [The Manual for *Phra Phum*], pp. 18–9 and Thong, ตำราปลูกบ้านตั้งศาลพระภูมิ [Manual to Erect a House and the *San Phra Phum*], pp. 26–7.

the meaning of the name and the realm over which he is guardian. Thus the Gandharva, in later Indian epic poetry usually seen as a celestial musician and in Pali sometimes known in connection with the conception of children, is well placed as guardian of bridal houses and of houses erected especially for festive reasons. Similarly, the epithet *dhārā* in Dāṣadhārā seems appropriate, *dhārā* meaning 'stream, current'. Most names, however, cannot be traced to proper names in Indian lore.

In the third column of Table 6 the different realms of the *Phra* Phum are enumerated. It can be deduced from this column that in the Thai textbooks the total physical surroundings are divided into nine parts: they include the main traditional buildings and the major types of land and water. The division appears somewhat inelegant and artificial as, for example, in the sixth realm, where rice fields and forests are lumped together. In the expression *Phra* Phum, the word 'Phum' is not used by the Thais in its literal meaning, 'earth', but may better be translated as 'guardian' or 'tutelary spirit'.

According to a popular myth, all nine Venerable Phum are brothers, sons of King Thotsarat (ทศราช) and his wife Santhathuk (สันทาทุกข). Other names recorded for the king are Sokarat (โศกราช) and Kayathat (กายทัศ); the queen is also known as Sunanthathuk (สุนันทาทุกข) and Manthathukathibodi (มันทาทุกธิบดี).[19] All three Thai versions in the handbooks report that this king ruled over Krungphali (กรุงพาลี). Thotsarat divided his kingdom into nine realms and gave each of his sons an area to guard. These nine realms have been enumerated in Table 6.

The myth continues:

> Later, the Lord of Krungphali did not live in righteousness and this caused much unhappiness among the people. The *avatāra*[20] of *Phra* Narai[21] came down to earth in the form of a small Brahman who came to ask from the Lord of Krungphali of plot of land, only three steps wide, so that he could perform a ceremony. The Lord of Krungphali did not hesitate, gave his permission and to solemnize this he poured *udakadhārā*.[22]
>
> [. . .]

19 See ตำราพระภูมิ [The Manual for Phra Phum], p. 17, n. 1 and 2, and ประเพณีไทย ฉบับพระราชครู [Thai Customs, the Rajaguru edition], p. 287.

20 An incarnation of a deity on earth, used in particular in relation to Viṣṇu. (M. Monier-Williams, *A Sanskrit-English Dictionary*, p. 99.

21 Sanskrit: Nārāyaṇa. In Thailand this name is commonly used to indicate Viṣṇu.

22 *Udaka* is a ceremonial water-offering, whilst *dhārā* means 'stream' or 'flow'. This seems related to the Thai *kruat nam*, the custom of pouring some water after a religious ceremony.

As soon as the water flowed, *Phra* Narai changed himself into Narai with four heads, and he started to step. With a single stride the whole earth was covered, and the Lord of Krungphali had to leave and live in a forest in the Himaphan.[23] When he set out for this remote region he felt extremely sad and returned to beg for mercy. *Phra* Narai told him as solace: 'From now on, all humans ought to offer some food at the beginning of their ceremonies to *Phra* Phum, because he was the original owner of the earth. When this offer is performed, there will be happiness . . . '.[24]

When this myth was told in Wat Sanchao,[25] the mysterious visitor to King Thotsarat was reported to be one of the former Buddhas.[26] After the immensely powerful Buddha had taken his steps and covered all of the world, thus dispossessing Thotsarat, the nine sons begged the Buddha to give them a place of their own. The Buddha assented and allotted to each of the sons the guardianship of a realm. Chayamongkhon obtained the guardianship of all residences and homes, and therefore all persons who build a house must make an offering to this power.

The myth doubtlessly derives from the famous story of Viṣṇu's deception of the *daitya* Bali, known in Indian mythology since Vedic times.[27] Viṣṇu, in the form of a dwarf dispossesses the demon Bali of most of his realm, leaving Bali only the underworld Pātāla. In the Thai version it is Thotsarat, the king of Krungphali, who is tricked, in some versions by Viṣṇu, but sometimes by a Buddha. In all the Thai versions Thotsarat is the owner of Krungphali, which comprises the whole earth.

The name Thotsarat can be traced to *daitya rāja*, king of the *daitya*, and this is in accordance with the Indian prototype. Krungphali may be derived from the words *krung* (กรุง), 'city' and the proper name Bali. It appears that the *daitya* Bali of the original version became the *daitya* king of the city Bali. It is possible that the mistake originated in Cambodia where Bali is called Krŏṅ

23 Sanskrit: Himāvant, lit. having frost or snow, a name often used for the Himalayas.

24 Translated from Urakhin, *op. cit.*, pp. 287–289.

25 Somkhuan Suthichai, 15 November 1968.

26 In Theravada Buddhism usually five Buddhas previous to Siddhārtha Gautama are known, with their Pali names: Vipassin, Sikhī, Kakusandha, Konagamuni and Kassapa. Only the latter three were known to the learned informants of Wat Sanchao. Landon (*Siam in Transition*, p. 186) also mentions only the last three among the previous Buddhas.

27 J. Gonda, *Aspects of Early Viṣṇuism*, pp. 145–146.

Pali.[28] The Cambodian honorific title *krŏṅ* may have been misunderstood by the Thais as referring to *krung*, 'city', 'metropolis'.

Another name frequently encountered in the ritual of building a house is Thorani (ธรณี). This word is derived from the Sanskrit *dhāraṇī*, meaning 'earth, soil, ground', In Thailand the word Thorani is often used with the honorific title *Phra* or *mae* (แม่) 'mother'. *Mae* Thorani is known to many villagers in several different contexts. Most villagers have heard of Mother Thorani in connection with the story of the life of the Buddha. Before the Lord Buddha completed his awakening, he was assailed by the evil Māra and his army. In order to defeat Māra, the Buddha lowered his right hand to the earth and called the earth to witness of the positive deeds in previous existences (the hand-gesture known in Sanskrit as *bhūmisparśamudrā*). *Mae* Thorani appeared as the personification of the earth beneath the Buddha, in the form of a beautiful young lady. She testified for the Buddha by wringing from her tresses of hair the amount of water that had flowed from pouring water after meritorious deeds in Buddha's past existences. The amount of water was so immense that Māra's army was drowned in it.

There can be little doubt that the theme of a river of water flowing from tresses of hair is also based on an ancient Indian story. One of the names of Śiva is 'upholder of the river Ganges'. According to the myth, when the rush of the Ganges fell from heaven Śiva interrupted her course with his matted locks. In Buddhist lore this theme was taken up to illustrate the Buddha's greatness. Many Thai monasteries possess a series of 32 pictures of the life of the Buddha, and the scene that depicts the lady Thorani out of whose hair pours the water testifying to the immense amount of the Buddha's past deeds is always included.

In the same series of pictures from the life of the Buddha, *Phra* Thorani occurs a second time, namely as punisher of the jealous and evil Devadatta. After Devadatta had made attempts on the life of the Buddha and tried to cause dissent in the order of monks, Thorani opened up and the earth swallowed him. The picture usually shows Devadatta, greatly startled, falling through a crack in the surface of the earth. Probably connected with the story of Devadatta's punishment is the custom of *thorani san* (ธรณีสาร) (Sanskrit: *dhāraṇī śānti*), the appeasing of the earth.

The *thorani san* ceremony is held in order to prevent the earth from opening up under a person's feet, namely when something terrible of a deeply polluting

28 E. Porée-Maspero, 'Krŏṅ Pali et rites de la maison', *Anthropos*, Vol. 56, 1961.

character has happened to that person. Occasions which warrant an appeasing ceremony are: the birth of a child, which is considered polluting and may cause both the mother and the midwife to hold such a ceremony; the occurrence of a very threatening omen, such as when a vulture descends on the roof of a house; the occurrence of a very unlucky event: for example, if by accident a monk drops his begging bowl in front of a house the owner of the house should have the ceremony held; or the occurrence of a disgraceful polluting event: if a man, for example, falls head down in a heap of dung, he should avert further mishap by purifying himself through the *thorani san* ritual.

The ceremony itself consists of the sacralization of a bowl of water with very intensive and difficult chanting by a chapter of monks, and the rinsing of the object or person with this purifying liquid. This ceremony may be seen as another example of the mechanics of magical power in rural Thai Buddhism. The sacred Pali words, chanted by the sacred persons, can be used to undo the effects of bad luck and evil power. During the periods of fieldwork totalling more than 16 months, no such ceremony was held in the immediate surroundings of Wat Sanchao and evidence rests therefore purely on hearsay.

Mother Thorani is also known to some villagers because she may play a part in one of the stronger types of love magic. It has been noted in the previous chapter that a young man may scoop up some earth, rub it on his head and invoke the power of *Phra* Thorani to assist in the acquisition of a specific bride.

The distinction between *Phra* Phum and *Phra* Thorani is greater than their respective names would suggest. A dictionary gives for both a meaning of 'the earth'. In the previous pages it has become clear that to the villagers *Phra* Phum is a power who has a legendary claim on a certain part of the surroundings. It is a tutelary spirit, and the best-known Phum is the guardian of homes. Mother Thorani, on the other hand, is the personification of the earth itself. During the elaborate rituals of house-building each of these powers is therefore placated in their own right.

A last power encountered in the building ritual is the king of serpents, *Phaya* Nag, the big snake who is given food at every place where a hole will be dug in the earth and whose 'belly' has to be pierced when digging the first hole. The idea of a chthonic serpent is widespread in Asia. In the thirteenth century A.D., the inhabitants of Cambodia were reported to believe in the spirit of a nine-headed snake, the owner of the soil of the whole kingdom.[29] In Chinese geomancy, the principle of a dragon, visible in the outlines of mountains and

29 P. Pelliot (translator), *Mémoires sur les coutumes au Cambodge par Tcheou Ta-Kouan*, 1902, p. 23.

hills, is considered before selecting a place to build a house.[30] However, that the Thai customs regarding the serpent have been derived from India (probably indirectly via Cambodia) becomes most likely when we read:

> In India, just before a house is built, the astrologer will decide which foundation stone must be laid upon the head of the serpent upholding the world. The master mason sticks a stake into the appointed spot, so as to 'fasten down' the head of the earth-serpent firmly, and so avoid earthquakes.[31]

Other ritual details which indicate a link between ancient India and modern Thai house-building ceremonies can be found in the *Gṛhya sūtras*. To illustrate this, a quotation from a translation of the beginning of the fourth *kaṇḍika* of the third *kaṇḍa* of the *Pāraskara Gṛhya sūtra* is given:

1. Now the building of the house.
2. Let him have his house built on an auspicious day,
3. Into the pits (in which the posts shall be erected) he pours an oblation with (the words), 'To the steady one, the earth-demon, svāhā!'
4. He erects the posts.[32]

During the elementary ceremony, placation of religious powers is foremost, but there the non-human powers are not differentiated. During the elaborate rituals, it is ascertained that the various powers who may have a claim on the plot of land or who are otherwise closely associated with the house are placated comprehensively: the spirit who lives in the timber, the guardian spirit of the house, the *daitya* Bali, the chthonic serpent and the personification of the earth itself.

The Ritual Baskets

During the elaborate ceremonies, two ritual baskets are used: a triangular container on the *san phiangta* and a square one that is deposited in the most important foundation hole. Each of these containers usually possesses nine compartments in which various items of food are placed. Similar receptacles are used in the house-building ritual of rural Cambodia, and Mme Porée-Maspero provides an illustration of one of them.[33]

30 This aspect of geomancy is discussed, for example, in Eitel's *Principles of the Natural Science of the Chinese*, pp. 48–54.

31 Mircea Eliade, *Patterns in Comparative Religion*, 1958, p. 380.

32 Translation by H. Oldenberg, *The Gṛhya-Sūtras; Rules of Vedic Domestic Ceremonies*, Part 1, *Sacred Books of the East*, Vol. XXIX, p. 345.

33 Porée-Maspero, *op. cit.*, Plate V, opposite p. 584.

Again, it is possible to relate the use of these ritual baskets to ancient customs of the Indian subcontinent. Wales describes the Ceylonese foundation deposit box, which usually comprises nine compartments, and is filled with paraphernalia to ensure by magical means that the building has the properties of a microcosm.[34] Later in the same work he refers to the placing of these boxes as 'the usual custom when Hindu shrines were built'.[35] The division into nine symbolizes there the nine heavenly bodies (Sun, Moon, Mars, Mercury; Jupiter, Venus, Saturn, Rahu, and Ketu). The use of these multi-compartmented food containers in the elaborate house-building ritual of the Thais may therefore be regarded as another indication of the continuation of the Indian traditions in rural Thailand.

Avoiding Inauspiciousness

While choosing building materials, preparing the site, and conducted the rituals of house-building, those concerned should avoid many actions that are *apamongkhon* (อปมงคล) (Sanskrit: *apamaṅgala*), inauspicious. If these recommendations are not followed, automatically some harm will come to the inhabitants of the future house. If, for example, a house is inauspiciously oriented, it is believed that eye disease will strike its inhabitants. A possible reason for this belief can be seen in the idea that a wrongly oriented home obstructs and offends the sun (*khwang tawan* ขวางตะวัน). The sun, popularly called *tawan* (ตะวัน), probably derives its name from the words *ta* (ตา) 'eye' and *wan* (วัน) 'day', the 'eye of the day'. Being struck with eye disease seems a punishment consequent on offending the 'eye of the day'. Usually, however, the harmful effects of breaking a recommendation are vague and unspecific: bad luck will occur, or somebody in the house may become ill or suffer from nightmares.

When analysing specific rules on the avoidance of inauspicious behaviour, various aspects can be stressed. Some prescriptions provide clues concerning the evaluation of different directions and the different parts of the human body. The ordering of objects, persons, and activities in a horizontal and vertical plane often indicates such an evaluation. It is not by accident that the magical drawings are placed on the very top of the supporting poles.

Some recommendations for avoiding that which is *apamongkhon* can be traced to associations of semantic character. An example of such avoidance is the case where a type of wood is not used as timber primarily because the

34 H. G. Q. Wales, *Dvāravatī*, p. 56.

35 *Ibid.*, p. 57.

name evokes the thought of violent death. Similarly, the inauspiciousness of the western direction is affirmed in the ears of the Thais through reference to its common name *tawan tok,* literally: 'sunfall'. The opposite also occurs. Some Thais regard Friday as auspicious, because the name of this day, derived from the Sanskrit name for the planet Venus, śukra, is homophonous to the Thai word *suk* (สุข) 'happiness', derived from the Sanskrit or Pali *sukha.*

Other rules seem primarily related to a body of practical knowledge. When it is said that building a house is inauspicious from the sixth until the twelfth lunar month, this can be taken to mean that it is impractical, because the rainy season falls within this period and neighbouring farmers would be too busy to come to help with the construction. Removing mounds and tree trunks from the building site may displace jealous spirits, but at the same time it is technically sound to build on a smooth, level surface. Wood that is considered inauspicious for construction often proves to be just that which makes poor timber. Elements of practical wisdom, acquired in the past through trial and error, are thus handed down with religious validation.

The idea of a range of magical powers, from harmful and aggressive, through ambiguous to beneficial, has proven valuable at several instances in this chapter. It aided in explaining why during the elementary ritual for house-building there was a difference between the actions of a monk and those of a lay specialist. It also proved highly illuminative in the analysis of the *thorani san* ritual, where the positive power of the monks is needed to offset the effects of pollution.

CHAPTER VIII

THE PRECEPTS AND RITUAL

The Five Precepts[1]

The first mention of the five precepts (Pali: *pañca sikkhāpadāni* or *pañca sīlāni*) is found in the canonical texts of the early Buddhist tradition.[2] Originally these precepts seem to have been 'a sort of preliminary condition to any higher development after conforming to the teaching of the Buddha (*saraṇaṃ-gamana*) and as such often mentioned when a new follower is "officially" installed . . . .'[3] When Buddhism spread among different peoples, the use of the five precepts must have gradually diversified. In areas where Buddhism co-existed and competed with other religious disciplines, the link between the five precepts and official installation could well have remained or have become even more pronounced. In China, for example, up to the present time, the five precepts have been taken as a solemn lay ordination.[4] In regions where Buddhism has been the state religion for many centuries, such as Thailand, asking for the five precepts may no longer be linked with an initiation into the Buddhist faith. The farmers of Wat Sanchao are not initiated into Buddhism; they are born as Buddhists.

In rural Thailand, the ritual of asking to receive the five precepts is a common event. It is called: *kho sin ha* (ขอศีลห้า), or 'asking for the five commandments'. Any person who takes part in the usual communal religious services that are

1 A previous version of the discussion of the five precepts was presented during the 28th International Congress of Orientalists, Canberra, Australia, and later published under the title 'The Five Precepts and Ritual in Rural Thailand' in the *Journal of the Siam Society*, 1972, Part 1, pp. 333–43.

2 For example, *Majjhima-nikāya*, I, 345; I, 521; *Samyutta-nikāya*, II, 68; II, 167; *Aṅguttara-nikāya*, IV, 10, 97.

3 *Pali-English Dictionary*, Pali Text Society, p. 712.

4 H. Welch, *The Practice of Chinese Buddhism 1900–1950*, pp. 361–5.

held in private houses as well as in the monasteries will have the opportunity to receive the five precepts many times a year. During special days, when a major religious festival is celebrated, the precepts can be given as often as several times a day, each time at the beginning of a new ceremony. Whenever a chapter of monks and a group of laymen assemble for a religious service, the five precepts can be given, and the order of events at the commencement of the service seldom varies.

At the outset, before the monks arrive, laymen prepare the dais on which the members of the Sangha will sit, by placing an image of the Buddha at one end of the room, and arranging mats and cushions in a single file on the left hand of the image. When the monks enter, senior monks will sit nearest to the statue of the Buddha, junior monks furthest away, novices at the end. Where possible they will be seated in single file, facing the laymen. If there is not enough space for all monks to sit in single file, they will have to sit two or more layers deep. In these circumstances the seniority rule is often maintained only for the first row, those behind being seated wherever there is space.

As soon as the elders among the laymen feel that the ceremony should begin, a spokesman will call everyone to attention by asking three times in Pali in a clear voice:

> Mayaṃ bhante visuṃ visuṃ rakkhaṇatthāya tisaraṇena saha pañca sīlāni yācāma.

In the relatively rare cases where only one layman is present to ask for the precepts, as for example in the ceremony of leaving the Sangha (described in Chapter VI), the formula is changed to the singular: *mayaṃ* is changed into *ahaṃ* and *yācāma* into *yācāmi*.

Bareau, writing about Cambodian religious practices, translates this formula as: 'O vénérables, nous demandons chacun pour soi les cinq précepts avec le triple refuge dans un but de protection'.[5] The three words *visuṃ visuṃ rakkhaṇatthāya* are therefore translated by him as: 'Each person for himself, in order to obtain protection'. Presently, after considering some Thai data, I will suggest an alternative translation of these words.

In central Thailand the five precepts can also be asked for using the shorter formula: 'Mayaṃ bhante tisaraṇena saba pañca sīlāni yācāma'. Similar to the formula above, if only one layman is present, this text should be changed into the singular. The second formula seems to be often used in urban centres. It

5 A. Bareau, 'Idées sous-jacentes aux pratiques cultuelles bouddhiques', in *Beiträge zur Geistesgeschichte Indiens*, ed. by G. Oberhammer, 1968, p. 29.

is, for example, the only version given by Phaichoet.[6] This second formula for asking the precepts differs from the first one mentioned only in that it omits the words *visuṃ visuṃ rakkhaṇatthāya.*

At first sight it could be expected that the more compact formula is used in preference to the first, it being easier to memorize. However, in rural regions this second version is only seldom heard. On one occasion when a lay spokesman accidentally proceeded to ask for the precepts with the second formula, a senior monk interrupted him and made him recite the first, longer formula.[7] According to this monk, the difference between the two formulae is substantial. After a layman has received the precepts by way of the formula with *visuṃ visuṃ rakkhaṇatthāya* there will come a moment when he who received them breaks a precept. If that happens, he still retains four of the five precepts; when he breaks another precept, three remain, and so on. If, however, a person takes the precepts without the words *visuṃ visuṃ rakkhaṇatthāya* he will be in a position where, if he breaks a precept, all five are broken. The reason why the second formula should be avoided in most circumstances is therefore that it is believed that the promise resulting from the second formula is much more difficult to uphold than the promise resulting from the first formula. It is only in exceptional cases, when all laymen agree that the more solemn promise is warranted, as on the day that *kathiṇa* robes are presented when the Lenten season comes to an end (a ceremony that is described in Chapter IX), that the second formula should be used.[8]

In light of this Thai interpretation of the difference between the two methods of asking for the five precepts, a re-examination of the words *visuṃ visuṃ rakkhaṇatthāya* seems warranted. The words *visuṃ visuṃ* mean: 'each on his own', but can also be translated as: 'one by one, separately',[9] and *rakkhana* has, apart from the meaning 'keeping, protection, guarding', also a second meaning: 'observance' (especially with relation to the *sīla*).[10] Thus an alternative to Bareau's translation: 'each person on his own for the sake of protection', may be: 'for the sake of observing them, one by one, separately'. This alternative translation corresponds closely with the beliefs of the Thais. It would be interesting to know whether this alternative translation would also be the most proper one in

6 Phaichoet Thapthimthun, หนังสือสวดมนต์แปล [The book of Chants in Translation], B.E. 2510 (1967), p. 88.

7 July 7, 1968. Wat Kungkrathin.

8 Personal communication with the Venerable Phlik, Wat Sanchao.

9 *Pali-English Dictionary*, Pali Text Society, p. 640.

10 *Ibid.*, p. 560.

other regions where they use the formula with *visuṃ visuṃ rakkhaṇathāya* – in Cambodia, for example.

In answer to either formula, one of the senior monks takes up an ornamental fan, and holding it firmly with the right hand in such a manner that its oval shape hides his face from the lay people, recites in a clear voice three times the sentence: *namo tassa bhagavato arahato sammā sambuddhassa.* This sentence constitutes the introduction to many Buddhist ceremonies, and can be translated as 'Reverence to the Lord who is worthy and fully awakened'. Immediately after the opening sentence the Three Refuges follow, in which the members of the community promise to take refuge in the Buddha, the Dharma and the Sangha. The monk halts after each sentence in order to give the lay community occasion to repeat after him. When the Three Refuges have been said three times, the five precepts are prompted and repeated:

Pāṇātatipātā veramaṇī sikkhāpadaṃ samādiyāmi
Adinnādānā veramaṇī sikkhāpadaṃ samādiyāmi
Kāmesu micchācārā veramaṇī sikkhāpadaṃ samādiyāmi
Musāvādā veramaṇī sikkhāpadaṃ samādiyāmi
Surāmeraya majjapamādaṭṭhāna veramaṇī sikkhāpadaṃ samādiyāmi

These precepts have sometimes been translated rather carelessly and hurriedly as 'I refrain from killing, stealing, wrong sexual conduct, lying and alcohol'. However, in order to convey the importance of the exact meaning for the Thais, a more cumbersome translation should be given:

I undertake [to observe] the rule of abstinence from taking life
I undertake [to observe] the rule of abstinence from taking what is not given
I undertake [to observe] the rule of abstinence from wrong sensuous pleasure
I undertake [to observe] the rule of abstinence from false speech
I undertake [to observe] the rule of abstinence from intoxicants that cause a careless frame of mind.

The laymen sit in polite fashion, with the hands joined palm to palm in front of the chest, the feet folded towards the back. During this interplay between the one senior monk and all laymen who wish to adhere to the five precepts, the other monks on the dais are not involved. Some may still smoke or softly talk to one another in obvious display that this is a matter that does not concern monks who, after all, are committed to so many more precepts than the five being given. Similarly, on occasions when a few laymen of the congregation ask for the eight precepts (discussed in the second part of this chapter), those who do not wish to join them keep their hands down and wait until this ritual is over before joining in the other ceremonies.

When the fifth precept has been prompted and repeated, the monk who presides over this part of the ceremony solemnly recites from behind his fan the following Pali words, while all laymen show great attention:

> imāni pañca sikkhāpadāni sīlena sugatiṃ yanti sīlena
> bhogasampadā sīlena nibbutiṃ yanti tasmā sīlaṃ visodhaye.

This means: 'These five precepts lead with good behaviour to bliss, with good behaviour to wealth and success, they lead with good behaviour to happiness, therefore [I will] purify my behaviour'. Although virtually nobody in the audience is able to translate these words, most laymen realize that this is the moment when they really undertake to follow the precepts. Some will softly murmur some Pali words that are known to be auspicious, others will remain quiet. One informant explained that this was the moment during which he said to himself for how long he would try to observe the precepts, 'for a few minutes, a few hours, or even longer'.[11] At the last syllable of the word *visodhaye*, which is usually drawn out by the officiating monk, all laymen bow their heads and raise their joined hands to the forehead, and the monk may now lay down the ornamental fan. From this moment onwards, now that the laymen have committed themselves, the ceremony proper can proceed, whether it be a sermon, a consecration of water, or any other religious activity which requires the presence of both monks and laymen.

From the description of the occasions when and the manner in which the *pañca sīlāni* are given by a monk and received by laymen, it is clear that a function of the ritual of promising to adhere to these precepts is that of the preparation of the laymen for the ceremony which follows immediately. Receiving the five precepts may be seen as a ritual cleansing, a purification that enables the laymen to maximize the benefits of the ceremony. It brings the laymen out of their secular world into a religious sphere; it moves them temporarily into a state approaching that of sanctity.

Since the whole verbal exchange takes place in the Pali language it is justified to ask whether the farmers know the import of their promise to adhere to these rules. In theory the people could utter the sentences without

11 Somkhuan Suthichai, 3 November 1968.

realizing that they are committing themselves to precepts, or without being aware of what the precepts exactly entail. It will become clear that this is not the case.

As early as elementary school the meaning of each precept is taught, but it is not expected from a child that it understands the full implications of taking the five precepts. Most adult laymen, especially the men who have spent at least one Lenten season in the Sangha, can give a coherent picture of the precepts; they can enumerate them in Thai. Among the old people, those who consider themselves to be devout, men as well as women, can give elaborate exegetical details. It is interesting to note how complex a moral code can be extracted from the five precepts. The views of some older people on this subject, collected at different stages of the fieldwork, can be summarized as follows:

1. The first precept is broken when life is taken: human life as well as animal life. Slapping a mosquito, or killing a germ in an egg by boiling it are certain breaches of this first rule. Torture or lesser forms of inflicting pain are also considered to fall under this rule by those who are most knowledgeable on ritual affairs.
2. Any form of stealing, whether it be taking goods against the rightful owner's wish, or borrowing without taking the trouble to ask the owner's consent consists of a breach of the second precept. It is generally conceived that gambling falls under this rule.
3. The third precept does not only forbid the obvious breaches of proper conduct like adultery, incest and rape, but also forbids acts showing intention to behave in a licentious manner, such as flirting with a woman who is already married or promised to another person.
4. The fourth precept is very easily broken. Abstinence from false speech is seen to cover a wide range of untruths, like exaggeration, insinuation, abuse, gossip, unrestrained laughter, deceitful speech, joking, and banter. This precept can often be broken together with another precept; a breach of promise involves the second precept and the fourth, flirting with a married woman involves the third and fourth.
5. The last of the *pañca sīlāni* forbids the use of alcoholic beverages, and all other stupefying substances like opium and drugs, unless taken for medicinal purposes.

The five precepts are thus interpreted much more widely than their literal translation would suggest. They have been built out to form the whole system of morality. Such views underlie much of the famous book *Benchasin Benchatham* by the late Supreme Patriarch Prince Vajirañāṇavarorasa,[12] which was written as a textbook for primary school, but which at present is widely used as a textbook for the *Naktham* III examinations, especially by lay devotees.[13]

A well-known story illustrates the evils of the fifth precept, and at the same time throws light upon the attitudes towards the *pañca sīlāni* as a whole:

> Once upon a time there was a man who was thoroughly good; he lived an exemplary life. One day he was challenged to break just one precept for once. The good man thought: 'The first precept I cannot break, having great compassion for all beings. With regard to stealing, no, I cannot take what is not mine, that would hurt the owner's feelings. The third precept is out of the question, as it would upset my wife whom I dearly love. As to false speech, I abhor it. However, the fifth precept does not harm anybody but my own brain, so if I have to break a precept, I had better take some alcoholic beverage'. The man took a bottle, and pouring himself a drink he felt rather curious as to the taste of this forbidden liquor. When he drank the first glassful he considered it rather innocent and tasted a bit more .... When the bottle was empty he noticed his neighbour's wife looking amazed at his behaviour. He staggered towards her and tried to rape her. When her husband came to help, he first denied that he had touched her, a fight resulted and his neighbour was killed. In order to escape revenge, our 'good' man had to flee and become a robber. Thus breaking the 'innocuous' fifth precept led to the breaking of them all.[14]

While it seems plausible to draw the conclusion that the farmers are usually well aware of the import of the promise to adhere to the five precepts, the question immediately arising is whether they do try to behave according to these rules, that is, whether the *pañca sīlāni* exercise a marked influence on Thai behaviour.

A crime like murder, armed robbery or rape certainly involves breaking a precept. If it were possible to prove that crimes involving breaking one or more of the precepts occur less among Buddhists than among non-Buddhists, then this could be an indication towards supposing that observance of the five precepts markedly influences behaviour. Lack of reliable statistical data regarding crime in rural areas precludes such a line of investigation. Moreover,

12 This work has been translated under the title *Five Precepts and Five Ennoblers,* 1963.

13 See the 'Foreword' to *Five Precepts and Five Ennoblers* by Phra Sāsanasophon.

14 Translated and paraphrased after a personal communication with Somkhuan Suthichai, Wat Sanchao.

even if such data were available, it would need substantial in-depth interviewing with criminals and would-be criminals in order to assess to what extent people abstained from committing a crime through fear of breaking a precept, and to what extent other considerations, such as fear of social sanctions play a role. It is necessary, therefore, to investigate other aspects of the situation.

In order to observe whether people in rural Thailand try to adhere to the five precepts, behaviour that unquestionably implies breaking a precept, but that does not automatically carry punishment by law, can be investigated. Examples of such behaviour include gossip, mild deceit, drinking alcoholic beverages and killing animals.

A community without gossip is almost beyond imagination. Talking about other people, especially about aspects that these others would like to remain not generally known is a habit in which many people occasionally indulge. On no occasion was it noticed that a layman refrained from talking about other laymen because he was afraid to break one of the five precepts. It would have been unfortunate for the researcher if gossip had not been available to provide him with illuminating case histories of misconduct. A notable exception is the reticence of many laymen to speak ill about a member of the Sangha. Although the conduct of monks in general can be the subject of conversation, people generally refrain from discussing the evil deeds of a monk. This restraint, however, seems to be part of the polite behaviour of ritually inferior towards ritually superior.

Mild forms of deceit are also part of daily life. A joke played upon an unsuspecting victim is appreciated by all (except perhaps by the victim); and whenever goods are sold or traded, some kind of deceit is almost unavoidable in order to make a profit. These mild forms of deceit are readily engaged in and, when questioned about the morality of such action, people will readily admit that they contravene a precept, but this is usually followed by the stipulation that a farmer cannot live naturally without breaking precepts.

Alcoholic beverages are sold openly, under government monopoly and for festivals a home-brew is welcome. Strong drink can be consumed in all public cafes and restaurants and drunken people are no rare sight. Unless an adult male guest has medical grounds upon which to appeal, it would be insulting to the host if he declined to share in a proffered drink. To make the appeal that one tries to observe the precepts would be bad taste indeed. A person who adheres so strictly to precepts should not mingle in a festive crowd. During some of the big community ceremonies in rural areas, liquor is drunk by many laymen, even within the precincts of the monasteries, and many a procession would not be so gay and spontaneous without the stimulant of intoxicating beverages. The farmers thus seem to break precepts frequently and without embarrassment.

Similarly, behaviour towards mosquitoes is merciless, and the man who can afford insecticide will not hesitate to spray a crop, thus killing countless small living creatures in flagrant contravention of the first precept. However, behaviour with regard to the killing of animals that are bigger than insects is often accompanied by a marked discomposure. A squirrel will be killed in a trap because it devours the best fruit, a poisonous snake will be beaten to death, rats that steal the provisions are disposed of similarly, but in all these cases the careful observer may notice that there is uneasiness about these acts of violence. The squirrel that is trapped, it may be argued by the farmer, does not meet with its death directly through human action; it has at least had the chance to avoid the lethal trap. Sometimes a farmer will evade the act of chopping a fish to death by letting it die out of the water or by ordering a servant to do so. When fish or a chicken has to be killed for domestic consumption, it will be done out of sight, well away from the house, so that even the spirits of the ancestors cannot see this act.

An illustration of the uncomfortable awareness of the evils of killing animals is the following record of a spontaneous conversation between the researcher (at the time he was still ordained as Buddhist monk) and a layman:

> Today, standing on one of the jetties waiting for a taxi-boat, a stranger struck up a conversation. At one point I asked him his profession at which he answered: 'I work on the water'. Mistakenly I thought he was a sailor, and consequently demanded to know whether he was attached to the navy or worked on a merchant vessel. Rather embarrassed the old man explained that he was a fisherman, but he had avoided saying so 'because it is not nice to tell a monk that you live by killing fish'.[15]

Possibly the evasion would not have been used in conversation with other monks. The fact that the monk in question was a Westerner may have caused the old man to be particularly deferential. However special the circumstances, the fact remains that the man, when choosing to be extra polite, used a euphemism to describe the profession of fisherman.

Animals bigger than chickens, like pigs and buffaloes, are usually not slaughtered by farmers. Sometimes, when draught animals are too old to work, they are permitted to remain on the farm until they die a natural death,

15 From field notes, Wat Sanchao, September 1968.

but often these big animals are sold to professional butchers. Most farmers shudder to think about the store of bad karma a butcher accumulates during his lifetime.

With regard to the question whether Thai people seem intent upon trying to evade breaking a precept, it must therefore be concluded that around Wat Sanchao this *appears to be the case* only with regard to the first precept. People engage freely in other acts against which there is no legal sanction and which obviously imply breaking a precept. The general attitude seems to be that full adherence to the five precepts is not compatible with ordinary daily life and that people should not be sanctimonious.

The five precepts, while providing an ideal code of behaviour, can be acted upon or ignored as is expedient. There are people in Thailand who do commit themselves fully to the *pañca sīlāni*. There are people, for example, who take a solemn oath (*patiyan* ปฏิญาณ) to observe these five precepts. Such people will be assured of an exceptionally good rebirth and all devout farmers would gladly follow their example if they were able to. However, farmers can seldom hope to imitate such people because, in order to follow the precepts properly, a person should be so wealthy that he can shelter himself from society so that no impure action or harmful thought will reach him. Realistically the farmer readily admits that, within a few hours after receiving the five precepts, he will have broken some of them. This realization may well be a reason for the preference in rural areas for using the formula containing the words *visuṃ visuṃ rakkhaṇathāya* when asking for the *pañca sīlāni*.

Other people who on ordinary days take great pains to follow the five precepts (and on special days as many as eight precepts) are the female religious virtuosi, the *mae chi* (แม่ชี), women who shave their heads, who dress in white robes and usually live a secluded life in the shadow of a monastery.[16] Again, a woman must be rather wealthy to be able to afford such a retreat from society.

The marked exception in the easy-going attitude towards minor offences against the five precepts is the behaviour with respect to killing animals bigger than insects. In light of the reasoning above, it can be hypothesized that it is not for fear of breaking a precept that people refrain from killing animals or are

16 There is a tendency in the literature to describe the white-robed women as people who continuously follow the eight precepts (for example, Bunnag, *Buddhist Monk, Buddhist Layman*, p. 88). This is not borne out by data from around Ratburi. Whilst the white-robed women do join the other devout laymen on special days to observe the eight precepts for one day and one night, on ordinary days they try to adhere to the five precepts, a task that is difficult enough when one takes the strict interpretation of the Thais into account.

rather embarrassed about doing so. After all, there is no apparent reluctance to break other precepts. The main reason why the killing of animals is surrounded with manifestations of guilt feelings appears to lie in the belief in the *karmic* repercussions of the killing act. The sanctions are clearly outlined in Buddhist lore, and they can hardly be ignored. The popular Jātaka stories abound with examples of extreme suffering that is ascribed to the fact that the person who is afflicted had in a former life killed an animal. Other stories deal with the great happiness that results from saving an animal from death. The axioms regarding rebirth, which do not exclude the possibility that a human can be reborn in the form of an animal such as chicken, or a dog, certainly add to the uneasiness with regard to the act of killing animals of that size.

Moreover, most adult Thais will be aware of the story of *Phra* Malai, the famous monk who, on the way to visit Indra, has the opportunity to inspect the different kinds of hell.[17] This tale is sometimes recited as part of the elaborate death ceremonies. Most Thais will know about *Phra* Malai through observing pictures in monasteries, because the details of the horrors seen by *Phra* Malai in the seven different hells are a recurrent theme in pictorial art. One of the seven hells is reserved solely for people who had killed animals, and this hell is depicted as a place where creatures with human bodies but heads that resemble those of buffaloes, cats, dogs, chickens, and ducks, suffer agonising torture.

Therefore it is plausible that fear of *karmic* ill-effects, rather than fear of breaking a precept, is responsible for the attitudes towards the first precept. The fact that farmers are often obliged to kill animals as part of the circumstances in rural areas can be seen as a source of guilt feelings. There are farmers who feel that they will never be able to escape their poor lot, who sense that they will probably never be reborn in better circumstances, because the farmer's way of life includes killing animals.

While the five precepts were originally probably intended to be given to a layman in order to initiate him into the Buddhist faith, the initiation aspect was bound to become less important in a country like Thailand, where since time immemorial most inhabitants have been born Buddhists. There is one instance where the initiation aspect of the ritual of asking for the five precepts seems to be recognizable. This is immediately after a man has left the Sangha, described in Chapter VI.

17 The theme of a visit of a mortal being to the heaven of Indra is quite common in Buddhist literature (see: Malalasekera, *Dictionary of Pali Proper Names*, Vol. II, p. 963). The poem of Malai (Pali: Maleyya) was written in the reign of king Boromokot (1733–1758) by the king's eldest son.

It has been observed that the ritual of asking for the five precepts occurs usually at the commencement of a ceremony whenever a group of monks and a group of laymen assemble. This ritual contains many signs pointing to the idea that it can be interpreted as a rite of purification, performed to prepare the laymen for the ceremony at hand. Exegetical details show clearly that each precept is interpreted as widely as possible. The emphasis on the idea that the five precepts are very difficult and hard to follow corresponds to a stress on the sacredness of the moment of taking the promise to adhere to the precepts; its function can be seen to be to accentuate the cleansing qualities of the ritual.

While the scope and meaning of the *pañca sīlāni* are aggrandized for ritual purposes, the precepts cannot retain much practical meaning for daily non-ceremonial life. Therefore, statements that the five precepts are 'the minimum duties of a householder',[18] or 'the moral code of Buddhism',[19] while in an ideal sense they are true, are not applicable for rural Thailand without major qualification.

The Eight Precepts

Just before sunrise, every *wan phra,* some elderly people leave their homes intending to adhere to the eight precepts for a period of one day and one night. They proceed towards the monastery, carrying a basket laden with ritual paraphernalia such as candles and incense sticks, with food to be offered to the monks, with provisions intended for their own consumption including food as well as a day's supply of areca nuts and betel leaves, and often also with a mat and a mosquito net. After they have given their contributions to the monks' meal and received their shares of beneficial *karma* via the chanting of all members of the Sangha who are present, these laymen gather in the *bot.* In this building they spread mats on the floor and arrange to sit in such a manner that they face the main Buddha image. The men sit in front with their *phakhaoma* arranged over the left shoulder as befits a solemn occasion, the women form the rows behind. When one of the men present is superior to all others in knowledge of ceremonial and in age, he is given the role of leader in this ritual. When several candidates for this role are present, the leadership may be shared. For example, one man will then lead the Pali chanting, another the singing in Thai, while a third may ask for the eight precepts. Like all rituals in front of the Buddha image, the ceremony begins with the lighting of candles and incense.

18 E. Conze, *Buddhism, Its Essence and Development,* 1951, p. 86.

19 C. Humphreys, *Buddhism,* 1962, p. 73.

Outside the Lenten season: the elementary ceremony

If the period of the year happens to be outside the Lenten period, the ritual of taking the eight precepts is devoid of most elaborations. At first the laymen chant a few Pali verses that are virtually identical with some of the texts that monks chant in the morning. Following these sacred words, the laymen usually chant a Thai translation. When the vernacular tongue is used, a style of chanting is chosen that is quite different from that in which Pali is recited. Meanwhile the monks will have terminated their first morning meal, and the abbot or his deputy goes to the *bot* in order to take up his part in the ceremony. The monk prostrates three times before the Buddha image and sits down on the dais reserved for the members of the Sangha, facing the laymen. Shortly afterwards, a spokesman for the laity formulates his request:

> mayaṃ bhante tisaraṇena saha aṭṭhanga samannāgata uposatha yācāma.

When only one lay person is present to receive the precepts, the formula has to be changed from plural to singular, thus, as with the request for the five precepts, *mayaṃ* has to be changed to *ahaṃ* and *yācāma* to *yācāmi*. The words *aṭṭhanga samannāgata uposatha* are typically used in the canon to indicate the eight precepts[20] and the formula can therefore be translated as: 'Sir, we ask for the Three Refuges with the Eight Precepts.'

The preliminary sentences prompted by the monk and repeated by the lay people are identical with those in the ritual of the five precepts mentioned earlier in this chapter. When the time arrives for the eight precepts to be prompted, the monk recites solemnly, leaving a short pause after each sentence in which the laymen can repeat:

> Pānātipātā veramaṇī sikkhāpadaṃ samādiyāmi
> Adinnādānā veramaṇī sikkhāpadaṃ samādiyāmi
> Abrahmacariyā veramaṇī sikkhāpadaṃ samādiyāmi
> Musāvādā veramaṇī sikkhāpadaṃ samādiyāmi
> Surāmeraya majjapamādaṭṭhāna veramaṇī sikkhāpadaṃ samādiyāmi
> Vikālabhojana veramaṇī sikkhāpadaṃ samādiyāmi
> Naccagītavāditavisūkadassanā mālāgandhavilepanadhāraṇana-
> vibhusanatthana veramaṇī sikkhāpadaṃ samādiyāmi
> Uccāsayanā mahāsayanā veramaṇī sikkhāpadaṃ samādiyāmi.

Most of the devout laymen who participate in this ceremony are well aware of the exact translation of these sentences:

20 *Pali-English Dictionary*, Pali Text Society, pp. 712–3.

I undertake [to observe] the rule of abstinence from taking life
I undertake [to observe] the rule of abstinence from taking what is not given
I undertake [to observe] the rule of abstinence from unchastity
I undertake (to observe) the rule of abstinence from false speech
I undertake [to observe] the rule of abstinence from intoxicants which cause a careless frame of mind
I undertake [to observe] the rule of abstinence from taking food at the wrong time
I undertake [to observe] the rule of abstinence from dancing, music, visiting shows, flowers, make-up, the wearing of ornaments and decorations
I undertake [to observe] the rule of abstinence from a tall, high sleeping place.

There are two aspects of this ritual that are often not mentioned in the literature dealing with the eight precepts. In the first place it cannot be said that the eight precepts are simply the five plus three additional rules, for the wording and the meaning of the third rule of the eight precepts differs from the third rule in the five precepts. Whilst ordinary laymen abstain from wrong sensuous pleasure (*kāmesu micchācārā*), the person who takes the eight precepts promises to be chaste. The second aspect that is not generally known is that the laymen engage to observe their eight precepts for a definite period of time. Immediately after the eighth rule they repeat the following sentence:

Imaṃ aṭṭhanga samannāgataṃ buddhapaññattaṃ uposathaṃ imañ ca rattiṃ imañ ca divasaṃ sammadeva abhirakkhitu samādiyāmi.

Translated:

I undertake to observe in harmony during this day and this night these eight precepts that have been designed by the wisdom of the Buddha.

A final, solemnizing sentence pronounced by the monk is not repeated by the laymen:

imāni aṭṭhasikkhāpadāni uposatha sīlavasena sādhukaṃ katvā appamādena rakkhitappāni sīlena sugatiṃ yanti sīlena bhogasampadā sīlena nibbutiṃ yanti tasmā sīlaṃ visodhaye.

These words may be translated as:

> Having performed these eight precepts with controlled behaviour, that are to be kept with vigilance; they lead, with good behaviour to bliss, with good behaviour to wealth and success, they lead with good behaviour to happiness, therefore (I will) purify my behaviour.

Each of the laymen then donates some money; in Wat Sanchao during the 1960s this was a minute amount: it often varied between one *salueng* and one *baht* per person. These gifts are collected by the lay leader who counts the total, places it on a tray together with some flowers, incense and candles, and presents the tray to the monk. Whilst presenting it he mentions the exact amount in a Thai formula that states that the laymen have collected money so that the monk may buy a new robe or a new begging bowl (this wording has been explained in Chapter V). The monk does not touch the money, for that would bring demerit on him and take some of the auspiciousness of the ritual away, but he indicates his acceptance by chanting some blessings in Pali. Later in the day one of the laymen may place the money in an envelope and take it to the cell of the monk to hand it over.

From the moment that the Pali blessings have been recited, the ritual of taking the eight vows has terminated, and it is proper to refer to the men as *ubasok*, (อุบาสก) and the women as *ubasika* (อุบาสิกา), titles derived from Pali meaning 'devout layman' and 'devout lay woman' respectively. Quite often these terms are used to indicate the people who are in the process of adhering to the eight precepts, and in rural areas lay people return to their previous status when the period of one day and one night has elapsed and when they are automatically released from their undertakings.

The monk who prompted the precepts often remains for a while in the temple, discussing religious subjects with the people in a relaxed manner until it is time to partake of the last meal of the day. While the monks eat their second morning meal, the *ubasok* and *ubasika* also use this last opportunity of the day to take solid food. These laymen can eat in any place they choose, under a veranda or in one of the meeting halls, but when they select the building where the monks take their meal, they must sit lower than the monks. All afternoon the laymen tend to stay in the *bot* or any other cool place where they can remain undisturbed. At night they sleep in one of the gathering halls and at sunrise they may return home, having fulfilled their promise to observe the eight precepts for a period of one day and one night.

During the Lenten season: elaborate ceremonies

During the religiously intensive period of the year, taking the eight precepts is a more solemn and elaborate ritual, mainly because the number of persons involved is much greater and also because many laymen are present to observe while the eight precepts are requested. While outside the Lenten period relatively few persons become *ubasok* or *ubasika,* as soon as *phansa* draws near, so many people wish to adhere to the eight precepts that the temple is sometimes hardly spacious enough to hold them all. For Wat Sanchao this is illustrated in Table 7. From this table it can be seen that during the eight days of religious observance preceding the Lenten season an average of 6.4 persons took the eight precepts, while the average during *phansa* was 34.7 persons. Although there are no reliable statistical data regarding the number of people who take the eight precepts in other communities, there is no reason why the picture should be different from that obtained in Wat Sanchao in 1968.

In order to understand the difference between taking the eight precepts during *phansa* and following this ritual outside the Lenten season, it is necessary to examine certain economic aspects of the relationship between monks and laymen. For a regular food supply, the inhabitants of a monastery depend on donations from laymen. Many members of the lay community are aware of the fact that it would reflect unfavourably on themselves if there were a shortage of victuals in the monastery. Every day the food supply must reach the monastery early in the morning because, if the monks and novices are not fed properly before noon, they are obliged by their code of life to go hungry until the following day.

The ordinary way in which provisions reach the precincts of the monastery is via the 'begging' of the monks. During most mornings of the year, monks, novices and *dek wat* walk past the houses of the laymen, carrying containers in which food offerings can be placed.

If a householder invites a chapter of monks to perform a ceremony during the morning hours, he knows that the invited monks, by accepting the invitation, may be prevented from collecting food early in the day, or that they will not be able to join the communal meal at their monastery. It is imperative, therefore, that the layman who arranges for a group of monks to chant Pali texts be clear in his arrangements so as to ensure that the food supply to the monastery will not be adversely affected. When he issues the invitation to the abbot and to the individual monks he wishes to join the chapter, he should specify whether the monks should join the begging round as usual, or whether there will be a special food donation in the house, during which ample provisions will be offered that can be taken back to the monastery. In the latter event, begging bowls and other food containers are brought along by *dek wat* and these will be filled during the recitation of the sacred texts. Part of this food will be eaten by the monks while they are in the house; the remainder is taken back to the monastery, sometimes to be included in the second morning meal of the members of the Sangha, but, if it is already past midday by the time the monks return, in any case to feed the *dek wat* and the animals that roam around freely in the monastery grounds.

Food-giving is therefore often part of the ordinary proceedings when monks perform rituals in the houses of lay persons. It seems to be little known in the literature that there exists in Thailand a special elaborate ceremony in which the donation of food is performed in such a manner that a much greater amount of beneficial *karma* is accrued than in ordinary circumstances. This ceremony is often referred to in Wat Sanchao with the rather general term *thawai sangkhathan* (ถวายสงฆทาน). The word *thawai* means 'to present, to donate' and *sangkhathan* can be traced to Sangha and *dāna*, so that the whole expression can thus be translated as 'to present a gift to the Sangha'.

Because the ritual centres around a meal, and monks are not allowed to eat after noon, *thawai sangkhathan* always takes place in the morning. The minimum number of monks present is four,[21] because this is the minimum number of monks required to make a valid legal decision in the name of the Sangha.[22] As soon as all the monks taking part are seated and the five precepts have been recited, a layman who knows the proper formula offers the food gifts amassed in front of the monks with the words:

> Imāni mayaṃ bhante bhattāni saparivārāni bhikkhusaṃghassa oṇojayāma; sādhu no bhante bhikkhusaṃgho imaani bhattāni saparivārāni paṭigganhātu amhākaṃ dīgharattaṃ hitāya sukhāya.

This is the standard formula for *thawai sangkhathan*[23] that can be translated as follows:

> We give as a present these foods and paraphernalia to the community of monks; may the community of monks accept from us these foods and paraphernalia with the word *sādhu* to our enduring benefit and happiness.

21 Bunrot Morarueang, ประเพณีทั่วโลก [Customs World-wide], 1968, p. 25.

22 The number of four monks is also the quorum needed to ordain a new monk, to chant the full version of the *Pāṭimokkha*, to expel a monk from the Sangha, or to receive *kathin* robes.

23 This formula is recorded at the end of *Suatmon Chet Tamnan*, p. 81, and in Somchit Ekayothin (ed.), หนังสือคู่มือ วิธีรักษาอุโบสถและทำวัตร์เช้า, เย็น, กับสมบัติขอวอุบาสก อุบาสิกา [Handbook for Keeping Holy Days, Morning and Afternoon and the Conduct of Devout Men and Women], B.E. 2510 (1967), pp. 116–7.

Table 7: Number of people receiving the eight precepts in Wat Sanchao from 11 May 1968 until 28 October 1968

Date	Men	Women	Total	Remarks
May 11	3	3	6	
May 19	2	2	4	
May 26	2	4	6	
June 3	2	2	4	
June 10	2	7	9	
June 18	2	5	7	
June 24	2	6	8	
July 2	2	5	7	
July 9	20	29	49	This, the fifteenth day of the waxing half of the eighth lunar month, was the beginning of *phansa*.
July 17	—	—	29	A dash indicates that the fieldwork data do not provide an exact number.
July 24	—	—	27	
August 1	—	—	22	
August 8	10	16	26	
August 16	13	16	29	
August 22	13	24	37	The contingent of *ubasika* was boosted by the visit of eight women from another community.
August 30	14	15	29	
September 6	—	—	30	The fifteenth day of the waxing half of the eleventh lunar month, the end of *phansa*.
September 14	—	—	28	
September 21	20	23	43	
September 29	17	28	45	
October 6	—	—	59	
October 14	—	—	45	Although phansa is over, the religious fervour lasts until the *kathin* festival.
October 21	—	—	10	
October 28	—	—	11	

The leader of the chapter of monks questions his fellow monks in Pali whether or not they can accept the gifts, and then asks them to indicate their agreement. Invariably all monks answer in unison: 'Sādhu' (the Pali exclamation that indicates approval).

The key to understanding the difference between an ordinary food offering and a *thawai sangkhathan* lies in the expression 'foods and paraphernalia'. It is understood by all parties concerned that everything used during the meal of the monks is included in the gift: the plates from which they eat, the vessels that contain food, glasses, cutlery, even the mats on which the monks sit, and the spittoons used. It is customary that the person who performs a private *thawai sangkhathan* at home purchases these goods especially for this occasion and takes care that only things of very good quality are used. This ritual can therefore represent a great expenditure. It is believed that the merit resulting from this ritual may greatly increase the life span of a person, and consequently it is mostly older people who are interested in performing it.

Apart from such a relatively rare, privately held *thawai sangkhathan* the community can also perform this ceremony to present food and paraphernalia in the monastery, and in central Thailand it is a regularly recurring ritual on *wan phra* during the Lenten season. On these days, the monks do not have to collect food. Instead, early in the morning, laymen come to the monastery in great numbers, laden with food so that they can take part in a collective *thawai sangkhathan*. This differs from the 'private' ritual in several respects.

Firstly, there is no main sponsor for the service in the monastery; anybody can bring food and join in the beneficial *karma* that results. In the second place, the ceremony is not held in a private home, but takes place as part of the rituals of *wan phra* in the communal monastery. Often the most spacious assembly hall is needed to house all participants. Thirdly, the 'paraphernalia' that are used during the ceremony and donated with the food to the Sangha are not especially purchased for this occasion, but are borrowed from the monastery stores itself. Thus the expense for the lay participants amounts to nothing more than the food donated. The communal *thawai sangkhathan* does not bring an individual the massive dose of merit he gains from the privately sponsored ritual. The use of the *thawai sangkhathan* formula is, however, not merely a means to accentuate an atmosphere of solemnity. It may be seen as a mixing of the wealth that has been accumulated in the communal monastery store with that of the present. The moment when the monks accept the accumulated food and the many objects in and on which this is displayed may be seen as a celebration of the strength and benefits of communality.

The amount of food donated on such occasions may be staggering. The abbot usually delegates an experienced monk to arrange and supervise the distribution of all the left-over foods. He will set aside some trays for members of the Sangha for their second meal, just before noon, some for the *dek wat* and reserve a portion for the animals of the monastery. The remainder is redistributed; some may be given to the poorest families, other bits to the devout laymen who stay behind to talk to the monks when most of the congregation has returned home.

The elaborate ceremonies of *wan phra* continue with a solemn chanting service of the monks in the *bot*. The texts recited are the same that are practised on ordinary days during the Lenten season, but the inexperienced monks will often feel handicapped because they are not allowed to read from the *Suatmon Chet Tamnan* while laymen attend the chanting. The laymen who fill the lower floor areas of the temple consist of those who will soon undertake to follow the eight precepts and some others who grasp the opportunity to gain beneficial *karma* by attending the morning ceremonies as a whole.

After the recitation of Pali texts, one of the monks ascends the ornate preaching chair, placing himself on an even higher level than his fellow monks. As soon as the is properly and comfortably installed among the cushions, the spokesman for the devout laymen formally requests the eight precepts, upon which the monk in the preaching chair takes up a fan and prompts the appropriate Pali words. This is followed by the formal reading of a sermon from a palm leaf text during which all monks and laymen keep up a polite attitude, with the hands raised palm to palm in front of the chest. A considerable amount of money is collected from the lay members of the congregation and this is officially presented as soon as the sermon has ended. The morning service ends with the *kruat nam* ritual and many of the laity return home, leaving the *ubasok* and *ubasika* in the monastery precincts.

Monks, novices and those who adhere to the eight precepts now have a last opportunity to take some solid food before the fast begins in the afternoon. During *phansa* the lay people will not be able to occupy the *bot* throughout the afternoon as the monks require this building for their chanting and meditation and often for the recitation of the *Pāṭimokkha*. Therefore, the group of *ubasok* and *ubasika* gather in one of the other halls. Early in the afternoon they can rest and relax a little, but after two o'clock their leaders usually decide to begin a lay chanting session. Their recitation may coincide with the rituals of the monks in the *bot*. If the hall in which the laymen are gathered is situated close by the temple the two groups can clearly hear each other: from the *bot* the well-trained voices of the monks and novices resound, while independently from the hall other texts are recited by the less skilled voices of the laymen. Later in the afternoon each group, following separate timetables, engages upon a period of meditation and closes the ritual with *kruat nam*. The texts chanted by the laymen are clearly based on the monks' *Suatmon Chet Tamnan*,[24] but it is notable that the lay people regularly chant the Thai translation immediately after having recited the Pali version.

In the evening the hall of the laymen becomes a centre of activity; a dais is prepared for a chapter of monks, and in addition to the big group of *ubasok* and *ubasika*, other laymen may come to attend the evening service. This service is centred around a preaching, the second sermon of the day. In contrast with the earlier preaching, not all monks are expected to attend the evening service; notably the older monks often prefer to remain in their cells and go to sleep early. The monk who has been chosen by the abbot for the evening preaching asks the laymen first whether or not there are any laymen other than *ubasok* and *ubasika*, and if the answer is affirmative, he proceeds to prompt the five precepts. Those who are still under the obligation to follow the eight precepts will not repeat the *pañca sīlāni* after him; they will only show their respect by politely raising their hands, palm to palm. After the reading of the sermon, the *kruat nam* ritual is once again performed and the laymen who wish to go to sleep can do so. Often some monks remain till a very late hour talking with a group of devout laymen. It is an excellent opportunity for some influential farmers to get to know some of the monks that live in their monastery. Not long after midnight the monks usually have all returned to their cells and those laymen who stay in the monastery sleep on the floor of the gathering hall. As soon as it becomes light enough to discern the small patterns of the epidermic folds on the palm of the hand, at around half past five in the morning,[25] automatically all are relieved from their eight vows and go home.

During the Lenten season, therefore, *wan phra* constitutes a major festival for the community as a whole. At this time of the year the number of monks is relatively great, and a throng of laymen of all ages gather early in the morning for a solemn food offering. This is an attractive social occasion, when there is

24 For a wealth of details with regard to the texts used by laymen, see Somchit, *op. cit.*, pp. 62–106.

25 This is the traditional method of deciding whether a new day has started. This method is also used by monks; during *phansa*, monks must wait until they can discern the small lines in their palms before setting out collecting food. If they left earlier, they would feel that they were breaking the rule that they should stay in their own monastery every night during the Lenten season.

ample opportunity to meet friends, exchange news, and look at other members of the community. The fact that *wan phra* during the Lenten season has such importance for the whole of the community cannot fail but have an impact on the number of people who wish to take the eight precepts. It is part of the general intensifying of religious activities during this part of the year that the number of *ubasok* and *ubasika* increases so markedly. There are laymen who try to follow the eight precepts on every *wan phra* of the Lenten season, an accomplishment only few manage and which is believed to assure great rewards in a coming rebirth. These persons feel that they are observing the lay version of the monks' *phansa*. In general, though, taking the eight precepts during the Lenten season implies a taking part in the intensive generation of beneficial *karma*.

Outside the Lenten season, *wan phra* often hardly differs from any ordinary day in a rural monastery. There are very few monks, there is no communal food offering, the monks do not chant as a chapter in the *bot*, and no sermons are held. Many laymen feel that it is not attractive to follow the eight precepts under such circumstances.

Throughout the year, people younger than 40 years of age seldom adhere to the eight vows. Although there is no rule which forbids young people to become *ubasok* and *ubasika*, nobody expects them to take the eight precepts. Of all the persons recorded in Table 7, there was only a single case of a young person taking part. This was a woman in her early twenties who accompanied her mother for personal reasons. All others were of ripe age. A retreat from the world does not correspond with the life of a young adult. Young people are expected to be concerned about their work, their children, the organization of an economical household, and the solving of domestic problems. Circumstances prevent young people from dedicating themselves to asceticism for a whole day and a whole night. Moreover, their minds are believed still to be too capricious and too alive, and their interests too earthly. Only those whose children have grown up, who are not capable of much manual work, and whose passions have calmed possess the qualifications for the communal retreat. Moreover, the older people become, the more they will realize that death approaches. The increasing awareness of the finality of the present life is often an incentive to grasp opportunities to obtain beneficial *karma* so that a good future in the next life becomes more likely,

Life as *ubasok* and *ubasika* is very attractive to some older people. It brings persons together who have their age and memories in common. During the periods of fasting, recitation, meditations and discussions of religious nature, discomfort is shared, a bond can be welded, and sincere friendship can result. There are few opportunities for older people to regularly meet their contemporaries outside the monastery, for the households lie scattered about along the waterways and people do not readily visit other compounds unless they have a good and generally accepted reason.

Older women and the eight precepts

Table 7 reveals that the number of *ubasika* generally exceeds that of the men. This may be related to several factors. In the first place there are slightly more women than men in the older age group of the community. Secondly, the number of available older men has been somewhat depleted because older men have the opportunity to join the Sangha as monks. In 1968 there were six older men in Wat Sanchao who had become monks, thus depleting considerably the contingent of older men who are most likely to become *ubasok*. In comparison, only one woman of the Wat Sanchao region had joined the full-time religious specialization open to women by shaving her head and donning white robes.

Nevertheless, the fact remains that women are well represented among those who undertake to observe the eight precepts. It seems one of the rare instances in the life of women in rural Thailand when they are accepted as equal participants in a religious institution. Women cannot become *dek wat* and they cannot join the novices or the monks (and indeed, until the early twentieth century, they could hardly gain access to the skills of reading and writing). They have therefore no way of learning the proper formulae and are excluded from wearing the strongest protective amulets. The reason for this exclusion from religious knowledge appears to be twofold: in the first place they form a threat to the sanctity of the monks by making the members of the Sangha hanker after temporary earthly pleasures and secondly they are excluded because of their monthly flow of blood which is considered to be dangerous and polluting.

Women who become *ubasika* can no longer be classified as dangerous and magically potentially harmful persons. With the passage of time not only do they gradually lose much of their physical attraction, so that they can no longer be regarded as a potential danger to the monks' concentration, but also they automatically become less dangerously charged upon reaching menopause.

The difference between women of childbearing age and the less dangerous older women is well illustrated in the modes of covering the lower part of the body. While young women usually wear a piece of material wrapped around hips and both legs, older females usually wear a loose garment tucked behind under a belt in such a way as to form loose 'trousers'. Young women are forced by their clothing to sit with both legs folded on one side, the knees pressed together, while the clothing of older women permits them to sit on their haunches with the knees wide apart, or to sit cross-legged, in the manner of men. Upon reaching menopause, a woman becomes 'less female' and needs no longer behave in the formal manner required from a younger member of her sex. In this respect it is interesting to note which new types of clothing were accepted in the late 1960s in rural areas for young ladies who had access to new fashions. Slacks were considered modern, becoming in a young girl who had been in Bangkok, and they could be so tight that they accentuated the shape of the leg. The short skirt was only proper for schoolgirls; a girl of the age of 14 onwards could no longer wear them, according to Wat Sanchao public opinion. Shorts were regarded as decidedly improper and the mini-skirt would have been classed as much too daring. Older ladies who wished to be dressed up in the most modern international fashion could wear skirts as the fashion prescribed; in 1968 this was well above the knee.

The great number of *ubasika* should therefore not be interpreted as a deviation from the usual reluctance to let women participate in religious knowledge, but should be seen instead as an indication of a change of status of women past childbearing age.

A comparison between the five and the eight precepts

The eight precepts are taken as a whole, and breaking one precept automatically causes them all to be broken. This is borne out by the fact that, in the formula with which the eight precepts are requested, no proviso for separation is made comparable to the words *visuṃ visuṃ rakkhaṇathāya* in the request for the five precepts. The wording of the first, second, fourth and fifth precept is identical in each set, and the general interpretation of these four precepts is the same. It has been noted, however, that the third of the eight precepts is differently worded from the third of the *pañca sīlāni*. Those who promise to adhere to the five precepts declare to abstain from wrong sensuous pleasures, but people who take the eight precepts commit themselves to refrain from unchastity.

Wrong sensuous pleasures cover adultery, incest, rape, and all behaviour related to such misdeeds. However, when adhering to the eight precepts, and vowing to refrain from unchastity, a person must avoid all behaviour leading to sexual intercourse. The five precepts do not forbid love-making between husband and wife; the eight precepts do. In this respect it is noteworthy that sexual intercourse should not take place between any laymen on a *wan phra,* and this rule of conduct is handed down to all married couples. An interesting parallel is discernible in Indian literature. In Indian history it seems to have been the rule that on *Parvan* days, which correspond with the Thai *wan phra*, one should be chaste.[26]

The sixth precept, abstinence from taking food at the wrong time, is interpreted in the same manner as the thirty-seventh *pācittiyā* rule of the monks.[27] Until noon the *ubasok* and *ubasika* can partake of a meal. Their behaviour during their pre-afternoon meal is a good imitation of that of the monks: all avoid demonstrating greed, items of food are offered politely to a neighbour, nobody asks for rice or sauce for personal use, nobody speaks with the mouth full and all prevent smacking the lips while eating. After the meal is over they can complete their imitation of monastic behaviour by raising the hands and chanting in unison the same Pali texts that monks recite after a meal. In the afternoon and during the night, the *ubasok* and *ubasika* may consume tea, coffee or soft drinks, and most of them have taken the precaution to bring sufficient money to be able to purchase these refreshments.

The seventh rule that forbids make-up, ornaments, dancing, music, theatre, and the like is usually not difficult to follow. When there is no major entertainment in the precincts of the monastery itself there is hardly occasion to break this precept. However, when entertainment is foremost, on days of important cremations for example, the rule is often interpreted in a somewhat relaxed manner, again in imitation of the monks. *Ubasok* and *ubasika* are often of the opinion that they do not have to hide from a film, shadow theatre, or acrobatics when these take place in the monastery grounds; as long as they keep away from the crowd they may take note of such events from the safe distance of their gathering hall. The rule is interpreted to mean: do not dance or enjoy yourself in an unrestrained manner, and this interpretation closely follows the accepted monastic discipline.

The eighth and last precept is very easy to follow. In their own homes rural people do not possess high beds. Most individuals sleep on a mat rolled out on the appropriate portion of the floor, a rich farmer may spread out a mattress filled with kapok. Therefore, the *ubasok* and *ubasika* do not have to modify

26 Mention of this, for example, is made in the *Manusmṛti* (111, 45), and in the *Mahābhārata* (XIII, 104, 89). When Monier-Williams translated the word *Parva-gāmin* as 'He who approaches his wife' (*A Sanskrit-English Dictionary*, p. 609) he may not have been aware of this rule, otherwise the translation would probably have been: 'He who approaches his wife on a wrong day', or words to that effect.

27 Ñāṇamoli, *The Pāṭimokkha*, pp. 54–5.

their usual sleeping habits; a mat spread out on the floor of their gathering hall provides a comfortable sleeping place.

Strictly speaking, there is no obligation for the laymen to remain within the precincts of the monastery during the time they follow the eight precepts. Indeed, sometimes there are devout laymen who return home because they prefer to sleep in the trusted atmosphere of their own house. The majority of older laymen frown upon this practice. It is seen as giving in to a weakness, but above all it undermines the communal effort of those who stay the full period in the monastery. Although, in theory, a layman can observe the eight precepts at home, most devout persons maintain that in practice it is hardly possible to do so. The risks of becoming involved in domestic life, the difficulty of refraining from listening to idle talk, and the problem of staying away from the evening meal, or refraining from feelings of annoyance or a quarrel are of such magnitude that the advice of conscientious laymen is that the eight precepts can only be safely observed in the guarded and sacred surroundings of the monastery, with the moral support of the fellow devotees.

The eight precepts have been shown to form a completely different complex of norms and behaviour from that of the five precepts. Some difference existed already in the times of early Buddhism. A document that goes back to the fifth century A.D. makes a clear division between the ritual ordination of the five precepts, and the period of retreat for older people who follow the eight vows.[28] While the ceremony of receiving the five precepts, after it was adopted in Thailand, has taken on many of the characteristics of a purification ritual, the manner of adherence to the eight precepts appears to have been preserved almost in an unchanged form from the early times of Buddhism.

The Ten Precepts

A third fixed number of precepts mentioned in the *Tipiṭaka* are the ten precepts or *dasa sikkhāpadāni.*[29] In the canon, as in present-day Thailand, the ten precepts are always reserved for members of the Sangha; it is the maximum number of general rules that govern moral behaviour. Monks as well as novices can be said to be adherents of the ten precepts, but since the monks have many specific prescriptions in the *Pāṭimokkha*, the ten precepts have more relevance for the novices and have become their hallmark. The ordination of a layman as novice consists mainly of a promise to adhere to the ten precepts. During the ordination

28 L. Wieger (translator), *Bouddhisme Chinois*, Vol. 1, *Vinaya, monachisme et discipline; Hinayana, véhicule inférieur*, 1951, pp. 146–151.

29 For example in the *Mahavagga*, I, 56.

of a fully-fledged monk the ten precepts are also recited in an early part of the ritual, and this is often regarded as the passing of the novice stage.

An aspirant novice requests to be prompted with the ten precepts with the words: 'Ahaṃ bhante saranasīlaṃ yācāmi', or: 'I, sir, ask for the Refuges and the Precepts'. After the Refuges have been prompted and repeated by the candidate, the ten precepts follow. The first six precepts are identical in wording with the first six of the eight precepts, but from the seventh precept onwards the wording is as follows:

7. Naccagītavāditavisūkadassanā veramaṇī sikkhāpadaṃ samādiyāmi
8. Mālāgandhavilepanadhāraṇamaṇḍanavibhūsanaṭṭhānā veramaṇī sikkhāpadaṃ samādiyāmi
9. Uccāsayanā mahāsayanā veramaṇī sikkhāpadaṃ samādiyāmi
10. Jātarūparajatapaṭiggahaṇa veramaṇī sikkhāpadaṃ samādiyāmā

In translation:

7. I undertake [to observe] the rule of abstinence from dancing, music and visiting shows
8. I undertake [to observe] the rule of abstinence from flowers, make-up, the wearing of ornaments and decorations
9. I undertake [to observe| the rule of abstinence from a tall, high sleeping place
10. I undertake [to observe] the rule of abstinence from receiving gold or silver.

As with the ritual of promising to adhere to the eight precepts, the candidate solemnly states that he intends to follow them, but in this case no time limit is indicated. The Pali words are: 'Imāni dasa sikkhāpadāni samādiyāmi', or simply: 'These ten precepts I undertake (to observe)'.

A comparison of the wording of the eight and the ten precepts reveals that (7) and (8) of the *dasa sikkhāpadāni* combined correspond with the seventh of the eight precepts. The ninth precept is identical with the final resolution of the *ubasok* and *ubasika*. Strictly speaking the ten precepts only add one rule to those of the devout laymen: the abstinence from receiving gold or silver. However little may seem the difference between the wording of the eight and the ten precepts may seem, the actual implications show a vast gap between the two formulae.

The eight precepts are followed for one day and one night; the ten vows carry no time limit. Novices are expected to adhere to their vows continuously, and whenever they feel that they have broken a precept they can go to any monk, kneel down and ask for the ten precepts anew. In actuality novices are not so preoccupied with the exact interpretation of precepts as laymen who follow eight precepts. The reason for this lies partly in the youthfulness of most novices but also in the fact that novices follow the example of the monks in so many details that they may safely surmise that they have more than followed just ten precepts. As members of the Sangha they live permanently in a monastery, they wear the yellow robes that set them apart from all lay folk, their shaven heads remind at all times that here are people set apart in society. Novices live in the shadow of the monks, and their daily behaviour is more an imitation of monastic comportment than a direct result of carefully analysing the import of the ten precepts.

From the Buddhist tradition the Thais thus received three distinct numbers of precepts: the five, the eight and the ten vows. It has been argued that the function of these different groups of moral rules may well have changed considerably during the many centuries that have elapsed since Buddhism was introduced in the region. Such a change has been suggested especially with regard to the five precepts. Originally probably part of an initiation ritual, they appear in rural Thailand to form some kind of purification ceremony. The eight precepts as well as the ten precepts appear to have retained more of their original meaning. The eight precepts are designed for older people to go into retreat for a specific period of time, whilst the ten precepts are firmly linked to the full monastic discipline of the members of the Sangha.

It has been demonstrated that it is wrong to apply simple mathematics to these three numbers. It may not be said that the eight precepts are the five plus three additional precepts,[30] or that the ten precepts add two to the eight. The subtle distinctions in the wording of the formulae surrounding the promises to adhere to any of these sets of moral rules point to the individual characters of each type. The functions of the rituals appear to be quite distinct, and the separateness goes back to of distinctions that were already recognized in early Buddhism.

30 This inaccurate description of the eight precepts has crept into many otherwise very scholarly books; such as Bunnag, *Buddhist Monk, Buddhist Layman*, p. 107, *et passim.*

CHAPTER IX

THE PURSUIT OF BENEFICIAL KARMA

The really poor farmer can take part only in very few ceremonies. Sometimes he has the chance to witness an ordination procession or a *kathin* cortege on its way to a monastery, and he is able to earn a minute share in the beneficial karma emanating from such an occasion by lifting his hands respectfully while saying: 'anumodana sādhu'. This Pali formula means 'I approve', or 'Assent indeed'. Other common ways of obtaining some good *karma* without much financial outlay are attending a sermon, listening to the chants of the monks, assisting a monk in the pursuit of his duties, or offering relief to travellers by placing a pot of fresh water at the side of a path. In general, however, it is accepted that the amount of beneficial karma that a person gains is directly related to the cost.[1]

Farmers who can afford it often spend hundreds and sometimes thousands of baht during a series of varied events that all are intended to increase good karma. Some rich farmers grasp every opportunity to contribute food for the upkeep of the monastery and on ordinary evenings they may tune their transistor radio to a station that transmits a sermon. In order to obtain the optimum amount of good karma, he takes care to behave in a suitable manner while listening to the broadcast of a famous monk. It is not unusual to see a villager sitting in front of his radio, listening to a sermon with his hands raised politely and his feet folded behind.

There are wealthy persons who readily join friends and family whenever they are invited to take part in a religious ceremony in their houses, especially if those friends and relatives can be depended upon to return the gesture in the future. They are also glad to take part in many communal ceremonies in the nearby monastery and to join excursions for religious purposes to other

1 As noted before, this has also been remarked by Hanks, 'Merit and Power in the Thai Social Order', 1962.

communities. When the well-to-do person takes part in a communal ritual during which money gifts are needed, it is expected that he will donate a greater amount than those in a less fortunate financial position. Such a person usually will invite a chapter of monks to chant Pali texts in his private house whenever an appropriate occasion arises. When visiting a monastery the man with money may spontaneously arrange a meal for all monks; or if the time when members of the order can take solid food has already elapsed, he may arrange for soft drinks to be brought in from the local cafe. He may decide to accumulate enormous amounts of merit by financing a whole *kathin* ceremony or pay for the construction of a building in a monastery.

The many different types of activity which carry beneficial karma from which a farmer can choose may be brought under four headings, along a scale of sociological complexity of events. Firstly there are religious actions that involve only one or two individuals. Then there are the family rituals. These are followed by the religious festivities of the whole community in a monastery, and finally there are ceremonial links between different communities.

Beneficial activities during which only a small number of people are involved

An individual can accumulate good karma by living a morally just life. For the Thai Buddhist this means behaving according to the five precepts, even if only for a short period. Very few farmers will hope to be able to follow these precepts because they cannot afford to abandon agricultural pursuits and also they may be reluctant to forego the many pleasant aspects of social life that a proper adherence to the five precepts would entail. A person can also gain merit by concentrating on sacred Pali words and meditating. This concentration is not reserved for monks, *ubasok* and *ubasika*, but can be practised by all laymen. Especially those who at some stage of their lives have been members of the Sangha for a prolonged period may have acquired the habit of meditating for a while at night, just before lying down to sleep. This practice usually consists of repeating a few sacred words while breathing deeply and calmly. Not only does the custom of meditation carry some beneficial karma that will have an effect at some unknown time in the future; it is believed to have an immediate effect as well in that it helps a person to sleep soundly without evil dreams.[2]

Another certain method of obtaining merit is the practice of munificence. At sunrise on all mornings when there is no special food offering in the monastery, members of the order leave their monastery in order to offer laymen

2 Somkhuan Suthichai, personal communication, 9 February 1969.

the opportunity to donate food. Any layman who thus helps in the upkeep of the monastery obtains a good amount of merit. However, in order to ensure that he obtains the maximum benefit, he must take care to behave in an exemplary fashion during the presentation of food. The rice should be well cooked and brought from the house in a clean container. Many families possess a copper or silver vessel that is reserved for such occasions. The person who donates the food should be reasonably well dressed; in rural regions work clothes, as long as they are clean, are considered to be quite proper. An adult man will also arrange a cotton *phakhaoma* over the left shoulder as befits a ritual occasion. Thus attired he awaits the approach of the monks. When they are in sight, he may squat down, lift the rice container to the level of his forehead, and softly say: 'Nibbāna paccayo hotu', or 'May it be a factor in reaching *nibbāna*'. In the literate Buddhist tradition the concept *nibbāna* is equated with the extinction of all passion, anger and ignorance. In rural, animistic Buddhism it means ultimate bliss, a total happiness without end. The farmers do not really aspire to reach *nibbāna*; they are aware of their firm links with daily life and the formula is used to move a little in the direction of *nibbāna* by being reborn in more favourable circumstances than the present existence.

A more elaborate formula that can be said before offering rice to the monks consists of the following sentence, which is repeated three times: 'Sudinnaṃ vata me dānaṃ āsavakkhayāvahaṃ hotu' or 'May this well-given donation lead to the extinction of the āsavas'.[3] The concept 'extinction of the *āsavas*' is also well known in scriptural Buddhism and usually it refers especially to the obtaining of *arahant*-ship.[4] In this case again, the farmers are likely to ignore the exact meaning of the words and to believe the formula to be of general beneficial impact. If a layman cannot remember such formulae he can use any other Pali words that come up in his mind, or say something appropriate in Thai. After the formula he will rise to his feet and make sure that he approaches the monk without wearing any footwear. It would be wrong to have the feet clad whilst the monk is obliged by the rules of his order to go barefooted when collecting food. While he deposits some rice in the begging bowl of a monk, the farmer usually refrains from talking; it is only when he has something urgent to communicate that he speaks, but without raising his voice.

The very poor farmer who has little to eat for himself and his family may add a piece of salt to the rice because rice alone is considered too frugal a gift

3 ประเพณีการทำบุญ [Customs connected with Making Merit], p. 8.

4 *The Pali Text Society's Pali-English Dictionary*, p. 115.

to the members of the Sangha. Most farmers place a piece of fish, some soup, a sauce, vegetables, some fruit or a sweetmeat, either on top of the rice in the begging bowl (from where the monk will transfer it before he gives the next layman a chance to donate) or directly in the food containers which the *dek wat* bring along for that purpose. In some areas where monks collect food by paddling in a small boat from house to house, the begging bowl is placed ornamentally in the bow, together with some containers for soups and sauces.

Gifts to the members of the Sangha are the preferred form of munificence, but a certain amount of beneficial karma is also attached to giving to fellow laymen. Therefore a person acquires merit by giving alms to beggars and by donating to charitable institutions. It must be understood that the practice of donating is not reserved for laymen only; a monk accumulates beneficial karma in the same manner every time he gives a book or an amulet to laymen or fellow monks.

Family rituals that include a recitation by a chapter of monks

A wealthy householder can elaborate upon his private family rituals by inviting a chapter of monks to come and recite Pali texts. The first haircutting of a child, the imminent ordination of a son, the first preaching at home of a son who has recently become a monk, a marriage ceremony, the first entering of a new house, a private *thawai sangkhathan,* the death of a relative, or the commemoration of the death of an ancestor are some of the best-known occasions that may be rendered more auspicious by the inclusion of the chanting of a chapter of monks.

In former times the recitation was a very lengthy affair that took place during the afternoon and was followed the next morning by a festive meal, thus obliging the monks to travel twice to the house. In present times the recitation and the meal of the monks take place during the same morning, and consequently the duration of the recitation of sacred texts has been shortened considerably.[5] Whilst traditionally the monks may have chanted several hours, they are now often pressed for time because they ought to take their final meal of the day before noon.

The preparations a householder has to make when a chanting session accompanies a ritual in his house are numerous. In the first place he has to decide how many monks will be invited. If fewer than five monks come to the house, the chanting of Pali texts is likely to sound too soft and inadequate; and

5 Phya Anuman Rajadhon, *Life and Ritual in Old Siam*, p. 84.

especially if inexperienced monks are among this small number, the ceremony will lack impressiveness. On the other hand, if a great number are invited, the householder will strain the resources of his household, and the house itself may not provide adequate space for so many monks and their audience. Another consideration is the fact that most ceremonies require the presence of an uneven number of monks. The head of the family therefore usually decides to invite seven, nine, eleven, thirteen or even more monks to come and chant.

An exception to the rule regarding the number of monks occurs at the time immediately after a person has died; on such inauspicious occasions a chapter of four monks can be invited to chant, with others, the story of *Phra* Malai. Uneven numbers are often considered more auspicious than even. A ladder ought to possess an uneven number of rungs, lest ghosts should climb it. Similarly, it is reported of some Thais that they believe that an uneven number of shouts from a gecko bodes well, whereas an even number is considered a bad omen.

Secondly, the head of the family has to decide which members of the Sangha he will invite. If any close relatives are members of the order, or if the householder is very friendly with certain monks, these will have to receive a personal invitation. After they have been contacted and have agreed to be present, the householder calculates how many are still needed to make up the full chapter and customarily he goes to the nearest monastery to request the abbot to send the number of monks needed. It is part of the duties of an abbot to select monks for these chanting sessions in private homes. Since these recitations are often generously rewarded with presents, invitations are much sought after and the abbot usually rotates the open invitations in a manner that ensures that each experienced monk obtains a fair share in the gifts.

If the chanting is to take place during the morning, the household must arrange for the preparation of a meal for all the monks and laymen who are expected to attend. Even if the chanting takes place in the afternoon the householder must reckon on great expense, because then the meal will be held on the following morning. Most rural households do not possess sufficient implements to prepare and serve food for more than a dozen persons, and the householder usually borrows pots and pans, spoons, and plates from the nearest monastery. Most monasteries possess a great amount of kitchenware, the accumulation of many donations. They are regarded as communal property of which the monks are but the custodians. One monk is often in charge of all such goods and he keeps a record of all articles borrowed by laymen or by neighbouring monasteries. Any goods that are damaged or lost should be replaced by the borrower.

In order to be able to receive the monks in a proper manner, the organizer has to buy an ample supply of soft drinks, cigarettes, betel leaves, and areca nuts. Within the house along the most auspicious side, the east wall, a dais is prepared. The mats and pillows needed for this dais are usually also borrowed from the stores of the nearest monastery.

Before the monks arrive, the householder approaches the shrine of the Venerable Phum, situated at some distance from his house. He lights a candle and some incense and informs the guardian spirit of the compound of the imminent ceremony. Customarily he fastens one end of the sacred cotton thread, the *sai sin*, to the top of the shrine and leads this thread towards his house, unrolling the ball of cotton as he goes. He hangs the thread high up, looping over branches so that it does not touch the ground and cannot hinder passers-by. When he reaches his house, he walks around it in the auspicious clockwise direction, all the time unwinding the *sai sin* which he fastens at or just below roof level. If more than one household living in the same compound combine their resources for the duration of the ceremony, the other houses may also be encircled with the same thread. Finally, the thread is taken through a window to the most auspicious corner of the house, usually in the north-east part of the room where a Buddha image has been placed on a pedestal.

When the monks arrive they are received in a manner befitting their superior ritual position. Sometimes this entails their feet being washed by members of the household. Upon arriving in the heart of the house, each monk chooses a place on the elevated dais. The most senior monk sits directly next to the pedestal with the Buddha image, while those who are of lower rank or who have been ordained at a later date sit on his left, facing the laymen. When the whole chapter has arrived and some polite conversation has been kept up for some time between the monks and the older men among the audience, the householder or his delegate requests to be prompted in the five precepts. Often the most senior monk delegates the giving of the five precepts to a colleague on his left, so that he has some time to prepare the ritual paraphernalia on the pedestal. He lights a candle and fastens it on the rim of a vessel containing clear water, or sometimes he lowers the lighted candle in the water itself so that it rests on the bottom of the vessel and rises above the water surface. He checks that the sacred cord has been wound in a clockwise direction around the Buddha image and also around the vessel with water. The remainder of the ball of cotton thread is passed down the line of monks and when it reaches the youngest member of the Sangha there is usually still some spare *sai sin* left, and this is placed on a plate or some such object, so that it does not directly touch the floor.

Figure 9.1: Making *nam mon* in a private house.

As soon as the five precepts have been repeated, the leader of the chapter of monks begins the chanting session and all monks raise their hands palm-to-palm to chest level, holding the *sai sin* between the index finger and thumb. The monks usually chant the auspicious texts that can be found in the *Suatmon Chet Tamnan*. The laymen appreciate it when the monks chant in loud voices, and the small house on stilts may vibrate with the rhythmical sonorous sound of the sacred words. It is believed that beneficial, protective power is emitted by the monks as they chant the Pali texts and that this travels through the cotton thread. This power is reinforced by the Buddha image and causes the water to be charged.

The use of the *sai sin* and the bowl of water is typical of ceremonies during which monks chant in private homes. Phya Anuman Rajadhon likens the cotton thread to an electric wire, within the orbit of which everything is consecrated.[6] When the monks chant similar texts for laymen within the precincts of the monastery, the sacred cord is not employed to channel the power of the monks. A likely reason for this may be that a monastery is *per se* sacred ground and it is so frequently the scene of Buddhist chanting and meditation that it may

6 *Life and Ritual in Old Siam*, p. 85.

be regarded as permanently beneficially charged. Therefore a bowl of water, placed in the *bot,* is believed to become filled with a beneficial power without the use of a *sai sin.*

During the ceremony in a private house, a lighted candle is used from which molten wax occasionally drips onto the surface of the water in the vessel. When the leader of the chapter of monks is of the opinion that sufficient texts have been chanted, he begins the *Ratana Sutta* and holds the candle almost upside-down so that more molten wax drips quickly into the vessel. Upon reaching the words *khīṇaṃ purāṇaṃ navaṃ natthi sambhavaṃ* ('it is destroyed and exhausted, no rebirth is produced'), he extinguishes the candle in the water. This concludes the sacralization of the water, which is now called *nam mon,* or *mantra* water. A few moments later the recitation of Pali texts ends. The *nam mon* is often used in the ceremony at hand; during a ritual hair-shaving the child may be sprinkled with it, when blessing a new house the oldest monk walks around profusely scattering drops of *nam mon* over doors and walls. On some occasions the householder may ask the senior monk to sprinkle the whole assembled congregation. On all occasions when *nam mon* is scattered, some twigs or leaves are used which carry auspicious names. In the course of this book several types of leaves have already been mentioned, such as 'silver-and-gold leaf', the hardy grass *ya phraek,* the feathery *mai mayom* branch, and the *rak*-leaves (the latter suitable for sprinkling a bridal couple because the word *rak* means 'to love, to cherish'). Other plant materials sometimes used to sprinkle *nam mon* are *ya kha* (หญ้าคา), the hardy cogon grass, and the leaves of the *matum* (มะตูม) and the *mayom* (มะยม) tree.[7]

The remainder of the *nam mon* can be used by the householder for various purposes. Some may be tipped into the containers of drinking water, or he may sprinkle his home with it. There are laymen who rub a bit of *nam mon* over their faces or over the top of their heads. The water that has been charged with beneficial power is considered capable of warding off illness, unhappiness and misfortune.

Public ceremonies in 'one's own' monastery

Farmers whose ancestors have helped build a monastery, who have themselves been monks there, and who contribute regularly towards its upkeep, are aware

7 The *matum* tree is the Aegle marmelos, the bael-fruit tree which has well-known medicinal value (McFarland's *Thai-English Dictionary,* p. 635); the *mayom* is *Phyllanthus distichus,* the star gooseberry tree, of which the fruit is commonly used for pickling and the roots are used in some medicines (McFarland, *ibid.,* p. 638).

of a close link between themselves and this particular monastery. Their feeling can be called joint-proprietary and – while recognizing that there are occasions when the monks cannot allow laymen near, such as during *sadaeng abat,* during the recitation of the *Pāṭimokkha,* and while the monks meditate – they know that the monastery is theirs. It is open to lay visitors at almost any time of the day or night. The lay people often realize that the monastery is totally dependent upon them, and therefore it is considered not more than proper that they are always able to influence its organization. All decisions concerning the future of the monastery are taken after consultation with the older members of the lay community.

Those attending ceremonies on a regular *wan phra* are almost invariably people who 'belong to' the monastery. Each year there occur some major rituals in the monastery during which almost the whole sustaining population comes to attend the morning service and the other communal rituals that then take place. The most important annual ceremonies have been set out in Table 8. These major festivals are usually marked by a solemn public food offering that is followed by a ritual appropriate to the occasion.

Makhabucha has been established relatively recently as a national Buddhist festival. It was only during the reign of King Mongkut (r.1851–1868) that this day was chosen to commemorate the miraculous meeting of monks during which the Buddha gave the *Pāṭimokkha* to the order.[8] Its relatively recent introduction, or possibly its timing during the religiously 'slack' period, may be a reason why this festival seems more popular in urban areas than in rural Thailand. Kingshill reports for a community in northern Thailand that *Makhabucha* was not celebrated at all during the year of research.[9]

During the month of April traditionally all Thais used to celebrate New Year in a festival known as *Songkran.* However, since 1941 the Thai government has brought the beginning of the year into line with that of most other nations and officially the new calendar year begins on the first of January. In the rural areas, which are more traditionally minded, it can be noticed that *Songkran* remains a major festival. The celebrations last for several days and the ceremonial use of water is always a conspicuous element of *Songkran.*

On April 13, 1968, the first day of *Songkran,* a large number of laymen came to the most spacious gathering hall of Wat Sanchao in order to participate in the ritual afternoon bathing of the monks. A dais was prepared, with a Buddha

8 Wells, *Thai Buddhism, Its Rites and Activities,* p. 13.

9 Kingshill, *Ku Daeng - The Red Tomb,* p. 196.

Table 8. The major annual ceremonies in the monastery

Thai name	*Pali or Sanskrit equivalent*	*Period of the year*
Makhabucha มาฆบูชา	Māghapūjā	January–February
Songkran สงกรานต์	Saṃkrānti	Mid-April
Wisakhabucha วิสาขบูชา	Visākhāpūjā	April–May
Buat phra บวชพระ	Upasampadā	All year[a]
Salakaphat สลากภัต	Salākabhattaṃ	May–September
Thawai pha apnamfon ถวายผ้าอาบน้ำฝน	Vassikasāṭikaṃ dānaṃ	June–July
Asalahabucha อาสาฬหบูชา	Āsāḷhāpūjā	June–July
Khao phansa เข้าพรรษา	Vassupanāyikā	June–July
Ok phansa ออกพรรษา	Pavāraṇā	September–October
Saibat dawadueng ใส่บาตรดาวดึง	Piṇḍapāta Tāvatiṃsa	September–October
Kathin กฐิน	Kathina	September–November

[a] While a man can, in principle, enter the order at any time of the year, in this table it has been placed just after *Wisakhabucha* because most men join the Sangha just before the Lenten season.

image on one end, and the abbot seated himself near this Buddha image. All other monks sat on his left ordered in decreasing order of seniority. The monks placed their hands with the palms turned upwards on their knees. A group of elder men, each carrying a vessel of water, approached the monks, all other lay people filed behind them. Each person first poured a little water on the Buddha image, then on the abbot and on each of the remaining monks. Some men had brought a fragrant paste that they rubbed over the hands, arms, shoulders, heads or backs of the Buddha image and the monks before pouring the water. The women among the throng of people had to refrain from rubbing fragrant matter. They should at all times avoid bodily contact with members of the Sangha, and therefore were limited in their activities to pouring a bit of water from a safe distance.

Since almost the whole lay community of Wat Sanchao thus filed past, the monks and their robes became thoroughly drenched. Notwithstanding the cold water all monks remained solemn and silent. In contrast, the lay people gradually became less deferential, and young people especially began

Figure 9.2: *Rotnam phuyai.*

splashing each other with water. The monks ended their part of the ceremony by chanting a blessing and retreating to their cells. While they changed into dry robes, the laymen created an atmosphere of jocularity and general water throwing. Nobody became angry at being soaked, for most buckets full of water were accompanied by a smile and a funny remark. It was an excellent opportunity for young unmarried men to attract the attention of girls.

The aspect of jocularity should not obscure the fact that pouring water over a senior person is essentially an act of great respect. It is called *rotnam phuyai* (รดน้ำผู้ใหญ่), literally 'pouring water over important people', and is not solely reserved for the traditional New Year. For example, when on October 27, 1967 the Reverend Phot, one of the Wat Sanchao monks, was promoted to a higher ecclesiastical rank the community organized a procession to the provincial capital and back to Wat Sanchao, and then further honoured the monk by placing him on a chair and pouring water over him. Similarly, after the elaborate ordination ceremony, a recently ordained monk may be honoured by having scented water poured over his hands and feet. Usually the *rotnam phuyai* is a solemn ritual and the wild splashing and licentiousness during *Songkran* is typical for the New Year ceremony only.[10]

On May 11, 1968, the full moon of the sixth lunar month, fell *Wisakhabucha*. In Wat Sanchao the day began like any other important *wan phra* with a communal food offering in the most spacious gathering hall, with a group of *ubasok* and *ubasika* promising to adhere to the eight precepts for a period of one day and one night, and with the recitation of the *Pāṭimokkha* in the *bot* for all the monks residing in the monastery. However, at seven o'clock in the evening the big bell of the monastery was beaten to warn the lay population that the *Wisakhabucha* evening service was impending. At around eight o'clock the temple was filled to capacity and one of the older monks read in a loud and clear voice the declaration of *Wisakhabucha* in the Thai language, halting after each phrase to give his audience the opportunity to repeat these words (amounting to a summary testimony of the life and teachings of the Buddha).[11] After this declaration everybody lighted a candle and some incense and, with all the monks leading, went slowly three times around the temple in a clockwise direction.

Around each temple in Thailand there are eight round stones deeply interred, and a ninth is buried in the centre of the building. The places where the eight outer stone balls rest in the earth are indicated by eight marking stones. After completing the third circumambulation everybody deposited the remnants of their candles and the half-burned incense tapers at the marking stone near the main entrance of the *bot*. Their circumambulation completed, the congregation re-entered the temple and listened to a formal preaching before returning home. Phya Anuman Rajadhon reports that in Bangkok the preaching sessions last throughout the whole night,[12] but this was not the case in Wat Sanchao.

The ritual of *buat phra*, the ordination ceremony, is not necessarily accompanied by a public festival. Customarily it is only the young man who joins the order for the first time in his life who makes this transition in an elaborate public

10 Further details of the *Songkran* festival may be found in Phya Anuman Rajadhon, *Loy Krathong & Songkran Festival*, Thailand Culture Series, No. 5, 1953, pp. 13–24, Urakhin ประเพณีไทยฉบับพระราชครู [Thai Customs, the Rajaguru edition], pp. 616–34 and Wells, *Thai Buddhism, Its Rites and Activities*, pp. 85–9.

11 An English translation of the declaration for *Wisakhabucha* can be found in Wells, *Thai Buddhism, Its Rites and Activities*, pp. 73–5.

12 *Life and Ritual in Old Siam*, p. 94.

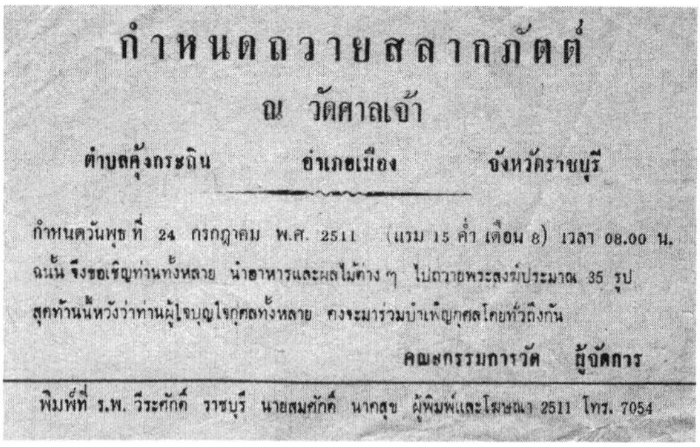

กำหนดถวายสลากภัตต์

ณ วัดศาลเจ้า

ตำบลคุ้งกระถิน อำเภอเมือง จังหวัดราชบุรี

กำหนดวันพุธ ที่ 24 กรกฎาคม พ.ศ. 2511 (แรม 15 ค่ำ เดือน ๘) เวลา 08.00 น.
ฉนั้น จึงขอเชิญท่านทั้งหลาย นำอาหารและผลไม้ต่าง ๆ ไปถวายพระสงฆ์ประมาณ 35 รูป
สุดท้ายนี้หวังว่าท่านผู้ใจบุญใจกุศลทั้งหลาย คงจะมาร่วมบำเพ็ญกุศลโดยทั่วถึงกัน

คณะกรรมการวัด ผู้จัดการ

พิมพ์ที่ ร.พ. วีระศักดิ์ ราชบุรี นายสมศักดิ์ นาคสุข ผู้พิมพ์และโฆษณา 2511 โทร. 7054

Figure 9.3: Announcing a *salakaphat*.

manner. On the day before the actual ordination, several rituals may take place in the house of the main sponsors, often the parents of the monk-to-be. First the hair of the young man is shaved, and the persons who contribute most lavishly to the ordination will make sure to cut the first locks. During the afternoon a chapter of monks may come to the house and chant Pali blessings. Then a lay specialist takes over who addresses the gods and holds a *tham khwan* ceremony to strengthen the morale of the candidate. Rich sponsors hire a band, and throughout the night there is music and dancing for the guests. These rituals are of a family nature and they are usually not held in a monastery building.

On the day of the ordination the ceremony becomes more public. First the ordinand is led in procession to the monastery. Anybody who wishes to contribute financially to the ordination is welcome to join. The traditional order of the procession is often observed. The musicians and some older members of the community who can dance well go in front, followed by three girls carrying the gifts for the ordainer and the two preceptors. Then come a series of beautiful girls in their best dresses carrying gifts for all members of the Sangha who will be present at the ordination. Immediately behind follow the main sponsors of the ritual who proudly carry the robes of the future monk, his begging bowl and his ritual fan. Then in the shade of a huge umbrella, comes the aspirant monk himself, sometimes on horseback, sometimes carried by friends, or on foot. At the rear are the people who carry various gifts for the new monk: his sleeping-mat, a pillow, a razor, a parasol, a sieve to strain water, a blanket, a kettle and any other object that has been purchased for this occasion.[13]

13 This order can be found in อนุสรณ์กตัญญูเนื่องในการฌาปนกิจ นายเบี้ยวเจริญจันท์ [In Grateful Memory at the Cremation of Nai Biaw Charoenchan], Bangkok: Withayalai khrusuansunantha, B.E. 2511 (1968), p. 32.

When the procession reaches the monastery, the monk-to-be must prostrate himself before the shrine of the guardian spirit of the monastery, informing him of his intention to become a resident monk. The whole procession, which at this time includes many friends and relatives, slowly moves three times in a clockwise direction around the *bot* before entering. The ordinand is aided over the threshold by his mother and father and he takes official leave from them inside the temple before going to the dais where the ordainer waits. The ordination ritual carries an immense amount of beneficial karma for the main sponsors and this is reflected in the great care with which the *kruat nam* ritual is performed immediately after the ordination. Whilst the monks chant their blessing, the main sponsors pour water from a vessel over the top of the index finger. Only those who have made a substantial contribution may place their finger in the stream of water. Near relatives who contributed not as generously may obtain a small share of the power by touching the arm or a shoulder of one of the main sponsors. Those who gave only a few *baht* receive their share without touching the central figures.

During the season when fruit is abundant, near the end of the hot period of the year and at the beginning of the rainy season, some important laymen confer with the older monks of a monastery in order to decide on which day their monastery will hold the annual *salakaphat*, the distribution of food by lot. This custom can be traced to the early days of the Sangha and may originally have been designed to avoid quarrels over food when the supply was scarce.[14] In Thailand most monasteries have always had an abundance of food and the distribution of food by lot is therefore of a character quite different from that of the *salākabhattaṃ* in the *Tipiṭaka*.[15]

The day chosen for this ceremony is made known to everybody usually by distributing printed leaflets, not only in the monastery itself but in the surrounding villages as well. The organizers have to be certain that neighbouring monasteries have not, by chance, already reserved the same day for a *salakaphat*. If two neighbouring monasteries were to hold it on the same day, the reciprocal invitation patterns that have over time come into existence would be upset. The organizers of a *salakaphat* in rural areas can predict fairly accurately how many individual gift baskets of food will be available for the ceremony, because there will be scarcely a household that will not participate in this traditional festival, and each household can be counted upon to bring a basket of food to be

14 T. W. Rhys Davids and H. Oldenberg (transl.), *Vinaya Texts*, Vol. III, pp. 220–3. (*Cullavagga*, VI, 21, 1–3.).

15 The ritual has been dealt with in some detail in my *Boeddhisme in de Praktijk*, 1977, pp. 78–90.

Figure 9.4: Waiting with the baskets during *salakaphat*.

distributed to the monks by the drawing of tickets. The number of households that sustains a rural monastery is invariably much greater than the number of its monks, and thus there will be many more baskets of food than can be readily consumed by the inmates. Traditionally, each gift should consist of several pounds of unhusked rice, onions, garlic, and shrimp paste, together with several kinds of fruit. Nowadays, however, it occurs only rarely in the region of Ratburi that a family prepares a gift for *salakaphat* that contains food other than fruit.

It is customary that the abbot of the monastery where a *salakaphat* is planned invites a number of monks from other monasteries to share in the ritual lottery. The invitations are sent to the abbots of many monasteries in the region, requesting the presence of a specified number of monks for *salakaphat*, but not mentioning any monks by name, thus leaving it to the abbots of the various monasteries to distribute the invitations. The number of monks invited varies from monastery to monastery and is based on a reciprocal relationship between the monasteries involved. The total number of monks that can attend a *salakaphat* depends on the number of baskets that will be distributed. For Wat Sanchao, the organizers can reckon on between one hundred and two hundred food gifts. It is important that the invited monks obtain a great deal of food; when they take only one or two baskets back to their monastery it would be interpreted as a sign that the Wat Sanchao people had been rather stingy. On the other hand, if more than four or five baskets had to be carried home, the monks might have difficulty transporting so much, and the community may be accused of trying to be ostentatious. Three baskets per monk constitute a proper generous result of a *salakaphat* ceremony. This implies that in Wat Sanchao the total number of monks attending the ritual seldom exceeds forty-five.

On the morning of *salakaphat* all the families take regular food to the monastery that will be presented in a solemn manner befitting a gift to the Sangha. At the same time the laymen take their special *salakaphat* gifts, approximately twenty pounds of fruit packed tightly in a bamboo basket. The lay organizers have prepared a great number of sticks of about one metre in length, and every basket is provided with such a stick. A piece of paper on which a number is clearly written is attached to the stick. These sticks have also been provided with a slit, in which the heads of the families from which the gifts originate will slide a banknote. Poor farmers will use the smallest banknote in circulation, in 1968 this was a five *baht* note, but others give ten or twenty *baht*. A rich man may conspicuously place a bright red hundred-*baht* note with his fruit basket. When all baskets have been labelled the lay congregation sits amongst a small forest of sticks, numbers and banknotes.

The five precepts are requested, prompted and repeated, and then a spokesman for the community offers the lottery gift to the Sangha with the following words:

> Etāni mayaṃ bhante bhattāni saparivārāni asukaṭṭhāne ṭhapitāni bhikkhusaṃghassa oṇojayāma; sādhu no bhante bhikkhusaṃgho etāni bhattāni saparivārāni paṭiggaṇhātu amhākaṃ dīgharattaṃ hitāya sukhāya.[16]

They can be translated as:

> We give as a present these foods and paraphernalia arranged in a certain place to the community of monks; may the community of monks accept from us these foods and paraphernalia with the word sādhu to our enduring benefit and happiness.

This formula is of a type generally used to present the Sangha with a gift. The wording is changed only slightly to fit the specific character of the donation. Another example was quoted in the previous chapter in discussing the ritual of *thawai sangkhathan* and a further version occurs in the ceremony of *thawai pha abnamfon*, discussed later in this chapter.

16 This formula occurs also in *Suatmon Chet Tamnan* p. 81 and in Urakhin ประเพณีไทยฉบับพระราชครู [Thai Customs, the Rajaguru edition], p. 833.

Figure 9.5: The monk receives a basket he drew during *salakaphat*.

The methods of distributing the baskets vary from region to region and from monastery to monastery.[17] The most common method of distribution in the region around Wat Sanchao was to place as many tickets as there were baskets in a container and let each monk select one ticket. The number on the ticket entitles the monk to a basket together with the money that is attached. The vessel with tickets is passed around several times, but when there are not enough tickets left to make a full round of monks the lay organizers add a number of blank tickets and the monks proceed to draw a final round. There is a general interest among the laymen as to who will draw the baskets that carry the greatest amounts of money, since it is seen as an indication which monks possess the greatest store of beneficial karma.

The presentation of bathing clothes is often the next major communal festival. *Thawai pha apnamfon* can also be traced to the early days of Buddhism. According to the *Vinaya Piṭaka*, some lay people appeared upset at the sight of members of the Sangha bathing naked in the rain. In the eyes of these devout laymen, such behaviour seemed more in accordance with that of some ascetics who believed in the sanctity of nakedness, and did not befit Buddhist monks. The complaint caused a problem in that that the monks could not be expected to bathe fully dressed, since this would have forced those who possessed only

17 For other methods of drawing by lot see Wells, *Thai Buddhism, Its Rites and Activities*, pp. 120–2, and Kingshill, *Ku Daeng – The Red Tomb*, pp. 204–6.

Figure 9.6: An abundance of fruit is passed on to the monks during *salakaphat*.

one set of robes to wear heavy, uncomfortable and damp clothing. Therefore the Buddha ruled that special garments of small size could be used for bathing purposes. It was laid down that the monks could only obtain these bathing clothes during the last month of the hot season.[18] This is the background of the twenty-fourth rule of the *nissaggiyā-pācittiyā* rules of the *Pāṭimokkha*. In the *Sacred Books of the East* series this rule has been translated as: 'When he sees that a month of the hot days has yet to run, let a Bhikkhu provide himself with the materials for robes for the rainy season … '.[19] Probably it would have been better to translate the words *vassika sātikacīvaraṃ* as 'materials for bathing robes for the rainy season'.

In accordance with the Buddhist tradition, the Thais designate the time of presenting monks' bathing clothes as somewhere between the first day of waning moon of the seventh lunar month and the day of full moon of the eighth lunar month.[20] As with the *salakaphat* ritual, monks and laymen consult each other before deciding upon the date of *thawai pha apnamfon*. Often it is decided to celebrate the giving of bathing clothes within the stipulated time, but sometimes it is considered advisable to postpone it to the first day after full

18 T. W. Rhys Davids and H. Oldenberg (transl.), *Vinaya Texts*, Part II, pp. 216–25 (*Mahāvagga*, VIII, 15, 1–15).

19 T. W. Rhys Davids and H. Oldenberg (transl.), *Vinaya Texts*, Part I, p. 28.

20 Urakhin ประเพณีไทยฉบับพระราชครู [Thai Customs, the Rajaguru edition], p. 635.

moon of the eighth lunar month so that it then coincides with the feast of the first day of the Lenten season.

Each family that wishes to take part in *thawai pha apnamfon* prepares or purchases a piece of material that is acceptable according to Sangha rules. It is a rectangular piece of cotton, about 130 cm in length and about 60 cm wide. In the canon the exact size of the bathing cloth has been laid down as six *sugatavidatthis* in length and two and a half *sugatavidatthis* in width.[21] Amongst commentators there is no unanimity with regard to the exact size of a *sugatavidatthi*. The controversy centres mainly around the ninety-second *pācittiyā* rule of the *Pāṭimokkha*, where monks are forbidden to have robes made of the size of the robes of the Buddha or larger, and the dimensions of the Buddha's clothes are given as nine by six *sugatavidatthi*. Legends about the huge size of the body of the Lord Buddha have caused commentators to estimate the *sugatavidatthi* to be much longer than the *vidatthi*, the span of approximately 23 cm commonly known in ancient India. One of the latest opinions of the Thais rejects the idea of a Buddha many times the size of an ordinary person, but compromises in making the *sugatavidatthi* one plus one third ordinary *vidatthi*, still leaving the Buddha's robe almost three metres long.[22] The size of the bathing clothes given to the monks on the occasion of *thawai pha apnamfon* would suggest that in this case the *sugatavidatthi* is reckoned to be equal to an ordinary *vidatthi*.

It seems quite plausible to accept that everywhere in the canon the word *sugatavidatthi* intends to refer to a measure of 23 cm. This would make the size of the robes of the Buddha 207 by 138 cm, quite ordinary robes for the average man 2,500 years ago. This interpretation of the rule implies that, strictly speaking, many monks nowadays would be wearing robes of a size forbidden to members of the Sangha.

To many householders, the gift of a bathing cloth together with incense, a candle and some flowers appears small and insignificant. Therefore most families enlarge their donations by adding some useful household goods that the monks may need during the Lenten season, such as soap, toothpaste, a box of matches, toilet paper and usually also a small amount of money. In order to make their present even more attractive some farmers purchase a bathing cloth that has been skilfully folded in such a manner that it resembles a lotus flower or a *haṃsa* (a mythological goose). The monk who receives such an

21 The ninety-first *pācittiyā* rule of the *Pāṭimokkha*.

22 The Venerable Ñāṇamoli Thera, *The Pāṭimokkha*, p. 114.

ornamentally folded cloth may place it among his prize possessions on his private altar in his cell.

On the morning of *thawai pha apnamfon* the laymen present these special gifts during the beginning of the morning meal of the monks. A spokesman offers the gifts to the Sangha with the appropriate formula, that differs from that of *thawai sangkhathan* only in that the word *bhattāni* is omitted and *vassikasāṭikacīvarānī* (bathing cloth for the Lenten season) substituted. The number of families participating in this ceremony is usually much greater than the number of monks and thus each monk may receive several bathing cloths. The distribution of the many gifts can be decided by lot in the manner described above for the *salakaphat* ritual.

Because the ceremony is held at the beginning of the rainy season, and also because the clothes offered are known as 'robes to bathe in the rain' (in actual fact they are used for bathing in general, in the river, from a big earthenware water container or in the rain, whichever is expedient), it is not surprising to find that many farmers believe that participation in this ceremony will help ensure good rains for the fields. It is another instance where taking part in a meritorious ritual is believed to have also a direct, almost simultaneous, practical result. The immediate aspect of the good karma arising from this ceremony is beneficial power. The magical interpretation of the Buddhist ritual makes for the causal link between the donation of rain clothes to the monks and the abundance of water soon afterwards.

From an organizational point of view, *thawai pha apnamfon* is very different from *salakaphat*. The former ritual is reserved only for those monks who reside in one monastery, while the latter is traditionally a ceremony whereby the abbot of a monastery invites monks from other monasteries. The first is basically a transaction between community and its own monks whilst the second is a much more outwardly directed ritual, whereby laymen are influenced by the thought that the prestige of the monastery is at stake.

Asalahabucha is a recently introduced festival, commemorating the Buddha's first disciples. It is celebrated on the day of full moon of the eighth lunar month. In years when there is a second, intercalary month in order to adjust the difference between the solar and lunar years, *Asalahabucha* falls on the day of the full moon of the second eighth lunar month. The rituals for laymen are similar to those of *Wísakhabucha* described earlier in this chapter. During the evening the big monastery bell is sounded to warn all laymen of the impending ceremony in the *bot*. After the declaration of *Asalahabucha* has been prompted and repeated by everyone present, the temple is circumambulated three times,

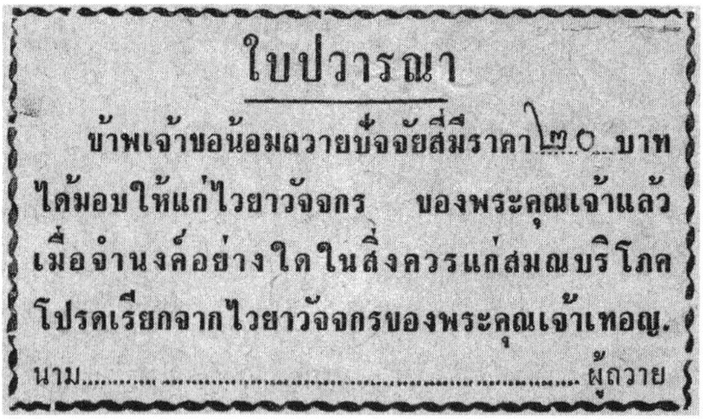

ใบปวารณา

ข้าพเจ้าขอน้อมถวายปัจจัยสี่มีราคา ๒๐ บาท
ได้มอบให้แก่ไวยาวัจจกร ของพระคุณเจ้าแล้ว
เมื่อจำนงค์อย่างใดในสิ่งควรแก่สมณบริโภค
โปรดเรียกจากไวยาวัจจกรของพระคุณเจ้าเทอญ.
นาม.. ผู้ถวาย

Figure 9.7: A declaration donating 20 baht for an *ok phansa* ceremony.

everyone holding a candle and some incense between the fingers of the two hands joined in front of the chest.

The following day, the first waning day of the moon, is known as *Khao phansa,* literally 'to enter the Lenten season'. On this day all monks gather in the temple, and one after the other in order of seniority they declare three times in a firm voice: '*Imasmiṃ āvāse imaṃ temāsaṃ vassaṃ upemi*'. This means: 'I enter upon Lenten season in this residence for these three months'. While many monks are not able to give an exact translation of the solemn declaration, all realize that they promise to bind themselves to this particular monastery for the duration of *phansa*. The Thais interpret this strictly along orthodox lines. Each morning at sunrise, just before the small lines in the hand can be discerned, all monks should be within the boundaries of the monastery they selected for *phansa*. From sunrise onwards, the monks can leave the monastery, but when they wish to depart from the immediate surroundings they must ask permission from the abbot or his delegate. If a monk travels beyond the boundaries of his monastery and is prevented from returning before the first moment of sunrise of the following day, he breaks his vow and will automatically forfeit the strongly beneficial karma of the *pavāraṇa* ceremony at the end of *phansa*. In the case of a serious illness a maximum of seven days' absence is permissible without forfeiting the benefits of completing a Lenten season.[23] *Khao phansa* is primarily a ritual of the Sangha; the lay congregation is only involved in the services of an ordinary sacred day in the Lenten season: food offering, the eight precepts, and sermons.

Three lunar months later, on the day of the full moon of the eleventh lunar month, it is *Ok phansa,* literally: 'Leaving the Lenten season'. The day is a *wan phra*

23 This is in accordance with the canon; see *Mahāvagga* III, 6, 2.

Figure 9.8: Every *wan phra* during *phansa,* the donation of food is a major event.

and the services for the laymen are almost identical with those of an ordinary sacred day during *phansa*. However, there are two subtle differences. In the first place many laymen offer flowers to the monks during the early morning meal of the Sangha. This may be regarded as a token of veneration and respect for individual monks on the day that they complete a Lenten season. In the second place, many laymen bring a bucket, pan, or other vessel to the temple, and make sure that each vessel contains an amount of clean water before the monks begin the *pavāraṇa* ceremony. These vessels are placed in an elevated position of the *bot,* near the main Buddha image. In the beginning of the afternoon a candle is affixed on the rims of each vessel in such a manner that, when alight, the candle will drip wax on the surface of the water. The actual lighting of the candles takes place immediately after the *pavāraṇa* formula when the monks hold a long chanting session.

For the *pavāraṇa* ceremony all monks who have successfully completed a Lenten season gather in the temple. The abbot's deputy opens the ceremony by declaring:

> Sunāṭu me bhante saṃgho ajja pavāraṇa yadi Saṃghassa pattakallaṃ saṃgho pavāreyya.

This is the prescribed formula in the *Vinaya piṭaka,* that has been translated as:

> Let the Sangha, reverend Sirs, hear me. Today is the Pavāraṇā day. If the Sangha is ready, let the Sangha hold Pavāraṇā.[24]

The most senior monk of the assembly has the right to answer first, and after him all other monks chant three times a prescribed formula, each monk for himself. The monks who have been in the order for a longer period than the abbot's deputy will use following polite Pali words:

> Sangham āvuso pavāremi diṭṭhena vā sutena vā parisaṃkāya vā vadantu maṃ āyasmanto anukampaṃ upādāya passanto paṭikarissāmi.

Those who have been members of the order for a shorter period than the spokesman must phrase this formula in a different manner, omitting the familiar *avuso*, and using the more polite term of address *bhante* instead.[25] This formula has been translated as:

> I pronounce my Pavāraṇā, friends, before the Samgha, by what has been seen, or by what has been heard, or by what has been suspected; may you speak to me, Sirs, out of compassion towards me; if I see (an offence), I will atone for it.[26]

After the youngest monk has completed the third repetition of his formula, the candles on the rims of all the vessels are lighted and the monks begin their chanting and meditation session. During this period, it is believed, some of the immense store of good karma of the assembly of monks who have just completed their *phansa* in amity attaches itself to the water and sacralizes it. After the final blessing the laymen can collect their containers and use it for auspicious occasions.

It is remarkable that the *pavāraṇā* formulae are executed faultlessly in a rural monastery such as Wat Sanchao. Without proper understanding of the Pali grammar, the declaration and personal statements are recited exactly as prescribed in the canon. It is indicative, not only of the capacity of the monks to memorize sacred words in these remote monasteries, but also of the fact that the Buddhist church in Thailand is strongly centralized and exerts its influence mainly via printed texts.

On the morning after the *pavāraṇā* ceremony, many laymen will go to the monastery for a very special food offering, called *saibat dawadueng* or the

24 T. W. Rhys Davids and H. Oldenberg. *Vinaya Texts*, Part I, p. 329.

25 Urakhin ประเพณีไทยฉบับพระราชครู [Thai Customs, the Rajaguru edition], p. 672.

26 T. W. Rhys Davids and H. Oldenberg, *Vinaya Texts*, Part I, p. 329.

Tāvatiṃsa begging bowl ceremony. Early in the morning all monks gather in the *bot*, and the lay people collect on either side of the footpaths of the monastery, having brought ample cooked rice and fruit. At a sign from the spokesman for the laity a slow procession takes place. The first to emerge from the temple is a strong man carrying an image of the Buddha 'in walking position' and the Buddha's begging bowl. Immediately behind in single file follow all the monks in order of seniority, also carrying their begging bowls. The whole procession makes the round of the monastery grounds, giving all laymen the opportunity to place rice and fruit in the bowls. The quantities of food are such that the begging bowls are soon filled to capacity and have to be emptied in other containers in order to give all people the chance to make the food offering.

Informants in Wat Sanchao were uncertain about the origin of this custom, but during subsequent research it could be ascertained that it must be related to the story that the Lord Buddha spent the seventh Lenten season after his Awakening in the *Tāvatiṃsa* heaven.[27] *Saibat dawadueng* is a commemoration of the return of the Buddha from his stay in heaven. This explains the name of the ceremony and also why the image of the Buddha with a begging bowl is carried in front of the monks. What appears to be a 'walking Buddha' actually should be seen as a descending Buddha, returning from his stay in heaven to earth.

When *phansa* has ended, the laymen know that within one month the *kathin* robes must be presented. The custom of the preparation and presentation of robes after the rainy season has ended is prescribed in the *Tipiṭaka*.[28] Several elaborate versions of giving these robes have developed in Thailand. In some of the most important monasteries of the country, a Great *kathin*, or *mahakathin*, can be held during which a fabulous range of goods accompany the robes of the monks. Another elaboration is the *chulakathin*, 'Small *kathin*', during which *kathin* robes were manufactured by the combined efforts of the lay community. All people would make sure that they would weave, dye, cut and sew at least one set of robes during the course of a single day. The robes had to be ready before dusk, and if there was reason to fear that the monk's clothes would not be fully prepared by that time, everybody, even the oldest and feeblest monk, had to come and assist. It is only rarely that the *chulakathin* can be witnessed in

27 G. P. Malalasekera, *Dictionary of Pali Proper Names*, Vol. I, 1960, pp. 1002–1003. See also S. J. Tambiah, *Buddhism and the Spirit Cults*, p.159.

28 *Mahāvagga*, VII, 1, 1–6; *Cullavagga*, V, 11, 3–7 and see also the *Pāṭimokkha*, *Nissaggiyā-pācittiyā*, rule 1–3.

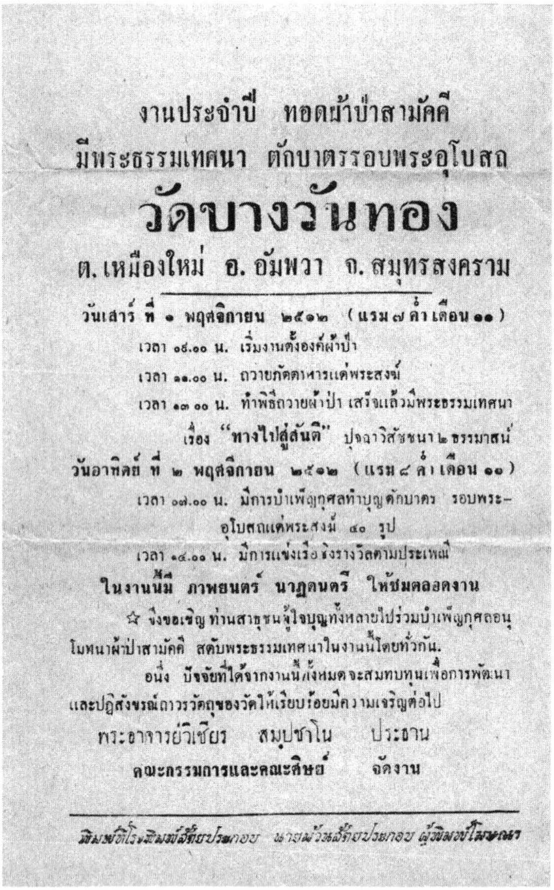

งานประจำปี ทอดผ้าป่าสามัคคี

มีพระธรรมเทศนา ตักบาตรรอบพระอุโบสถ

วัดบางวันทอง

ต. เหมืองใหม่ อ. อัมพวา จ. สมุทรสงคราม

วันเสาร์ ที่ ๑ พฤศจิกายน ๒๕๑๒ (แรม ๗ ค่ำ เดือน ๑๑)

เวลา ๐๙.๐๐ น. เริ่มงานตั้งองค์ผ้าป่า

เวลา ๑๑.๐๐ น. ถวายภัตตาหารแด่พระสงฆ์

เวลา ๑๓.๐๐ น. ทำพิธีถวายผ้าป่า เสร็จแล้วมีพระธรรมเทศนา

เรื่อง "ทางไปสู่สันติ" ปุจฉาวิสัชชนา ๒ ธรรมาสน์

วันอาทิตย์ ที่ ๒ พฤศจิกายน ๒๕๑๒ (แรม ๘ ค่ำ เดือน ๑๑)

เวลา ๐๗.๐๐ น. มีการบำเพ็ญกุศลทำบุญตักบาตร รอบพระ-อุโบสถแด่พระสงฆ์ ๔๐ รูป

เวลา ๑๔.๐๐ น. มีการแข่งเรือชิงรางวัลตามประเพณี

ในงานนี้มี ภาพยนตร์ นาฏดนตรี ให้ชมตลอดงาน

☆ จึงขอเชิญท่านสาธุชนผู้ใจบุญทั้งหลายไปร่วมบำเพ็ญกุศลอนุโมทนาผ้าป่าสามัคคี สดับพระธรรมเทศนาในงานนี้โดยทั่วกัน.

อนึ่ง ปัจจัยที่ได้จากงานนี้ทั้งหมดจะสมทบทุนเพื่อการพัฒนาและปฏิสังขรณ์ถาวรวัตถุของวัดให้เรียบร้อยมีความเจริญต่อไป

พระอาจารย์วิเชียร สมฺปชาโน ประธาน

คณะกรรมการและคณะศิษย์ จัดงาน

พิมพ์ที่โรงพิมพ์ลี้ยิ่งประกอบ นายผ่วนลี้ยิ่งประกอบ ผู้พิมพ์โฆษณา

Figure 9.9: An invitation to join a *phapa* ceremony.

modern times. Nowadays, the new robes are usually purchased in a provincial capital.

The presentation of the *kathin* robes is a ceremony reputed to bring a great amount of beneficial karma to the donor, and therefore it is not unusual to find laymen interested in becoming the main sponsors of such a ritual. One of the reasons why this ceremony carries great prestige and brings honour to the sponsors is that it is extremely expensive. A private individual is expected to give, apart from the new robes, many useful goods and a great amount of money. It is not uncommon to find a rich farmer saving for more than ten years before he can become the main sponsor of a *kathin* ritual. In 1968, only a man who could spare several thousands of baht would think of becoming the holder of such a festival, and rich donors from municipal areas were reported to attach sums of tens of thousands of baht to their robe giving.

Each year the lay community sustaining a monastery waits full of suspense to know whether a private individual will offer to become sponsor of this year's *kathin*. In return everybody is willing to give such a person a hero's welcome and treat him with utmost respect. If no private individual offers to sponsor the *kathin* festival, the community will have to raise money to buy some robes themselves. In order to bring a money gift together with the new robes they will organize a fund-raising ceremony in the monastery, attracting small gifts by holding a dance or a film show.

It has been noted by Tambiah that during the presentation of *kathin* robes sometimes a 'money tree' is presented.[29] He failed to note, however, that the offering of a tree forms part of a ceremony that can be held in conjunction with *kathin*, but is wholly separate and may also be celebrated at any other time of the year. It is the ritual of presenting *phapa* (ผ้าป่า), forest clothes. The donation of *phapa* involves much less expenditure than that of *kathin*, and consequently it carries less prestige. A small tree is provided with banknotes and under the tree is a collection of goods of a kind useful to the monastery in its daily running. Thus the *phapa* gifts often include new pots and pans, brooms, vessels with oil, petrol and paraffin as well as some durable fruits such as coconuts. Usually it is the abbot who takes possession of the gifts in the name of the Sangha.

Public ceremonies in monasteries 'other than one's own'

Some of the ceremonies described in the previous section need not necessarily be sponsored by the laymen who live in the immediate vicinity of the monastery where the rituals are performed. Quite often a *kathin* festival is instigated by somebody who is not directly related to any of the regular supporters of the monastery. When outsiders channel their resources into an ordination or a *kathin* or *phapa* presentation, the receiving monastery is under no obligation to return the gesture. When the sponsor has been received in a proper and adequate manner, the community is under no further obligation for the sponsor will have been amply rewarded by the prestige he has gained and by the great store of beneficial karma that accrued to him by donating his money to such a good cause.

While the farmers can accept outsiders as main sponsors for ordinations, *kathin* and *phapa* presentations in their own monastery, they may similarly

29 Tambiah, *Buddhism and the spirit Cults*, p. 159.

decide to celebrate such a ritual in a community other than their own. This occurs regularly especially with regard to *kathin* and *phapa*. Often the wealthier farmers pool their resources and become the main sponsors in a monastery that has caught their attention. Then they make it known to their friends and relatives that anybody who wishes to share the merit should pay some money to the main organizers and thereby become part of the retinue of the main sponsors during the presentation. In central Thailand it has become the custom to select for such occasions a monastery in a region that many villagers may want to visit, so that the presentation of robes is combined with a holiday. As soon as the Lenten season is over, the roads and waterways are therefore the scene of many processions. Buses and lorries, tugboats and water-taxis, gaily decorated with flags and banners, carry large groups of villagers to monasteries other than their own. The farmers in the region of Wat Sanchao had the opportunity to participate in two very adventurous *kathin* presentations, one in 1966 to the Phuket peninsula about 600 km south of Ratburi and another in 1967 to Chiang Mai, a similar distance north.

Whilst ordinations and *kathin* festivals do not involve the main sponsors in reciprocal relationships, many other rituals in which outsiders participate do involve the recipients of gifts in an obligation to return the donation at some time in the future. This can be clearly seen in the big fund-raising ceremonies that take place approximately once a year in almost every monastery in rural central Thailand. It is difficult to predict what occasion the elders of a community will choose for a fund drive. Sometimes, when no outside sponsor has been found to present *kathin* robes, they are forced to raise money for this event, but they may choose any of the other major annual ceremonies as an excuse to raise money.

They may think of an unusual ceremony in order to create interest: a famous monk may be found willing to give a public preaching, a new building of the monastery may be inaugurated, or a ceremony to endow amulets with beneficial power may be organized. As soon as the laymen, in consultation with the monks, have decided which occasion will be used to try and raise capital, the event must be advertised widely. Notices stating the event, the date, the place and the major attractions are printed and sent to relatives and friends who live far away. At the entrance of the monastery a big placard may announce the same information. Nowadays it is quite common for the lay organizers to hire a boat or a car that has been fitted with loudspeakers and thus publicize the fund-raising ceremony in neighbouring communities. On the day of the event, free transport to the monastery may be offered to all groups who are interested to take part and all participants may be brought home free of charge.

In the course of time these regular events have resulted in an intricate network of mutual relationships between different communities. When a fund-raising festival is to take place at a monastery which is situated at a large distance, but with which there exists a reciprocal relationship, the leaders of the community make sure to hold a collection well before the event takes place. All contributions are attached to a small tree, or to a symbolic representation of a tree that is manufactured of wire, coloured paper and glue. Presenting gifts on a tree (which we have already encountered as part of the *phapa* ritual) is commonly recognized in Thailand as a solemn and formal deed, in accordance with ancient customs. It is related to the concept of heavenly plants such as the *kapparukkha,* which reputedly yield any object that people may wish them to yield. The people who carry the money tree to the monastery where the fund-raising festival is held are received with great respect; they are treated as ambassadors from the other community. The amount of money on the tree is publicly announced and recorded, so that on a similar occasion in the monastery from where the communal gift came, a deputation with a gift not markedly greater, but certainly not less, can be sent in return. Thus, when a whole array of tree gifts accumulates during a fund-raising ceremony, this reveals part of the network of formal obligations between different communities in a wide region.

Establishing a scale of merit

Some anthropologists have tried to measure the villager's evaluation of different ceremonies through questionnaires. Kaufman, for example, asked 25 Thai adults to place ten items that he had selected for that purpose, in order of 'maximum merit'. The results of his questionnaires were computed until a single list of items appeared, noting from high to low:

1. Becoming a monk.
2. Contributing enough money for the construction of a monastery.
3. Having a son ordained as a monk.
4. Making excursions to the Buddhist shrines throughout Thailand.
5. Contributing towards the repair of a monastery.
6. Giving food, daily, to the monks and giving food on holy days.
7. Becoming a novice.
8. Attending a monastery on all holy days and obeying the eight precepts on these days.

9. Obeying the five precepts at all times.
10. Giving money and clothing to the monks at presentation of *kathin* robes.[30]

The value of this type of research appears rather limited. In the first place the sample seems rather small; only 25 adults were asked out of a population of 744 persons. Also one may object to the narrow range of choices given to the villagers. Many common meritorious acts such as listening to a sermon, circumambulating a temple, charity to laymen, listening to the chanting of the monks or helping to finance a cremation were not included. The most serious objection, however, lies in the fact that some items that were presented to the villagers must have seemed unrealistic, sometimes impossible and in other instances ambiguous. For example, the construction of a whole monastery is totally beyond the scope of villagers. While a rich farmer may finance ceremonies that cost him several thousands of baht, building a monastery involves a person in a outlay of the order of millions. Similarly, obeying the five precepts at all times is incompatible with a farmer's way of life, and while there are a good number of people who observe the eight precepts during the Lenten season, there is nobody who would contemplate doing so throughout the year. Items 5 and 10 must have puzzled the informants for they may be interpreted at different levels. There is a fundamental difference between contributing a sum of money towards a good cause and becoming the main sponsor of a major ceremony and it is not possible to see in the wording which of the two Kaufman intended to be answered.

A similar exercise is reported by Tambiah whose sample was markedly bigger, but who offered an even more limited choice of activities to be ranked. His 79 family heads came up with the following ranking:

1. Financing entire building of a monastery.
2. Becoming a monk oneself.
3. Having a son become a monk.
4. Contributing money to the repair of a monastery.
5. Making gifts at a *kathin* ceremony.
6. Giving food daily to monks.
7. Observing every *wan phra* at the monastery.
8. Strict observance of the five precepts.[31]

30 Kaufman, *Bangkhuad*, pp. 183–4. I have changed the wording of the list slightly to fit in with the terms used in this book.

31 Tambiah, 'The Ideology of Merit', p. 68, reprinted in *Buddhism and the Spirit Cults*, p. 147.

The criticisms that were expressed in relation to Kaufman's list apply to an even greater extent to the one drawn up by Tambiah. The list cannot be regarded as exhaustive, and some of the items must have seemed unrealistic or highly ambiguous to the informants. It need therefore not surprise us that the two lists show discrepancies. Whilst Kaufman's informants placed contributions to the *kathin* ceremony lowest on the scale (probably thinking of a communally organized *kathin*), Tambiah's villagers (probably thinking of the chief sponsor of such a ceremony) evaluated it much higher.

With regard to the fact that items of 'ethical and moralistic conduct' are placed very low on the list, Tambiah comments:

> Strict observance of the five precepts (especially that exhorting avoidance of killing) and meditation on the philosophical assertions of the *Dhamma* have little positive interest for the villager, either because lay life is not possible without breaking some of the prohibitions or because one must renounce lay life altogether to pursue such aims. He therefore rates these pursuits, in so far as they have relevance for his life, low on the merit-making scale; this is not because he devalues them but because they are not normally open to him. ...[32]

In contrast to Tambiah, I do not think that the villagers placed these items so low on the scale because these pursuits were not normally open to them. After all, constructing a whole monastery is even less open to the farmer, but he places it on top of the list. It seems that the farmers tried, difficult though it must have been with some items, to apply the criterion of financial sacrifice to all items. That is why the construction of a monastery ranks high, and the ethical conduct comes low on the scale. After all, the observance of *wan phra* need not involve participants in great expense, as just a few coins may be offered during an official sermon. Similarly, the five precepts need not involve people in financial losses; on the contrary, by refraining from gambling and intoxicating beverages many a farmer would even be better off financially.

The line of enquiry taken by Kaufman and Tambiah, attempting to establish a scale of meritorious activities, would gain in interest if a much longer list with much more specific items were presented to the informants. For good measure it should include detailed descriptions such as: 'A man donates 100 *baht* towards a cremation but does not present it personally, sending it by mail' and another item which shows a subtly different situation: 'A man donates 100

32 *Buddhism and the Spirit Cults*, p. 148.

baht towards a cremation using the proper dedication when handing it over'. Merit is a very complex idea and each case may be judged taking all aspects surrounding the activity into account. I therefore sympathize with Bunnag who refrains from grading types of meritorious activities because she realizes that aspects such as the purity of the actors' intentions and the usefulness of the act itself must be taken into account.[33]

As a general guideline towards understanding the different acts of obtaining beneficial karma it is useful to remember that greater financial outlay results in a greater return in good karma. Since virtually all farmers possess only a limited income and because during the year there will be many occasions to take part in ceremonies that carry considerable merit, each farmer has to decide many times whether he will attend a certain ceremony and, if so, how much he will contribute. Often the farmer is obliged to attend and assist with a ritual, simply because the ceremony is given by friends or relatives with whom he wishes to maintain good contacts. On such occasions the fact that he will thereby increase his store of good karma may well be of secondary importance.

During public ceremonies in 'one's own' monastery and when there are fund-raising rituals in monasteries with which the community keeps a formal relationship, people contribute not only because they gain merit, but also so as not to be seen to lag behind others. The organizers of a fund-raising ceremony are well aware of this secondary motivation and, in addition to writing down all contributions in a book open for inspection, they often announce each donation over a loudspeaker. A rich man cannot hope to give a small amount unnoticed. If he decides to do so notwithstanding the publicity, his decision will be respected, however. It is not proper to directly shame a person into increasing his contribution: each person should give as much as he wishes and it is considered bad manners to indicate that a person should have donated more. Nevertheless, while *mores* prevent the villager from stating openly that a person is trying to shirk his social obligations, most farmers are well aware of what is expected of themselves and of others in order to escape the verdict of being stingy.

There are occasions when the prime motivation for contributing to a ceremony seems to lie in the special power that is believed to be emitted during the ritual. Many of the yearly recurring major festivals seem to be characterized by some kind of force that carries rewards in the immediate future. When bathing clothes are given to the monks, it is believed that it will rain in the fields, not in the unspecified future, but in the following weeks and months.

33 *Buddhist Monk, Buddhist Layman*, p. 145.

Similarly, a chanting session in a private house is expected to ensure prosperity in that year. It is in this light that a famous monk who had preached during a fund-raising ritual ended his blessing to the crowd with the words: 'May all of you win the lottery this week'.[34] In the ears of the contributors this remark quite naturally was uttered directly after the concluding Pali blessings were chanted by that monk. There are many instances known of farmers who had a stroke of good fortune immediately after contributing to an important event that carried good karma. In fact, many will postpone trying their luck until after such a ritual. This idea is closely related to that of the emission of beneficial power by monks uttering sacred words. It is the immediate force that purifies the house via the sacred cord and that charges the vessel of water whilst the monks chant in a private home; the same power, but probably even stronger, is transferred to the water in the vessels which stand in the vicinity of the monks during and immediately after the *pavāraṇā* ceremony.

The people who do not experience any immediate beneficial result from having come into contact with the power of the chanting monks can rest assured that their financial contributions were not in vain. The doctrine of karma assures a person that each good deed will have its reward, if not in this life, then in the life hereafter. This latter aspect, being at best in the background of the thoughts of many adults, gains in importance as a person becomes older. When a man or woman has reached an age when death becomes likely, it may become a motivation of prime importance.

34 Wat Phodok, September 26, 1968. A similar event occurred in Wat Bangwanthong, November 1, 1969.

CHAPTER X

OLD AGE, DEATH, AND THE HEREAFTER

When their physical powers diminish and people become unfit for heavy work in the fields, they usually transfer most of their assets to some younger relatives in return for food, company and a place to sleep. The elderly often play an important role in the life of the family with whom they live: they willingly care for the very small children, they often look after the vegetables in the compound, they help with the lighter household tasks, and they occupy themselves with some useful handicraft. At all times they can be a mine of information for their younger relatives.

With increasing age, their interest in religion may be enhanced. While there are aged people who do not go to the monastery on *wan phra,* who are prevented from attending or otherwise prefer to stay home, many elderly persons regard the periods that they are devout *ubasok* and *ubasika* as highlights of the year. On those occasions when they follow the eight precepts they are forced to refrain from idle talk, gossip or angry words, they should not laugh loudly or speak rashly. Their conversations invariably turn to serious religious subjects. Among this group of older persons who stay together for a whole day and night a common topic of conversation is the life hereafter.

The gruesome details of the many hells of Buddhism are well known to them from sermons based on the *Traiphumikhatha,* from the story of the Venerable Malai and from depictions in books and paintings. It may be safely surmised that the old people do not like to envisage the possibility that they themselves may suffer in one of these hells. This horrible fate is reserved for people who commit hideous crimes, who, for example, kill their own parents or a monk, or who commit a less heinous deed with great frequency. To be on the safe side, many farmers have assured themselves against going to a hell by attending seven different inaugurations of temples. It is generally believed that a person who has pressed gold leaf on all the stones which are ritually buried in and around the *bot* on seven individual occasions cannot go to hell immediately after the present existence finishes. Apart from pressing gold leaf on all the nine round stones, most people drop a packet, containing a small candle, some incense, a flower, a miniature booklet, a pencil, a needle and some thread into the hole where the central stone will be lowered. These objects ensure that in the next existence the person performing the ceremony will obtain access to knowledge, represented by the paper and writing instrument, whilst the needle and thread symbolize a sharp and keen brain.

There are other pitfalls to be avoided in rebirth. One of the unfortunate possibilities, one that especially applies to people who have been avaricious throughout their life, is to be born as a *pret*, an unhappy being roaming around the world as some kind of ghost consisting mainly of an enormous stomach who craves for food, but has no adequate means to assuage its hunger. A state even more unpleasant than that of a *pret* is that of an animal. The animal world may be seen as an existential trap, a dead-end, since even domestic animals have very little opportunity to accumulate the good karma that is needed for an improved rebirth. An existence preferable to that of a *pret*, but still an unfortunate rebirth for a human is that as a *yak* (ยักษ์) an ogre commonly seen as the victim of emotional drives and passions, who possesses considerable magical power. Another possibility is the *asura* (อสูร) a figure that can change its shape at will, can travel through the air, and who can, in exceptional instances, come to the aid of human beings in distress.

While most older people will admit that it is theoretically possible to become a *pret*, *yak* or *asura*, virtually nobody envisages such a rebirth for himself. Most people expect that they will be reborn in circumstances very similar to those of their present lives. They imagine that they will be rural people who will speak Thai and that they will meet all their friends and relatives, as well as their enemies. This view stems from the idea that the interpersonal relationships of a former life, of the present, and of lives in the future are not accidental, but are the direct result of interlinked karma. The person who befriends another individual knows that this developing relationship is the outcome of some action in one or more of past lives and also that it will have consequences in their respective future lives. Therefore, people who love each other will offer each other a share in beneficial karma, and people who hurt each other may expect to continue to do so beyond the span of the present life. Thus it is believed that a man who kills somebody will be killed himself, during a future life, by his reborn victim. These views have relevance for parts of the marriage ceremony, for when the couple give food to the monks they hold the spoon or the plate simultaneously, linking their karma. Similarly, if there is a strong dislike between two persons in a community, they take trouble to avoid making merit together,

While the farmers are of the opinion that their destinies are linked with the fate of the persons with whom they interact, it is considered an open question in what relative position the actors will stand towards each other in a future existence. A woman may well be reborn as a male; if a person is at present the father of another individual he may become that person's sister or neighbour,

In general, those who think that the balance of good and bad karma of the present life is loaded in favour of the bad karma will expect to be reborn as people who are slightly lower on the social and financial ladder, or, if they consider that the present life is already so full of misfortunes that some of the past bad karma has worked itself out, they may expect to be reborn in almost the same position in society. Those who feel that their beneficial karma outweighs their bad karma can hope to be born in a position better than the present. They may envisage becoming wealthy merchants, rich landowners or secure government officials. A person who during his lifetime repeatedly performed ceremonies of major significance may expect great rewards. A man who, while he was a monk, learned to recite the *Pāṭimokkha* and often led the Sangha in its formal chanting, a person who was main sponsor of a *kathin* donation, or somebody who contributed with largesse to the building of one or more monasteries, may temporarily even go to one of the heavens to reap the rewards of having accumulated such an extraordinary store of beneficial karma. A person can live in heaven either in human form, for example, as a guest of the gods in the *Tāvatiṃsa* heaven, or he may become one of the gods himself.

It is interesting to note that in animistic Buddhism no farmer aspires to reach *nibbāna*. This exalted state is reserved for the Buddha and the *arahants*. While, in the eyes of the farmers, *nibbāna* is something like eternal bliss, they feel decidedly that no ordinary human can aspire to reach such a state of perfection. Most of them only hope that they may, during the course future existences, improve their circumstances to such an extent that they are reborn as wealthy persons. They also hope that, if they ever reach that goal, they will be wise enough to invest a considerable amount of wealth in meritorious activity in order to ensure that they do not fall back to the level of struggling agriculturalists.

Therefore, Thai farmers do not aspire to escape rebirth; they are satisfied to be reborn in better circumstances. *Moksa* (โมกษะ), the well-known term for salvation or deliverance in Buddhist literature,[1] is understood by Buddhist philosophers as a freeing from the eternal cycle of birth and death; for the Thai farmers, who are not at all oppressed at the thought of continuing rebirth, the term has a different meaning. Many unsophisticated Buddhists understand *moksa* to mean a delivery from misery as a direct result of the acquisition of merit. *Moksa* can be experienced temporarily; according to the farmers it simply means an intense feeling of wellbeing. In future lives, *moksa* can thus be experienced by being reborn in very fortunate circumstances.

When assessing the past, older people may realize that they have accumulated a great amount of bad karma. They know that evil deeds of the past cannot be erased by a good deed in the present, and that each bad action inevitably will result in some kind of misfortune. This knowledge does not motivate them to a fatalistic resignation; on the contrary, it often results in an increased feeling of responsibility. After all, every meritorious act will carry benefits, and the person who adds to his store of good karma increases his chances of fortune in his rebirth. Considerations of this kind sometimes induce people to consider joining a group of religious specialists. Men may think about joining the Sangha, and women may want to join a group of female religious virtuosi, the *mae chi*.

The older monks

While the accumulation of good karma may have become so important to an elderly man that he decides to become a monk, other considerations may also play a role. The high status and exalted position of a member of the Sangha attract all but the humblest men in rural communities. In addition, the position of a monk is protected and secure: a monk can rely upon receiving food and shelter, and every monk receives free medical treatment in all state hospitals. Moreover, some of the aspects of monastic life that may deter younger men from remaining a long time in the Sangha do not seem so forbidding to a person of ripe age. It is especially those rules of monastic behaviour that accentuate the fact that a monk should always be calm, passionless, and at peace that may attract an older man rather than discourage him. Older monks do not have to prepare for the yearly *Nak tham* examinations, and they will often be able to chant all common Pali texts effortlessly, so that their learning tasks are markedly lighter than those of younger monks.

1 As noted with the term *phiksu*, Thai Buddhist terminology adopted some key terms from Sanskrit rather than Pali. Thus they use *moksa* (from Sanskrit *mokṣa*) rather than the Pali *mokkha*.

Before an older man can become a monk he needs to be assured of continued support of at least one family. Most rural monasteries are not wealthy and depend for their food solely on the daily gifts from the lay supporters. The abbot of a monastery has the legal power to refuse a monk to live in his monastery,[2] and he will only assent to the entrance of a new monk when he knows that this will not constitute a risk to the food supply available to those already in his charge. It is only when a monk can claim that a group of laymen will continually present extra food because of his presence in the monastery that a rural abbot will consider permitting an additional monk to come and live there. The wise abbot will also assess whether or not the new monk will fit in with the rest of the monks, but usually he will not exclude a man who has lay sponsors. In urban areas, where the link between laymen and monks is much more diffuse, such considerations may not be relevant.

After the older aspirant monk has found out that he will be allowed to live in a certain monastery, he has to approach a monk who has the power to ordain. The Department of Religious Affairs in the capital recommends that ordainers should not admit men into the Sangha who are sick and feeble, or those over eighty years old, but the decision in each individual case rests upon the judgment of the ordainer. Usually an older man who has obtained permission to live in a certain monastery will be able to find an ordainer without much difficulty. His ordination ceremony is often a simple affair, with only the nearest relatives attending and the minimum number of monks. There will be no *tham khwan*, no public procession, and the ordination itself may even take place in the private office of the ordainer instead of in a *bot*.

Like all monks, once ordained, the older *phiksu* can decide for himself whether he will remain in the order or return to lay status. In general, however, older men remain members of the Sangha for a long time, in many cases until they die. It is not uncommon for a man who joins the order at a ripe age to live as a monk for a further decade or even longer. The longer he is a monk, the more exalted becomes his ritual position, and as more senior monks die or leave the order and newly ordained men enter the Sangha his relative position in the hierarchy rises. A monk who remains in the same monastery for many years may withdraw almost completely from the world, content with the monastic routine, watching from a distance every year how religious life intensifies during *phansa*, to ebb away into quieter months outside the Lenten season. Usually the older monks form solid friendships with other

2 Article 38 of the 1962 Act on the Administration of the Sangha, p. 54.

aged members of the order and rely upon each other for support and an understanding ear.

There are some older monks who will not be content to withdraw from the world. They may cultivate their relations with laymen, especially those who continuously support the monastery for their sake. These monks may at all times be sought out by laymen to give advice on matters of ritual, but also on economic transactions between farmers. They may even be asked to give advice in quarrels and disputes. Their cells are always open to friends and relatives and in time such places become a focal point for many people where they may drop in to discuss the daily events.

Some of the older monks may cultivate their relations with laymen to an even greater extent. They are the monks who are willing to help the abbot in organizing and preparing the major ceremonies. They are sought out by the lay leaders to discuss the possibilities of another fund-raising ceremony. Whenever a pilgrimage is arranged or a *phapa* offering to a different community is prepared, their opinion weighs heavily. The abbot may delegate some administrative tasks to such monks. They may take charge of the daily distribution of food, ensuring that every monk, novice, *dek wat* and animal obtains a fair share. Such a monk may be asked by the abbot to supervise the borrowing from the store of household goods of the monastery. He will have to write down in detail what goods leave the monastery and see to it that they are returned in good condition. Sometimes the older monk may be asked to enter all sources of income in a book especially set aside for this purpose, and to supervise all purchases. The abbot of a monastery may thus come to depend heavily upon his senior monks for the daily administration of his monastery, and reserve for himself only the most important decisions and the receiving of the more distinguished visitors.

Traditionally, an older monk with aptitude for public relations and administration would end up by becoming abbot himself. Occasionally the laymen may put up the name of one of their oldest monks to become abbot, and if there is no other suitable candidate, an appointment may result. It has, however, become the policy to appoint younger experienced monks, notably those who showed a remarkable aptitude for monastic life and ecclesiastical studies when they first became members of the Sangha in their early twenties and who then chose to stay in the order. Modern abbots may be as young as thirty when they are chosen for this office.

Among the specializations of older monks that of medicine ranks high. Fully consistent with the animistic interpretation of Buddhism is the practice of asking for *mantra* water, *nam mon*, in order to cure aches and pains. When a monk has male patients he may rub sacral water over the sore parts, but women, of course, have to take the *nam mon* home. Apart from the use of powerful *nam mon*, there are several other fields of medicine open to members of the Sangha. There are some older monks who are famous for the healing power of their pills, manufactured from ground-up sacred objects. Others have a regular clientele for their bundles of herbs from which the patient should brew a medicinal tea. The monk's name as a doctor depends mainly on his success in difficult cases. He does not receive a fixed payment for his services; it is up to the client to decide on the remuneration. A small gift is usual before the treatment begins, but a greater amount can be expected as soon as the patient feels better.

Some older monks specialize in esoteric knowledge. They may, for example, draw *yan* on rectangular or triangular pieces of cloth. After they have drawn the diagrams and inscribed the proper letters and ciphers, all the while pronouncing appropriate *khatha*, these pieces of cloth are believed to be capable of protecting a person. The monk who wishes to specialize in this kind of lore frequently obtains his knowledge from another monk who already is an established expert. If no such expert is available, he may learn from some of the popular textbooks on *khatha* and *yan*, but usually he will take care not to be seen whilst consulting such a publication, because most specialists proclaim that these books do not transmit the full knowledge. If a book were printed with a complete *khatha*, or with a *yan* fully drawn in all details, the magical effects would immediately be noticeable, heat would accumulate, making the book too hot to be held casually in the hand.

Pieces of cloth inscribed by an expert are valuable. Some should be hung in the house in a properly elevated position, while others are reputed to protect a boat from collision and must be fastened in the stern. There are special ones made to protect cars and buses and others may be rolled up and put in a small cylinder that may be worn around the neck. The monk whose magical drawings have reputedly saved people from accidents may be sought out to perform many small prophylactic ceremonies. He may be asked to sprinkle the area of the house with *nam mon* where a woman will give birth; it is this monk who will be asked to make a metal *takrut* for a young boy. He may tattoo a young man or a recently ordained monk with beneficially charged ink. If someone buys a new cart, he may ask such a monk to bless the vehicle by drawing protective diagrams over it whilst muttering the proper spells. He is also the monk who makes the small Buddha images that can be worn around the neck. If these images acquire a reputation for their power, they may make his monastery famous throughout the region. During a fund-raising ceremony the lay committee may decide that a medallion be cast with this monk's face on one side and a simple *yan* on the back and thousands of people may treasure possessing one.

Women as religious specialists

In Thailand, generally, no females are admitted to full membership of the order.[3] This is in accordance with the animistic form of Buddhism in which women are regarded as antithetic to the monks' sacred beneficial power. As a result of the regular contact with the literary Buddhist tradition, most adults know that once this was not the case. The text of the *Pāṭimokkha* is frequently recited in even the remotest monasteries and in it there are many rules which prescribe the monk's behaviour towards women who are members of the Sangha, namely the *bhikkhunīs*. While all such rules are regarded as obsolete, the repeated mentioning of such a class of persons may cause some to formulate their views regarding the admittance of women to the order. Thus the late *Phrakhru* Wimonkiti:

> In the remote past there were indeed women in the Sangha but this practice has been given up long ago. The Lord Buddha in his wisdom never wanted women in the order, but when he was persuaded he put so many safeguards up that it became virtually impossible for women to enter. In the first place a woman has to go into a prolonged novitiate that may last several years. In the second place the ordination ceremony itself would be most embarrassing for women because of the long and intimate questioning prescribed in the *Vinaya Piṭaka*.[4]

These statements cannot be simply dismissed as the anti-feminine prejudices of a celibate Thai monk. There are indeed indications that the Buddha had to be persuaded to allow women to become *bhikkhunīs*. There are also many regulations and safeguards in the canon, ensuring an effective separation of monks and nuns[5] that, if these rules were interpreted in its strictest form, it would be virtually impossible to set up this branch of the order anew. The segregation prescribed in

3 Some emancipated women obtained full ordination, first in Taiwan and more recently in Sri Lanka, but as of 2011 they have not yet succeeded in being formally accepted as members of the Thai Sangha.

4 The Venerable Wimonkitì, personal communication, Wat Phanoenplu, 31 August 1968.

5 See the chapter of the *Cullavagga*, of which an English translation can be found in T. W. Rhys Davids and H. Oldenberg, *Vinaya Texts*, Part III, pp. 320–69.

the *Cullavagga* makes for two different organizations within the Sangha, one for men and the other for women. With regard to the embarrassment in the event of a woman being ordained, the Venerable Wimonkitì probably referred to the formal Pali questioning of the candidate, which, in the case of women refers to a number of abnormalities, deformities and diseases of the womb. Since the wording of these questions is couched in an obsolete terminology the embarrassment factor would constitute a much smaller impediment.

Whatever the reason given, the fact remains that women are still barred from being members of the Sangha. The closest a woman can get towards sacred living is by joining the ascetics, by becoming a *mae chi*. The word *chi* is probably related to the Sanskrit *jīva*. In Hindi there exists a similar word, *ji*, a title attached to names as a mark of respect.[6] These women who carry the title *chi* are not *bhikkhunīs*, they are not members of the Sangha and therefore they ought not be referred to as nuns. Often the *chi* live in an organization of recluses and undoubtedly they model their behaviour upon the example of the monks. Generally, but not always, they shave their heads every month as an indication that they renounce vanity. They also have a uniform. They cannot wear yellow, red or brown robes, since these would make them indistinguishable from monks and novices, and therefore they have to be satisfied with wearing white robes. There are some solitary *chi*, but often they live in small groups, where they observe an order of seniority. The eldest *chi* is responsible for the general appearance of the communal abode and makes sure that all her charges present a neat and clean appearance.

That they are a long-established institution in Thailand is demonstrated by the account of Schouten, more than three-and-a-half centuries ago:

> Besides these Priests, there are a sort of old Nuns shorn, lodged in Chappels near the greatest Temples, who assist very devoutly in all their preachings, singings, ceremonies, and other Church services, but all voluntary, being tied to no rules or prescriptions.[7]

At present it is a fairly widespread institution. The *Yearbook for Religious Affairs* reported just over 10,000 *chi* in 1967, but this number had decreased to 9,348 in 1970.[8] One of the main reasons why the number is not greater is the fact

6 M. Monier-Williams, *A Sanskrit-English Dictionary*, p. 442.

7 J. Schouten, *A Description of the Government, Might, Religion, Customes, Traffick, and Other Remarkable Affairs in the Kingdom of Siam, 1636*, translated into English by Roger Manley in 1671, p. 141.

8 รายงานการศาสนาประจำปี ๒๕๑๐ [Annual Report on Religious Affairs, 2510], p. 97 and รายงานการศาสนาประจำปี ๒๕๑๓ [Annual Report on Religious Affairs, 2513], p. 159.

that it is not customary for *chi* to collect food like the monks and novices, and therefore they must be able to sustain themselves financially.

There are some inconsistencies in the literature concerning the number of precepts that these female religious specialists follow. Whilst Schouten states that they are tied to no rules or prescriptions, Kaufman, more than three centuries later, reports that they follow 'only eight of the 227 rules'.[9] Kingshill, on the other hand, maintains that the *chi* 'are required only to keep the ten precepts which the novices keep'.[10] In the region of Wat Sanchao none of these views held; the female recluses considered themselves bound to the five precepts in all its ramifications. Only on special days, like other devout laymen, they would join the group that vows to adhere to the eight precepts for a period of one day and one night.

In contrast to ordinary farmers, the *chi* try to follow the five precepts strictly and meticulously and this compels them to avoid most contact with the secular world. Usually they live just within the precincts of a monastery or in a house in the immediate vicinity. Thus they are able to attend all public ceremonies, they often donate food to the monks and seldom miss an opportunity to hear a sermon. In their private surroundings they may add to their store of beneficial karma by reading sacred books, by meditating and by learning Pali texts by heart. The chanting of sacred Pali words is thus not forbidden to them, and some groups of *chi* become quite famous for their beautiful way of chanting. At major cremation ceremonies, a group of *chi* can be invited to chant some sacred texts appropriate to the occasion. This occurs rarely in rural areas because there are seldom sufficient *chi* attached to a rural monastery to make up a chapter, and it would, of course, be unthinkable to mix monks and *chi* in the same chapter. Moreover, many farmers, whilst appreciating the chanting skills of the female recluses, prefer the monks. The, latter, after all, are full members of the Sangha, they follow many more precepts, and are therefore expected to emit a much stronger beneficial force whilst uttering the sacred words.

Death

The various ways of dealing with the phenomenon of death can be brought under two headings: there are procedures for handling deaths that are predictable and expected, and there are different methods for treating those that occur suddenly, tragically and unpredictably.

9 Kaufman, *Bangkhuad*, p.121.

10 Kingshill, *Ku Daeng*, p. 73.

The expected demise

People who live to a ripe age and who, having become very feeble, expect to die soon should remain in their own homes. If they are staying somewhere else, for example if they are undergoing treatment in a hospital, and death appears imminent, they should be transported to their homes. It is considered inauspicious to carry a corpse into a private house and therefore the person who dies while away from his usual residence would have to be brought straight to the monastery where all final rituals would take place. It is much better to perform these ceremonies in the house, so that the spirit of the deceased will not be upset and will let itself be coaxed gently and naturally into the world of the dead, from where a link with the *phi ban* (ผีบ้าน), the class of ancestors who are still attached to their old property and interested in the welfare of their descendants, may be established and maintained.

When the relatives of a person are aware that death is approaching and inevitable, they must try and make the dying person think of some activities of the past that were highly auspicious. Thus a man may be reminded of the fact that he was ordained as a monk many years ago, or that he once performed a *kathin* ceremony. A woman can be reminded of the ordination of her sons, the many times she gave food to the monks or the time she spent in the monastery as an *ubasika*. When the end is near, in general it is advisable to make a dying person repeat some auspicious words like the Triple Gem, or the words '*arahant, arahant*'. In Buddhist philosophy, an *arahant*, literally 'deserving', is a person who has destroyed all karmic influences, who will not be reborn and will therefore reach *nibbāna*. The repetition of this word does not mean that the farmer hopes to become an *arahant*. It is simply a highly auspicious word that is used because it puts a person in a frame of mind in which meritorious subjects prevail. It is believed that a person who at the moment of death thinks about his beneficial karma will reap the fruits of this merit by heading eventually towards a good rebirth, whereas a person who dies remorseful of his past will reap the results of his evil deeds through an inauspicious rebirth.

When a person has expired in his own home, surrounded by his close relatives, signs of excessive grief should be suppressed. If there are members of the family who are overcome by grief and who can no longer control themselves, they should be led away from the corpse for it is inauspicious to let tear drops fall on the body of a dead person. It is said that the soul of the dead person may not yet have realized what has happened, and the crying relatives may make it difficult for the soul of the deceased to depart from this existence.

When the eyes of the dead person remain wide open this is interpreted as a sign that the soul is anxious about his relatives and reluctant to leave the body. One of the bystanders should close the eyes whilst saying in a soothing voice words like: 'It is all right, don't be anxious, you shall go well'.

The bereaved family will usually call on the services of a man who is prepared to act as undertaker in return for a small fee. He will instruct that water be fetched and that the body be washed. The body is then dressed in clean clothes and all relatives are invited to take part in a further ritual washing. In this context the act of sprinkling with water is not one of cleansing but must be regarded as paying homage, and at the same time it is an asking forgiveness for any bad feelings that still may exist between the deceased and the living. The closest relatives pour water over hands and feet of the dead person, but all other persons pour water only over the hands.

In the mouth a coin is placed, which the soul of the dead person needs in order to pay the fare to cross the underworld river, guarded by *Phra Ketkaew Culamani,* (เก็จแก้วจุฬามณี) or 'Lord Bright Gem Jewel'. Probably this is Yama, the Hindu god who presides over the dead and who is described as 'with a glittering form, a crown on his head'.[11] If the person who dies was fond of areca fruit and betel leaves, a small quantity of this may also be placed in the mouth. Further preparation of the corpse entails the colouring of the face with turmeric, the arranging of the hands on the chest, palm to palm, with a candle, incense and a flower placed between them.

This is followed by the ritual of *tra sang* (ตราสัง), 'binding the corpse'. The undertaker uses a piece of white unspun cotton thread to bind the neck, feet and hands whilst saying the Pali formula: '*Putto gīve, dhano pade, bhariya hatthe*'. This is interpreted as a spell with which to free a person from the three strongest ties in this world: from the tie of children (whilst putting a loop with the cord around the neck), from wealth (when binding the feet), and from the tie of the spouse (while the hands are tied).[12] One end of the *sai sin* is kept hanging free for a length of about one metre. Then the body is placed in a wooden coffin, and the loose end of the cotton thread is hung over the side so that later, when the monks come to chant, it is easy to knot another cord to it. In the coffin a small ladder with four rungs may be placed, made from the stem of a banana tree. This little ladder should enable the soul of the dead man to leave the coffin at any time. It is necessary that it should have an even number

11 M. Monier-Williams, *A Sanskrit-English Dictionary*, p. 846.

12 Bunrot ประเพณีทั่วโลก [Customs World-wide], p. 121.

Figure 10.1: A chapter of four monks is appropriate for the chants for the dead.

of rungs because it is believed that spirits cannot climb a ladder that possesses an uneven number, such as the ladder leading up to the house.

While the corpse remains at home it is believed that the soul hovers in or around the body. At all times candles and incense are kept burning to keep the spirit in an amiable state, and the inhabitants of the house have to adjust their behaviour in order to prevent offending the soul which wanders about. At all mealtimes one of the relatives must place a tray holding a little plate with food and drink near the corpse, rap softly on the wood of the coffin, and warn politely that it is time to eat. After a suitable time has elapsed, during which the spirit can partake of the essence of the food, the plate can be removed and the contents can be thrown away, for example to the domestic animals.

During the evening a wake is observed by the relatives and their friends. If the family can afford the expense, they may elaborate on the ritual by inviting a chapter of four monks to come to chant during one or more nights. It is only during ceremonies dealing with the spirits of the dead that an even number of monks is needed, in contrast to the uneven number needed during auspicious occasions. This is part of the inversion with regard to the world of the dead, hence a ladder with four rungs, and also a circumambulation of a coffin is changed from the auspicious clockwise direction to an anti-clockwise movement. When the monks arrive at the house, a relative of the dead person

Figure 10.2: *Mae chi* can also be invited to chant for the dead.

should again knock on the coffin and inform the soul that the monks have come. During the night the monks chant appropriate texts from the *Suatmon Chet Tamnan* and any other text they may know that deals with broad philosophical questions. In former days, the monks would bring a box with the text of the story of the Venerable Malai and his adventures in the heavens and hells. This epic account was chanted in the Thai language. At present, however, very few monks know how to chant Thai texts in the proper traditional manner and the story is not told any more. A further elaboration consists of an orchestra that plays suitable music in between the periods of chanting.

The corpse may remain in the house up to seven days. According to one informant, it is on the seventh day that the dead person suddenly realizes that he cannot remain in the decaying body. This is the moment when he has to go to the world of the dead and wait till he is reborn. The farmers are often of the opinion that this waiting time may be last very long. While they will admit that theoretically it is possible for a spirit to be reborn almost immediately, they do not think this happened to their own ancestors. Thus they solve the apparent paradox between the cult of the spirits of the ancestors and the Buddhist teachings. Whilst the ancestors wait to be reborn they can be placated in the house. It is only seldom, for example when a child is born in the community who displays a strong characteristic of a person who died some time in the past, that the farmers can calculate the exact time between death and rebirth. Apart from these rare cases the time between death and rebirth may be as long as several generations.

Other Tai peoples, especially the White and Black Tais of northern Vietnam, who do not seem to be influenced by Buddhism, have quite different views. In their eyes, a person has many *khwan* that, upon death, divide themselves in groups; some *khwan* go to the spirit world above, some are conducted to the house and can be worshipped on the ancestral shrine, while the remainder stay in the grave.[13]

During the time that the corpse rests in the house, no food or incense should be offered to the Buddha image of the house or to the guardian spirit of the compound. Both these powers may be informed of the bereavement only after the dead body has been removed. The moving of the corpse from the house to the monastery usually requires the supervision and assistance of the ritual expert. He binds some *sai sin* around the wrists of the persons who help carry the body in order to reassure their *khwan* and to prevent these from being frightened and chased away. He then walks three times in an anti-clockwise direction around the coffin, rapping several times on it and urging the spirit of the dead man to remain in the body for a while during transport. The door and stairway have been temporarily transformed with branches to look like a jungle, so that the spirit does not recognize from which house it is carried. As soon as the coffin has been lowered onto the ground, the undertaker will say a spell, while drawing a line in the sand with his knife, to make sure that the spirit will not re-enter the house. The same procedure takes place at the point where the remains of the person leave the compound. As soon as the corpse has left, all water containers of the household should be emptied and filled with fresh water. If the coffin on its way to the monastery must cross a bridge, the corpse has to be told of this fact, and in addition the undertaker must bind some incense, a candle and some flowers to one of the bridge posts. In the region of Wat Sanchao, a piece of paper with some streaks of gold and silver paint is attached to a pole of a bridge, a custom the farmers say they derived from Chinese religious practice.

The financial circumstances of the family determine what kind of cremation shall take place. If the dead person came from a poor family it may be arranged with the abbot to organize the cremation as soon as possible. In the countryside it is believed inauspicious to cremate on a Friday or a Saturday, or to burn the

13 See P-B. Lafont, 'Notes sur les familles patronymiques Thai Noires de So'n-la et de Nghĩa-lô', *Anthropos*, Vol. 50, 1955, p. 807.

Figure 10.3: Leading the coffin to the cremation grounds.

body of a person who died on a Saturday immediately on the following Tuesday, because those are the days when the 'spirits of dead people are strong'. An evil person who has the ritual knowledge could capture a spirit and this would give him great magical power. Or a spirit such as the *phi krasue* may on these inauspicious days seek shelter in a living human being without showing any signs of its presence until that person is asleep. In the city, however, Saturday is considered a good day for a cremation, as many people are then free from work; in urban areas cremations are avoided on Friday and on *wan phra.* On the day of the cremation a chapter of monks should chant a few appropriate Pali texts and, immediately after the chanting, the procession towards the funeral pyre takes place. In front walk the monks, who hold a *sai sin* that is knotted to the white cord with which the corpse is bound. Then follow the bearers with the coffin, family members and friends. At the cremation grounds, the procession circumambulates three times in an anti-clockwise direction and the coffin is placed on top of the pyre.

In front of the funeral pyre, relatives will place several trays with household goods and tools. On these trays should be a lamp, some fuel, a box of matches, a knife, some medicine, seed rice, onions and garlic to plant, and some tools to work the soil. Sometimes a piece of paper is included, on which it is written that the bearer is entitled to receive a plot of land from *Thotsarat*, the mythical original owner of all earth. The trays with goods are dropped from a small height onto the ground at the moment the pyre is lighted. It is believed that the dead person is finally despatched at the moment of cremation, and the dropping of useful objects is probably a symbolic destruction in the belief that anything destroyed during cremation will accompany the dead person on his destination. When a monk is cremated, no objects are dropped on to the ground. After all, a monk needs no special equipment and he is not allowed to work on the land. Modern funeral customs, imported from the towns, tend to leave out this offering of useful objects.

After the cremation, the tools and objects, of which the essence has been given to accompany the dead person, become the property of the monastery where the man was cremated. It is always a layman who lights the pyre in rural monasteries, for if a monk did so, he might inadvertently kill the many insects that live in the wood. With the rapid spread of modern incinerators that use petrol this prohibition is no longer observed. The cremation on a traditional wood pyre lasts several hours and needs constant supervision by some older men who make use of long poles to control the burning. They make sure that the body remains in the heart of the fire and that it is properly consumed. When the fire is finally allowed to die, the ashes are raked and small pieces of bone that remain are collected. Somewhere near these pieces are arranged roughly in the shape of a miniature human body along an east-west axis, and an older, experienced monk is usually invited to perform the final ritual of the cremation.

A piece of cloth is draped over the pieces of bone, and the monk holds an edge of this cloth between thumb and index of the right hand while reciting in a solemn voice the famous Pali lines:

> aniccā vata saṃkhārā uppādavayadhammino uppajjhitvā
> nirujjhanti tesaṃ vūpasamo sukho.

This is the ancient Buddhist proverb that is closely connected with death. It has been translated as follows:

> O transient are our life's experiences!
> Their nature 'tis to rise and pass away.
> They happen in our ken, they cease to be.
> O well for us when they are sunk to rest.[14]

The laymen turn each piece of bone a half-circle, again forming the rough small shape of a human along the east-west axis. The first time the bones were

14 C. A. F. Rhys Davids, *Psalms of the Early Buddhists*, 1964, p. 385.

Figure 10.4: 'Aniccā vata saṃkhārā . . . .'

arranged with the head of the human shape towards the west, pointing in the direction of death, but the second time, after rearranging, the head is towards the east, symbolizing rebirth.[15] The same piece of cloth is laid over the bones again and the monk proceeds with another famous appropriate saying:

> Aciraraṃ vata yaṃ kāyo paṭhaviṃ adhisessati chuḍḍo apetaviññāno Niratthaṃ va kalingaraṃ.[16]

This can be translated as:

> Before long, alas, this body will lie upon the ground; cast aside, with no consciousness, like a useless thing.

15 Somkhuan Suthichai, personal communication, 5 December 1968.

16 *Dhammapada*, 41.

The monk who has recited these verses receives the piece of cloth. The presentation of cloth during cremations, which is greatly elaborated upon during important cremations, is clearly related to a practice of the early days of Buddhism, when cloth was scarce and monks were instructed to obtain robes from discarded rags at funeral pyres. After the presentation of cloth is over the laymen can now put a few of the ashes and small pieces of bone in an urn and throw the remainder back into the smouldering ashes.

There are many variations on custom of arranging the ashes and bones just described. The bones that have been arranged in the shape of a body may be honoured by the relatives of the dead person with a ceremonial sprinkling with perfumed water. The bones may be strewn with flowers and some members of the family may put coins among the remains. Later they collect the coins for they are considered to become luck-bringing. When filling the urn, the relatives may take care to take one piece from each part of the 'body'. The remainder may be collected in a white piece of cloth and later dropped in the river.

Cremations can be very elaborate rituals. Families that can afford to spend thousands of baht would lose face if they were to dispose of the body of an honoured member of the family in a quick and simple manner. Many farmers gladly spend for such a purpose because they believe that not only will an elaborate cremation send a great amount of beneficial karma to the deceased, but also it is an excellent opportunity for the living to make merit for themselves. For elaborate cremations usually a long period of preparation is needed and the corpse will therefore be stored in a temporary grave for a period that may range from a month to over a year. During the time that the deceased lies in the temporary grave, the chief organizers of the planned cremation will collecting donations from members of the family and close friends and painstakingly keep a record of all these financial contributions. In general, the more elaborate the ceremony the greater the number of people attending and contributing to the cost. Thus the most influential members of the community are cremated with the accompaniment of an orchestra, and there may be classical theatre performances or film shows.

The coffin is enveloped in ornamental panels and surrounded by beautiful tables with many bouquets of flowers. The chapter of monks chanting Pali texts can be expanded to fifty or more and in addition there may be hundreds of members of the Sangha invited to come, each to receive a piece of cloth draped over the coffin. All lay guests may come forward and place a candle, some incense, and a sliver of sandalwood in the open coffin, a gesture usually

Figure 10.5: The donor of the new robes stands close by.

interpreted as a personal leave-taking, an asking for forgiveness for any ill feeling that they may have caused the deceased. On this occasion copies of booklets may be distributed among the guests. These memorial books usually contain a short biography of the deceased and some articles on ethics and Buddhist philosophy. Often a list of persons who sponsored the cremation and the amount of money donated is published on the final pages of such booklets. Before the pyre is lighted, the ornamental panels that are the property of the monastery are removed. Fireworks may accompany the setting alight of the pyre. After the corpse has been consumed, the relatives may collect two containers of bones and ashes, one to take home, the other to be deposited under a shrine erected for that purpose in the vicinity of the temple.

At regular intervals, the wealthy family may invite a chapter of monks to come to their ancestral house and chant for the dead. All the urns of deceased relatives will be placed at the right hand of the leader of the chapter, at the place where otherwise the customary bowl of water is found. At one stage of the chanting, the *sai sin* is attached to the urns and all monks take this cotton cord lightly between thumb and index fingers of the right hand, which they keep resting on the dais immediately in front of their folded legs (an attitude reminiscent of the receiving of the burial cloth). Solemnly they chant again the famous lines: '*aniccā vata saṃkhārā* . . . ', mentioned above.

The sudden, unpredictable death

In all cases of accidental death some modification of the ritual that has been discussed in the preceding section is necessary. When a person expires suddenly while he is far away from his community, he will be carried to a nearby monastery since a corpse should not be heaved into any house. All rituals have to be performed in this monastery. An undertaker prepares the corpse in the usual manner and a relative of the deceased will have to arrange a day for cremation with the abbot or his deputy. If the accidental death involved no violence from another person, for example in the case of a sudden illness, or a suicide, a wealthy family may defer the cremation until they can organize several elaborations.

When somebody dies as a result of a violent action by another person, the spirit of the killed individual is a 'ghost who died wrongly' or *phi taihong*.[17] Dealing with such corpses is considered rather dangerous. The most malicious type of *phi taihong* comes into existence when a woman dies while pregnant or during childbirth. The body of a person who died in such a tragic and inauspicious way must be cremated as soon as possible, so that the spirit is safely despatched before it revenges itself on innocent people, or before a magician uses the occasion to draw *namman phrai*, or performs other necromantic rituals. Formerly the monks were not prepared to chant Pali texts for people who died so inauspiciously, but in present times this restriction is no longer in force and the unfortunate victim is no longer deprived of the benefit of the chants.

For a rural monastery it would be a terrible thing if a murder took place within the precincts. Although the ecclesiastical authorities would not normally intervene in the matter, it would bode badly for the monastery's future. The farmers would feel that the reputation of their sacred meeting place would be stained, its ceremonies would no longer attract crowds, and laity would be ashamed to be associated with it. Many people are sufficiently realistic to know that rural monasteries are not wholly perfect places; laymen sometimes drink alcohol there and the monastery is for many a centre for gossip. They

17 See Chapter III.

draw the line, however, at physical violence. As soon as there is a danger of an outbreak of a violent quarrel among men who have been drinking, there will be laymen ready to intervene or to shoo the combatants away from the monastery grounds. A murder committed just one yard outside the monastery gate would be sad for the victim's relatives of the victim and it would also create a new *phi taihong*, but at least, it will be said, it would not stain the reputation of the monastery since it happened outside its sacred grounds.

Special arrangements should be made if a miscarriage or a stillbirth occurs. The family or a ritual expert will bury the small corpse under a tree in the name of the family. To prevent the corpse's spirit from becoming troublesome, the lay ritual specialist may coax the spirit of the child into an earthenware vessel. This container is carefully closed and the use of strong spells and magical diagrams should ensure that the spirit cannot escape from the vessel. Finally the earthenware pot is disposed of by being gently placed in the river where it is allowed to float seawards. No special cremation services are therefore required if the dead person was a baby. The same rule applies to cases where small children die of illnesses or accidents; in rural areas, a child of less than seven years is unlikely to be cremated.

All the ceremonies surrounding death reveal something of the worldview of the living. Some of the ceremonies indicate aspects that are little in tune with a strict interpretation of Buddhist doctrine, but that correspond closely with the animistic worldview. Thus the preoccupation with despatching the spirits of those who died inauspiciously seems to imply that the ritual acts have the power to influence the spirits of the dead. The realm of the dead, as can be deduced from the use of even numbers, the preponderance of the western direction, and the anti-clockwise circumambulation, is the inversion of the world of the living.

Even if the dead roam in a strange world, they appear to need the same basic tools upon which the living depend. This is clearly seen in the offering of a coin, and the token destruction of a lamp, fuel, rice and agricultural tools. One informant volunteered the information that some generations ago the monks who would chant in the house of a person who had recently died, engaged in practices that are now forbidden. On the nights that they chanted the story of the Venerable Malai, they would drink alcohol and dance throughout the night.[18] If this statement is based on the truth, it might be related to a ceremony of guiding the spirit to the world of the dead, not unlike shamanistic practices widely known in Southeast Asia, a theme that also seems to be the inspiration

18 The Venerable Bunrot, 28 August 1968, personal communication at Wat Sanchao.

of the story of the Venerable Malai himself. The abandonment of such practices is a natural outcome of the growing influence of the central administration in matters of monastic discipline. In modern Thai Buddhism the idea of monks using alcohol for ritual purposes is unthinkable.

While the cremation rituals ensure that the spirit of the dead person is sent towards the world of the dead, at soon as this has been achieved, new links are established between the living and the dead. After cremation, some ashes and bones are brought back to the house and placed in an honourable position, often together with a photograph of the deceased. The living inhabitants regularly light incense and a candle near where these remains are kept and inform the spirits of their ancestors of all important events in this world: when the new rice is sown, when an ox is bought, and when the roof is repaired. The ancestors are always told when a guest stays overnight, if a marriage has been decided upon, or when a new member of the family is born. The dead are thus considered not only to be able to understand what happens in the house, but to maintain an interest. The forebears are also seen capable of receiving beneficial karma whenever the descendants perform a *kruat nam* ceremony during which they include a thought for these ancestors. The idea of rebirth is staved off when one is thinking about one's own dead relatives: their rebirth may not take place yet. At any rate the concept of time among the dead is likely to be quite different from that of the living. A human year may correspond with only a single day in the realm of the ancestors.

The tendency to regard the moment of rebirth as rather distant is connected with the belief that the direct links with a previous existence are severed when a person is reborn. While the dead may experience a continuation of life in some manner, not unlike that they have just left, and are conscious of the love and respect of their relatives, this bond is broken with rebirth. From that moment onwards the new individual does not receive a share in the merit bestowed upon the ancestors. The newly formed memory will in normal circumstances not be able to recall the details of a former existence. That is why the farmers tend to exaggerate the duration of the period between rebirths. Life appears to most of them to proceed, not so much in a continuous cycle, as in an endless spiral, each new turn built on the previous one, but with large sectors of this eternal coil obscured. These dark sectors represent the time spans from death to rebirth.

CHAPTER XI

CONCLUSIONS

The study of Thai religion is an exceptionally wide field. Even by limiting the subject to the rural interpretation of Thai Buddhism the subject is too large to cover adequately in one book. No attention has been given to the many agricultural rituals, the healing practices, the relative positions of the different non-human powers, the details of placating rituals, and the ceremony of the erection of a shrine for the *san Phra Phum*, to name some obvious gaps. Fieldwork data covered all these areas and these will have to be dealt with separately. At the time when this, the fourth edition of this book was being prepared, in October 2012, the author realises that the direction of his research interests took a different turn. Possibly the awareness of the existence of these data may inspire a future scholar to delve in them.

The choice of rituals in this book deliberately centred around the religious practices and beliefs of rural people that are closely related to the Buddhism of the canon. Since the main theme of this book has been to demonstrate the fundamental difference between the intellectual, elitist conception of Buddhism and the rural, magico-animistic interpretation of Buddhism, this basic difference should be particularly visible in the beliefs and ceremonies that most closely remind us of textual Buddhism. If I had dealt with spirit propitiation only this treatment could have been interpreted as an argument for a compartmentalist approach to rural religion. It is relatively simple to demonstrate the magico-animism of ceremonies that centre around the offering of a pig's head to the unseen powers, but this would not aid us in understanding the magico-animistic orientation of the whole of rural religion. Many scholars who are well versed in the literature on Buddhism would classify it as a stream apart, as an aspect antithetical or at least separate from 'pure' Buddhism that they would assume also to be present in the village.

Thus it was deliberate that much attention was given in this book to the ritual activities that involve the Buddha image, the role of the sacred Pali words, and the perception of the Buddhist monk in the village. It has been demonstrated that even those aspects of religion that are obviously at the very heart of the Buddhist tradition are interpreted by both the farmer and the rural monk in their own characteristically magico-animistic manner. Thus the ritual of receiving the five precepts, which is prescribed word-for-word in the canon, has taken a new meaning in the rural setting and has been described as a type of purification ceremony. Similarly, Buddhist monks, who ideally should be striving to eliminate the causes of new karma, are in the rural monastery primarily engaged in creating a specifically good type of karma, that which has an immediate effect of conveying luck and good fortune to its surroundings. The Buddhist key concepts such as *mettā, nibbāna,* and rebirth are all interpreted in such a manner that they fit the animistic worldview.

Several secondary themes contributed to the format of this book. In the first place, the fact that there is a great variation in the religion of individuals has been underlined by the choice of an ontogenetical pattern in the chapters; an attempt has been made to show how individuals grow and develop in their culture. A young child's religion often consists of ideas concerning the spirits, the monks, the monasteries, and ethics. Adolescents obtain access to a great variety of magically charged objects. After reaching the age of twenty, a man can expect to become a monk and thus learn some sacred chanting and obtain a thorough knowledge of rituals of all kinds. Being a member of the Sangha does not imply that one becomes a recluse. For a rural person, the withdrawal from the world consists of an abstention from certain types of worldly behaviour only; his involvement with the community as a whole remains intense. Adult laymen have many opportunities to participate in private and public ceremonies, in the nearby monastery as well as far away. Most laymen feel obliged to participate in the public fund raising ceremonies. Old men can be ritual experts, and they may often lead the lay community in rituals that are celebrated together with the monks. They may become the healing specialists, those who tattoo young men, or serve as undertakers. Their opinion is sought out whenever a decision has to be made that involves ceremonial activity. Some of these older people have a regular intimate contact with each other when they become recluses for periods of one day and one night. A few of the older men join the Sangha for a second or third time in their lives and enjoy the quiet and secure existence of a monk. By this means they have no worry about obtaining food, shelter or medical care, they occupy highly respected positions in the community and at the same time have a better chance than most other rural people of achieving a good rebirth.

Another theme that has been developed throughout this book is the distinction between the religious knowledge of men and that of women. From the time of their earliest education, little girls are admonished to keep a physical distance between themselves and the monks. They are excluded from becoming *dek wat,* and also from joining the novices. The most powerfully charged amulets are out of their reach and no tattooing specialist is prepared to give them permanent religiously charged markings. At the time that their male age-mates join the order, girls have only indirect access to religious knowledge. They can attend ceremonies, but always in a passive role, only as recipients of merit and not as primary generators of beneficial karma. It has been argued that in the animistic worldview there is a good reason for excluding women from much of the important religious practice and knowledge. Menstrual blood is regarded as antithetical to the protective power and women are thus periodically a source of pollution; they have to be kept away from the best amulets and strongest tattoos. In addition, many women endanger the luck-bringing power, for by their attractive appearance they may cause a monk to leave the order and marry, thus depriving him of a chance to accumulate enormous quantities of beneficial power.

It is thus only when women are past childbearing age and when they are less attractive sexually that they are able to obtain detailed religious knowledge. Many older women join the devout older men on sacred days during the Lenten season and adhere to the eight vows. During these periods of asceticism they can learn to recite Pali texts, meditate and participate as equals in discussions about religious topics.

The order in the animated world

The analysis of ceremonies in this book has led to a catalogue of regularities and a description of some important characteristics of the magico-animistic worldview. In the first place, it was found, magical power appears to be centred in certain objects and connected with specific activities. Secondly, the farmers believe that the intensity of the power diminishes drastically when the physical distance from the source increases. A third characteristic of magical power there is a wide range in quality. Fourthly, there appears to be a variation in the operatic level of power: sometimes the animistic aspect is hidden, in other cases it is central and overt. Each of these four features deserves a short note

Sources of magical power

There is no sharp division between physical powers of nature and magical power. The earth, which possesses the capacity to make plants grow and thrive, is sometimes seen in the shape of a beautiful female, *Mae* Thorani. Under the earth is the domain of the chief of the Nak, a serpent-like shape with the face of a dragon. The wind, the river, a tree, a house, and the monastery, each of these is connected with one or more unseen powers, conceived of in anthropomorphic form, and each of these unseen powers has its specific likes and dislikes. A farmer learns to attract their attention with candles, incense, and flowers, and develops skills in addressing and pleasing them.

Nature has provided men with unexpected seats of power. For example, a termite hill may acquire a reputation for bringing luck; or when lightning strikes a building, the scorched plaster is regarded as magically powerful. A lump of resin that shows the shape of a Buddha is sacred, and a big stone that is dragged up from the river brings prosperity when laid in the rice-storage hut.

The most important activities of men that are reputed to generate magical power are the uttering of sacred words and meditation. Both monks and laymen can perform these activities. The monk's power is generally considered to be stronger than that of the layman, but the former is limited in his application of this power. Because of his superior ritual position a monk should not lower himself to supplicate the unseen powers. That is why monks can, by reciting sacred texts, consecrate a bowl of water at a marriage ceremony, but only a lay ritual specialist may present the couple to the ancestors. Lay experts politely raise their hands when asking favours from one of the powers around them, but when a monk, if he were to address such a power, he should make sure not to raise his hands.

Secondary sources

The closer to the seat of magical power, the stronger is the influence of that force. Any object of the appropriate shape that is exposed to a strong dose of magical power will become a secondary seat of the force. This has been amply demonstrated in the rituals surrounding amulets. When, for example, medallions with the face of a famous monk and sacred syllables are cast in a factory, these small objects have no innate power whatsoever. Also a small Buddha image or a medallion bought in the market must first be activated before it will ward off evil. This is why the bundles of such objects are placed near a monk who is preaching, why the begging bowl of an ordinand contains them, and why bowls of water stand near the monks who complete their *pavāraṇā* ceremony. The principle is apparent in the rituals designed to sacralize amulets as well as those where a bowl of water is charged.

The range of powers

It has been shown that, in addition to the protective power that emanates from people who utter sacred words or who meditate, there are ambiguous forces in the animated world, forces that may protect, but that could also be harmful. Examples of the ambiguous powers are the gods, the spirits of the ancestors, the anthropomorphic and theriomorphic powers that live in nature and are the legendary original owners of the environment, and guardian spirits. Esoteric knowledge, with its many spells and diagrammatic drawings, also belongs mainly to this ambiguous class. Finally, there are powers that are nothing but dangerous and wholly aggressive. Dangerous forces encountered in the course of this book are evil spirits, corpses (especially those who died inauspiciously), polluted substances, and some of the rare spells that reputedly have the power to kill.

Variations on the operatic level

The fourth aspect of the magico-animistic worldview concerns the level of awareness of the notion of magical power during religious actions. In some rituals the acquisition and manipulation of the invisible force is the foremost reason for holding a ceremony and many actors are aware of this. On other occasions, although research indicates the same principle to be at work, the actors appear much less conscious of it. Examples of religious behaviour in which considerations of animistic nature appear to be foremost are the final 'waking-up' of magical tattoos, the consecration of a bowl of water through the recitation of Pali texts, and the rituals with which bundles of amulets are charged with protective power.

An example of religious behaviour that the researcher may link with underlying animistic principles, but which in practice is seldom directly related to magical forces by the actors themselves, is the special rural interpretation of the monastic discipline. It has been noted that the official rules that are regularly broken are rules that are not in accordance with animistic principles. Thus rural monks are almost obliged to handle money. Other monastic rules are followed more closely than the texts would lead us to expect because they are re-enforced by those principles. A good example is the monks' extreme avoidance of touching women.

Merit and good fortune

Another important finding in the Wat Sanchao data concerns the relation between the concepts of beneficial karma and good luck. Merit is generally

Table 9: The role of merit in the life cycle of the adult farmer

Time perspective	*Stage*	*General ideas about merit*
In retrospect	Past lives	Meritorious deeds of the past will have resulted in the more fortunate aspects of the present circumstances of an individual, such as good health, rich relatives, and an attractive countenance. Some of the past merit may still have effect at some date in the future.
	Birth	The basic character of a child, the sex, its position in the family, and its innate abilities are dependent upon the amount of merit that was active when conception took place.
Present	Adulthood	When someone performs a morally just deed, attends a ceremony, or is otherwise in close contact with a primary source of beneficial power, he does not only increase his chances of immediate rewards, but he is certain to favourably influence his total balance of merit and demerit
Prospects	Immediate future	Not long after gaining merit there is a good chance that things go well, the harvest may turn out abundant, the price of rice may be increased by the government, or at least illness and bad luck may be averted.
	Death	At the moment of death, a person ought to try and activate his store of merit by thinking of ceremonies attended, by uttering Pali words, or by considering the time when he was a monk, in order to ensure a favourable rebirth.
	Future lives	The course that future lives will take depends to a great extent on the configuration of dharma elements of an individual when he is ready for rebirth. Relatives may influence the configuration in a favourable manner by elaborate cremation ceremonies, and by regularly sending some merit to those already deceased.

seen as a beneficial and protective force that extends over a long period of time and that links individuals together. Table 9 represents a summing-up of the ideas concerning the role of merit in the life cycle of farmers. It is characteristic of the concept that it may have a long-term effect. The protective magical power, however, can be seen as the immediate, specifically temporary aspect of merit. In this respect this can be seen as another instance of a concept from doctrinal Buddhism being linked up with a basically animistic idea.

Just as the development of a foetus shows stages that are reminiscent of the evolution of the whole species, so the individual in central Thailand develops in his religious outlook from a preoccupation with magical power to a concentration on the long-term effects of merit. When competing for a wife, the young adult is concerned with improving his chances, and in his eyes the actions of the monks who generate beneficial power may well be used to his advantage. To the farmers it is no coincidence that the most crucial period of the agricultural cycle falls at the time when religious activities in the monastery are also at their peak. The frequent chanting and meditation sessions in the Lenten season have a good influence on the abundance of rain and the growth of rice. Similarly, a man believes that he stands a better chance of winning the lottery immediately after attending a major ceremony in the monastery.

It is only in the later stages of life that the diachronic aspects of making merit take precedence. While a young person may know that, in theory, the beneficial karma obtained may have effect at an unspecified time in the future, it is only when a person becomes aware of the fact that death is rapidly approaching, that the wish to obtain a fortunate rebirth becomes a prime motivating force.

The overall approach to Thai religion in this book seems essentially different from that in the standard literature on the subject. Instead of choosing between syncretism and a compartmentalized model, I have argued that both are adequately represented in Thailand. Syncretism appears to fit the religious outlook of the unsophisticated sections of the population, whilst a more or less rigid distinction between 'pure' Buddhism and religious practices that have little to do with Buddhism is most likely to be found among the educated and sophisticated Thai elite. Even the few scholars who mention a difference between rural Buddhism and Buddhism of the elite fail to notice the fundamentally different orientations of the two. The orientation of the Wat Sanchao farmers is basically animistic and they have adopted aspects of Buddhism that suit their animistic outlook, just as they adopt elements from Brahmanism and Chinese religion. The farming community accepts any spell, any horoscope and any magical procedure as long as it appears efficient.

Members of the elite are often aware of the fact that some of their actions are in accordance with the Buddhist canon and that other religious practices must be classified under different headings. Only among the highly educated classes can be found people who fully appreciate the philosophical and practical consequences of the teachings of Siddhārtha Gautama. It is only in urban centres that doctrinal Buddhism occupies a superior sphere in the religious outlook and it is here that the Thai elite finds tattooing, magic and the power of sanctified water of somewhat lesser value than the subtle teachings in the canon.

These two fundamentally different interpretations of Buddhism within a Buddhist country are not intended as an exhaustive typology; they are a description of two extremes. It is an incomplete model that probably could be developed further with research in the provincial capitals and in the capital city. Among the rapidly expanding middle classes there are probably some who adhere to the animistic rural religion and others who feel more at home in the sophisticated compartmentalized religious outlook, but it can be expected that many waver between one and the other. In addition, it is probable that the compartmentalized elitist orientation covers a wide spectrum of religious approaches, from the sceptical to the deeply involved. In any case, the two fundamentally different approaches to Buddhism amongst the Thai believers may provide a useful vehicle with which to study the changes in Buddhist religious orientations. The model that recognizes animistic Buddhism as well as a compartmentalized religion with a Buddhist superstructure has the advantage of being dynamic. It helps put into perspective the changes that occurred in rural religion during previous centuries, when the overt behaviour of the Buddhist monks has been modified to fit better the ideals developed by the central organization, but where the basic attitudes of many farmers may have remained relatively unaltered.

The model is thus useful when applied to the history of Buddhism in Thailand. Too often the development of religion is depicted only as a matter that concerns only the ruling classes, and therefore the historical sources have been used that present a purely compartmentalized point of view. The dichotomy between rulers and ruled, between town and hinterland is highly relevant for the study of religious development. It has been argued in this book that the two fundamentally different approaches to Buddhism may well originate from the time of the very first introduction of Buddhism in the rural scene.

POSTSCRIPT

One of the chief motivations to conduct the research that eventually resulted in writing *Monks and Magic* was the wish to find out how Buddhism was practised. The preparatory readings of sections of the Tipitaka and its commentaries had yielded a fascinating picture of the Sangha as one of the world's most successful long-term organizations, but had not provided me with much relevant information on how this could be translated in religious behaviour of devout lay people. I had also become aware of the fact that Buddhism has never had a permanent central authority and that already in its early days different schools developed around varying interpretations of core philosophical concepts. The occasional Buddhist Councils had not succeeded in ironing out these differences and in the course of time quite distinct regional variants had developed. Consequently Buddhism in mainland Southeast Asia is not the same as Buddhism in India, Tibet, China, Korea or Japan.

In each of these regions the establishment of Buddism involved a coming to terms with existing creeds. In India sections of the Hindu pantheon were encorporated in Buddhist lore and when Buddhism spread northwards to Tibet at the end of the first millennium, it blended with what scholars assume to have been the Bön religion, adopting features of its methods of fortune telling, as well as various animistic and shamanistic practices. The introduction of Buddhism in mainland Southeast Asia similarly did not eradicate previous religious beliefs: it must have accomodated many local beliefs. In the following, some aspects of the religion in rural central Thailand are mentioned that appear to me to be the result of a mix between Buddhism and an earlier, indigenous religion. Thus, the ceremony of arranging and re-arranging bone remnants after a cremation, described in Chapter X, is reminiscent of the custom of a 'second burial', still practised in some parts of Southeast Asia.

It has been seen in this book that the Buddhists living around Wat Sanchao conceive of merit not only as the karmic result of a good deed, but as a commodity that at certain times emanates from monks and that may attach itself to certain objects in the vicinity of monks performing a ceremony. This emanation is seen as a luck-bringing force, a power that attaches itself to certain suitable objects, that may be led through the cotton thread (*sai sin*) and that can be infused into water to make *nam mon*. If this interpretation of the effect of positive karma is not part of Buddhism as it is described in the Tipitaka and if the practises described in this book in relation to the manipulation of this force are not encountered in other forms of Buddhism, it may well rest upon a local underlying Southeast Asian belief system.

In Chapter IV it was described how amulets were made and how they were kept and treasured. This preoccupation with small protective, luck-bringing, shielding objects is an unusual regional phenomenon. Now, many years after the original fieldwork, the subject is of continuing interest for understanding modern Thailand. Not only is the world of collectors still thriving, as witnessed by a plethora of journals, but there is avid interest in finding out where the rare most powerful of these objects can be found. In December 2009 I came across an article in *The Nation* that described the string of amulets worn by Abhisit Vejjajiva, then Prime Minister of Thailand. It was described that the Premier wore some ten amulets, some his own, others loaned to him. In the first category was a Luangpho Thuat M16, known all over Thailand as providing invulnerability to its wearer.[1] Another highly valued amulet worn by Abhisit was one reputed to be one of the first batch of Jatukam Ramathep amulets, widely regarded at the time of assuring that the wearer would have success and meet with good fortune.[2] The article continues with a description of various instances of amulet-presentations to the Premier.[3]

Another major striking idiosyncrasy in Thai religion is that a man's ordination to become a fully-fledged member of the Sangha is not only reserved to people who wish to renounce the world, but is also taken as an ideal temporary

1 Luangpho Thuat is a legendary Buddhist monk who is reputed to have lived in the seventeenth century in southern Thailand. In the 1950s the first amulets with his countenance were made to help finance the rebuilding of a monastery. The fame of the M16 version of amulet derives from an incident in the South of Thailand, when bandits attacked a lorry and sprayed the driver cab with rounds from an M16 automatic rifle. The driver's shirt was torn by bullets, but he himself, wearing a Luangpho Thuat amulet, was not hurt.

2 The first batch was made in 1987. The Jatukam Ramathep amulets became much sought after in 2006, after the death of the man who first made them. At one time a single amulet of the proper silvery-black colour reputedly passed hands for as much as 1,800,000 baht. The Kasikorn Research Centre, in an article dated 21 June 2007, reported that already 300 series of the talisman had been printed and that business around the sale of the amulet for the year 2007 was estimated to amount to 40 billion baht.

3 Traithep Krai-ngu, 'PM Protected by Amulet Shield', *The Nation*, December 13, 2009.

retreat for the young adult male, preferably undergone before taking on the responsibility of founding a family of his own. This *rite-de-passage* seems to be one of such above-mentioned local adaptations of the Buddhist creed. As far as I could determine, it is practised in this way only in Thailand, Laos and Cambodia and it is not based on the Buddhist canon. The question of why this should be so is vexed. We have only a vague inkling of the mix of indigenous religions in mainland Southeast Asia at the time that Buddhism was established. My hypothesis is that the institution of the Buddhist monastery blended with an indigenous institution, that I – for simplicity's sake – shall call the 'men's house'. In order to account for the large number of young men who serve only for a single rainy season, I assume that the Buddhist monastery absorbed a local institution in which young men were initiated before being accepted into the adult world. The strict Buddhist monastic discipline with its abstinence of food, alcohol and sex has much in common with the types of ordeals that may be expected in initiation rituals and this may have been the reason why the Thai Sangha has become so generous towards young adult males by allowing them to be ordained, well-knowing that they will soon return to pursue their career as lay people.

Also, as an anthropologist I have been struck by the shape of the chief buildings in Southeast Asian Buddhist monasteries, with their massive, often multi-layered roofs. These structures reminded me of the large bamboo constructions found in Southeast Asia. The architecture of Southeast Asian Buddhist monasteries of Southeast Asia only rarely conforms to Indian prototypes. Gradually I have come to adopt the idea that the Buddhist monastery absorbed not only the indigenous institution where young men were initiated but also the very building – the 'men's house' – in which this initiation had taken place, shape and all.

Furthermore, it has been noted in this book that the formal rules governing the monks' behaviour sometimes are interpreted in a rather lax manner (not just the rules governing male access to the Sangha just mentioned, but notably those related to the prohibition to touch money and the relaxed attitude towards smoking) and that in contrast some rules are kept even more assiduously than the letter of the law prescribes. The latter is particularly true with regard to the many formal rules that prevent contact between Buddhist monks and women. It has been argued in this book that the finicky dealing with matters feminine is related to the notion that women, not only because of their association with procreation and their allure that may disturb monastic equanimity but more specifically because of their monthly exuding menstrual fluids, are seen as antithetical to the most valued for of luck-bringing magical power.

It is this usually unstated aspect that makes it difficult for women to rise above the status of *mae chi*, and to re-instate the order of the *phiksuni*, the fully ordained, yellow-robed Buddhist nuns. In the 1920s already two sisters took the bold step of getting themselves ordained. This caused a furore and the Sangha reacted rapidly with the Supreme Patriarch officially forbidding monks to ordain women. The civil authorities followed suit: both women were arrested and forcefully disrobed. In 1933 a law was passed formally prohibiting women's ordination. This law has never been repealed.

Modern Thailand naturally also has its feminists, and among them there are some who are of the firm opinion that the Sangha ought to be enriched with fully ordained women. In the early 1970s I met Thailand's only *phiksuni*, a full female member of the Sangha, who resided in her private monastery, named Watra[4] Songtham Kanlayani, in the town of Nakhon Pathom. This was the Reverend Voramai Kabilsingh, who told me that in 1971 she had been ordained in Taiwan. While she impressed me by her sincerity and determination, I also observed that she remained rather isolated from the immediate surrounding population. When I asked whether she went collecting food in the early morning, she told that that was not possible, because many people would not accept her nun's role. Many ordinary Thais felt uneasy with her, some saying that she did not belong to the Theravada tradition, others stating with indignation that a female in monks' robes was an impossible situation, an inacceptable anomaly. The Reverend Voramai, protected by her wealth and upper-class connections, managed to edit her own journal and remained a devout Buddhist nun till she passed away, aged 96 in 2003.

Since those days there have been many more women who felt that the male dominance of the Thai Sangha needed to be challenged, and like the Reverend *phiksuni* Voramai, they made use of the multiplicity of Buddhist schools around the world to gain access to the order. They selected Sri Lanka, a wise choice because there they found a Theravada tradition that made them feel welcome. Early in 2001, Voramai's daughter, the well-known academic Chatsumarn Kabilsingh was there ordained as a novice and took the name of *samaneri* Dhammananda and two years later she became a fully ordained Buddhist nun. At that time there may have been as much as 13,000 *mae chi* in Thailand but, in view of the continuing hostility that yellow-robed females

4 By using the word *watra* (วัตร meaning 'practice') instead of *wat* (วัด 'monastery') she avoided an open conflict with the clerical authorities.

meet in Thailand, only a small number (at the time of writing this more than 20) decided to follow and became ordained. Most *mae chi* prefer to avoid a direct confrontation with the general public and exploit the chances offered by remaining in the traditionally accepted *mae chi* role.

The only contribution that *Monks and Magic* offers in this on-going debate is to point out the often suppressed, seldom openly stated belief that males are by nature privileged in that they can (amongst other things and with the proper effort) create luck-bringing power and women are by nature handicapped and sometimes destructive in this respect.

Wat Sanchao Revisited

Some of the readers of earlier editions have asked me how I came to choose Wat Sanchao and, indeed, I had omitted that information in former editions of *Monks and Magic*. This is a summary account of what happened.

In 1962 I lost my way in Bangkok, standing in a backyard, rather bewildered not seeing a way out in the maze of wooden structures around me. Soon some Thais, regarding me with curiosity, spoke to me in their native language. When I asked in English for the way out, nobody understood my words or gestures. Then someone rolled out a mat and insisted I sit down on their porch. Gradually a crowd gathered around. Every attempt I made to get up and quietly disappear was met with a firm gesture that I should sit and wait. Eventually a girl of my age was pushed forward. She asked me in English what I was doing in their back garden. Under the admiring eyes of her relatives we conducted an animated conversation, after which she assisted me to find the street. At our parting, she asked whether I would be willing to become her penfriend, to which I gladly agreed. During the following years, back in the Netherlands I regularly wrote to her and occasionally sent small presents.

At that time I was studying anthropology. As part of my courses I had to focus my attention on a region of the world of my own choice. In a friendly conversation with Dr Robert van Gulik, who was one of my teachers, I mentioned that I was considering to choose Thailand, and with his customary enthusiasm, van Gulik not only expounded on his own adventures there, but also revealed that he had long wished to learn Thai and that he possessed a course book together with the appropriate set of gramophone records, written by Mary Haas during the Second Word War. Van Gulik himself had by then given up the plan to learn Thai and he generously donated the whole course to me. In the preface to the first edition, above, I indicated how I shared this course with some of my fellow students.

Thus, after finishing my undergraduate courses and having been awarded with a PhD scholarship from the Australian National University, I returned to Bangkok after an absence of almost five years. The family of my penfriend received me with touching hospitality; they were delighted that I was able to conduct a simple conversation in Thai. When I told my friend that I was looking for a monastery where I could be ordained, she immediately suggested the village where her father had been born and where her old aunt still lived. This aunt, who recently had become widowed and who was well aware of the fact that her spell of life was nearing the end and that she should do all she could to prepare for the next, was glad to become a chief sponsor of a monk, a foreigner at that. My ordination was thus prepared and it grew into a major event: the learned Phrakhru Wimonkiti was willing to be my preceptor, and an unprecedented crowd joined my procession towards the monastery. The provincial newspaper reported the event with a photograph on the front page. After having served for more than six months as a Buddhist monk, the terms of my scholarship still allowed me ample time to continue the fieldwork. Thus it came about that, after leaving the order, I went to live in the farm of my friend's aunt, my former sponsor. She was kind enough to treat me as a younger relative and I gladly helped her not only in the house but also on her rice fields.

In the nine months that I had the privilege to live in her house, I got to know, appreciate and love this truly remarkable person. She had never learnt to read or write, but possibly this allowed her keen mind occasionally to display a phenomenal memory. During the evenings in the dim light of a sooty oil lamp we talked for hours and when the prosaic daily events had been dealt with, some evenings she treated me with stories of the past, for she was a storyteller par excellence. She had cause to be proud: although her husband (who had died not long before I arrived in the village) had been born a slave,[5] the couple had successfully raised four sons; all four had become soldiers. After the second son had gained officer rank he had assisted his two younger brothers to enter upon a career in the army as well. This family had become the most influential in the wider area and at present are the chief sponsors of the modernization of the monastery.

The community where the fieldwork took place was therefore not selected: it was presented to me. It can by no means be regarded as typical or representative of a central Thai village. On the contrary, when I first visited the region

5 The abolition of slavery was officially announced in the early 1880s but its implementation was a gradual one so that only in the first decades of the twentieth century did this class of people disappear.

surrounding Wat Sanchao, I found this unusually depressed and poverty-stricken. Most farmers lived on the far side (as seen from the provincial capital) of the Khwae Om river. In the early '60s the community had had high hopes of prosperity when a bridge was built connecting them with the provincial road network. However, during the first rainy season after completion the pylons of the new bridge had caught a drifting tree, other material became entangled, and before the mass of driftwood could be removed the pressure caused the new bridge to be swept away. (It was murmured in the community that inferior building materials had been used.)

Be that as it may, at the time my research began, the villagers were constructing a rickety makeshift bridge with bamboo poles and narrow wooden planks. When it was finished even bicycles had to be carried across. This was also the reason why all farms on the east side of the Khwae Om were deprived of modern developments. Electricity was obtained only at special occasions during festivals when a noisy generator was rented; drinking water rested in huge earthenware pots, filled with water scooped from the river and supplemented by collecting rainwater. Private houses had no toilet: people relieved themselves at certain spots distant from the house.

Economic life was conducted much as in previous generations. Rice growing remained the main source of income: every farmer depended upon rainfall and flooding, each deciding for himself when to sow or transplant seedlings, and with what type of rice. Large clay pits on the west branch of the village showed that once there had been a kiln, now long abandoned. The only manufacturing industry I noted took place in a large shed where bronze religious images were cast, chiefly depictions of Brahma and of the Buddha. These images were artificially made to look ancient with the aid of a short bath in acid, followed by a period being buried in the ground. One may safely imagine that gullible tourists would take them to be treasures, recently dug up, and that intrepid ones would smuggle them out of the country.

The main transport ways were riverine and all houses were built along the riverbanks. The river Khwae Oom presented a lively scene with fishermen heaving their nets and housewives paddling to the provincial market with fresh fruit, herbs, vegetables from the kitchen garden or baskets woven from thin strips of bamboo. On the river Maeklong, there was a lively scene of large boats making their way up and down and barge-trains being pushed by a push-tug. Frequently the deafening noise of long-tail boats reverberated against the dense vegetation, warning all smaller boats that a splashing wave was imminent. Over land there was only a single raised footpath, running about a hundred

Figure 11.1: In 1967, rice fields were prepared with buffaloes.

meters parallel to the waterways. There almost everyone walked, most of them on thongs or barefoot, only stepping aside to let through an occasional bicycle.

In order to illustrate the stupendous changes that have taken place I present a number of photographs, the first five taken in the 1960s, followed by a set taken illustrating the situation in 2010. In the more than four decades the community has been catapulted from an almost archaic situation into the modern world.

The first major modernization impetus came in 1966 and 1967 as a result of the building of a new pumping station and its connected water channels. This pump freed the farmers from the anxieties of hoping for a suitable rainfall at the appropriate time. It also forced them into a cooperative society, where they had to pay for the petrol to run the pump and to keep the water channels clear.

Figure 11.2: Harvest time, a community labour.

The most fundamental change was, however, that in future the higher fields – formerly the poorest on which rice was only sown broadcast – now should be flooded first, as befits an irrigation system. This reversed the traditional value system where the lowest fields had been the most valuable, for they had been the least risky for raising a crop in the time that they depended on rainfall. As the first three photographs show, the tilling of the fields, the harvest and transport of the rice crop was done with time-honoured methods.

In the 1960s the monastery possessed two stone edifices: a main temple building (the *bot*) and a large monument (a *chetiya*). A large wooden gathering hall on concrete stilts, flanked left and right with rows of monks' cells was the busiest place of the whole monastery. Here the early morning chanting took

Figure 11.3: 1968, transporting the harvest to the threshing ground.

place and it was the scene where the annual major ceremonies described in Chapter IX were staged. One major footpath and a few shortcuts through the grassy areas connected these buildings with the farming areas and those who chose to reach the place by boat chose the middle of the three landings at the river side, the other two being rather rickety. Figure 11.4 is taken from the café nearest the main entrance over land, a simple bamboo structure with home-made furniture, a roof made of pandanus leaves providing shade. From here anyone passing on the elevated footpath would be in clear view and could be hailed with the standard question: "Pai nai ma?" (ไปไหนมา). Figure 11.5 gives a good impression of the river approach to Wat Sanchao, with the main open-air

Figure 11.4: Opposite the entrance to the monastery, the café in 1967.

rest-house (*sala*), where on school days an itinerant trading woman would sit waiting for the midday break to sell some sweets to the children.

Figure 11.6, whose photograph was made in the mid-70s, records the first major change in the monastery: a new modern meeting hall with cremation

Figure 11.5: Wat Sanchao seen from the Maeklong river in the 1960s.

Figure 11.6: In 1974: the old *bot* to the left, the new meeting hall and cremation furnace on the right.

facilities attached had been erected. Henceforth corpses were no longer burnt in the open air and Wat Sanchao's monastery committee could now expect to derive a fair amount of income as families would want to make use of these modern funeral facilities.

More than forty years after the period of fieldwork, Wat Sanchao and its immediate surroundings had been enveloped by Ratburi's expansion. Dozens of electricity wires now crossed the river Kwae Om (see Figure 11.7). The monastery grounds were no longer visible from the road, a solid wall now enveloping the whole area. Near the entrance a large marmor plaque records that on August 28, 2006 the building of the new wall had begun and that the work was finished on May 12, 2008; it also lists the full names of 240 donors. Once inside, a visitor sees that the grassy areas have now all disappeared, the lower grounds raised and a smooth concrete floor now allows access to motorised vehicles. Where formerly the large wooden gathering hall dominated the scene a two-story building in the style of a modern Thai palace now stands (see Figure 11.8). The next picture shows that also the waterside is included in the total renovation with a beautiful ornate *sala* and a new bell tower, in between a brand-new statue of Luang Pho Taa (see Chapter III).

Parallel to the changes in Wat Sanchao, the surrounding countryside has been transformed. Former footpaths are now broad asphalted roads, parts of

Figure 11.7: The new bridge, electricity wires above.

them lined with suburban-style houses and shops. Much of the rice-growing area had been transformed into gardens, where now vegetables and fruit crops were raised, and one large factory building now changed the skyline. The view in Figure 11.4 has been changed to that now seen in Figure 11.10.

The river now has fallen silent; goods are more efficiently transported over the roads. Traffic noise has shifted upwards to the roads. In short, Wat Sanchao and its community are now part of an outer suburb of the provincial capital. The rural community has disappeared: young people orient themselves to Ratburi town and from there are part of Thailand and the wider world. In the 1960s in Wat Sanchao there was no reading material and the postman seldom crossed the river Khwae Om; now there are kiosks selling local and national newspapers that are widely read. This accelerated development, this precipitation into the complex modern world has occurred not only in Wat Sanchao, it is the experience of millions now growing up in completely different circumstances than those in which their parents and grandparents lived. A remarkable element in this transformation is that the monastery was not left behind: the massive investment in new buildings demonstrates this. It still houses a number of monks, every year boosted by youngsters who intend to stay only one rainy season. In the modern world the Buddhist monastery

Figure 11.8: Wat Sanchao, with concrete floor, 2010, at the right the 'uposatha hall' (*bot*).

Figure 11.9: The new access to the river Maeklong.

Figure 11.10: Opposite the entrance to the monastery, in 2010, transformed into a suburban scene.

remains a quiet haven, it retains its reflective atmosphere and remains a refuge where the hectic world is left behind. The inhabitants of Wat Sanchao still remind the community that the human span of life is short and that in contrast to those who pursue the acquisition of wealth or power there are those who find fulfilment in renouncing the mundane world.

Wat Sanchao then and now

1967	Present
• Landscape: Rice fields, houses and gardens along rivers	• Suburban Ratburi, roads, cars, houses
• No electricity	• Light, TV, fridge
• Rainwater	• Connected with Ratburi
• Rivers were highways	• Riverways almost unused
• Marriage within ca. 20 km radius	• Marriage radius vastly expanded

GLOSSARY OF THAI, PALI AND SANSKRIT WORDS

Thai words are presented in transcription, followed by the term in Thai. When an expression is in Pali this is indicated with (P), Sanskrit words with (S).

abhisek, อภิเษก, abhiṣeka (S)	anointing, consecrating
achan sak, อาจารำย์สัก	tattooist
amphoe, อำเภอ	area, subdivision of a province
apamongkhon, อปมงคล, apamaṅgala (P)	inauspicious
arahan, อรหัต, arahant (P)	person who achieved Arhatship
Asalahabucha, อาสาฬหบูชา, Āsāḷhāpūjā (P)	festival that falls in June–July
asura, อสูร, asura (P, S)	a class of mythological beings
avatāra (S)	incarnation of a god, often Viṣṇu
baeng kuson, แบ่งกุศล	sharing merit
baht, บาท	Thai monetary unit
bai chak, ใบจาก	leaf of the Nipa palm tree
bai ngoen, ใบเงิน	leaf of the caricature plant
bai si, ใบศรี	receptacle folded from banana leaf
bai thong, ใบทอง	leaf of the caricature plant
bhūmisparśamudrā (S)	gesture, calling the earth to witness
bot, โบสถ์, posatha (P), poṣadha (S)	temple
buat phra, บวชพระ	the monk's ordination
buat rian, บวชเรียน	ordination in order to gain knowledge

changwat, จังหวัด	province
chaokhana changwat, เจ้าคณะจังหวัด	monk in charge of provincial affairs
chaophi, เจ้าผี	tutelary spirit
chaopho lakmueang, เจ้าพ่อหลักเมือง	central pillar of a town or city
chaping, จะปิ้ง	small girl's metal *cache-sexe*
chedi, เจดีย์, cetiya (P), caitya (S)	tumulus, sepulchral monument, cairn
Chayamongkhon, ชัยมงคล	guardian spirit of residences
Chayasop, ชัยสพ	guardian spirit of food storage houses
chi, ชี, jīva (S)	female recluse
daitya (S)	demon
dek wat, เด็กวัด	boy servant of the monks
dhāraṇī (S)	mystical verse or charm
dharma (S), dhamma (P)	essential Quality
dukkhatā (P)	ill deeds
garuḍa (S)	mythical bird
gāthā (P; S)	verse, stanza
haṃsa (P; S)	goose, mythical bird
Huai Ko Kho, หวยขอคอ	former popular lottery
kam, กรรม, karma (S), kamma (P)	the cause of existence, effect of action
kapparukkha (P)	mythological tree
kathin, กฐิน, kaṭhina (P)	robes offered at end of Lenten season
kavaca (S)	amulet, mystical syllable
kha, ฆ่า	to kill, to murder
khao phansa, เข้าพรรษา	to enter the Lenten season
khatha, คาถา, gāthā (P; S)	verse, stanza
kho sin ha, ขอศีลห้า	to ask for the five commandments
khon dìp, คนดิบ	an unripe (not yet formed) person
Khonthap, คนธรรพ, Gandharva (S)	guardian of ceremonial buildings

Khom, ชอม	Khmer, Cambodian
khru, ครู	teacher
khru sak, ครูสัก	tattooist
khrut, ครุฑ	garuda
khwang tawan, ขวางคะวัน	to offend the sun
khwan, ขวัญ	spirit, soul, morale
kradong, กระด้ง	large round tray
kruat nam, กรวดน้ำ	ritual transfer of merit
krung, กรุง	city
Krungphali, กรุงพาลี	realm of King Thotsarat
kuti, กุฏิ, kuṭi (P, S)	a monk's cell
linglom, ลิงลม	the wind monkey, the slow loris
Loi krathong, ลอยกระทง	November water festival
luang phi, หลววพี	reverend older brother
luang pho, หลววพ่อ	reverend father
luang ta, หลววตา	reverend uncle
mae, แม่	mother
mae chi, แม่ชี, jīva (S)	female recluse
mai charoensuk, ไม้เจริญสุข	'prosperity and happiness' – wood
mai mayom, ไม้มะยม	the star gooseberry shrub
mai makha mong, ไม้มะค่ามอง	name of a timber tree
mai rang, ไม้รัง	small timber tree
mai ruak, ไม้รวก	a type of bamboo
mai takhian, ไม้ตะเคียน	a large timber tree
mai teng, ไม้เต็ง	hardwood, widely used as timber
mafueang, มะเฟือง	fruit of the cucumber tree
Maha nikai, มหานิกาย	Thai Buddhist sect
Makhabucha, มาฆบูชา, Māghapūjā (S)	festival in January–February
mantra (S)	mystical verse, magical formula
māsaka (P)	ancient coin of low value
matum, มะตูม	the bael-fruit tree
mettā (P)	compassion, love, sympathy

moksa, โมกษะ, mokṣa (S)	release, salvation
muban, หมู่บ้าน	hamlet
nak, นาค	serpent
Nak tham, นักธรรม	skilled in the Buddhist teachings
Nakhonrat, นครราช, Nagararāja (P)	guardian of fortifications
namman nga, น้ำมันงา	sesame seed oil
namman phrai, น้ำมันพราย	liquid extracted from a corpse
nam mon, น้ำมนตร์	sacred water
Nang Kwak, นางกวัก	image of a beckoning woman
Nang Mai, นางไม้	female spirit of the wood
Nawakowat, นวโกวาท, navakovāda (P)	advice to the newly ordained monk
nibbāna (P)	final extinction, salvation from rebirth
nissaggiyā-pācittiyā (P)	evil which has to be expiated through forfeiture
ok phansa, ออกพรรษา	the end of the Lenten season
oṃ (S)	sacred exclamation
pa paeng, ปะแป้ง	covering the face with white dots
pācittiyā (P)	evil deed which has to be expiated
pañca sikkhāpadāni (P)	the Five Precepts
pañca sīlāni (P)	the Five Precepts
pārājikā (P)	evil which merits exclusion
parien, เปรียญ, pariñña (P)	higher degree in Buddhist learning
paritta (P)	charm, safeguard, protection
Pāṭimokkha (P)	collection of monks' precepts
patiyan, ปฏิญาณ	to take a solemn oath
phakhaoma, ผ้าขาวม้า	rectangular cloth used by men
phansa, พรรษา, vassa (P)	the Lenten season
phanung, ผ้านุ่ง	lower garment
phapa, ผ้าป่า	'forest'-robes
Phaya Nak, พะยานาค	the king of serpents
phi, ผี	ghost, spirit
phi ban, ผีบ้าน	ancestor spirits

phi krasue, ผีกระสือ	ghosts which feed on excrement
phi ruean, ผีเรือน	ancestor spirits
phi taihong, ผีตายโหง	ghosts of people who died inauspiciously
phiksu, ภิกษุ, bhikkhu (P), bhikṣu (S)	Buddhist monk
phra, พระ	title of sacred persons or things
phra phim พระพิมพ์	pressed sacred objects
Phum, ภูมิ, Bhūmi (P; S)	(guardian of the) earth
phuthaphisek, พุทธอภิเษก	sacralization ritual
Phuthaprawat, พุทธประวัติ	the biography of the Buddha
Phuthasasanasuphasit, พุทธศาสนาสุภาษิต	a book of Buddhist proverbs
pinto, ปิ่นโต	multi-layered metal food box
pluksek, ปลุกเสก	to sacralize
prakhen, ประเคน	to offer ceremoniously
pret, เปรต, preta (S)	a type of ghost
rak, รักยม	to love
rakyom, รักยม	a type of love charm
rai, ไร่	a square surface measure
riang mon, เรียงหมอน	arranging pillows during marriage ritual
rotnam phuyai, รดน้ำผู้ใหญ่	aspersion of honoured persons
ṛṣi (S)	mythological sage
sadaeng abat, แสดงอาบัตติ	to confess transgressions
sai sin, สายสิญจน์	white cotton thread used in rituals
saibat dawadueng, ใสบาตรดาวดึง	ritual Tāvatiṃsa food offering
salakaphat, สลากภัต, salākabhattaṃ (P)	ritual food lottery
salueng, สลึง	small coin, worth one-fourth of a baht
saṃsāra (P)	the endless cycle of transmigration
san phiangta, ศาลเพียงตา	shrine on eye level
san Phra Phum, ศาลพระภูมิ	shrine for the guardian of houses
Sangha (S), สังฆ์	the Buddhist order of monks and novices
sao aek, เสาเอก	the 'first pole' in house-building
sida, สีดา	the fruit of the cucumber tree
Songkran, สงกรานต์, saṃkrānti (S)	traditional April new year festival

suk, สุข, sukha (P; S)	happiness
suk, ศุกร์, śukra (S)	the planet Venus, symbol for Friday
ta, ตา	eye
takrut, ตะกรุด	type of charm or amulet
tambon, ตำบล	precinct, subdivision of amphoe
tarpaṇa (S)	offering a libation to the spirits
Tāvatiṃsa (P)	one of the heavens in Buddhist mythology
tawan, ตะวัน	the sun
tawantok, ตะวันตก	the west
tha paeng, ทาแป้ง	to whiten the face with powder
tham khwan ทำขวัญ	to strengthen the spirit or morale
tham wat yen, ทำวัตร์เย็น	the late-afternoon chanting
Thammahora, ธรรมโหรา	guardian of fields and forests
Thammayuthika nikai, ธรรมยุทธิกานิกาย	Thai Buddhist sect
Thammikarat, ธรรมมิกราช	guardian of gardens
thang, ถัง	unit of capacity, equal to 20 litres
Thathara, ทาษราชา	guardian of swamps and rivers
thawai pha apnamfon, ถวายผ่าอาบน้ำฝน	donating bathing cloth to the monks
thawai sangkhathan, ถวายสงฆทาน	donating to the Sangha
Thephen, เทเพน or Thewathen, เทวเถร	guardian of stables
thorani, ธรณี, dharaṇī (S)	the earth
thorani san, ธรณีสาร, dharaṇī śānti (S)	appeasing the earth
thūlaccaya (P)	serious transgression
tra sang, ตราสัง	binding a corpse
ubasika, อุบาสิกา, upāsikā (P)	devout woman
ubasok, อุบาสก, upāsaka (P)	devout layman
udakadhārā (S)	ceremonial water-offering
unalom, อุณาโลม	conically shaped sacred symbol
vassa (P), varṣa (S)	the Lenten season, see *phansa*
Vinaya (P)	canonical code of ethics and rules of behaviour

wai khru, ไหว้ครู	ritual homage to mythical teachers
wat, วัด	monastery
Wayathat, วัยทัต	guardian of monasteries
wan, วัน	day
wan kon, วันก่อน	the day before *wan phra*
wan phra, วันพระ	holy day, day of worship
winjaan วิญญาณ, viññāṇa (P)	principle of conscious life
Wisakhabucha, วิสาขบูชา, Visākhapūjā (P)	annual festival in April–May
ya kha, หญ้าคา	cogon grass
ya phraek, หญ้าแพรก	Bermuda grass, dub-grass
yajñopavīta (S)	sacred thread worn over left shoulder
yak, ยักษ์	ogre
yan, ยันต์, yantra (S)	mystical diagram
yan ubakong, ยันต์อุบากอง	table for calculating auspicious times
yok khru, ยกครู	ritual invoking the teachers
yom, โยม	title of a person who supports a monk
yu faj, ยู่ไฟ	lying by a fire after giving birth

BIBLIOGRAPHY

All works mentioned in the text and in footnotes are enumerated. Thai authors are listed under their first name

Part I. Works with specific reference to Thailand

Acts on the Administration of the Buddhist Order of Sangha [sic], Published on the occasion of the Convocation Day 29th December B.E. 2506 (1963) by the Mahāmakuta Educational Council, The Buddhist University.

Andaya, Barbara Watson, 'Statecraft in the Reign of Lü Thai of Sukhodaya (ca. 1347–1374)', in Bardwell L. Smith (ed.), *Religion and Legitimation of Power in Thailand, Laos and Burma*, Chambersburg: Anima Books, 1978, pp. 2–19.

Ayabe, Tsuneo, '*Dek Wat* and Thai Education: the Case of Tambon Ban Khan', *Journal of the Siam Society*, Vol. 61, Part 2, 1973, pp. 39–52.

Barlow, J. G., 'The Zhuang Minority Peoples of the Sino-Vietnamese Frontier in the Song Period', *Journal of Southeast Asian Studies*, Vol. 18, No. 2, Sept 1987, pp. 250–69.

Bhirasri, Silpa (C. Feroci), *Thai Buddhist Art (Architecture)*, Thai Culture, New Series, No. 4. Bangkok: The Fine Arts Department, 1970.

Blackmore, Michael, 'The Ethnological Problems Connected with Nanchao', in *Symposium on Historical, Archaeological and Linguistic Studies on Southern China, South-East Asia and the Hong Kong Region* (F. S. Drake general editor), Hong Kong: Hong Kong University Press, 1967, pp. 59–69.

Bourlet, Antoine, 'Les Thay', *Anthropos*, Vol. 2, 1907, pp. 355–73, 613–32 and 921–32.

Broman, Barry M., 'Early Political Institutions of the Thai: Synthesis and Symbiosis', Master of Arts thesis, University of Washington, 1968.

Bunnag, Jane, *Buddhist Monk, Buddhist Layman: A Study of Urban Monastic Organization in Central Thailand*. Cambridge Studies in Social Anthropology, No. 6., Cambridge at the University Press, 1973.

Bunrot Moraruetang, ประเพณีทั่วโลก [Customs World-wide], Bangkok: Odiankan-phim, 1968.

Caldwell, J. C., 'The Demographic Structure', in T. H. Silcock (ed.), *Thailand, Social and Economic Studies in Development*, Canberra: Australian National University Press, 1967, pp. 27–64.

Caron, Francis and J. Schouten, *A True Description of the Mighty Kingdoms of Japan and Siam. Written Originally in Dutch by Francis Caron and Joost Schouten, and Now Rendred into English by Capt. Roger Manley*. Printed for Robert Boulter at the Turks-head in Cornhill over against the Royall Exchange, 1671. Partly reprinted by Chalermnit, Bangkok, Chalermnit Historical Archives Series, 1969. (The material on Thailand is based upon Schouten's *A Description of the Government, Might, Religion, Customes, Traffick, and other Remarkable Affairs in the Kingdom of Siam*, 1636).

Cartwright, B. O., 'The Huey Lottery', *Journal of the Siam Society*, Vol. 18, Part 3, 1924, pp. 221–39.

Chamberlain, James R., 'A New Look at the History and Classification of the Tai Languages', in J. G. Harris and James R. Chamberlain (eds), *Studies in Tai Linguistics in Honor of William J. Gedney*, Bangkok: Central Institute of English Language, 1975.

Coedès, Georges, 'À propos de deux fragments d'inscription récemment decouverts à P'ra Pathom', *Comptes-Rendus de l'Académie des Inscriptions et Belles-Lettres*, 1952, p. 146.

——— and Charles Archaimbault, *Les trois mondes (Traibhūmi Brah Ruaṅ)*, Publications de l'École Française d'Extrême-Orient, Vol. 89, Paris: École Française d'Extrême-Orient, 1973.

Credner, Wilhelm, *Cultural and Geographical Observations Made in the Tali (Yunnan) Region with Special Regard to the Nan-chao Problem*, translated from the German by E. Seidenfaden, Bangkok: The Siam Society, 1935.

———. *Siam, Das Land der Tai*, Osnabrück: Otto Zeller, 1966. First published in Stuttgart: J. Engelhorns Nachf., 1935.

Cripps, Francis, *The Far Province*, London: Hutchinson & Co. Ltd, 1965.

Damrong Rajanubhab, H.H. Prince, 'History of Siam in the Period Antecedent to the Founding of Ayuddhya by King Phra Chao U Thong', *Selected Articles from the Siam Society Journal*, Vol. III, Bangkok, 1959, pp. 35–100.

Dhanit Yupho, *The Custom and Rite of Paying Homage to Teachers of Khon, Lakon and Piphat*. Thai Culture New Series, No. 11. Bangkok: The Fine Arts Department, 1970.

Dupont, Pierre, *L'Archéeologie Mône de Dvāravatī*. Paris: Publications de l'École Française d'Extrême-Orient, Vol. XLI, 1959.

Gerini, G. E., *Chūlākantamangala or the Tonsure Ceremony as Performed in Siam*, Bangkok: The Siam Society, 1976. First published in 1893.

Griswold, A. B. and Prasert na Nagara, 'An Inscription in Old Mòn from Wieng Manó in Chieng Mai Province', Epigraphic and Historical Studies, No. 6. *Journal of the Siam Society*, Vol. 59, Part 1, 1971, pp. 153–6.

———. 'The Inscription of King Rāma Gamhèn of Sukhodaya (1292 A.D.)', Epigraphic and Historical Studies, No. 9. *Journal of the Siam Society*, Vol. 59, Part 2, 1971, pp. 179–228.

———. 'King Lödaiya of Sukhodaya and his Contemporaries', Epigraphic and Historical Studies, No. 10. *Journal of the Siam Society*. Vol. 60, Part 1, 1972, pp. 21–152.

Guide to the National Museum, Bangkok, Bangkok: Fine Arts Department, Third Edition 1970.

Halliday, R., 'Les inscriptions mon du Siam', *Bulletin de l'*École Française d'*Extrême-Orient*, Vol. 30, 1930, pp. 86–105.

Hanks, Lucien M., 'Merit and Power in the Thai Social Order', *American Anthropologist*, Vol. 64, 1962, pp. 1247–61.

Hardouin, C. 'Traditions et superstitions siamoises', *Revue Indo-Chinoise*, 1904, pp. 333–42 and pp. 415–25.

Heinze, Ruth-Inge, *The Role of the Sangha in Modern Thailand*, Asian Folklore and Social Life Monographs, Vol. 93, Taipei: The Chinese Association for Folklore, 1977.

———. *Tham Khwan: How to Contain the Essence of Life*, Singapore: Singapore University Press, 1982.

Ingersoll, Jasper C., 'The Priest Role in Central Village Thailand', *Anthropological Studies in Theravada Buddhism*. Cultural Report Series, No. 13, Southeast Asia Studies. Yale University, 1966, pp. 51–76.

Kachorn Sukhàbanij, 'ถิ่นกำเนิดและแนวอพยพของเผ่าไทย' [The Origin and Migration of the Thais],' in T. Bunnag and M. Smithies (eds.), *In Memoriam Phya Anuman Rajadhon*, Bangkok: The Siam Society, 1970, pp. 111–28.

Kaufman, Howard Keva, *Bangkhuad. A Community Study in Thailand*. Monograph No. 10 of the Association for Asian Studies. Locust Valley, New York: J.J. Augustin Inc., 1960.

Khantipālo, Bhikkhu. *Buddhism Explained; With Special Reference to Siam*, Second, revised edition, Bangkok: Social Science Association Press of Thailand, 1968.

Kingshill, Konrad, *Ku Daeng – The Red Tomb, a Village Study in Northern Thailand*. Chiangmai: The Prince Royal's College, 1960.

Klausner, William J. 'Popular Buddhism in Northeast Thailand', in F.S.C. Northrop and Helen H. Livingston (eds), *Cross Cultural Understanding, Epistemology in Anthropology*, New York, Evanston and London: Harper & Row, 1964, pp. 70–92.

Kraiśrī Nimmānahaeminda, 'Ham Yon, the Magic Testicles', in Ba Shin, Jean Boisselier and A. B. Griswold (eds), *Essays offered to G. H. Luce by his Colleagues and Friends in Honour of his seventy-fifth birthday*, Ascona: Artibus Asiae, 1966, Vol. II, pp. 133–48.

Kromkansasana, รายงานการศาสนาประจำปี ๒๕๐๘ [Annual Report on Religious Affairs, 2508], Bangkok: Rongphim kansasana, B.E. 2508 (1966).

———, รายงานการศาสนาประจำปี ๒๕๐๙ [Annual Report on Religious Affairs, 2510], Bangkok: Rongphim kansasana, B.E. 2509 (1966).

———, รายงานการศาสนาประจำปี ๒๕๑๐ [Annual Report on Religious Affairs, 2510], Bangkok: Rongphim kansasana, B.E. 2510 (1967).

———, รายงานการศาสนาประจำปี ๒๕๑๓ [Annual Report on Religious Affairs, 2513], Bangkok: Rongphim kansasana, B.E. 2513 (1970).

———, รายงานการศาสนาประจำปี ๒๕๑๘ [Annual Report on Religious Affairs, B.E. 2518], Rongphim kansasana, B.E. 2518 (1975).

Kumut Chandruang, *My Boyhood in Siam*, second edition, New York: F.A. Praeger, 1969.

Lafont, Pierre-Bernard, 'Notes sur les familles patronymiques Thai noires de So'n-la et de Nghĩa-lô', *Anthropos*, Vol. 50, 1955, pp. 797–809.

Landon, Kenneth Perry, *Siam in Transition, a Brief Survey of Cultural Trends in the Five Years since the Revolution of 1932*, New York: Greenwood Press, 1968. Originally published in 1939 by the University of Chicago Press.

Lévi, Paul, 'The Sacrifice of the Buffalo and the Forecast of the Weather in Vientiane', in R. de Berval (ed.), *Kingdom of Laos*, Saigon: France-Asie, 1959, pp. 162–73.

Likhit Hoontrakul, *The Historical Records of the Siamese-Chinese Relations Commencing From Ancient Times up to the Time when the Siamese People Formed Themselves into a State Called Siam with the Town of Sukhothai as Capital*. Bangkok, privately published, 1953.

McFarland, George Bradley, *Thai-English Dictionary*. American Edition, Stanford University Press, 1944.

Mole, R. L. *Thai Values and Behavior Patterns*, Tokyo: The Centre for East Asian Cultural Studies, 1973.

Moerman, Michael, 'Ban Ping's Temple: the Center of a 'Loosely Structured Society', *Anthropological Studies in Theravada Buddhism*. Cultural Report Series, No. 13, Southeast Asia Studies, Yale University, 1966, pp. 137–74.

Mote, F. W. 'Problems of Thai Prehistory', *Social Science Review*, Vol. II, No. 2, Bangkok: 1964.

Mulder, Jan A. N., *Monks, Merit, and Motivation: Buddhism and National Development in Thailand*, Center for Southeast Asian Studies, Northern Illinois University, Special Report No.1, Second revised edition, 1973.

N.N., ประเพณีการทำบุญ [Customs connected with Making Merit], Cremation Volume for Nai Thawin Kiatkoetsuk, Bangkok: Borisat Sahasayamphathana, B.E. 2511 (1968).

N.N., อนุสรณ์กตัญญูเนื่องในการฌาปนกิจ นายเบี้ยวเจริญจันท์ [In Grateful Memory at the Cremation of Nai Biaw Charoenchan], Bangkok: Withayalaj khrusuansunantha, B.E. 2511 (1968).

Ñāṇamoli, Thera. *The Pāṭimokkha, 227 Fundamental Rules of a Bhikkhu*. Bangkok: The Social Science Association Press of Thailand, 1966.

Notton, Camille, *Annales du Siam, Première Partie: Chroniques de Suvaṇṇa Khamdëng, Suvaṇṇa K'ôm Khăm, Siṅhanavati*, Paris, Limoges, Nancy: Imprimeries Charles-Lavauzelle & Cie, 1926.

Phaichoet Thapthimthun, หนังสือสวดมนต์แปล [The book of Chants in Translation] published in honour of the seventy-second birthday of Chupsi Suprathit na Ayudhya, Bangkok: Rongphim S. Phayunphon, B.E. 2510 (1967).

Prajaub Thirabutana, *Little Things*. Sydney, London: Collins, 1971.

Pussathewa, Supreme Patriarch (ed.), ปฐมสมโพธิ [First Step to Enlightenment], Bangkok: The Mahāmakuta Educational Council, The Buddhist University, B.E. 2510 (1967).

Rabibhadana, Akin. *The Organization of Thai Society in the Early Bangkok Period, l782-l873*. Data Paper No. 74, Southeast Asia Program, Department of Asian Studies, Cornell University, 1969.

Rajadhon, Phya Anuman. *Loy Krathong & Songkran Festival*. Thailand Culture Series, No. 5. Bangkok: The National Culture Institute, 1953.

———. *Life and Ritual in Old Siam. Three Studies of Thai Life and Customs*. Translated and Edited by W. J. Gedney. New Haven: HRAF Press, 1961.

———. 'The Khwan and Its Ceremonies', *Journal of the Siam Society*, Vol. 50, Part 2, 1962, pp. 119–64.

———. 'Data on Conditioned Poison (A Folklore Study)', *Journal of the Siam Society*, Vol. 53, Part 1, 1965, pp. 69–82.

———. *Essays on Thai Folklore*, Bangkok: The Social Science Association Press, 1968.

———. *Thai Traditional Salutation*, Thai Culture, New Series, No. 14. Bangkok: The Fine Arts Department, 1969.

Reynolds, Frank E. and Mani B. Reynolds, *Three Worlds according to King Ruang: A Thai Buddhist Cosmology*, Berkeley Buddhist Studies Series, No. 4, Berkeley: University of California and the Institute of Buddhist Studies, 1982.

Sa, Supreme Patriarch, พุทธประวัติ เล่ม ๓ [The Life of the Buddha, Part III], Bangkok: The Mahāmakuta Educational Council, The Buddhist University, B.E. 2511 (1968).

Sarasas, Phra. *My Country Thailand; Its History, Geography and Civilization*. Tokyo: Maruzen, 1942.

Sathian Koset (pseud. Phya Anuman Rajadhon), ประเพณีเก่าของไทย [Old Customs of the Thais], Bangkok: Prae Pittaya, B.E. 2500 (1957).

Schouten, J. See under: Caron, Francis and J. Schouten.

Somchit Ekayothin (ed.), หนังสือคู่มือ วิธีรักษาอุโบสถและทำวัตร์เช้า, เย็น, กับสมบัติขอวอุบาสก อุบาสิกา [Handbook for Keeping Holy Days, Morning and Afternoon and the Conduct of Devout Men and Women], Bangkok: Liangsiang, B.E. 2510 (1967).

Suatmon Chet Tamnan สวดมนต์เจ็ดคำนาน นะมะการะสิทธิคาถา- โยจักขุมาวิธีบรรพขา อุปสมบทแบบธรรมยุตติกนิกาย-มหานิกาย คำอาราธนาศิล-ธรรม และคำถวายทาน [Chanting the Series of Seven: The chant of Venerating the Powers, The Method of Ordination in the Mahanikaya and Thammayuttikanikaya Way, The Formulas of Asking the Vows and the Dhamma and the Words for Presenting Offerings], Bangkok: Rongphim Thammabannakhan, B.E. 2510 (1967).

Subhadradis Diskul, M.C., *Art in Thailand: A Brief History*. English-Language Series of the Faculty of Archaeology, Silpakorn University, Vol. I. Third revised edition, Bangkok, 1972.

Tambiah, Stanley J., 'The Ideology of Merit and the Social Correlates of Buddhism in a Thai Village', in E. R. Leach (ed.), *Dialectic in Practical Religion*, Cambridge Papers in Social Anthropology, No. 5. Cambridge University Press, 1968, pp. 41–121.

———. *Buddhism and the Spirit Cults in North-East Thailand*. Cambridge Studies in Social Anthropology, No. 5. Cambridge at the University Press, 1970.

———. *World Conqueror and World Renouncer, A study of Buddhism and Polity in Thailand against a Historical Background*, Cambridge Studies in Social Anthropology, No. 15, Cambridge: Cambridge University Press, 1976.

Tanabe, Shigeharu, 'Spirits, Power and the Discourse of Female Gender: The *Phi Meng* Cult of Northern Thailand', in Manas Chitikasem and A Turton (eds.), *Thai Constructions of Knowledge,* London: School of Oriental and African Studies, 1991, pp. 183–212.

Terrien de Lacouperie, A,E.J.B. 'The Cradle of the Shan Race', in A.R. Colquhoun, *Amongst the Shans*. New York: Paragon Reprint, 1970, first published in 1885.

Terwiel, Barend Jan, 'The Five Precepts and Ritual in Rural Thailand', *Journal of the Siam Society,* Vol. 60, Part 1, 1972, pp. 333–43.

———. 'Leasing from the Gods (Thailand)', *Anthropos,* Vol. 71, 1976, pp. 254–74.

———. 'A Model for the Study of Thai Buddhism', *The Journal of Asian Studies,* Vol. XXXV, 1976, pp. 391–403.

———. *Boeddhisme in de Praktijk,* Assen: van Gorcum, 1977.

———. 'The Development of a Centrally Organized Education System in Thailand', in K. Orr (ed.), *Appetite for Education in Contemporary Asia,* Development Studies Centre Monograph, No. 10, Canberra: The Australian National University, 1977, pp. 39–6l.

———. 'The Origin of the T'ai Peoples reconsidered', *Oriens Extremus,* Vol. 25, Pt. 2, 1978, pp. 239–58.

———. 'The Rotating Naga: A Comparative Study of an Excerpt from the Oldest Tai Literature', *Asemi,* Vol. 16, 1985, pp. 221–45.

———. 'การค้นหาแหล่งกำเนิดของชาติไทย' [Reconsidering the Origin of the Thais], in B. J. Terwiel, Anthony Diller and Chonthira Sattayawathana, คนไท(เดิม)ไม่ได้อยู่ที่นี่ [The original Thais did not live here], Bangkok: Muang Boran, B.E. 2533 (1990), pp. 8–78.

———. *The Ram Khamhaeng Inscription: The Fake that did not Come True,* Gossenberg: Ostasien Verlag, 2010.

———. *Thailand's Political History: From the 13th Century to Recent Times,* Bangkok: River Books, 2011.

Textor, Robert B., *An Inventory of Non-Buddhist Supernatural Objects in a Central Thai Village*. Unpublished Ph.D. dissertation. Cornell University, 1960.

Thammasenani, Phra. ระเบียบการลาสิกขาบท [The rules of Leaving the Discipline], Ratburi: Rongphim Wirasak, B.E. 2496 (1953).

Thawat Fueangpraphat, ตำราคัมภีเพชรัตนมหายันต์ [Manual of Gems of Yantras], Bangkok: Prachakwithaya, B.E. 2509 (1966).

Thep Saríkabut, พุทธาภิเษกพิธี พิธีกรรมปลุกเสก พระเครื่องรางของขลัง [The Ceremony of Sacralization, Rituals of Blessing Objects that Cause Invulnerability], Bangkok: Prachakwithaya, B.E. 2509 (1966).

Thong, *Achan*, ตำราปลูกบ้านตั้งศาลพระภูมิ [Manual to Erect a House and the *San Phra Phum*], Bangkok: Odiankanphim, B.E. 2513 (1970).

Thongkham Yimkamphu, and Phit Phenrat, ตำราพระภูมิ [The Manual for *Phra Phum*], Bangkok: Fueangakson, B.E. 2513 (1970).

Trittel, W., *Thailand.* Second edition. Kleine Auslandskunde, Deutsches Auslandswissenschaftliches Institut. Vol. XI, edited by F.A. Six. Berlin: Junker and Dünnhaupt Verlag, 1943.

Urakhin Wiriyaburana, คัมภีร์ยันต์ ๑๐๘ ชำระโดยพระราชครูวามเทพมุนี [The Book of 108 Yantras, Revised by phraratchakhru Wamthephamuni], Bangkok: Rongphim Luk S. Thammaphakdi, n.d.

———.พรหมชาติ ฉบับหลวง ประจำบ้าน ดูด้วยตนเอง [The Brahman, Major Edition for the Household, for Self-use], Bangkok: Rongphim Luk S. Thammaphakdi, B.E. 2500 (1957).

———. คัมภีร์คาถา ๑๐๘ ชำระโดยพระราชครูวามเทพมุนี [The Book of 108 Spells, Revised by phraratchakhru Wamthephamuni], Bangkok: Rongphim luk S. Thammaphakdi, B.E. 2509 (1966).

———. ประเพณีไทยฉบับพระราชครู [Thai Customs, the Rajaguru edition], Bangkok: Prachakwíthaya, B.E. 2510 (1967).

Vajirañāṇavarorasa, H.R.H. Prince. *Ordination Procedure*, Bangkok: The Buddhist University, 1963.

———. *Five Precepts and Five Ennoblers (Pañcasīlapañcadhamma)*, Bangkok: The Buddhist University, 1963.

———. นวโกวาท [Advice to the Newly Ordained], Bangkok: The Mahāmakuta Educational Council, The Buddhist University, B.E. 2511 (1968).

———. พุทธประวัติ เล่ม ๑ [The Life of the Buddha, Part I], Bangkok: The Mahāmakuta Educational Council, The Buddhist University, B.E. 2512 (1969).

———. พุทธประวัติ เล่ม ๒ [The Life of the Buddha, Part II], Bangkok: The Mahāmakuta Educational Council, The Buddhist University, B.E. 2512 (1969).

———. พุทธศาสนสุภาษิต เล่ม ๑ [Buddhist Religious Proverbs, Part I], Bangkok: The Mahāmakuta Educational Council, The Buddhist University, B.E. 2512 (1969).

Velder, Christian, 'Die Palmblatt-Manuscriptkultur Thailands', *Nachrichten der Gesellschaft für Natur- und Völkerkunde Ostasiens / Hamburg*, Vol. 89/90, 1961, pp. 110–4.

Wales, Horace G. Quaritch, *Siamese State Ceremonies, Their History and Function.* London: Bernard Quaritch, Ltd, 1931.

———. 'Siamese Theory and Ritual Connected with Pregnancy, Birth and Infancy', *Journal of the Royal Anthropological Institute of Great Britain and Ireland*, Vol. LXIII, 1933, pp. 441–51.

———. *Ancient Siamese Government and Administration*, New York: Paragon Book Reprint Corp., 1965. First published in London, 1934.

———. *Dvāravatī, the Earliest Kingdom of Siam*, London: Bernard Quaritch, Ltd., 1969.

———. *Early Burma – Old Siam, A Comparative Commentary*, London: Bernard Quaritch, Ltd., 1973.

———. *Divination in Thailand; The Hopes and Fears of a Southeast Asian People*, London: Curzon Press, 1983.

Wells, Kenneth E. Thai *Buddhism, Its Rites and Activities*, Bangkok: by the author, 1960.

Wood, W. A. R. *Consul in Paradise*. London: Souvenir Press, 1965.

Worakawinto, Phra Maha Thongyoy (Thongyoy Saengsinchai), *A Village Ordination*, translated from the Thai by T. H. Silcock, Scandinavian Institute of Asian Studies Monograph, No. 25, London: Curzon Press, 1976.

Wright, Michael A., 'Some Observations on Thai Animism', *Practical Anthropology*, Vol. XV, 1968, pp. 1–7.

Yanawimut, C., หลักวิชามวยไทย [The theory of Thai Boxing], Bangkok: Chamroensueksa, B.E. 2509 (1966).

deYoung, John E., *Village Life in Modern Thailand*, Berkeley and Los Angeles: University of California Press, 1955.

Part II. Other references

Abhay, Thao Nhouy., 'Marriage Rites', *Kingdom of Laos*. Edited by Rene de Berval. Saigon: France-Asie, 1959, pp. 137–43.

Ames, M. M., 'Magical-Animism and Buddhism: Structural Analysis of the Sinhalese Religious System', *The Journal of Asian Studies*, Vol. 23, 1964, pp. 21–52.

Bareau, André, 'Les idées sous-jacentes aux pratiques culturelles bouddhiques dans Ie Cambodge actuel', in G. Oberhammer (ed.), *Beiträge zur Geistesgeschichte Indiens*, Wiener Zeitschrift fur die Kunde Südasiens und Archiv für indische Philosophie, Vol. XII/XIII, 1968–1969, pp. 23–32.

Barua, Golap Chandra (transl. and ed.), *Ahom Buranji (with parallel English translation) from the Earliest Time to the End of Ahom Rule*, Calcutta: Baptist Mission Press, 1930.

Bechert, Heinz, *Living Buddhism in East Bengal: A Comparative View*, mimeographed, n.d.

———. *Buddhismus, Staat und Gesellschaft in den Ländern des Theravāda-Buddhismus, Vol. II, Birma, Kambodscha, Laos, Thailand*. Vol. 17/2 der Schriften des Instituts für Asienkunde in Hamburg. Wiesbaden: Otto Harrassowitz, 1967.

Bizot, François, 'Notes sur les yantra bouddhiques d'Indochine, in M. Strickmann (ed.), *Tantric and Taoist Studies in Honour of R. A. Stein*, Mélanges Chinois et Bouddhiques, Vol. 20, Bruxelles: Institut Belge des Hautes Études Chinoises, 1981, pp. 155–91.

Boeles, Jan J., 'The Migration of the Magic Syllable Oṃ', in *India Antiqua, a Volume of Oriental Studies*, presented by his friends and pupils to Jean Philippe Vogel on the occasion of the 50th anniversary of his Doctorate, Leiden: Kern Institute, 1947, pp. 40–56.

Bühler, G. (translator) *The Laws of Manu*. Sacred Books of the East Series, edited by F. M. Müller, Vol. XXV, Delhi: Motilal Banarsidass, 1970.

Coedès, Georges, 'Documents sur l'histoire politique et religieuse du Laos occidental', *Bulletin de l'*École Française d'*Extrême-Orient*, Vol. 25, 1925, pp. 1–202.

———. *The Making of South East Asia*, translated by H.M. Wright, London: Routledge & Kegan Paul, 1966.

Conze, Edward, *Buddhism, Its Essence and Development*. London: Faber & Faber, 1963.

Dutt, Sukumar, *Buddhism in East Asia*. New Delhi: Indian Council for Cultural Relations, 1966.

Eitel, E. J., *Principles of the Natural Science of the Chinese*. Hong Kong and London: Trübner, 1873.

Eliade, Mircea, *Patterns in Comparative Religion*, translated by R. Sheed, London and New York: Sheed and Ward, 1958.

Endicott, K. M., *An Analysis of Malay Magic*. Oxford Monographs on Social Anthropology. Oxford: Clarendon Press, 1970.

Ethnic Groups of Northern Southeast Asia, Cultural Report Series, No. 2. Yale University Southeast Asia Studies, 1950.

Gonda, Jan, *Aspects of Early Viṣṇuism*. Delhi: Moilal Banarsidass, 1969.

Homans, G. C., *The Human Group*. London: Routledge & Kegan Paul, 1951.

———. *Social Behavior, Its Elementary Forms*, New York: Harcourt, Brace & World Inc., 1961.

Humphreys, Christmas, *Buddhism*, Penguin Books, 1962.

Jayavardena, C., 'The Psychology of Burmese Supernaturalism: A Review Article', *Oceania*, Vol. 41, 1910, pp. 12–9.

Kane, P. V., *History of Dharmaśāstra, Ancient and Medieval Religious and Civil Law*. Bhandarkar Oriental Research Institute, Government Oriental Series, Class B, No. 6. 5 Vols in 1 Poona: 1932–1962.

Leach, Edmund R., 'Pulleyar and the Lord Buddha: An Aspect of Religious Syncretism in Ceylon', *Psychoanalysis and the Psychoanalytical Review*, Vol. 49, Part 2, 1962, pp. 81–102.

———. 'The Politics of Karma', *The New York Review*, November 18, 1971, pp. 43–5.

LeBar, F. M. *et al.*, *Ethnic Groups of Mainland Southeast Asia*, New Haven: HRAF Press, 1964.

Le May, Reginald, *The Culture of South-east Asia, the Heritage of India*, London: George Allen & Unwin Ltd, 1964.

Malalasekera, G. P., *Dictionary of Pāli Proper Names*, Vols I and II, London: Luzac & Company Ltd, 1960.

Manderson, Lenore, 'Roasting, Smoking and Dieting in Response to Birth: Malay Confinement in Cross-Cultural Perspective', *Social Science and Medicine*, Vol. 15 B, 1981, pp. 509–20.

Maspero, G. (ed.), *Un empire colonial français: l'Indochine*, 2 Vols, Paris: Les Editions G. van Oest, 1929–1930.

Mendelson, E. M. 'The Uses of Religious Scepticism in Modern Burma', *Diogenes*, Vol. 41, 1963, pp. 94–116.

Meijers, J. A. and J. C. Luitingh, *Onze Voornamen, Traditie, Betekenis, Vorm, Herkomst*, Amsterdam: Moussault's Uitgeverij N.V., 1963.

Monier-Williams, M, *A Sanskrit-English Dictionary Etymologically and Philologically Arranged with Special Reference to Cognate Indo-European Languages*. Oxford, at the Clarendon Press, 1964.

Nash, J. C., 'Living with Nats: An Analysis of Animism in Burma Village Social Relations', *Anthropological Studies in Theravada Buddhism*. Yale University Southeast Asia Studies, No. 13, 1966, pp. 117–36.

Obeyesekere, Gananath, 'The Great Tradition and the Little in the Perspective of Sinhalese Buddhism', *The Journal of Asian Studies*, Vol. 22, Part 2, 1963, pp. 139–53.

Oldenberg, H. (translator), *The Gṛhya-Sūtras, Rules of Vedic Domestic Ceremonies*. Sacred Books of the East Series, edited by F. M. Müller, Vol. XXIX/XXX. Delhi: Motilal Banarsidass, 1967.

Pelliot, P. (translator), *Memoires sur les coutumes du Cambodge par Tcheou Ta-Kouan.* Hanoi: F.-H. Schneider, 1902.

Porée-Maspero, Eveline, 'Kròṅ Pāli et rites de la maison', *Anthropos,* Vol. LVI, 1961, pp. 179–251; pp. 548–628 and pp. 883–929

Rhys Davids, C. A. F. (translator), *Psalms of the Early Buddhists,* Pali Text Society, London: Luzac & Company Ltd., 1964.

Rhys Davids, T. W. and W. Stede, *The Pali Text Society's Pali-English Dictionary,* London: Luzac & Company Ltd., 1966.

——— and H. Oldenberg (translators). *Vinaya Texts.* Sacred Books of the East Series, edited by F. M. Muller, Vols XII, XVII and XX. Delhi: Motilal Banarsidass, 1968–1969.

Spiro, Melford E., 'Religion and the Irrational', *Symposium on New Approaches to the Study of Religion.* Proceedings of the 1964 Annual Spring Meeting of the American Ethnological Society, Seattle: University of Washington Press, 1964, pp. 102–15.

———. 'Religion: Problems of Definition and Explanation', *Anthropological Approaches to the Study of Religion,* edited by H. Banton. A.S.A. Monograph No. 3, London: Tavistock Publication, 1966, pp. 85–126.

———. *Burmese Supernaturalism, A Study in the Explanation and Reduction of Suffering.* Prentice Hall College Anthropology Series, edited by D. M. Schneider. Englewood Cliffs, N.J.: Prentice-Hall, 1967.

Trager, Frank N., 'Reflections on Buddhism and the Social Order in Southern Asia', *Burma Research Society Fiftieth Anniversary Publications,* Vol. I, 1960, pp. 529–43.

Welch, Holmes, *The Practice of Chinese Buddhism, 1900–1950.* Harvard East Asian Studies, No. 26. Cambridge, Mass.: Harvard University Press.

Wieger, L. (translator), *Bouddhisme chinois,* Vol. I, Vinaya, monachisme et discipline; Hinayana, véhicule inférieur. Serie Culturelle des Hautes Études de Tien Tsin, Paris: Cathasia, 1951.

INDEX

abbot, 22, 57, 99, 108, 119, 132, 134, 210, 215, 220, 242 . *See also* monks: hierarchy

accidents, prevention of, 69, 116, 127, 133, 244

achan sak, 79–81, 140, 283. *See also* tattooing

acrobatics, 51, 202

agriculture in Wat Sanchao. *See* Wat Sanchao

Ahom Buranji, 9, 298

alcohol, 28, 67, 76, 111, 141, 164 181, 183–5, 258, 260, 271

amulets, 55, 70, 72, 74, 87–8, 116, 136, 140, 270. *See also phuthaphisek*

ancestor spirits, 20, 53, 141–2, 144, 148, 151, 155, 186, 248, 250, 251, 260. *See also* spirits

Aṅgada, 83

Angkor, 7, 14

animism. *See* Buddhism; magico-animism

animal sacrifice, 17, 20. *See also* buffalo sacrifice

apamongkhon, 176–7, 283

arahan, 119, 207–8, 240, 283

Araññavasi, 10–11. *See also* Sīhalabhikkhus

areca nut, 10, 26, 43, 112, 143–4, 149, 153, 164, 189, 211, 249

Asalahabucha, 215, 225–6. *See also* festivals and ceremonies

āsavas, 208

Assam, 8, 19

astrology, 15, 44, 132, 147, 150–1, 156, 160, 175

asura, 239

auspiciousness, 151, 155, 176–7. *See also* inauspiciousness; *yan ubakong*

Ayutthaya, 14, 18, 120

bad dream. *See* nightmare

baeng ha system, 27. *See also chao khat tua* system; Wat Sanchao: agriculture

baeng kuson, 135. *See also* karma

bai chak, 153

bai ngoen bai thong. *See* silver-and-gold leaf

Bali (*daitya*), 172, 175. *See also* gods; Viṣṇu

bamboo, 26, 44, 46, 67, 81, 153, 157, 160, 221, 271, 275, 277

banana

- the fruit, 43, 47, 142, 161, 164
- leaves, 46, 47
- the plant, 165
- tree trunk, 161, 249

bathing cloth, 59, 214, 222–6

begging bowl, 61, 73–4, 116, 127, 133, 144, 174, 192–3, 209, 218, 229, 264. *See also* monks: and food

Benchasin Benchatham, 183–4

betel leaf, 26, 112, 143–4, 149, 164, 189, 211, 249

betrothal, 143–4

bhikkhunī, 125, 245–6, 272–3. *See also mae chi*; *phiksuni*; women